The Essence of
BUDDHISM

The Essence of
BUDDHISM
JO DURDEN SMITH

**CHARTWELL
BOOKS, INC.**

Published by
CHARTWELL BOOKS, INC.
A Division of BOOK SALES, INC.
114 Northfield Avenue
Edison, New Jersey 08837

First published by Arcturus Publishing Limited

This edition published 2004

British Library Cataloguing-in-Publication Data: a catalogue record for this book is available from the British Library

© Arcturus Publishing Limited
26/27 Bickels Yard, 151–153 Bermondsey Street, London SE1 3HA

ISBN 0-7858-1862-6

Printed in China

Contents

Introduction

Buddhism is not a religion in the sense in which the term is commonly understood in the West. Buddhists are indeed the followers of the Buddha and of his teachings, but not in the same way that Christians are said to be the followers of Christ. The Buddha did not begin to see himself, and is not seen by Buddhists, as a God; nor did he offer his disciples any sort of path to God. No claims were made by him to any unalterable truth, nor did he demand that his teachings should simply be accepted, taken on trust or acquired through an act of faith. Instead he encouraged those who wished to make the spiritual journey he himself had undertaken to experiment for themselves as individuals, retaining what was useful to them and abandoning what was not. As he is reported to have said some 2,500 years ago to the Kalamas people in north-east India (what is now Nepal):

> Don't be satisfied with hearsay or tradition or legend, or with what's come down from your scriptures, or with conjecture or logical inference or weighing evidence or a particular liking for a view . . . or with the thought: 'The monk is our teacher'. When you know in yourselves:

'These ideas are unprofitable . . . being adopted and put
into effect they lead to harm and suffering', then abandon
them. [But] when you know in yourselves: 'These things
are profitable . . .' then you should practise and abide in
them.

The goal announced by the Buddha, in other words, might be one and
the same – the experience and understanding of ultimate truth – but
each man, woman and child is enjoined to follow his or her own path
there. This necessarily entails a tolerance of others, however different
their methods and conclusions may be. What binds Buddhists
together into one community, or *Sangha*, is this mutual tolerance,
which is sometimes called spiritual friendship. From its beginnings
until the present day, the Buddhist *Sangha* – the word originally meant
a community of monks – has remained notably free from the violent
schisms and sectarian battles, as well as witch-hunting and the rooting
out of heresies, that have been so much a part of Western religious
history.

The second thing that binds Buddhists together is respect for
the Buddha and for the trajectory of the journey that he himself took
towards spiritual truth. This involved, as we shall see, a prolonged and
directed conscious effort. Because his teachings reflect this journey,
they are much less concerned with belief than with behaviour: how to
live; how to cultivate virtue and avoid vice; and, above all, how to
unlock, through meditation, the wisdom and compassion that lies
within us all. His precepts and example, in this context, represent
both a guide-book to the the paths that should be followed and a
primer in how to arrive at the truth without the mediation of either
faith or dogma. Religious experience can be apprehended directly, so
the teaching goes, as long as – like the Buddha – the individual is

prepared to undergo a spiritual transformation and to direct his gaze within himself rather than outside into the transient material world.

The third element that unites Buddhists is expressed by the word *Dharma* (in Sanskrit) or *Dhamma* (in Pali). *Dharma* or *Dhamma* is a complex carpet of a word in which the skeins of the words 'truth,' 'teaching' and 'law' can all be found. Within its two pregnant syllables, therefore, can be found the information that the Buddha's teachings point the way to the truth and that the truth is part of a natural law which is applicable to all human beings, wherever they may be. Practising the *Dharma*, in fact, is precisely what brings us together as brothers and sisters into one *Sangha*.

The concepts of Buddha, *Dharma* and *Sangha*, known as The Three Jewels, are the three cornerstones of the Buddhist's beliefs and are the most valuable possessions in his or her spiritual armoury. A formal, ceremonial commitment is made to all three whenever an individual decides to follow the path of Buddha, as expressed in a compilation of his teachings, the *Dhammapada*:

> Not to do evil
> To cultivate good
> To purify one's mind.

By making this commitment to The Three Jewels, each new Buddhist is in effect formally renouncing the three main enemies (sometimes known as the three poisons) that stand in the way of his or her path to enlightenment: greed (desire); hatred (disgust); and ignorance (delusion). He or she is also announcing that from now on Buddha, *Dharma* and *Sangha* will be a refuge within which safety and the possibility of personal growth can be found: in fact, the Three Jewels are also known as The Three Refuges. It is, then, precisely by repeating the following formula three times that one finally declares oneself to be a Buddhist.

> I go for refuge to the Buddha
> I go for refuge to the Dharma
> I go for refuge to the Sangha

After that – after 'going for refuge' – a Buddhist can then, like the Buddha himself who left his family's palace in search of wisdom two and a half millennia ago, 'go forth' and finally become a seeker, a journeyer towards truth.

Chapter One:

The Historical Background

According to tradition, the man who was to become the Buddha – the name means 'awakened' or 'enlightened' one – was born in about 560 BC in a place called Lumbini, which was situated on the northern edge of the plain of the River Ganges, just below the Himalayas, in what is now Nepal. He was given the name Siddhartha and the clan-name Gautama ('descended from the sage Gotama') and he inherited considerable privilege. His father Suddhodana was a leader (or *rajah*) of the Shakyas, one of a number of independent peoples who occupied this corner of north-east India. Like his father, therefore, the Buddha was born a member of the immutable *kshatriya* caste of aristocrats and warriors. It is worth examining for a moment the religious and social legacy he inherited.

About a thousand years before the Buddha's birth, a race of nomadic herders, commonly known as Aryans, had migrated into northwest India from the central Asian steppe and there they had encountered the last remains of a civilization that had once rivalled the Egypt of the Pharaohs: the so-called Indus River Civilization, which seems to have been egalitarian and matriarchal and to have practised an early form of Hinduism. (The word *Hindu* derives from the Persian name for the river.) The pipal tree (*ficus religiosa*) was apparently an object of veneration, asceticism and ritual cleansing appeared to be important and the figures of a mother goddess and a male god, surrounded by animals – perhaps an early manifestation of the Hindu god Shiva – have also been found.

The Aryans, who spoke an early form of Sanskrit, gradually spread out from the Indus Valley (what is now Pakistan) into the rest of the subcontinent, carrying with them a system of beliefs and social structures that were variously imposed, rejected, modified and adapted to produce the multiplicity of beliefs and practices of later Hinduism and the ordering of Indian society. These were in fact closely interrelated from the beginning of what is now known as the Vedic Age (c. 1500–500 BC) for the Aryans brought with them a rigid and hierarchical form of society (*varna*), in which different classes were divided from each other according to their level of ritual purity. Sacrifice was absolutely central to the religious life of the period, yet the necessary rituals could only be undertaken by a priest of the highest class, the hereditary brahmin priesthood, which jealously guarded its secrets.

The Caste System

From this core developed the caste system (*jati*) that still survives in modern India and which, in its earliest and most basic form, was divided into *brahmana* (the brahmin priesthood), *kshatriya* (warriors and aristocrats), *vaishya* (traders and other professionals) and *shudra* (aboriginal cultivators and farmers). Once a person was born into one of these castes, there was – and still is – no way of leaving it. Upward mobility was simply not an option: the whole system was underpinned by that familiar word *Dharma*, which in this context meant universal law, duty to family and fealty to the system, both religious and social – in other words, knowing one's place and harmoniously occupying it. If an individual lived his life meticulously according to this sense of *Dharma*, then he might be rewarded with reincarnation into a higher caste. But this was his only chance of improvement.

By maintaining this system the brahmin priesthood displayed an element of self-interest, because it made the other castes dependent upon them for their spiritual welfare. This system of control was further reinforced by the language of the Vedas; religious texts of enormous antiquity which were passed down orally through generations of the priesthood until they were finally written down in a form of Sanskrit that had become familiar to them.

The Vedas – the word *Veda* means knowledge – gave their name (retrospectively) to the Vedic Age. There are four Vedas in all, three of which are concerned with sacrificial formulae, the rules governing the conduct of religious services and spells. The oldest of them, the Rig Veda – which is believed to go back, at least in part, to the thirteenth century BC or beyond – is a collection of more than a thousand poetic hymns. Some of these are addressed to nature gods and goddesses, but some represent profound meditations on the origin of the world and the nature of the Supreme Being or Ultimate Reality: Brahman.

Brahman was one and indivisible, all-pervading and formless, a mystery at the heart of the universe: it later came to be regarded as identical with the limitless and indefinable mystery that lay at the heart of every human being. In this context Brahman was called *Atman*, but all of its aspects were really one and the same. The divine, that is to say, was perceived as being both universal and immanent – it was within us all while we were within it. Soma, an intoxicant, seems to have been often used in Aryan religious rituals in order that the celebrant could experience the continuity of Brahman and *Atman* directly, through an altered state of consciousness.

Alongside the brahminic control of the Aryan community's spiritual welfare – as made manifest in the Vedas – another religious tradition grew up, which probably had its roots in both the indigenous, pre-Aryan local culture and the Aryans' shamanistic past. This was the tradition of the ascetic, who was usually a member, not of the *brahmana*, but of the *kshatriya*, the warrior and aristocratic caste. Such warrior-ascetics – barred from an unmediated and unpatrolled relationship with the divine by the caste system – would renounce the world and, either singly or in groups, would hide themselves away in mountain or forest *asramas* (or *ashrams* – places of spiritual striving). Some were the forebears, no doubt, of modern *fakirs*, in search of supranormal powers. Most of them, however, were trying to find another and more personal way to the divine by abandoning the *Dharma* of the community. They mortified the flesh in various ways so that it could be subjugated by the mind. Meditation seems to have been practised and perhaps even yoga – images of figures sitting cross-legged in typically yogic fashion date from as far back as the period before the Aryan invasion.

The Four Stages of Life

What these ascetics were seeking was direct knowledge of the interpenetration of Brahman and *Atman* by means of self- (rather than drug-) induced states of exalted consciousness. It is reasonable to assume that many of those who were successful returned to their communities with a newly-acquired wisdom that flew in the face of the brahmin priesthood's proclaimed control over the gateway to religious experience. The response of the brahmins, though, was anything but aggressive. Instead, they began to incorporate elements of the ascetic philosophy into their own teachings and to lay down new rules that came to govern the ascetic path. They introduced the idea of the Four Stages of Life, by which a man was first a student, next a householder and then a patriarch who was finally able to start shaking off the bonds that tied him to the world. Only when he had done this – when he had fully paid his dues to *Dharma* – was he to be allowed to follow the *sanyassin's*, or renunciate's, way.

The texts in which the ascetics' philosophy and practices came to be enshrined were the Upanishads (or the Vedanta), composed between 800 and about 400 BC. Together with the Veda they encapsulate the two main Indo-Aryan paths to the divine: the priestly and the personal/ascetic. The Upanishads, though – particularly the later ones – represent a decline from the lofty and speculative mysticism of the early sages and poets. Brahman gradually became formalized and eventually took on the shape of the masculine Hindu creator-god Brahma; and *Atman*, instead of being both ineffable and universal, shrank in scale to become the permanent personal self or immortal soul (the *jivatman*) that transmigrates from one body to another after death according to the ancient law of *karma*.

The Sanskrit word *karma* has its roots in 'action', the willed action of body or speech or mind. The cosmic law of *karma* decreed – and still decrees in modern Hinduism – that the effects of past actions accumulate and disperse over several lifetimes. In the Upanishads, this law was conflated with the idea of the personalized *Atman*, so that from then on the status of a reborn individual was seen as being determined by the effects of his or her actions in past lives. (Thus an individual could be reborn as an animal, a human or even a spirit or minor god in a different dimension, depending on past deeds.) Today, different Hindu cults and sects have different notions of the ending of the soul's reiterative journey from one life to another. However, in the Upanishads it is the realization of the indivisibility of Brahman and *Atman* that finally releases an individual from the endless cycle of rebirth and suffering and nullifies once and for all the effects of past *karma*.

This, then, was the religious and social background against which prince Siddhartha Gautama, the future Buddha, was born. The nomadic Aryans had by this time (c.560 BC) spread out over India – although not without facing the sort of resistance recorded in such epics as the *Ramayana* and the *Mahabharata*, beloved of modern Hindus – and had settled down as agriculturalists. They had, in so far as the caste system allowed, integrated themselves with the local populations and had adopted many of their gods. There were thirty-three of these in the Brahmanist pantheon by the time of the Buddha's birth, all of them seen as separate manifestations of, and channels towards, the abstract Brahman. The creator-god Indra, for example, was believed to have sacrificed himself in order that the cosmos could be created out of his remains – thus necessitating the endlessly complicated sacrificial rituals of the brahmin priesthood, designed to guarantee its survival.

There was also considerable conflict, as we have seen, between the two religious traditions – priest-mediated and personal/ascetic – and it is tempting to believe that this may have been exacerbated by the great clearing of the Ganges plain which, by the time of Buddha's birth, had opened up vast and rich agricultural lands and had led to a new prosperity. The population had shot up, cities had emerged as important trading centres and there were new forms of political association, some of them tribal republics with leaders elected from the *kshatriya* caste – among them the Buddha's father. These may well have looked less kindly on brahminic orthodoxy than the iron-age kingdoms that were appearing elsewhere. But there were other pressures, too, that might have led many to favour the ascetic path in this new centre of Indian civilization – among them increased leisure, created by the accumulation of resources and personal insecurity brought on by a time of extreme change.

The Ascetic Groups

Whatever the pressures, though, it seems clear that more and more men were leaving home and becoming ascetics or *sramanas* (strivers) at around the time of the birth of Siddhartha Gautama. Identifiable heterodox sects, or groups of ascetics, were beginning to emerge by this time – each with its own philosophy and disciplines and each gathered around an individual teacher. Five main groups can be identified, according to John Snelling, the author of *The Buddhist Guidebook*:

1. Ajivakas: The teacher of the Ajivakas (or 'homeless ones') was Makkhali Gosala, who preached a totally determinist philosophy: The universe was a closed causal system but was little by little drawing each individual in it towards ultimate perfection – though the process would take aeons of time.

2. Lokayatas: The Lokayatas (or Materialists), gathered around Ajita Keshakambalin, believed that humans were composed of the four elements, into which they were re-resolved when they died. Death was the final ending for both the wise man and the fool, so in life men should seek all pleasures possible.

3. The Sceptics: The Sceptics held that brahminical doctrines were mutually contradictory and that ultimate truth was utterly unattainable. 'They are said to have wriggled like eels out of every question put to them', writes Snelling, 'but believed in cultivating friendliness and peace of mind'.

4. The Jains: The Jains, like the Lokoyatas, were contemporaries of Buddha in the sense that their philosophy seems to have been systematized by Mahavira in the second half of the sixth century BC – although its roots may go back a further thousand years. The Jains, in Snelling's words, 'held life to be an extremely painful business and aspired to attain *moksha* or liberation from the painful cycles of endless rebirth by withdrawing to a high, rarefied spiritual state'. They practised extreme forms of austerity and attached the highest value to the ethical life – a life of total honesty, chastity and non-attachment. They were also preoccupied with the karmic consequences of doing harm to any other living creature. They therefore rejected the sacrificial rituals that underpinned the Aryan/Brahmanic/Hindu view of the world; and many of them took the principle of *ahimsa* (or harmlessness) to extreme lengths to avoid violence towards even microscopic animals. Some would sweep the ground in front of them as they walked or wear masks over their mouths. They would go without clothes and filter their water. Some would even refuse to eat at all – and would starve themselves to a meritorious death. Although the Jains are still part of the religious life of India, few today, it is fair to say, are such radical ascetics.

5. The fifth sect – ultimately to spread over the whole continent of Asia – was that founded by Siddhartha Gautama, the Buddha, born, according to tradition, in the fourth month of the Indian calendar, a hundred miles north of the holy city of Benares, beneath the foothills

of the Himalayas – and it was in many ways the most radical and anti-clerical of them all. Although what later came to be called Buddhism had many features in common with the philosophy of the Jains, *Sakyamuni* – or the sage of the Sakha people, as the Buddha came to be called – went further. He forbade all intoxicants (such as *soma*); preached that there were no gods; and denied not only the existence of an eternal soul, essence or *Atman*, but also its ability to merge with the ultimate mystery of Brahman. He set his face against the blind following of teachers, including himself, preached in the ordinary language of the people and founded egalitarian communities that harked back in spirit to those that had existed before the Aryans had arrived. He was in his way, then, a social – as well as religious – revolutionary.

Chapter Two:

The Life Of Buddha:
The Path to Enlightenment

Such versions of the life of Buddha as we have were composed 500 years or more after his death. Even the earliest scriptures, those of the so-called Pali canon, which gathered together his teachings and precepts, contain nothing that can be called a biography. This is because the lore and traditions of Buddhism, during its first half-millennium, were passed on from one generation to another almost entirely by word of mouth. Stories were told and retold by wandering priests, monks or storytellers in a way that mixed theatre and religion. That is to say, village audiences learned Buddhism through the same sort of fabulous characters and divine beings that inhabit the *Ramayana* and the *Mahabharata*. The actual life of the Buddha himself was irrelevant to this process, *except in so far as it was enshrined in the telling of his teachings.*

Buddha's Life and Journey

By the time the first biography was actually written down – by a Sanskrit poet called Asvaghosa in the first or second century AD – the Buddha's life-story had accumulated an accretion of myth, legend and derring-do, which had turned its central character into a demigod, a supernatural figure out of epic. So, in the many later versions written after the *Buddhacarita* (or *Acts of the Buddha*), he was to remain. For all that, though, Buddha's very first biographer (as we know from the fragments of the *Buddhacarita*, in several Asian languages, that survive) regarded him as a real historical character. Beneath all the supranormal decoration of his own and later variations, there are the lineaments of a dramatic human story: of a man undergoing conflicts and temptations; trying out and rejecting different courses of action; exercising choice; and finally winning through – not by accident, or through any intervention of the gods, but by what he himself chooses to do. He is driven into action by compassion for suffering humanity. He is courageous, tough, supple-minded and, above all, extremely self-disciplined. He behaves throughout his long ordeals with the utmost sensitivity, delicacy and dignity.

Whatever else overlays this basic story – the trajectory of Buddha's life and journey – is also there for a purpose, we must assume, however far-fetched and fantastical it may seem to us today. The life is not only historical at root and highly moral in development but it is also a guidebook of the path towards enlightenment – in other words, it is a teaching manual.

Birth and Early Life

Great lives deserve great and important births – and so it was with Siddhartha Gautama, the prince and later sage (*Sakyamuni*) of the Sakya people, for he was conceived when his mother, Mahamaya (or Maya) dreamed that a Bodhisattva ('Buddha-to-be') came down from Tushita Heaven – the home, by tradition, of contented gods – and entered her body in the form of a white elephant with a red face.

During her pregnancy, which lasted for ten months, Mahamaya often meditated in Lumbini forest: it was there, in a grove of trees, that she finally gave birth from her side as she held on to the branch of a sacred tree. A great light covered the earth as the baby appeared, unstained and fully aware, and rain fell to wash both mother and child. Then the baby took seven steps, looked to the four corners of the world and said (in one of several versions): 'For enlightenment I was born, for the good of all that lives. This is the last time that I have been born into this world of becoming [*samsara*]. There is now no existence again.'

His mother died seven days later, her work in the world done, and from then on Siddhartha was raised by her sister Mahapajapati, who was perhaps another of his father's wives. It was soon clear that hers was no ordinary charge. At the baby's naming ceremony, his father arranged for his future to be predicted by a wise man called Asita, who found thirty-two auspicious marks on his body and prophesied that he would either become a powerful ruler – perhaps the monarch of the whole of India – or a great sage. If he took up the religious life and turned his back on his birthright, he said, Siddhartha could become a teacher of both men and gods, even the saviour of the world.

Father Suddhodana was not best pleased by this second possibility: he wanted Siddhartha to be a king. So, from then on, he did everything he could to make sure that he followed the warrior's rather than the ascetic's path. Arguing that his son's mind would only turn to religion if he saw and experienced the harsh and ugly realities of life, he created an environment of comfort, beauty and ease in which real life played no part. As Siddhartha got older, his father had three marble palaces built for him, one for each of the seasons, and in these he was confined to the upper floors, surrounded by every luxury and amenity wealth could buy – Benares silks, the finest oils, musicians, dancers and courtesans. Suddhodana wanted his son to be so ensnared in a life of privilege that he would never think to leave it.

For all this – all the pampering and spoiling – Siddartha grew up into a well-balanced, kind and studious young man, who was not only gifted in mathematics but also in sports and martial arts. It was by deploying these last talents of his that, at the age of sixteen, he won the hand in marriage of his beautiful young cousin Yasodhara. Yasodhara had been courted by a whole army of young princelings and aristocrats, but Siddhartha beat them all in a series of contests, in one of which he confidently drew a longbow that had belonged to an ancestor of his. The others couldn't even lift it.

In all this time, only one event disturbed the even tenor of Siddhartha's life. At the age of about seven, he went to a ploughing festival with his father, whose duty, as leader/king, was to plough the first furrow. As he watched from under the shade of a rose-apple tree, he saw how hard the men and animals worked and how the ploughs damaged plants and injured or killed small animals. He also saw a lizard eat an ant, only for it to be gobbled down by a snake, which was in turn soon snatched up by a vulture. As he pondered on these things, he experienced a sense of deep compassion and fell, almost without knowing it, into a pleasant meditative trance.

Perhaps it was the memory of this, preying on his mind throughout the years he spent in his palaces, within what was a happy marriage, that caused him to name his son, born when he was twenty-nine, Rahula (or 'fetter') – and to leave his life of luxury four times on four journeys of discovery.

The Four Sights

These expeditions into the outside world, made while his wife

Yasodhara was pregnant, were known to Buddhists everywhere as The Four Sights. On his first excursion, travelling with his charioteer Channa, he saw a frail old man. When he asked Channa what made the old man so weak and doddery, he was told that this was the eventual fate of all human beings, including himself. On the second journey, he saw a sick person: the response to his enquiry on this occasion was that illness could strike even the strongest and healthiest of individuals and there was nothing that could be done to prevent it. The third time he left the palace precincts he saw a corpse being stretchered to the cremation ground. When he asked what it was, he heard about death – an everyday event in human life, said Channa, since death itself was inevitable.

These three encounters had a deeply traumatic effect on Siddhartha, for he had become aware of the true facts of the human condition for the first time. Sickness, ageing and death were inescapable. Human life – all life – was dogged by impermanence, fear and pain. People had no control at all over their own fates and destinies. So how on earth could they pursue a life of pleasure or learning, thought Siddhartha, without coming to terms with this dreadful knowledge?

This was the starting-point for the longer journey that Siddhartha was ultimately to take, that of Seeing directly to the heart of the matter, just as it is for all Buddhists – clearing the mind of all its trivial preoccupations and pursuits and bringing into focus what is really important: that life is characterized by suffering. What happens after that point, in terms of the life one leads and the decisions one takes, is rooted in the knowledge that this is an absolutely fundamental problem that needs to be dealt with. Something must be done about it, but fatalism (passive acceptance) is not an option. The world that we routinely accept without thought is in reality a bizarre, cruel place and it is only by concentrating on this point, while determining to transform our understanding of what it means to lead a human life within it, that we can fulfil our human potential.

The fourth journey that Siddhartha took with Channa provided him with the beginnings of a personal solution to this problem, for he saw for the first time a *sadhu* (a wandering holy man) who, although alone and dressed in rags, was apparently content with his lot. Even though he possessed nothing but a begging bowl, there was a tranquillity about him that other men, for all their possessions and family connections, lacked. Siddartha wanted to know the *sadhu*'s secret, but when he returned to the palace he realized that he could never do so without leaving his own pampered existence behind. If the *sadhu* was as unaffected by the fear of change and suffering (the realm of *samsara*) as he seemed to be, then it had to be because he had abandoned the material life to which he was attached. No spiritual solace was to be found in merely fulfilling one's social duties. The brahminic interpretation of *Dharma* was simply not enough.

The Great Renunciation

In other words, Siddhartha realized that if he was to find any sort of truth in life – if, like the *sadhu*, he was to learn to become indifferent to suffering – he would need to suffer himself. Not only would he have to give up his life of luxury but also the ties of duty and responsibility that linked him to his clan, his family, his father and his wife. He would have to make a commitment: it is with this act of commitment and renunciation that the life of each Buddhist begins. He would have to become a wanderer himself, a simple seeker after truth.

On the very night on which his son Rahula was born – according to the story – Siddhartha secretly left his palace with his charioteer for the last time. They rode to the river Anoma, the border of the Sakyas' territory with a neighbouring kingdom, and there Siddhartha took off his robes and jewels and handed them to Channa, telling him to return them to his father with news of his decision to search for salvation or die in the attempt. His father, he said, was not to grieve, since sooner or later they would have been separated by death anyway. Not knowing how much time he had left for his own life meant the search had to begin immediately. Channa tried to argue him out of it, but Siddhartha would not be moved. Asvaghosa in his *Acts of the Buddha* gives Siddhartha a speech in which departure for the homeless life is justified as fidelity to an even higher *Dharma* than the one he had been brought up in.

With this, he cut off his hair and crossed the river, where he exchanged the clothes he still had for a passing hunter's. Siddhartha had now 'gone forth' in the same way that his followers were to do later. His search had started.

Siddhartha's Studies

For the next six years, according to the story, Siddhartha followed the ascetic path, begging for food and apprenticing himself to a succession of teachers who taught meditational techniques designed to achieve enlightenement (*bodhi*) and emancipation (*nirvana*). The first was Arada Kalama, who taught a form of meditation leading to 'the attainment of the state of nothing at all' and the second was Udraka Ramaputra whose aim was 'the attainment of neither perception nor non-perception'. It was clear, in other words, that as Siddhartha began his mendicant life he was not merely interested in the sort of contemplative identification of the individual soul and Brahman that was laid out in the Upanishads nor in the purgative and purifying abstinence of the Jains. What he sought was something more fundamental, the achievement of his goal of understanding through deep states of meditative concentration (*samadhi*). In later Hinduism this path became known as *raja-yoga* ('the royal discipline') – it was first outlined in the *Bhagavad Gita* in around 200 BC and was given its place of honour in the systematization of yogic practices in *the Yoga Sutras* five or six centuries later. But although Siddhartha became an adept at both forms – and was invited by his teachers to become a teacher himself – he ultimately abandoned them, unsatisfied, for *samadhi* alone could not provide him with the complete solution to his spiritual problem. It didn't reach far enough towards direct and perfect knowledge.

Next, he took himself off to the jungle, near a place called Uruvela, and began to submit his body to the cruellest of austerities and deprivations in an attempt to overcome the general suffering through his own and to exorcize all thoughts from his mind through self-denial. He spent long periods alone and naked – in 'the sky-blue state', as it was called. He endured every extreme of weather; he slept on beds of thorns; he experimented with an extreme form of meditation, holding his breath for as long as he could until he passed out and woke to blinding headaches; and he starved himself to the point of death. So extreme was his commitment that five other ascetics asked if they could join him in his strivings.

Little by little, though, Siddartha, who was by now all skin and bone, began to understand that he was getting nowhere. He was gaining in psychic powers but at the cost of his health – his survival, even – and he was getting no nearer to his goal of perfect understanding. He tried to think of another way, and he cast his mind back to the incident at the ploughing festival when, at the age of about seven, a feeling of compassion had spontaneously cast him into a pleasant meditative trance, a state of dispassionate equilibrium that was the first of the four stages of *dhyana*. Perhaps, he thought, this happy vision of childhood, free from all desire and sensuality, might provide an alternative way.

He also realized that if he went on mortifying his flesh in extreme ways, he might die and simply never find out, so when a woman came to the tree under which he sat and offered him food, he took it. When the five ascetics saw him eating – and continuing to eat – they soon left him in disgust, announcing that he had given up and abandoned the true path. But in fact Siddhartha had come to a profound decision.

The Middle Path

The memory of the childhood incident had begun to convince him that there was nothing wrong with being spiritually happy and he went on to understand, as he continued to eat each day, that a healthy body was also necessary to the pursuit of wisdom. Sensual self-indulgence might be a spiritual cul-de-sac – as he'd discovered for himself through The Four Sights – but so was mortification of the flesh. There was, however, a Middle Way – and this step towards enlightenment became central to the Buddhist *Dharma*. Happiness was important, after all, for the individual was not some sort of soul-substance carried by a greedy, machine-like body from which it had to be freed. Body and *Atman* formed an organic unity in which physical and psychic forces had their own parts to play.

The Temptation of Mara

According to the story of his life that is enshrined in the Buddhist tradition, Siddhartha then had five dreams that seemed to show that he was about to become a Buddha. At a place called Bodh Gaya in what is now the state of Bihar, he made himself a cushion of grass under a pipal tree, sat down facing east, and vowed never to rise again until he had reached enlightenment.

This vow – 'I will not rise from this spot until I am enlightened. Flesh may wither away, blood may dry up, but until I gain enlightenment I shall not move from this seat' – immediately attracted the attention of Mara and his hordes of demons. Mara, 'The Killer', is a sort of Buddhist Satan or Tempter, whose role is to maintain everything – desire, illusion and ignorance – that contributes to the realm of *samsara*, and he could not possibly tolerate the presence of a man who might not only find a way out of *samsara* but also a way to cheat Death himself. During the six years of striving, Mara had merely tried to whisper insinuations in Siddhartha's ear, but now he launched an all-out attack. As one colourful account has it:

> Mara ordered his army to attack Siddhartha with spears of copper, flaming swords and cauldrons of boiling oil. They came riding decaying corpses, and lashing out with hooks and whips and spiked wheels of fire. Some sprouted flames from every hair or rode mad elephants through the treetops. The earth shook and the regions of space flashed flames. Yet whenever anything touched him, it turned into a rain of flowers, fragrant and soft to the touch.

Siddhartha was protected by his merit, accumulated over several lifetimes, and by loving kindness, so the demons had to beat a retreat.

At this point Mara himself went into action by using his magical powers. But he too was rebuffed and he was soon calling on his retinue to bear collective witness to the force of Siddhartha's merit. Siddhartha, having no witness of his own, touched the ground with his right hand – a familiar gesture in all Buddhist art – and called on the witness of

Mother Earth, who is said to have quaked in response to him.

Mara, having failed to force, scare or cow Siddhartha, had one last shot. He now sent in his three beautiful daughters – Discontent, Delight and Desire – to conjure up another army, this time of goddesses.

> Some of the goddesses veiled only half their face; some displayed their full round breasts; some teased him with half smiles; some stretched and yawned seductively; some deliberately appeared dishevelled; some sighed deeply with passion; some undressed slowly before him; some fingered their golden girdles; some swayed their hips like palm trees. And all whispered to him: 'Come and taste the delights of the world and forget nirvana and the path of liberation till you're old'.

Once more, though, the Buddha-to-be (*Bodhisattva*) remained impervious, and when dusk fell Mara's forces finally withdrew.

This story, a late addition to the Buddhist canon, contains a number of important psychological truths – for all its mythological form and shape. For there is no doubt that once a seeker decides to make his or her integrated, determined attempt on truth, the demons of fear are soon summoned. It is not only that old ingrained habits begin to shriek protest at their coming destruction, but there are other questions, such as 'What if I go mad or project myself into some bizarre psychic state'? There is terror in the face of the supernatural, death, and the entering of some sort of existential limbo. Good habits and preparation will, of course, see the seeker through, but then doubts about whether a seeker is up to the challenge begin to arise, doubts that can only be allayed by supreme self-confidence. The last peril of all, in the words of Richard H. Robinson and Willard L. Johnson, in their book *The Buddhist Religion: A Historical Introduction*, 'is of course the rosiest and the deadliest. Perfect love (*maitri*) may cast out fear, but it all too easily changes into personal pleasure'.

The Great Awakening

During the night, with a full moon over him and the temptations of Mara behind him, Siddhartha slowly climbed through the four stages of trance or *dhyana*, the first of which he had experienced as a child, gradually gaining greater concentration and control over his mind as he did so – a process sometimes described by Buddhists as 'letting go'. He was, we must imagine, using techniques taught him by his first two teachers, but he was reaching beyond them to the fourth stage, which was free from all opposites like pain and pleasure, knowledge and ignorance and where there was nothing but pure awareness, spiritual peace and direct unmediated insight meditation (*vipassana*), without any point of view.

There are few details in the narratives of Buddha about what he 'saw' or 'achieved' through this radical reshaping and redirection of perception, for it was obviously considered to be impossible to describe: in other words it was ineffable. All that is said is that Siddhartha remembered all his previous existences during the first watch of the night. In the second watch, he acquired the 'divine eye,' saw the whole universe as if in a mirror and penetrated right to the heart of its endless cycle of birth and dying. He acquired direct knowledge of *karma*, and saw how those who do good are given a happy rebirth while those who commit evil are doomed to a new round of misery.

In the third watch, says the narrative, he gained knowledge of the destruction of the *asavas* ('cankers', 'taints', 'binding influences'), generally understood as physical desire, desire for existence and ignorance. He perceived what came to be known as The Four Holy Truths: 'This is suffering, this is the source of suffering, this is the cessation of suffering, and this is the path that leads to the cessation of suffering'. His mind floated free of the *asavas* and, in the words of the Sutra, quoted by Robinson and Johnson, he saw that 'In me emancipated arose knowledge of my emancipation. I realised that rebirth has been destroyed, the holy life has been lived, the job has been done, there is nothing after this'. As the morning star rose after his long night, he looked out at the world with new eyes, like a man waking up from a dream. He had become the Buddha (the 'emancipated' or 'awakened' one), and he again touched the ground for the earth to bear witness.

Chapter Three:

The Legacy of Enlightenment

Various supernatural events are supposed to have occurred at the moment of the Buddha's Enlightenment. The earth, it was said, swayed like a drunken woman. There were claps of thunder; rain fell; breezes blew; and blossoms and fruit dropped from the sky as Buddha's ancestors applauded his victory and offered him reverence from paradise.

Afterwards, according to the legend, the Buddha remained under the pipal – now the *Bodhi* or Enlightenment – tree for another week, and then spent a further forty-two days in the vicinity, meditating and doing yogic exercises. He was debating within himself whether, and how, to pass on what he had learned, what he had now become. At first he was reluctant, for he knew, on the basis of his own two apprenticeships, that truth cannot be taught, only experienced directly. He also believed that people would find it hard to understand his *Dharma* or live by it, so attached were they to their illusions and wordly ties. Inviting them to accept a truth that undermined and threatened their whole way of life would be nothing but a waste of energy.

In the end, though, his compassion for their unnecessary

suffering tipped the balance – as did a visit from Brahma, the highest god in the popular pantheon of the time. Brahma left the Brahma-world, and appeared before him to announce:

> May the Blessed One teach the Dharma. May the Well-gone One teach the Dharma. There are living beings with a little dust in their eyes who fall away through not hearing the Dharma. They will be recognizers of the Dharma.

At this point, it is said, Buddha opened up his Buddha-eye to survey the world and saw that it was indeed true – many people were impure and dull, but there were some people with keen minds and considerable purity of heart who might well accept his message. Where, though, to begin? He thought of his two teachers, but saw that they had recently died. Then he thought of the five ascetics who had earlier shared his extreme austerities. When he located them in the Deer Park at Isipatana (modern Sarnath) near Benares – over a hundred miles from where he was – he decided to join them.

On his journey to Isipatana, the story continues – as told in the *Sutras*, the collected writings of the Buddhist canon – he met a wandering ascetic who remarked on his clear eyes and shining complexion, and asked what discipline he followed. The Buddha replied that he was a Victor (*Jina*) and that he had no equal in the world of gods and men – he was omniscient and had reached *nirvana*. The mendicant answered with a single syllable – which meant 'It may be so', or 'Let it be so' – and promptly walked away to take another road. In other words, the Buddha was rejected by the first man to whom he offered himself.

When he finally reached the Deer Park at Isipatana (Sarnath) and met up with his one-time fellow-strivers, they too were at first dismissive. He was, after all, the backslider who had given up the ascetic path to indulge his body. But they were soon overwhelmed by his newly-acquired charisma, and in the end they welcomed him, took his bowl and staff, prepared a seat for him among them and gave him water to wash his feet. They called him 'Friend Gautama', but the Buddha immediately stopped them and said that he was now a *Tathagata* ('Teacher', 'one who has reached what is really so'), a perfectly enlightened *arhant* (usually translated as 'saint'). He had reached the ultimate, immortal truth, the *Dharma*, he said, and he was going to preach it. If they followed what he taught, they could then realize it for themselves. Finally, after much initial scepticism, the five men agreed to listen to him.

The Four Noble Truths and the Eightfold Path

We cannot know whether what is called by tradition the Discourse (*darsana*) of the Four Noble Truths actually took place on this occasion – we know as little about it as we do of Jesus's Sermon on the Mount – although it does seem appropriate enough for Buddha's audience of five ascetics. Part of his message was the message of The Middle Way: sensual indulgence was world-tied, illusory and spiritually useless, but mortification and self-torture were no better. It was the Middle Way, requiring vigilance but avoiding extremes, that led to enlightenment and *nirvana*. This Middle Way, he said, was the way of the Holy Eightfold Path, which he described as:

1. right understanding
2. right intention
3. right speech
4. right conduct

5. right livelihood
6. right effort
7. right mindfulness
8. right concentration

He then declared the Four Noble Truths to his audience. The first was the truth of *dhukka*, a Pali word that means 'suffering' but also contains within it overtones of impermanence, imperfection and unsatisfactoriness. This kind of suffering, he said, was to be found at every level and in every aspect of existence. Birth, illness, decay, death, living with one's enemies, being separated from one's loves – the whole world as it is experienced through the five *skandhas* (forms of perception) – was marked and dogged by this suffering.

The second Noble Truth was the truth of the cause of suffering – the intolerable neural itch of desire or craving, for pleasure, for life, sometimes even for death – and the third Truth was the truth of its cessation. When such desires or cravings were completely extinguished – by renunciation, dispassion and non-dependence – then the suffering, too, would come to an end. The fourth Noble Truth was the truth of the path leading towards this cessation of suffering – and with this the Buddha, in what may well have been his first sermon, seemed to come full circle. For this was the truth of the Eightfold Path, which would bring freedom from desires, end suffering in this life and interrupt the endless cycle of an individual's birth and rebirth into the world.

In this way, Buddha revealed for the first time the purified true knowledge he had seen at the moment of his Enlightenment. He did not claim to have created it – it had always existed. But by apprehending it and now teaching it – as others, now forgotten, had done in the past – he was beginning to turn the wheel of *Dharma* once more. One of his audience, a man called Kaundinya, grasped the totality of this as the Buddha was still speaking: he was said to have suddenly acquired the pure *Dharma*-eye. 'Kaundinya has got it! Kaundinya has got it!' exclaimed the Buddha, and when Kaundinya asked to be ordained as a disciple, the Buddha confirmed him with the simple words: 'Come, *bhikkhu* ['monk'], the Dharma is well proclaimed. Walk the holy pathway to the perfect termination of suffering.' *Sangha*, the Buddhist community, had been born.

The Building of the *Sangha*

The Buddha later gave another sermon to his small, select audience, this time on the five so-called *skandhas* – form, feeling, conception, dispositions and consciousness – the interpenetrative ways in which we perceive the material world and the world presents itself to us (a theme to which I shall return later). All of these, he said, were *anatman* ('devoid of self'): they were part of the realm – and causation – of suffering. On hearing this, the other four men in the Deer Park not only became members of the Buddha's order of *bhikkus*, but – according to the tradition – free from the world of illusions: *arhants*, or saints.

Soon, others came to the Deer Park to hear him, among them a young man called Asa, the world-weary son of a rich Benares merchant, to whom Buddha taught a version of the *Dharma* suitable for laymen, before introducing him finally to the Four Truths and allowing him to be ordained. Asa's father soon followed his son, and it was he who became the first Buddhist lay follower (or *upasaka*) by making a formal commitment to the Three Refuges as a rite of entry, reciting three times:

I go for refuge to the Buddha
I go for refuge to the Dharma
I go for refuge to the Sangha

He was followed in turn by his wife and daughters, who became the first female lay followers (*upasika*), and by fifty of Asa's young male friends, who listened to the Buddha and were subsequently ordained, having freed themselves from the shackles of perception to become *arhants* – as had Asa.

Asa and his friends, the five ascetics and Buddha himself formed the core of what became a missionary movement in northern and central India. They left Sarnath and travelled from village to village and city to city, proclaiming the Buddha's teachings 'for the the the benefit of the many, out of compassion for the world, for the welfare of gods and humans'. Men and women 'with keen faculties will attain liberation', said the Buddha, 'if – and only if – they actually hear the *Dharma* message'.

Right from the beginning, the great strength of Buddhism was its openness to all, regardless of race, caste, class or gender. The Brahmanic schools kept their teachings as esoteric and secret as possible and the masters maintained close control over their students. They also used an archaic form of Sanskrit. By contrast, the early Buddhists spoke in ordinary demotic dialect and broadcast their message to anyone and everyone to whom it could be communicated. The result was electrifying. People began travelling long distances for ordination: so many of them, in fact, and at such hardship to themselves, that Buddha soon gave his monks permission to confer ordination themselves wherever they went. The result was that the *Sangha* became self-replicating: word spread like wildfire over wide distances, far wider than could be controlled by any single authority.

And it wasn't only individuals who were prepared to give up their lives to the Buddhic *Dharma* – there were also whole sects. For example, one early convert was the leader of a fire-worshipping sect of ascetics, Uruvela Kasyapa, whom the Buddha so impressed with his supranormal powers that he and his five hundred followers immediately entered the Buddhist fold – to be followed soon afterwards by his two ascetic brothers and five hundred devotees of their own. Two members of another sect, who were later to become Buddha's chief disciples – Sariputta, famous for his wisdom, and Moggallanna, celebrated for his psychic powers – brought with them into the *Sangha* two hundred of their fellow-strivers who had become unsatisfied, as they themselves had, with the teachings of the master they had followed.

At first the Buddha made no strict rules for new converts like these. He simply asked ordinands to commit themselves to the Three Refuges and to an ethical life. They had to promise:

- not to harm any living thing
- not to take anything that wasn't freely given
- to forsake the world of fleshly pleasures and stay celibate
- to speak and think truthfully, kindly and compassionately
- to shun all intoxicants.

Later Buddha instituted a more formal ordination ceremony, which consisted of shaving off head and facial hair, ritually taking up the yellow robe and promising to obey certain simple monastic rules (subsequently expanded and written up in great detail in the *Vinaya Pitaka*). But in the early days the code of the monks seems to have remained simple, their purpose clear. For nine months of the year

41

they were to travel as mendicants, pursuing their own paths and spreading the word as missionaries. But for three months, during the Monsoon or rainy season, they were free to go into retreat – which they did, often in each other's company. This was the seed-bed out of which grew the Buddhist monastery.

The First Monasteries

Buddha spent the first rainy season at Sarnath and soon afterwards travelled to Rajagaha, the capital of Magadha, where he was welcomed by King Bimbisara and a great crowd of people, all of whom – says tradition – became lay followers. The next day the king himself waited on the Buddha and his *bhikkhus* at the alms meal, and afterwards he gave a pleasure garden to the *Sangha* outside the city called The Bamboo Grove, where a rich merchant later put up shelters. Here, in the first makeshift monastery, the Buddha spent the next two Rains Retreats, as they came to be called. But for the fourth he was invited to Savatthi, the capital of the neighbouring kingdom of Kosala. His host there was a rich philanthropist called Anathapindika, who bought for the purpose another pleasure-garden owned by a nobleman called Jeta – and hence called Jetavana or 'Jeta's Grove'. A second monastery was subsequently built here and was soon followed by a third, the Pubbarama or 'Eastern Park', built on land, also near Savatthi, donated by a rich laywoman named Visakha. When the Buddha settled permanently at Savatthi, he spent alternate Rains Retreats at the Jetavana and the Pubbarama.

After the fourth Rains Retreat, the Buddha made a journey back into his past: he went to visit his family and people in the Sakya capital of Kapilavatthu. For his father Suddhodana the visit of the *Sakyamuni* (the 'sage of the Sakya people') was a bitter-sweet occasion, for though he himself was set on the Path by his son, he lost another of his children, Nanda (the son of Buddha's aunt and foster-mother, Mahapajapati), as well as his beloved grandson, Buddha's son Rahula, to conversion and ordination. (Rahula went on to become a leading light among the trainers of new monks and novices.) He complained bitterly to the Buddha about this and won from him a small concession: he agreed that children would no longer be ordained without their parents' agreement.

These, though, were not the only relatives who chose to follow the Buddha, for around this time his cousin Ananda – who was to remain his faithful attendant for the rest of his life – became an ordained monk. Also, after Suddhodana died the following year, his widow Mahapajapati, who had raised the Buddha, begged to be accepted as a nun. She asked three times and was three times refused. But so determined was she that she cut off all her hair, put on the yellow robe and followed him along the road to a neighbouring kingdom with a retinue of ladies-in-waiting. There, Ananda took pity on the women's wretched, travel-worn state and intervened with the Buddha, who finally, and reluctantly, consented. He told Ananda that women had exactly the same spiritual potential as men, but he imposed eight stringent rules on Mahapajapati and the nuns (*bhikkhunis*) who were to follow her into the *Sangha* – among them her attendants and the wife of King Bimbisara – one of which was the acknowledgment that even the most senior nun was still junior to a monk, even one who had been ordained that very day.

His concern, he later told Ananda, was that the presence of women would distract the monks – and indeed he later warned his *bhikkus* to be vigilant in their presence. When Ananda asked how monks should behave when nuns were about, Buddha is recorded as having said they should not talk and they should keep their eyes open. It may have been around this time that he began to increase the number of promises each ordinand, male and female, had to make before admission to the *Sangha*, and to lay down the complex rules – governing every aspect of their behaviour – that are recorded in the Vinaya Pitaka. These rules were considered to be so all-important that, in the early history of the Buddhist community, they even took precedence over the Buddha's teachings. Morality – right conduct – came before everything else.

Buddha's Mission

For almost half a century the Buddha worked as a missionary, wandering from village to village for nine months of each year. When he arrived at a settlement, he would wait quietly with his alms bowl at its inhabitants' doors until he had gathered enough food for his one meal of the day. Then he would go off to a mango grove on the outskirts to eat, and would be joined there afterwards by anyone and everyone who wanted to hear him preach. Virtually his whole life, in other words, consisted of encounters with ordinary people of every caste and class, either met on the road or at village meetings. Many of these encounters passed into the Buddhist canon, each with its own moral or spiritual lesson. One of these, for example – as retold in Ven. Sangharaskshita's *A Guide to the Buddhist Path* – was with a brahmin:

> Journeying along the high road, the Buddha met a man called Dona [who was] skilled in the science of bodily signs. Seeing on the Buddha's footprints the mark of a thousand-spoked wheel, he followed in his track along the road until he eventually caught up with the Buddha, who was sitting beneath a tree. As the Buddha was fresh from

his Enlightenment, there was a radiance about his whole being. We are told that it was as though a light shone from his face – he was happy, serene, joyful. Dona was very impressed by his appearance, and he seems to have felt that this wasn't an ordinary human being, perhaps not a human being at all. Drawing nearer, he came straight to the point, as the custom is in India where religious matters are concerned. He said, 'Who are you?'

Now the ancient Indians believed that the universe is stratified into various levels of existence, that there are not just human beings and animals, as we believe, but gods, and ghosts, and yaksas, and gandharvas, and all sorts of other mythological beings, inhabiting a multi-storey universe, the human plane being just one storey out of many. So Dona askled, 'Are you a yaksa?' (a yaksa being a rather terrifying sublime spirit living in the forest). But the Buddha said, 'No'. Just 'No'. So Dona tries again. 'Are you a gandharva?' (a sort of celestial musician, a beautiful singing angel-like figure). Once again the Buddha said 'No', and again Dona asked, 'Well then, are you a deva?' (a god, a divine being, a sort of archangel). 'No'. Upon this Dona thought, 'That's strange, he must be a human being after all'. And he asked him that too, but yet again the Buddha said 'No'. By this time Dona was thoroughly perplexed, so he demanded, 'If you are not any of these things, then who are you?' The Buddha replied, 'Those mental conditionings on account of which I might have been described as a yaksa or a gandharva, as a deva or a human being, all those conditionings have been destroyed by me. Therefore I am a Buddha'.

Another much-celebrated encounter was with a woman called Kisagotami whose only son had died and who was wandering about, distraught, with his body in her arms – here told in an embellished version quoted by Clive Erricker in his *Teach Yourself Buddhism*.

> Kisagotami was almost driven out of her mind by her sorrow. A wise man saw her . . . and realised how much she needed help. He had heard some of the teaching of Gotama Buddha, and thought that he might be able to help her come to terms with her grief. He approached Kisagotami gently and told her that the Buddha was staying nearby and that he might have medicine for her son. 'Go and ask him', he said. Kisagotami went to find the Buddha and stood on the edge of the crowd, listening to him. When she had the chance, she called out to him, 'O, Exalted One, give me medicine for my son'.
>
> Part of the Buddha's greatness lay in his skill in knowing how to help other people. He told her kindly to go to the city nearby and visit every house. 'Bring me some grains of mustard seed from every household in which no-one has ever died.'
>
> Kisagotami was delighted. Here was someone who took her seriously. She went to the city, knocked [at] the first house and asked for some grains of mustard seed from the householder, if no-one had ever died there. The householder told her with great sadness that he had recently lost his wife. Kisagotami listened to his story with growing sympathy, understanding his grief from her own. She eventually moved on, but found that in every house there was a story of sickness, old age and death. Her own

grief seemed different now that she shared that of others, and she realised that the Buddha had known when he sent her out that she would find that her predicament was the common experience of human beings. Death is the law common to all that lives. She now took the body of her dear little son to the cremation ground and let it be cremated, fully realising that all is impermanent.

Kisagotami then returned to the Gotama Buddha. He asked her whether she had brought him the grains of mustard seed. She told him what had happened, and what she had realised. She then asked him to accept her as his follower and to teach her more about the nature of reality and the path to understanding . . .

Early Buddhic literature teems with encounters of this kind. There was Katyayana, a Brahmin court-priest sent by the king of Avanti in western India to find out more about the Buddha – he was sent back as monk and *arhant* to spread word of the *Dharma* in the West (and to become the first Buddhist commentator, 'foremost of those who analyze at length what the Buddha has stated concisely'). There were kings and queens, Jains and Brahmanists – and even a well-known and murderous bandit called Angulimala, or 'Finger-Necklace', so called because he wore his victims' fingers in a gruesome trophy round his neck. One day he gave chase to the Buddha as he was travelling on a deserted stretch of road, but however fast he ran he still could not catch him. So he shouted out, 'Hey! Stop, monk!', at which the Buddha coolly replied, 'But I have stopped, Angulimala. Isn't it time you stopped [using violence] too?' Angulimala promptly threw away his sword and, like so many others in the Canon, begged to be allowed to become one of Buddha's followers.

The Death of the Buddha

By the time he was seventy-nine, the Buddha knew that his body was failing, but he still would not let up. That season he travelled from Rajagaha by a series of stages to Vaisali in the northwest, preaching along the way. He stopped at Nalanda, where a great Buddhist university was later built, and at Pataligama, where he prophesied the creation of a great new city – now modern Patna.

Once at Vaisali, though, he became seriously ill with 'violent and deadly pains', and it was only by an act of supreme will that he was able to suppress them. He had not yet made any formal farewell to the *Sangha* – on whose survival his thoughts seemed to be running at that time, for he told his faithful cousin and attendant Ananda that he did not want the community to be personally dependent on him in any way. Each *bhikkhu* had to be as self-reliant as possible, he said, and should turn to the *Dharma* if in any doubt. He had taught them everything they needed to know. There were no extra dimensions, no esoteric teachings that had been somehow withheld. They already knew everything that was necessary.

When the rains let up, he moved on to one of the first monasteries, Jeta's Grove in Savatthi, where he heard the news of the death of Sariputta, one of his most cherished disciples. (Another, the adept psychic Moggallanna, seems to have died at about the same time.) This may have dispirited him, for back in Vaisali, according to *The Sutra of the Great Decease*, he hinted to Ananda that he had the power to prolong his life more or less indefinitely, if (and only if) he was asked. Ananda failed to seize the moment – for which he was later much blamed by the *Sangha* – and from then on the Buddha seems to have lost the will to live, for the death process began in earnest. When Mara ('The Killer') came near and told him it was time for him to attain *paranirvana* (perfect, or final *nirvana*), the Buddha simply agreed. He said, 'Don't fuss, Evil One. Very soon – within three months – the Tathagata's *paranirvana* will take place.'

Once more he set off, however, travelling from village to village, preaching at a place called Pava before receiving the meal that finally killed him, from a man called Cunda the Smith. It was of minced pork or mushrooms – scholars disagree – and it caused 'violent sickness, bleeding and acute stomach pain'. Somehow he managed to travel onwards towards Kusinagara, an insignificant village in the country of the Mallas (now Kasia in Uttar Pradesh), but outside it, in a grove of sala trees, he collapsed. He asked Ananda to make him a bed between two of the trees and he lay on it on his right side, with his head, supported by his hand, to the north and his face to the west, in a posture widely celebrated in Buddhist iconography.

He went on teaching through the night, according to the legend, even giving instruction to a wandering ascetic called Subhadra, who became the last of his converts to be accepted into the *Sangha*. Ananda was upset by this interruption of his last hours and wept. But the Buddha said to him, 'Don't mourn. Haven't I told you it's in the nature of things that we're separated from those we hold most dear? So why be upset?' He promised Ananda, who was not yet an *arbant*, that he would be 'liberated' soon. As to the question of his successor, he said to Ananda in the words of the *Digha-Nikaya*:

> As I have never sought to direct or subject the community
> to my teachings, I leave no such instruction to the Sangha.
> I am reaching my end. After my death each of you will be
> your own island, your own refuge. Take no other refuge.

The *Dharma* itself, in other words, was to be the Buddha's true successor.

By this time the Buddha was surrounded by monks, by local tribespeople and, according to legend, the lamentations of nature and of the gods, who were gathered around him so densely 'that a hair could not be slipped between them'. When his teaching was done, he asked three times if his disciples had any last questions or doubts. They were all silent. Then he spoke his last words to them: 'All created things are impermanent by nature. Work diligently towards your own salvation.' He then went into trance and climbed through the stages of *dhyana* until he reached the fourth, from which he passed into *paranirvana*. He died at the age of 80, free from rebirth, on the night of the July full moon, in the meditative calm in which he had learned to live.

The Funeral of the Buddha

The next day the people of Kusinagara and the surrounding area arrived to bury him according to the old Aryan tradition. The wake went on for six days with music, dancing and the offering of garlands and scents. The body was washed and anointed with oil and then wrapped in alternate layers of cotton wool and cloth. Eight chiefs of the Mallas then carried it on a bier to a tribal shrine, and there it was cremated – though not without some difficulty for the pyre, traditionally lit by the eldest son, would not catch fire until his senior living disciple, the ascetic Mahakasypa, arrived to light the first torch.

Before he lit it, though, Mahakasypa wanted to say goodbye and to pay homage to his beloved teacher by kissing his feet – still a practice in modern India. Immediately the bindings on the Buddha's feet unravelled, it was said, and after Mahakasypa had made his obeisance, the pyre caught light spontaneously and burned itself out without any human intervention. The Buddha's bones, though, turned out to be indestructible, according to the Canon, and some of them at least were buried in a *stupa* (memorial mound) raised at a nearby crossroads.

It was a funeral fit for an Aryan king. In fact, the rites echoed those of Homeric Greece – Hector's funeral in *The Iliad*, for example – and the *stupa* was exactly the same sort of 'round' barrow that was used to house the bodies of bronze-age kings and chieftains in places that were as far apart as Orkney and the East. It was also royal in another sense, too, for no distinction was made between the sacred and the secular realms at all – neither in Sanskrit nor in Pali nor in Ardamagadhi, the colloquial language the Buddha probably spoke. The same word, *arya* (Aryan), was used for both 'noble' and 'saint', and *puja* was used for both 'honour, respectful reverence' and for 'worship'. Buddha, then, was the true equivalent or equal of 'a king' or 'a noble' since the two spheres were undifferentiated – as were, in the popular view, the holy men whose *stupas* and shrines (*caitya*), where honour/reverence/worship was offered, dotted the countryside.

Because of this, there seems to have been considerable squabbling about the final disposition of the Buddha's relics, before the funeral party went its way. The Mallas laid claim to them, since the Buddha had died on their territory and they had arranged and conducted the funeral. But powerful leaders from other areas also wanted to lay their hands on them, since not only were they sacred, but they would also convey prestige and the mantle of authenticity – closeness to Buddha – on their caretakers. (They were also, one has to say, a potential source of revenue from worshippers and pilgrims.) The matter was decided, on the brink of a very un-Buddha-like battle, by an agreement to divide the relics, which were later granted their own individual monument or temple. The great building programme of the Buddhist community – and the myriad representations of the Buddha in sculptural form – had begun.

The Life as Example

The life of the Buddha is the cornerstone of Buddhism, just as the life (and death) of Jesus is that of Christianity, for his is literally the model life, the life on which the life of Buddhists is modelled. In this sense, his life and teachings are one, as he himself recognized when he said: 'Whoever sees *Dharma* sees me; whoever sees me sees *Dharma*.'

The trajectory of his life – presented as that of an epic hero in the battle for spiritual knowledge and self-realization – is a demonstration of the way actions and values are co-dependent. In its first part, the young Siddhartha, as his father's heir, is set to inherit the physical world. He is indulged, given everything that could possibly satisfy him. His palaces and lifestyle represent the fleeting world of materiality (*samsara*), the realm of impermanence, suffering, death and inevitable rebirth in an extreme, and perhaps enviable, form.

The first three of the Four Sights – his very first contacts with old age, sickness and death – enable him to realize that everything he has held to be of value up until this time is, in fact, meaningless. The fourth of the Sights – his encounter with the ascetic 'striver' – points to the way out. By completely changing his life, he is now able to begin to take personal responsibility for his values and actions. He learns self-discipline and steeps himself in the techniques of self-transformation that were available at the time. Like a spiritual physician, he has now not only identified the disease and realized that it can be cured, but he is also beginning to find where the cure lies.

The six years he spends as an ascetic and *yogi* are a time of intense self-reflection, of learning, and lead to the choices implicit in the Middle Way. He resolves for himself what values will govern his life, and through the visions of the Enlightenment he is ultimately transformed. The disease that he has identified at the root of human life has now been finally – and permanently – beaten.

After the Enlightenment, he decides to return to the world, to share these new values of his – his cure – and to exemplify for his fellow countrymen the spiritually considered and humane actions that spring from them. After almost fifty years of work as a missionary, he faces death with equanimity and dies with immense calm, without any of the anxieties of those still tied to the world.

His life, therefore, exemplifies the three-fold nature of what is known as the Buddhist Path. Everyone is born into a particular family or culture and makes accommodations and adjustments to them, gradually accumulating habits and tastes in the process which foreordain that we will behave in a particular way. Our lives, in other words, become progressively circumscribed and depotentialised. All we can do about it is to start again – either passively, by means of rebirth, or actively, by confronting this fact and taking counter-action. If we refuse to take this second option – refuse to become aware of the problem as the Buddha did – then there can be no spiritual maturity in this or any other life. We can never be free as individuals.

The ideal Buddhist way of dealing with this is patterned directly on the Buddha's own experience. It starts with a curative morality (*sila*), a set of ethical rules designed to purge and purify the individual and bring him or her closer to his or her essential nature. The following of this moral path is the beginning of transformation, since it increases self-knowledge and awareness (or mindfulness, *smrti*), without which we can never come to terms with the underlying illness – the causes and effects of our own past actions and assumptions. Essential too is mental discipline (*samahdi*), the cultivation of meditative calm (*samatha*) and what is called one-point concentration.

Samahdi leads, in a sense, to the third element, *prajna*, or wisdom, which consists in directly perceiving the truth of the *Dharma* and of Buddhist life-values. But wisdom – and its getting – is not really seen as separable, a different kind of milestone, from either *sila* or *samahdi*, for each is unattainable without the other two. The moral life, for example, cannot be sustained without both mental discipline and wisdom, and wisdom itself is also acquired cumulatively rather than in an all-at-once sort of way. It is a quality that grows as thought and understanding become gradually freed from ignorance, and this unchaining of the individual can only be achieved by following the three-fold path as a whole. The end result, the ultimate goal, was described by Buddha to his faithful Ananda not long before he died (in a version quoted in Clive Erricker's *Teach Yourself Buddhism*):

> Those who have died after the complete destruction of the three bonds, of lust, of covenance, and of the egotistical cleaving to existence, need not fear the state after death. They will not be in a state of suffering; their minds will not continue as a Karma of evil deeds or sin, but are assured of final deliverance. When they die nothing will remain of them but their good thoughts, their righteous acts, and the bliss that proceeds from truth and righteousness. As rivers must at last reach the distant main, so their minds will be reborn in higher states of

existence and continue to press on to their ultimate goal,
which is the ocean of truth, the eternal peace of Nirvana.

The ideal Buddhist course, then, for lay person and monk alike, follows a progression closely modelled on the life and mental development (*bhavana*) of Buddha – except that for the lay person, of course, the final destination will take longer.

Chapter Four:

Buddhism as Taught by Buddha

Thus have I heard. The Blessed One was once living in the Deer Park at Isipatana [the Resort of Seers] near Varanasi [Benares]. There he addressed the group of five *bhikkhus*.

So begins the first discourse of the Buddha, as it appears in the collected writings of the Buddhist canon, the Sutras. The word *sutra* means thread – each Sutra is thus a thread in the whole tapestry of Buddhic thought, and this discourse is perhaps the most important thread of all, since it lays out the Four Noble Truths and the Middle Way, the kernel of everything the Buddha had learned in the years up to and including his Enlightenment. In that time he had gained intimate experience of both sensual pleasure and self-mortification and he described both here as 'unworthy and unprofitable'. (Self indulgence was also 'low, common and the way of ordinary people', and self-mortification was 'painful'.) The correct path to follow, he said, was the Middle Way between them, which alone led to 'vision, knowledge, calm, insight, enlightenment and *nirvana*'.

The Middle Way was also the fourth of the Four Noble Truths and it is worth looking at them in turn in order to see Buddhism clearly for what it is: a doctrine of salvation.

The First Noble Truth: All Is Suffering

'Suffering' is a very approximate, and somewhat misleading, translation of the complex word *dukkha*, for Buddha acknowledged that life was not just one long vale of tears: it also had its moments of happiness. What he was saying was that when a human life is looked at overall, it is clear that what we might call a permanent state of *angst*, which stems from what we want and hope for ourselves, is *systematically* built into it. This desire for ourselves causes *angst* (or *dukkha*, suffering), because even if we get what we want we are aware that we cannot have it for ever: so we not only suffer in the anticipation of our desires but also in their loss. If we do not get what we want we still suffer, but this time from dissatisfaction and thwarted longing. A fundamental, built-in anxiety is part of the human experience, in other words. If we set goals for ourselves and fail to reach them, we become miserable; and if we do reach them, we want more – enough is never enough. And over all this web of desire and frustration hangs the presence of sickness, old age and death which casts a pall of anxiety over ourselves and all our relationships. Life, to sum up – and to appropriate Oscar Wilde's epigram about the smoking of cigarettes – may sometimes be exquisite, but it still leaves you (spiritually) unsatisfied, unfulfilled.

The answer to this problem, said the Buddha, cannot lie in changing the world to accommodate our desires and dreams. It must instead lie in ourselves, for the condition of the world is part of the problem, not part of the solution. The world is, by its very nature, impermanent (*anicca*) and subject to change. A state of endless fluctuation is systematically built into it which prevents everything and anything from enduring, so that nothing at all – no moment, no feeling, no thought, no action, no person – can last. However hard we try to create permanence for ourselves, therefore, it must always slip through our fingers. The Buddha said that death is, of course, the major under-cutter of this permanence, but little deaths and new beginnings fill every minute of existence – it is simply the nature of the world we live in, in which change is both necessary and inevitable. In the realm of *samsara*, therefore – the world of daily life – there *can* only be impermanence and *dukkha*. This description, from the Buddhic point of view, is neither happy nor sad, neither optimistic nor pessimistic. It is simply *so*.

The Second Noble Truth: The Origin of Suffering (or *Angst*)

The Second Noble Truth goes deeper into the roots of *dukkha*, into the way in which we confront the world through an organized personality we call 'the self' or 'I'. It is, in a sense, a psychological theory of relativity.

Put into its simplest form, the essential cause of *dukkha*, said Buddha, was *tanha* (or thirst). This thirst can be described as a fundamental, in-wired longing for something outside ourselves, and it ranges from gross manifestations like greed, lust and miserliness to more subtle and seemingly benign ones – like wanting to do good in the world or to know the truth. One way and another, Buddha said, we are victims of what the poet W. H. Auden called, in another context, an 'intolerable neural itch,' a constant desire to move our 'selves' out into the world in order to direct, change or understand 'it'.

But what exactly are these 'selves'? And what is the 'it' out there that we want to intervene in? In ordinary parlance we routinely separate the two concepts. We talk of 'the world I live in' and take it for granted that this 'I' of ours is somehow detached from its environment, and that the self or ego is a privileged, inside observer of people and events; the whole passing show. But how true can this be in reality, when everybody else 'out there' is carrying around their own selves, their own egos, and believing exactly the same thing? We ordinarily compensate for this unsettling fact by making remarks like 'Well, everyone has their own point of view' and other bromides, but we fail to fully examine its implications. Instead, we continue to believe – in a muddled, anxious and *systematic* state of *dukkha* – that we are somehow the centre of the universe.

But are we? And *can* we be? This, essentially, was Buddha's question – and it is a question that recurs in our daily lives, insinuating itself willy-nilly into our consciousnesses. Relativity, that is to say, keeps creeping in. Imagine the 'I', for example, as a person standing alone on a station platform when a train comes through. Believing that he is fixed in some way, permanent, assured of his 'I'-ness, he observes the train, the engine, the carriages, the people travelling between departure and destination, their lives changing in the process. Yet to a person on the train looking out of the window, his 'I' is just a momentary presence, then a past image, a distant memory. For each 'I', in other words, it is the other which is fleeting, transient – their realities are contradictory.

What Buddha said in effect was that neither of these two people, these two 'Is', is at all permanent in the way in which we imagine as individuals that they must be. What is moving is neither the train nor the person left behind on the platform, but that other great vehicle that sweeps through both platform and train – all life – alike: time.

Let us create another analogy by imagining the 'I' as a person standing on earth looking up at the sky, examining a star. He knows enough about astronomy to know full well that what he is seeing is hugely distant from him, both in space and in time, because of the time it takes for light to travel all the way to his eye. Within himself, at that moment, he may well feel that he is at the centre of the universe. But if another 'I' on that same star were to look for him at the very same moment, he would not yet even exist for his observer, since the light carrying information about his existence would only just be starting its long journey.

As Buddha was saying in the Second Noble Truth, an irreducible 'self' or fixed personality cannot logically exist, for it too is part of the universe's relativity – its constant change, or 'becoming'. Thus the ego, generally perceived as the source of consciousness, is in reality a false construct, a fiction designed to cloak its own inherent instability. This Buddhist doctrine of *anatta* (no self) is the third aspect of *dukkha*; and *dukkha*, *anicca* (impermanence) and *anatta* are together called the three marks in the Sutras, or the fundamental characteristics of existence.

Given all this, however, the question arises: 'If there's no such thing as a self, then what on earth constitutes an individual consciousness or personality?' And Buddha gave his answer through his version of the *skandhas*, the five groups or 'aggregates' of forces and energies that tie us to the world.

1. The Aggregate of Matter. This grouping includes the body, analyzed in terms of four elements (solidity, fluidity, heat and motion) and their derivatives, which include the five sensory organs: eyes, ears, tongue, nose and skin.

2. The Aggregate of Feeling (or Sensation). This grouping includes all sensations that are classified as pleasant, unpleasant or neutral, and arise through the encounter of the physical and mental organs with objects in the world. (The mind or brain is regarded here as one of

these.) They include the creation of visual forms, of sounds, smells, tastes, tactile sensations and – with the addition of mind – ideas, mental images and so on.

3. The Aggregate of Perception. Perception is the faculty which actually recognizes something in the world by picking out its characteristic features and distinguishing it from other things. It arises from the interaction of the sensory organs and the mind with the object in question.

4. The Aggregate of Mental Formations. This grouping includes all mental constructs: volitions and intentions; determination; heedlessness; intuition; and the idea of the self. These constructs also include the three poisons noted earlier: desire, ignorance and aversion. All these things are the raw material of *karma*, because they are the root cause of why and how we act. Mental formations and behaviour, in fact, cannot really be separated, for in a sense they are one and the same thing. As the *Dhamapada*, quoted in Clive Erricker's *Teach Yourself Buddhism* (for which I am grateful for this account of the *skandhas*) explains:

> What we are today comes from our thoughts of yesterday, and our present thoughts build our life of tomorrow. Our life is the creation of our mind.
> If a man speaks or acts with an impure mind, suffering follows him as the wheel of the cart follows the beast that draws the cart . . . If a man speaks or acts with a pure mind, joy follows him as his own shadow.

5. The Aggregate of Consciousness. This is an awareness of all the other four aggregates that supervenes out of their conjunction, *but is*

not – and cannot be – independent of them. 'There is no arising of consciousness without conditions,' said the Buddha to Sati the Fisherman's Son, who saw otherwise. Consciousness, that is to to say, cannot exist separately from the other *skandhas* – and just as they are impermanent, constantly on the move, so must consciousness be. What we perceive as the self, the 'I' – a sort of fixed, central command-centre and immutable point of reference – is, then, an illusion. All 'we' have access to is an impersonal succession of sense-impressions and awarenesses. In their constant flow, these may create a sense of 'identity' as a by-product, because they seem to be happening to 'us'. But the idea of a fixed independent selfhood – or ego – is an ongoing fiction. The Buddha understood how sensations, endlessly following one another, might create the impression of a self which seems to 'possess' the senses which apprehend them, but denied that there was any organizing principle at all 'behind' or 'above' either.

In other words, the raw material out of which we construct the world is nothing more – and *can* be nothing more – than a continual succession of mental and physical phenomena. Each individual is a compound of components, that is to say, which are constantly changing. Clive Erricker in *Teach Yourself Buddhism* gives an example, which is also an example of the *skandhas* in action:

> I am hungry and I am presented with a plate of food. I see it, smell it, and anticipate the taste. I am aware of what is in the dish. Sensations arise and perceptions follow, with the recognition of what it will be like to taste it. Volition is brought into play, I wish to eat. I pick up my knife and fork; all other concerns vanish from my mind as I indulge in the pleasure of eating. As my stomach becomes full, my desire decreases. My mind turns to other things. New sensations,

perceptions and mental formations arise. I am more interested in my partner's conversation, dwell on the discomfort in my stomach. I wish to do other things. I suggest it is time to leave. I look forward to what happens next, or I view it with disappointment – the end of an enjoyable evening and a new working day. I am enveloped in the never-ending process of continual arising (or 'dependent origination'), a chain of cause and effect that never ceases.

Life, the Buddha taught, does not have to be this way, forever shifting between aversion and desire in a maze of mental images and perceptions and volitions, in the middle of which I somehow confusedly identify something I call 'myself'. Desire and aversion, he said, are two sides of the same coin: the one inevitably leads to the other, and worldly happiness can never be more than a fleeting sensation – with dissatisfaction built into its very core. The only way to escape from this constant see-saw – or vicious circle – is to confront the fact that the 'I' which longs for happiness and ease is precisely the obstacle which stands in the way of obtaining either. Self is, in fact, *dukkha*. Only by giving up self can happiness be truly achieved.

If there is no such thing as self, though, and it is the fate of all individuals to undergo rebirth, what exactly, according to the teachings of the Buddha, is it that is reborn?

Rebirth

The Buddha firmly rejected the idea of eternalism: that is, he denied the prevailing belief that the soul or self somehow survived death intact. If physical form, feelings, perceptions and mental formations were all impermanent, after all, how could the self, which was merely their by-product, be anything more permanent than they were? Even in life, there is no abiding aspect of a person that is solid and unchanging enough to house what we call a self. When that person dies, therefore – and the other four *skandhas* pass away – there simply cannot be any residue or leftovers to pass on.

At the same time, though, the Buddha also rejected eternalism's metaphysical opposite – so-called annihilationism. That is, the idea that when a person dies, 'bang, that's that' – there is no afterlife at all. For that would have been to accept that human life lacks all meaning and purpose – and under those circumstances it wouldn't matter how anyone behaved, for there would be nothing to lose. Hedonism – total abandonment to every passing lust or caprice – would be the order of every day. Yet the Buddha saw this option as bringing about the worst possible of all conditions. Why? The answer lies in *karma*, a concept which is absolutely central to Buddhist ethics and to Buddha's teachings on the matter of rebirth.

Karma

Put at its simplest, *karma* is the law of cause and effect. It says that anything at all that happens has been caused by something else, and in turn causes other things. All living things are links in this continuous chain of cause and effect – births and deaths are simply small events in an endless cycle. Birth brings the *skandhas* together into a particular formation and death dissipates them again, but past actions and intentions – including those we 'ourselves' have injected (or will inject) into the stream – continue to play themselves out, rolling on regardless. *Karma*, therefore, should be understood as being – at one and the same time – what 'we' inherit from the past and what 'we' contribute to the future.

In the West, the word *karma* has had a bad press – it has been assumed that it refers to a deterministic and fatalistic view of life, or to some immutable destiny that we can do nothing to alter. But the Buddhic idea of *karma* – the on-rolling tide of cause and effect – is a great deal more than that. Yes, it is used in Buddhism to explain the differing conditions of people in the world – past good or bad deeds in other lives being responsible for their station or position in this one. And yes, it is used to help explain mass deaths and disasters (collective *karma*). But that is only because the law of *karma* decrees that everything *must* have a cause, even if it lies outside our ability to grasp it – this rule lies right at the heart of Buddhist ethics. It is not only the answer to everything-that-is, but also to the essential question of morality, which is 'Why should we be good'? *Because what we do and how we act produces personal, communal, human and spiritual consequences.*

One can see this principle at work on a personal level without any difficulty. For it is a truism that what we do has consequences which profoundly affect how we feel and what subsequently happens to us. A sudden outburst of anger, for example, can sour relations with others for hours, days or weeks – it might even be the cause of a permanent break and either leave us guilt-ridden or full of a defensive (or crowing) self-justification. ('Losing my temper was both right and effective; in the same circumstances I'd do it – even use it as a tactic – again.') Equally, a sudden moral lapse can have truly devastating consequences, such as the loss of a fortune or a career.

It is not only the bad things we do, however, that produce an effect. It would be a mistake if we only laid stress on the effect of so-called 'bad' karma, which in the traditional view may lead to rebirth as a poor or sickly person, an animal or an insect, or even an occupant, for aeons of time, of one of the Buddhist hells. That way lies guilt and terror of life. The Buddhist monk Ajahn Sumedho, quoted in John Snelling's *The Buddhist Handbook*, explains:

> We worry: 'I've done so many bad things in the past; what kind of result will I get from all that?' Well, all you can know is what you've done in the past is a memory now. The most awful, disgusting thing that you've ever done, that you wouldn't want anyone to know about; the one that, whenever anyone talks about karma and rebirth, makes you think, 'I'm really going to get it for having done that' – that is a memory, and that memory is the karmic result. The additions to that like fearing, worrying, speculating – these are the karmic result of unenlightened behaviour. What you do, you remember; it's as simple as that. If you do something kind, generous or compassionate, the memory makes you feel happy; and if you do something mean and nasty, you have to remember *that*. You try to repress it, run away from it, get caught up in all kinds of frantic behaviour – that's the karmic result.

Sumedho goes on to say that the only way to get rid of this sort of karmic result – or karmic formation, as it is often called – is to confront and recognize it fully. In meditation, karmic formations are encouraged to rise into the mind and then to disappear and die – without being acted upon, stresses Snelling. For whenever a karmic formation is acted upon in any way – good or bad – its life is prolonged and its power is increased. Habits of mind and behaviour that become harder and harder to break out of are created little by little.

Since breaking out – escaping from an endlessly reduplicated state of ignorance and *angst* – was absolutely central to the Buddha's mission to humanity, *karma* also plays a fundamental role, for it represents a demonstration-in-action of the practicability of his insight. Ethical considerations are paramount, because liberating oneself from the realm of *samsara* is ultimately a karmic matter, one that is rooted in our everyday activities and behaviour. We are not, that is to say, merely the passive prisoners of our past and of our karmic inheritance, but we have free will and the freedom to act in ways that can and will counter the burden of *karma* we carry. By freely and intentionally choosing how to behave, in other words, we can opt either to improve our lives or call down future misery upon ourselves. Living an ethical (or unethical, careless) life will alter the conditions of our rebirth through the *karma* it generates. Any conduct that lessens attachment to the physical world will lessen desires and lead to a better existence when the wheel turns next time, but if we remain wilfully ignorant of this fact and subject ourselves to oblivious craving, we will turn out to have been our own worst enemies both in this and future lives.

Karma, responsibility for one's own actions and the prospect of rebirth, then, are intimately tied together into a single system. They are the three great pillars that support the Buddhic insistence on the importance of ethics. For if rebirth – which is axiomatic for Buddhists since it was seen and experienced directly by the Buddha – were to be removed from this triad, then though it would still be possible to conduct oneself morally, the morality would be a narrow one and the idea of *karma* would be reduced to the level of a philosophy, a way of explaining, predicting and improving our own and others' behaviour. It is the prospect of rebirth, however, that ultimately buttresses Buddhist ethics and gives Buddha's message real purchase, for once we recognize that our ignorance and craving have consequences and the state of affairs that produces them in us goes on forever, the value of happiness and creature comforts as an alternative to living ethically takes a very sharp nose-dive indeed.

What is the point, after all, of a present, relatively comfortable existence if the struggle has to continue lifetime after lifetime with no escape except by your own efforts? What does it matter that the cell in which you're currently serving time is comfortable enough if you're permanently condemned to the prison of *samsara*? Something must be done, and it must be done now. It's 'your' responsibility to 'yourself' and to the whole world of creation. It's a matter – literally – of life and death.

Why, though? And here we have to return to the question we started out with: if the self is impermanent, what exactly is it that is reborn, and what relation does it have to the life being led now? What Buddha said was that although there was no transmigration between the lives of palpable selves or souls, there was still *a causal connection* between one life and another. The karmic accumulations of a particular life – itself the end-product of endless numbers of previous causally-linked lives – condition in their turn a new birth. Sequences of lives interconnected in this way form a continuum, though nothing is passed on but the conditioning, the karmic charge.

Put another way, our past actions and intentions continue to play themselves out even when the characteristics 'responsible' for them has disappeared. The good or bad *karma* accumulated then flows into a new set of characteristics which will neither be the same as the old one, nor completely different; its form and nature will depend on the quality of the unexpended *karma* which remained when the previous set died or disintegrated. The energy of this karma, not yet dissipated, will continue to play itself out in a new life.

The concept of rebirth without identity was, the Buddha knew, a hard one to grasp, so he drew an analogy with a drop of water taken from a great river. The drop, once extracted, seems to have a separate 'life' or identity of its own. Later, though, it is returned to the river and a second drop is taken, and although this second drop is made from exactly the same constituents as the first, there is no continuity of identity between it or any other drops.

Other metaphors have come to be used for this reconstitution of elements without the identicalness of a transferred eternal 'self'. One is of a flame that is passed from candle to candle. It is not exactly the same flame that is passed down the line, but it is not exactly a different one either. Another example comes from the cannoning of billiard or pool balls. The first ball hits a second and stops dead; the second ball hits a third and does the same; but the third ball continues. A single charge of kinetic energy, in other words, passes through a number of temporary vehicles.

Dependent Origination

Linked to *karma* – and, in a sense, indivisible from it in Buddhic thought – the great rolling tide of cause and effect is what is called the doctrine of dependent origination (*Paticassamuppada*). Buddhism does not (unlike Hinduism, for instance) acknowledge the existence of a creator god; and Buddha himself made it clear that nothing in the world is self-creating. His disciples, then, needed to know how and why phenomena came into existence at all under these circumstances. Also, where did cause and effect emerge from and why did some things seem to be eternal and uncaused – to have a 'life' of their own – while others seemed to leave no trace after being extinguished?

Buddha explained this in terms of a closed system of causal links – a circle of causes and effects that inevitably leads back to its own starting point in order to kick-start the chain reaction once more. There are (according to the usual interpretation) twelve elements or stages in this self-generating and self-perpetuating loop:

1. *Ignorance.* This is the state we are born into when we enter the wheel of becoming. It is the root cause of our false sense of self, our separation from the world and our desperate clinging to life. For ignorance leads to

2. *Will-to-Action.* Innate tendencies arise which lead all sentient creatures to act intentionally in a particular way, either good or bad. Will-to-action gives rise to

3. *Consciousness,* which in turn leads to

4. *Name and Form.* Without consciousness, or a sense of 'self', there would be no objects for us to find ourselves relative to. An object is meaningless, inert, without a subject to perceive and apprehend it. Name and form might be called psycho-physical interaction between an organism and the world, and it leads to the creation of

5. *The Six Bases.* These are the five senses and the mind; and they in turn give rise to

6. *Sense-impressions (or Contact).* This is the information about the world derived from sight, smell, hearing, taste, touch and the activity of the mind; and it causes

7. *Feelings.* From feelings (or emotions) come

8. *Attachment.* Attachments to things and ideas in the world are created by a desire which can never fully be satisfied. The organism clings to these attachments – to objects, ideas, ideals – and experiences suffering, which in turn condemns it to

9. *Being or Becoming,* the inevitable result of which is

10. *Rebirth.* Rebirth – being born at all – leads to

11. *Ageing and Death.* And ageing and death – the whole sorrowful experience of living – leads back once more, unless intervened in, to the beginning of the circle of dependent origination in ignorance. One life-cycle thus inevitably leads to another – and so on and on through vast aeons of time. This is 'the fearful cosmic roundabout', to borrow John Snelling's memorable phrase, to which we are all doomed – unless we do something about it.

The Wheel of Becoming

The entire realm of *samsara*, as described in the first two of Buddha's Four Noble Truths, is pictured in what is called the Wheel of Becoming. The wheel is clamped in the jaws of Yama, the Lord of Death, a dragon-like figure with three eyes, fangs and a crown of skulls, and its outer rim is an aide-memoire for the doctrine of dependent origination. The figure at the top is a blind man, representing ignorance, the inability to see. Moving clockwise, there follows a potter, representing the will-to-action of the potter's wheel, and a monkey, who stands for the constant restlessness of undirected consciousness. Next are three men in a boat – the boat of karmic inheritance – being carried across a stream towards interaction with the world of living things, and houses with doors and windows, which represent the opening of the doors of the six senses that let that world in.

The image of the lovers which follows symbolizes the contact between these senses and objects in the world that results in sense-impressions, and the man with an arrow in his eye stands for the fact that the feelings aroused by this contact are often so strong that they partially blind us – we lose sight of the way and stumble into desire. The man drinking, who is next, depicts the continuous craving (or thirst) that this produces, and the monkey clinging to a fruit tree (for dear life) illustrates the slavish attachment to objects of desire (and/or aversion) that are formed in life as a result. The inevitable outcome of this attachment is the pregnant woman who follows – a new embryo, condemned to becoming, has been formed, and when it is born into the world from the woman giving birth, who is next, it is doomed to decay over time into the last image of all, an old man carrying a corpse. The corpse-carrier, directly beneath the jaws of Yama, is carrying his burden towards a lake – perhaps representing death, the dissolution of the body – from which the blind man, under the same jaws, seems to have just stepped. The long carousel of life and death, then, continues to whirl on without stopping.

At the centre of the wheel, its controlling hub, are three animals: a pig, a snake and a cock. These, sometimes known as the Three Poisons or the Three Fires, are the vices which keep the world of *samsara* spinning on its axis. The pig is ignorance (unawareness, delusion); the snake is hatred (anger, aggression, violence); and the cock is greed (craving, lust, unslaked desire). In a circle of their own, they are shown as swallowing each other's tails (or else spewing each other up) in yet another endless and continuous cycle – the implication of which is that any one of them can and does generate the next, and that the energy created and expended in their hectic pursuit (or creation) of each other both powers the spinning world and is 'self'-consuming.

(This – as a psychological insight – is clear enough, for ignorance of the way in which the world turns encourages us to believe that the fulfilment of our desires will lead to enduring happiness, at no cost to ourselves. Realizing that this is not so, in the end, can have extreme reactive consequences, as can failing to get what we want in the first place. In turn, anger, by its nature, leads to the perpetuation of ignorance and desire can result in violence. They really do belong, all three of them, in the same dog-eat-dog spin.)

Surrounding the wheel's energetic hub is another circular domain, which is divided into two equal sectors, sometimes distinguished by their black and white colouring. In one half (white), figures are seen climbing upwards; in the other (black), they are descending towards free fall. This represents the karmic movement of all organisms, which are either intent on struggling upwards to a higher state of being or descending willy-nilly to a lower existence under the gravitational pull of illusion. The fact that this vignette is also circular and continuous means that those who climb will sooner or later fall; those who fall will 'survive' to climb once again, and so on and so on, to use Shakespeare's phrase in *Macbeth*, 'to the last syllable of recorded time'.

The remainder of the wheel between the central circles and the surrounding rim is divided by its spokes into (usually) six separate *samsaric* realms into which rebirth is possible. At the top are the gods (*devas*) in paradise, a place of pleasure and ease. To their right is the realm of the titans (jealous gods, *asuras*) who are constantly doing battle in an attempt to reach the top spot. (A tree that grows out of their realm provides fruit for the gods above, and a titan is shown trying to chop the tree down to get at it: his heart's desire.) The three sectors below this are the three lower realms: those of animals, of the damned suffering purgatory and of the so-called hungry ghosts (or *pretas*). These ghosts haunt the earth in a permanent state of hunger and thirst, but can never take in enough to satisfy their swollen bellies through their scrawny necks and tiny mouths. The small and unnourishing fruits they are competing for are protected by thorns and spiky branches.

The final realm, at the top left of the Wheel – and occupying a central position between the three lower realms and those of the gods and titans – is that of humans conducting their ordinary, everyday lives under the sway of karmic desire and conditioning. They eat, drink and work; they give birth and are treated for sickness; they grow old and die in ignorance with no chance of salvation. The only sign of hope is the presence of two ascetics under a tree, meditatively reflecting on the scenes around them. They are there to show that only in the human realm can virtue and wisdom be increased.

The six realms are a pictorial demonstration of the inevitability of rebirth and of the various conditions in which it can take place. No organism – not even a god – can remain for ever in one realm; every creature – once its karmic reward or punishment has been played out – is doomed to travel successively through all of them. But the realms, as depicted together in the Wheel, are also a sort of mnemonic for the chains which keep every organism locked within the *samsaric* system. In the case of the gods, it is pride which is their besetting sin; for the titans, it is jealousy; for the animals, brutish instincts; for the denizens of hell, pain and fear; for the hungry ghosts, the constant gnawing of appetite. As for humans, who ought to know better and have the greatest chance of release, it is self-preoccupation – obsessional concern with their ordinary daily lives – that prevents them from seeing clearly. This is the mirror that Yama holds up to us, a mirror in which we can not only see our own fate but also the drives, traps and delusions that keep us tied to the Wheel.

There is, however, one further figure featured in the ikon – and that is the Buddha himself, pictured within a circle, sometimes in each one of the *samsaric* realms, and sometimes standing outside the

Wheel, pointing away from it in another direction. His presence is there to indicate that although the Wheel may represent life-as-it-is, there is still a way to break out of the circle, a way he first outlined for the ascetics in the Deer Park at Sarnath in his Third and Fourth Noble Truths.

The Third Noble Truth: The Cessation of Suffering

If the Third Noble Truth had not been enunciated by Buddha, all he would have left us would be a metaphysical description of the world-as-illness: a collection of syndromes – and a bleak diagnosis – still in search of a cure. What he held out in the Third Truth, however, was the fact that the chronic, everlasting illness of *dukkha* could be treated. He invited all individuals – *so long as they recognized the truth of the disease* – to become, in effect, their own doctors and treat themselves. There was, in other words, a means of escape from *samsara*.

> Bhikkhus [monks], there is an unborn, unoriginated, unmade and unconditioned. Were there not the unborn, unoriginated, unmade and unconditioned, there would be no escape from the born, originated, made and conditioned. Since there is the unborn, unoriginated, unmade and unconditioned, there is escape from the born, originated, made and conditioned.

The key to this escape, he said, lay in control (*nirodha*): control over the craving or thirst (*tanha*) for attachment. If attachment was first rooted out, he went on, then the thirst itself would be extinguished. Once that had been done, a state of *nirvana* could be reached, a state in which there would be no further suffering.

For many people, one of the problems when confronting the prospect of this treatment is with the Buddhic conception of *nirvana*. Although it is clearly a condition in which something very important has been achieved, there is little description in Buddha's teachings of what it is actually like. Buddhists say this is of no importance: what *is* important is simply to begin the treatment as soon as you can. Once you have been offered a cure, after all, for an apparently incurable disease, it is absurd to demand to know first what it will feel like when it has been successful. If it cures you, they say, you will simply know for yourself that you are well, because the suffering and *angst* that is *dukkha* will have come to an end. *Nirvana*, then, is described only metaphorically: it has been variously illustrated as the laying down of an immense load, freedom from prison or, more disturbingly, in the famous *Fire Sermon*, as a last-minute escape from conflagration:

> Bhikkhus [monks], all is burning. And what is the all that is burning? Bhikkhus, the eye is burning, visible forms are burning, visual consciousness is burning, visual impression is burning, also whatever sensation, pleasant or painful or neither-pleasant-nor-painful, arises on account of the visual impression, that too is burning. Burning with what? Burning with the fire of lust, with the fire of hate, with the fire of delusion; I say it is burning with birth, ageing and death, with sorrows, with lamentations, with pains, with griefs, with despairs.

The reason why Buddha consistently discouraged questions into the true nature of *nirvana*, one might imagine, was that any answer he might have given would inevitably have been seen as definitive. All it would have achieved would have been the setting-up of expectations in the minds of his disciples. Expectations, in the Buddhic scheme, create attachments; and these would be just another burden that those who chose to follow his path would have to lay down. He knew, therefore, that any attempt to describe *nirvana* would be doomed to failure, just as Albert Einstein did when asked to explain his theory of relativity in a few words on his first arrival in America. 'Madam', Einstein is reported to have said:

> Two men, one of them blind, were walking down a long and dusty road, and the man who could see said, 'God, what I wouldn't give for a glass of milk!' And the blind man said, 'Glass I know. But what is this milk you speak of?' And the man who could see said, 'Milk is a white liquid'. And the man who was blind said, 'Liquid I know. But what is this white you speak of?' And the man who could see said, 'White is the colour of a swan's feathers'. And the man who was blind said, 'Feathers I know. But what is this swan you speak of?' The man who could see said, 'A swan is, um, well, a bird with a crooked neck.' And the blind man, persisting, said, 'Bird I know, and neck I know. But what is this crooked you speak of?' Finally, in exasperation, the man who could see took the blind man's arm and pulled it out straight from his shoulder. 'That,' he said, 'is straight.' Then he bent it at the elbow. 'And that,' he said, 'is crooked.' And the blind man breathed a sigh and said, 'Ah, now I understand what milk is!'

Nirvana, according to the Buddha's teachings, is equally far beyond the reach of ordinary language and experience. It cannot be described verbally, because words would only limit it. It has to be apprehended directly. In fact, one can only say what it is not. It is not, for example, some form of 'nothingness', for that would be to fall into the trap of annihilationism (complete non-existence) which the Buddha rejected, just as he rejected the possibility of any form of eternal life. It is not, equally, some sort of heaven to which good Buddhists go. For heaven (*svarga*) is merely, in Buddhic thought, another part of *samsara* ('that which goes round forever'). No, the Buddha made it plain that it can only occur in *worldly* conditions and, in the case of humans, within the human body:

> In this fathom-long body, with all its perceptions and thoughts, do I proclaim the world, the origin of the world [and] the cessation of the world . . .

Perhaps *nirvana* is best thought of, first of all, as a state of letting-go: letting go of all false beliefs, all illusions of permanence, any idea of the existence of the self as a fixed point of view. The 'self' disappears and the angle of the devotee's vision becomes universal rather than limited and particular. Thus an individual who now sees the world panoptically – as it is, in and of itself – can act disinterestedly, without any desire for a particular result and without identifying a 'self' in action. Indeed, in the words of Gillian Stokes in her excellent *Buddha: A Beginner's Guide*, 'Such a person knows that there is no self who is the doer or who can die . . . Psycho-physical death cannot touch the person who achieves *nirvana*, because such a person dies to each moment.'

Put another way, then, *nirvana* is transcendence: transcendence beyond the either-or categories of 'existence' and 'non-existence', and the finite, worldly contraries of suffering and happiness, misery and bliss. What is attained is a condition of perfect felicity, a condition that was enshrined in the life and disposition of Buddha and his liberated disciples, according to the *Dhammapada*:

Let us live happily, hating none in the midst of men who hate. Let us live happily, then, free from disease. Let us live happily, then, free from care. Let us live happily, then, we who possess nothing. Let us dwell feeding on joy like the Radiant Gods.

The Fourth Noble Truth: The Path to the Cessation of Suffering

The Fourth Noble Truth, as enunciated by Buddha, represents the practical steps that have to be taken if our inveterate thirst or craving for attachment (*tanha*) is finally to be eliminated – and the ground is to be made fertile for the attainment of *nirvana*. It takes the form of what is known as the Holy or Noble Eightfold Path: eight groups of attributes and/or modes of mental and behavioural conduct, which will help lead his disciples to their final goal. They are:

1. Right Understanding
2. Right Orientation or Thought
3. Right Speech
4. Right Action
5. Right Livelihood
6. Right Effort
7. Right Mindfulness
8. Right Concentration

These are generally construed as covering three main areas. Right Understanding and Thought come under the heading of wisdom, or *prajna*. Right Speech, Action and Livelihood cover the ethical or moral behaviour (*sila*) that is essential for any aspirant; and Right Effort, Mindfulness and Concentration must be deployed in the mental discipline of meditation (*samadhi*), when practised in the correct way.

The Path should not be interpreted as a hierarchical structure of some sort, however – for all its lay-out and division as a spiritual ladder with eight ascending steps. Buddha made it clear that its three main elements (wisdom, ethical behaviour and mental discipline/meditation) had to be developed in concert. Ethical conduct was as necessary to the getting of wisdom as wisdom was to the achievement and interpretation of meditational states. Without the mental discipline of meditation, both a considered moral life and wisdom would remain out of reach.

Ethical Conduct

The importance of a life led ethically has always been at the heart of Buddhic teaching. It is not, however, regarded as an end in itself, but as a means of developing compassion and lessening the amount of suffering in the world, both one's own and that of others. It represents a determination on the part of an individual to help solve the problem of *samsara* at its root by both taking personal responsibility for it and contributing as little as is humanly possible to the world of karmic conditioning. Humility – the abasement of self and the recognition of mistakes – is crucial to this. So are loving kindness, generosity and forgiveness, for by cultivating these things, the individual can keep the damaging reverberations of his or her behaviour – its fall-out – to a minimum.

Right Speech is a necessary part of this karmic self-disarmament, for it involves the avoidance of anything and everything that might take the speaker in harmful directions: swearing, gossiping, backbiting, slandering and wasting other people's time with idle chatter. It also means telling the truth at all times and keeping silent rather than saying something that is neither productive nor helpful.

Right Action is aimed, equally, at spiking the guns and defusing the karmic consequences of behaviour – especially unconsidered behaviour. It promotes peaceful and harmonious conduct at all times, and acknowledges that harm done to others represents both personal damage and an out-rippling echo of destruction in the general scheme of things. Certainly, then, one should not take life, nor steal nor immorally appropriate what belongs to other organisms, but one should also not misuse one's own senses by over-indulging in food, or beautiful sights and sounds, or intellectual pastimes. Intoxicants should be avoided at all times. Celibacy, though not mandatory in lay members, was essential to monks pursuing the Path, for an even tenor of mind without distraction and external embroilment – the Middle Way between indulgence and asceticism, according to Buddha's teachings – was the key.

Right Livelihood is a generalized injunction not to practise any trade at all that is in any way harmful to living things, and is in a sense inapplicable to ordained monks and nuns, since they have already embraced it. In the Buddha's own time, its application would have been fairly limited: to butchers, perhaps; soldiers; makers of or dealers in weapons and intoxicants; bandits; thieves; and those who lived by deception. (Now the net, of course, would spread much wider.) But it also represents an encouragement to Buddhists to take up callings, professions or trades that actively promote good and counter the playing-out of karmic conditioning in wars, violence, illness or damage to the environment. Again this is to do with the taking of personal responsibility, and with the recognition that these things have their roots in *dukkha* – to which *sila* (the ethical life) is in the end the only collective antidote. Buddha taught that *sila* is a vital stepping-stone in the path towards felicity and release and this was also recognized by aspirants.

Mental Discipline/Meditation

Meditation, in the words of John Snelling in his book *The Buddhist Handbook*, is:

> the specialized activity that helps us to fully realize the Buddha's teachings – to make them an integral part of our being rather than just a new set of ideas to be entertained theoretically in the mind. It weans [us] away from out usual habit patterns, particularly our involvement with our thoughts and their emotional sub-themes. At the same time it sharpens and intensifies our powers of direct perception: it gives us eyes to see into the true nature of things. The field of research is ourselves, and for this reason the laser of attention is turned and focused inwards.

In this context, *Right Effort* means making the effort to apply oneself conscientiously to the task ahead and to be awake and aware at every moment; to prevent wrong states of mind from arising and/or to dispel them; and to focus only on wholesome and useful states of mind. This requires an act of will, a decision to remain single-minded, for being single-minded is the only way to conquer laziness, doubt, faint-heartedness and the swarming-in of extraneous thoughts and sensations.

Right Mindfulness is to do with application to the here-and-now, to immediate states of consciousness. It involves careful awareness of the activities of the body, and the movements of the mind. It is the watcher, the overseer, of what is going on, the director of Right Effort – with which it is interdependent and co-reliant. Without Effort it would have nothing to produce – just as without Mindfulness, Effort would be random and lead nowhere. Both

Mindfulness and Effort, it should be noted, are not – and should not be – qualities just reserved for the inward examination of the meditation cushion. They are also fundamental to living ethically.

Wisdom

The essential ground-base of wisdom, as outlined by the Buddha, is *Right Understanding*. Anyone who wishes to follow Buddha's Path, in other words, must first have become familiar with his teachings – and have understood them correctly, both in theory and in practice. Any commitment that is made, then, is based on informed confidence in his teachings rather than on blind faith or any superficial attraction. *Right Understanding* is, therefore, the essential background to all other aspects of the Path – the ultimate motivator, for example, of Right Effort.

Right Thought or *Orientation* involves the necessary switch that has to take place in our patterns of thought if we are to reach towards the elimination of self and see the world panoptically. We have literally to reform our minds in order to escape from our periscope-like blinkeredness. We must learn to adopt *other*-directed modes of thought and to understand that the Path is not being followed for any reason of self-advancement but in order to move away from our egocentric world-view and towards self-obliteration – to be reached by the practice of the Path as a whole.

Wisdom, the combination of Right Understanding and Right Thought or Orientation, can be – and often is – seen as the culmination of the Path, its ultimate goal. Its acquisition is gradual and cumulative, though, and it requires overall mental development (*bhavana*). It demands commitment, absolute awareness in the form of meditation and expression that reaches outwards into the world in the form of action. Different schools of Buddhic thought have laid emphasis on one or another of these elements, but have universally agreed on the importance of all three.

The Eightfold Path, then, does not represent any sort of separation of approaches to *nirvana*. It is merely the teasing-out into categories of an all-at-once, directed passage towards final truth. This truth – the end-result of the Path – was described by Buddha to his faithful servant and cousin Ananda shortly before his death:

> Those who have died after the complete destruction of the three bonds of lust, of covetousness, and of the egotistical cleaving to existence, need not fear the state after death. They will not be in a state of suffering; their minds will not continue as a Karma of evil deeds or sin, but are assured of final deliverance. When they die, nothing will remain of them but their good thoughts, their righteous acts, and the bliss that proceeds from truth and righteousness. As rivers must at last reach the distant main, so their minds will be reborn in higher states of existence and continue to press on to their ultimate goal, which is the ocean of truth, the eternal peace of Nirvana.

The Five Hindrances

Elsewere in his teaching, as recorded in the Canon, the Buddha listed the major obstacles to progress that any committed follower would have to confront during his or her journey on the Eightfold Path.

1. Sensual desire
2. Ill will or aversion
3. Sloth or torpor

4. Restlessness and worry
5. Doubt

Sensual desire - with its drive towards attachment - is obviously the enemy of total commitment and concentration, as is *ill will or aversion*. But there are antidotes. Meditation, for example, can be directed towards the more repulsive aspects of the body and conscious good will towards the antipathetic person or object in question, in a way similar to Jesus's admonition to 'love your enemy'. *Sloth or torpor* can also be counteracted, this time by awareness and by the conscious monitoring of the body's intake and activities (what we would now call 'diet' and 'exercise').

Restlessness and worry, for their part, are seen as stemming essentially from a clinging to, and preoccupation with, past misdeeds. This preoccupation can usually be cured by confession and repentance and by a firm resolution never to repeat the misdeeds. A more chronic and persistent form of the obstacle (commonly held to be ubiquitous in the modern world) is simply a sign that the devotee has not yet begun to shake off the shackles that tie him to illusion and to the idea of 'self'. It can only be gradually laid to rest by the experience of the Eightfold Path itself.

The cause of the last of the Hindrances, *Doubt* – dithering and vacillation rather than healthy scepticism – was seen as being incomplete familiarity with the Buddha's teachings. This could be counteracted by further study, by a fuller commitment to the *Dharma* and by talking the matter through with those already on the Path. Guides such as as meditation-monitors, teachers and advisers on conduct were, and have always been, of central importance in Buddhism. It takes two, at the very least, to reach salvation – except, of course, in the case of Buddhas.

Buddhas and the Ordering of Enlightenment

Only Buddhas – fully 'enlightened' or 'awakened' ones – can arrive at Enlightenment without receiving the gift of the *Dharma* from another person and even they, according to a doctrine that emerged after the lifetime of Sakyamuni, have received it many lives previously from a former Buddha (generally believed to appear once every 320,000 years). No-one but Buddhas, in other words, can work out personal salvation unaided. As the *Dhammapada* says:

> You yourself must make an effort. The Buddhas, for their
> part, are the revealers.

Making this effort and following the Eightfold Path may at last bring the initiate a first glimpse of *nirvana*, in which case he or she, according to the Buddha, leaves the ranks of ordinary mortals to become a stream-winner, or *sotapanna*. It would take a stream-winner – one who has 'won' contact with the Path – only seven lifetimes, he said, to reach fully-achieved Enlightenment. At later stages of the Path there were also a variety of saints-to-be – known as once-returners (*sakadagami*) and never-returners (*anagami*) – as well as the saints (or worthy ones, *arhants*) themselves.

Arhants, of whom there were many, it seems, during Gautama Buddha's own lifetime – perhaps because of their earlier experiences as ascetics and seekers – are those who have finally thrown off, once and for all, the so-called 'binding influences' of sensual desire, the desire to exist, wrong views and ignorance. No longer producers of new karmic formations, they persist in the world because old ones still have to be worked out, and they spend what remains of their time teaching the *Dharma*.

To achieve arhantship, an enlightened teacher is necessary. This is not true of a so-called *pacceka buddha*, a solitary devotee of the Way who achieves Enlightenment alone, but does not teach. The Buddha combined in himself the qualities of both a *pacceka buddha* and an *arhant* – in as much as he achieved Enlightenment alone and went on to teach the *Dharma* – and therefore stands above both.

The last in the hierarchy of those who have glimpsed or achieved *nirvana* is the *Bodhisattva*, or Buddha-to-be – as Gautama Buddha was when he entered his mother's womb in the shape of a white elephant. The process of becoming a Buddha takes immense numbers of lifetimes, during which the *Bodhisattva* is reborn to and remains in the world, not because of any outstanding karmic debts, but due to the sheer force generated by the compassion of the decision to free all organisms from *dukkha*. Later, as we shall see, the concept of the *Bodhisattva* became increasingly important as Buddhism developed.

The Ordained and the Secular in the Buddhic Community

The oldest documents in the Buddhist Canon – generally recognized as originating from the period soon after the Buddha's death – relate to monastic discipline (*vinaya*). One document, the *Skandhaka*, which probably dates back to the fourth century BC, lays out the basic institutions of monastic life: the ceremonies of admission and confession, the rules governing retreats and punishments, clothing, food and the use of medicines. Another, the *Pratimoshka* – which is almost certainly even older – contains a list of two hundred and fifty ecclesiastical offences and it provides an insight into the *Sangha*, or community, which Buddha created and left behind him.

At first – as I have indicated elsewhere – all those entering the community simply had to swear to the Five Precepts. They had to promise that they would:

- avoid harming any living thing
- avoid taking anything not freely given
- forsake the pursuit of sensual pleasures and be celibate
- speak and think truthfully, kindly and compassionately
- avoid all intoxicants

These rules applied to monks, nuns and lay people alike, except that lay people were not required to be chaste – they simply had to avoid both excessive sex and adultery.

Later the Five Precepts were doubled to Ten, and all ordained monks and nuns were enjoined to follow them. Solemn promises were now made to:

- avoid eating solid foods after midday
- avoid frivolous entertainments, such as dancing, singing, music and mime
- avoid perfumes, garlands, jewellery and other personal adornment
- avoid using high seats or beds
- avoid handling gold and silver and all forms of trading

By the time the recitation of the *Pratimoshka* took on its present written form – it has to be recited once a fortnight before a chapter of monks – huge number of sub-clauses had been added to the Ten Precepts and the punishment of infractions was severe. The first four offences – sexual intercourse, theft, murder and false claims, either to supernatural powers or high spiritual attainment – warranted immediate expulsion. The next thirteen – relating to sexual misconduct, creating dissension within the order and building personal huts – deserved suspension. Two sexual offences followed that were punishable according to the circumstances, and thirty other offences resulted in the forfeiture of the right to wear clothing belonging to the order – and made the offender, moreover, liable to an unfavourable rebirth. These particular transgressions of the monastic code included the handling of gold and silver, engaging in trade and appropriating goods intended for the community for personal use.

The next ninety infractions were also punishable by an unfavourable rebirth, unless repented and atoned for. They involved such offences as telling lies or slandering or mocking other monks and they also covered relations with the lay community. Further offences included teaching the Buddha's scriptures word for word to any unordained person and gossiping to lay people about offences committed by monks. The remaining offences added up to an extraordinarily motley collection of misdemeanours which included, among other things, destroying vegetation, digging in the earth, drinking alcohol and possessing a bed or chair with legs more than eight inches high! There were also rules governing correct behaviour and the settling of disputes.

These rules were all introduced, of course, to promote the protection of other living creatures and to provide the best possible conditions for meditation and withdrawal from the everyday nagging temptation of attachment. The frugality and simplicity imposed on the monks was designed to foster their independence, as was their necessary separation from the ties of property, clan and family. In the Buddha's time, the order might well have been composed of no more than wandering mendicants, beggars for alms, who lived in forests or caves away from the towns and villages, feeding and dressing themselves as best they could. They were, however, required by the

Buddha to come together during the rainy season, and out of this practice, no doubt, developed the first monasteries. As the *Sangha* became richer, these monastic foundations spread and remaining together year-round became, at the same time, an increasingly practical option for the ordained monks and nuns. Not only did it sustain their necessary separation from social concerns without the daily rigours of a hand-to-mouth existence, but it also gave them a permanent presence among a lay community which, from then on, became not only their congregation but also their providers.

What was the relationship of ordained monks and nuns to lay members in the early *Sangha*? The laity, after all, had 'taken refuge' in exactly the same way as the ordained, by proclaiming the Three Jewels and taking up the Five Precepts. It seems that the relationship, from the beginning, was a rather condescending one, for 'visible' and 'invisible' *Sanghas* were distinguished at an early stage. The 'visible' *Sangha* consisted of ordained and lay members alike, but there arose within it an élite, known as the 'true' or 'invisible' *Sangha*, which was made up of the *arhants* ('noble' or 'holy' ones). These were regularly contrasted with ordinary worldlings, who were known as 'the foolish common people' (*bala-prthag-jana*). Since ordained monks, with their yellow robes, were at least on their way to achieving *arhant* status, the lay community was regarded by many of them as belonging, essentially, to another species.

The difference between the two member-classes was built into eartly Buddhist thought, for they were seen (by *arhants* and therefore by monks) as occupying two entirely separate planes of existence, the 'wordly' and the 'supramondane'. Only *arhants* were truly alive, since only they had experienced a spiritual rebirth – they were sufficiently detached from the world of conditioning to approach *nirvana*. 'The foolish common people', on the other hand, were so mired in *samsara* that all they could do was muddle along through life in a state of permanent fuddlement. Once in a while, of course, one of them, through prolonged teaching and meditation, might systematically be able to see worldly objects for what they really were – that is, mere hindrances. By then, though, he or she – now able to apprehend *nirvana* as the ultimate objective – was said by definition to have 'ceased to belong to the common people' and to have become transmogrified into one of 'the family of the *arhants*'.

This early perception of the laity as somehow representing a different order of life – for all its support of monastic communities – later became a matter of some dispute, as we shall see, as Buddhism spread across the whole subcontinent of India. So, too, did a large number of doctrinal points which had seemed so authoritative in the mouth of Buddha and yet appeared to need, once he had died, much further elaboration. It was not long before these doctrinal points caused the Buddhist *Sangha* to split into a number of different sects.

Part Two:
Buddhism after Buddha

Chapter Five:

The First Five Hundred Years

The Scriptures

The Buddha in life had never suggested that he was indispensable, either as a leader or as a canonical authority. Though he preached a doctrine of salvation, he was neither a Caliph nor a Pope and he made no arrangements for his successor. Only his teaching, his *Dharma*, he repeatedly told his disciples, was necessary to those who wished to follow the Path. Soon after his death – according to Buddhist tradition – five hundred of his most senior monks gathered in a cave at Rajagaha to determine what exactly that teaching had been. Their aim was to hammer out an exact account of it, as nearly as they could – an authorized version.

The story goes that one of the monks, Upali, passed on the details, under questioning, of when and under what circumstances the Buddha had laid down each rule that governed the lives of his monks (the *Vinaya*). Although the Buddha had once remarked that the *Sangha* could abolish the minor rules, if it so wished, no-one had actually asked him what these were; so Upali's listing of regulations, both major and minor, effectively passed into scripture. His intimate

95

disciple Ananda then recalled the Buddha's basic teachings, the *Sutras*, as exactly as he could. These were afterwards debated in open session, when a form that was acceptable to a majority of the monks present was finally found.

The story of this conclave may well be a myth, but it reflects what is very likely to have occurred soon after Buddha's death – an attempt to standardize Buddhist teaching and practice at a time when few could read and even fewer could write. Both of the texts that are said to have been discussed at the conclave lie somewhere at the heart of later (written) Buddhist literature. One can easily imagine them being taken back to the scattered communities of the *Sangha* by 'living books' – individual monks who set out to memorize all or part of them in the manner of Ray Bradbury's story *Fahrenheit 451*. They must have been gradually translated into local languages and dialects over the next generation or two: the beginning of a process that saw them transmitted orally within communities, from one monk to another, for fully three, perhaps four, hundred years.

As far as we can gather from the first written texts – recorded some time in the first century BC in what is now Sri Lanka – considerable efforts seem to have been made to maintain their purity during this oral period. Inevitably, however, distortions and local variations crept in, particularly in the record of the Buddha's teachings, which came to combine – as far as the laity were concerned – instruction and village entertainment. Since there was also considerable merit attached to their learning and recitation, the teachings appear to have ballooned at an early stage, not only with mnenonic devices such as strategically-placed repetitions but also with poetic embellishments and rhetorical flourishes. It was perhaps felt that the longer they were spun out, the more benefit was attached to their memorization. Another reason was that their acceptance as a canonical entity had not been universal, so some Buddhist communities (perhaps unrepresented at the conclave) had adopted their own versions.

The *Sutras*, then – to a far greater extent, as it turned out, than the rule-book of the *Vinaya* – gradually gave up their authoritative status as a kind of holy writ and became a burgeoning and spiralling series of descants on Buddhic themes. Within them, of course, there still remained the core of the *Dharma*. However, the idea of some sort of received doctrinal infallibility was abandoned (as the Buddha himself no doubt would have wished, given the *ad hoc* quality of his teachings in life) in favour of a generalized freedom to interpret, at both a communal and an individual level. The ideal of Enlightenment, it came to be widely accepted, could be reached by different roads. It was up to each initiate to find the path that best suited him, among the multiple choices represented in the gathering maze of the existing oral literature, which soon became too vast for a single 'living book' to learn and transmit.

Early Schisms and Sects

Given this latitude of interpretation, it is not surprising that divisions within the *Sangha* appeared – sooner rather than later – nor is it remotely surprising that the first of these divisions involved the relationship between Buddhist monks and the lay community which supported them. The Buddha, as we have seen, had allowed in his teachings that laypersons could – and indeed did – achieve the first three levels of sainthood ('stream-winner', 'once-returner' and 'never-returner'). Whether an ordinary citizen, unbound to the monastic life, could reach the ultimate level and become an *arhant* remained a matter of some dispute – although the *Sutras* in fact list twenty individuals who have done so – and it soon became generally accepted that no mere householder could achieve this, the highest status.

The early monasteries came to be regarded more and more as privileged spiritual hothouses for the propagation and conservation of *arhants*, particularly by the monks who inhabited them. Those accepted as such began to see themselves as achieved embodiments of the true *Dharma*, living at the top of an aspirational pyramid, so that only they could pronounce judgment on matters of doctrine and the holiness of others. As a result, they soon formed a kind of spiritual oligarchy, an oligarchy in which other monks became less and less important and lay people played a walk-on role as obedient provisioners and caterers.

Divisions within the Sangha

According to Buddhist tradition, this drift in the affairs of the *Sangha* came to a head on two occasions in the 150 years or so that followed the death of the Buddha. The first crisis, in about 380 BC, was caused by the relaxation of a number of *Vinaya* rules by the monks of Vaisali, thereby allowing themselves to handle gold and silver (in defiance of the Buddha's instructions). They started to collect money instead of food from the lay community and when one of the monks objected – and even went so far as to tell local villagers (successfully) not to donate – he was suspended for preaching without authorization. A council of eminent monks was convened when he passed this news on to other communities, that both ordered his reinstatement and severely censured the Vaisali monastery for its high-handed, non-Buddhic behaviour.

Another, not dissimilar, dispute arose about forty years later –

this time striking at the power of the *arhants*. A number of propositions began to circulate, designed to undermine their claims to omniscience and their self-proclaimed dissimilarity to other mortals. An *arhant*, after all – these new schismatics pointed out – could still be seduced by another person or in a dream; could doubt; could be ignorant and require teaching; could use human speech as a means to enter the Way; and could even spontaneously utter the word *dukkha* (suffering) while meditating. Of course, this hardly constituted a major bill of attainder, but it was the opening salvo, as it turned out, of what became a war of sorts between the traditionalists, the *Sthaviras* (or Elders) and what came to be known as 'the Great-Assemblyites' (the *Mahasanghikas*).

The Mahasanghikas

Inspired by a Buddhist teacher called Mahadeva, the *Mahasanghikas* regarded the *Dharma* as something more than merely a pathway designed for a limited few who lived in seclusion and were subject to strict rules – their aim was to open it up to ordinary people, to increase the chances of a general salvation. They invited non-*arhant* monks and householders to their gatherings and responded to popular religious concerns, claiming that in doing so they were being far truer to the Buddha's teachings than was the exclusive, high-priest-like bureaucracy of the Elders with its mantle of self-proclaimed orthodoxy.

The *Mahasanghikas* differed from the Elders, too, in their views on the essential nature of the Buddha and it is worth examining these for a moment, since they later fed into a general movement within Buddhism which was to become known as the *Mahayana* ('The Great Vehicle or Course'). They downplayed the Buddha's status as a historical human figure and instead turned him into an object of religious faith: transcendental and supramondane, without imperfections, omniscient, all-powerful and eternal. (The historical Buddha, they maintained, had simply been created by the transcendental Buddha in order for him to be able to appear in the world as a teacher.) At the same time — paradoxically, to some extent – they placed him firmly back into the world as a source of constant aid to suffering beings of every kind. He had in no sense, they said, simply 'disappeared' into *nirvana*. Instead, he was an unsleeping watcher, eternally vigilant, and his boundless compassion continued to reverberate in the world in all sorts of different ways: by means of the messengers he would continue to despatch into all the realms of the world until the end of time and through the manifestations of himself that occupied every corner of the universe.

The *Mahasanghikas*, and those that followed their pathway towards the *Mahayana*, also began to raise what turned out to be increasingly important philosophical questions: about the nature of reality and consciousness, for example; the status of knowledge; and the existence (or non-existence) of the self. They maintained that thought – which might be called consciousness-in-action – was in its essence lucent and pure, but that all impurities within it were adventitious contaminations. In line with their downgrading of *arhants*, they also questioned the value of any and all knowledge that could be expressed verbally or in conceptual form. The world and all worldly things, they announced with varying degrees of passion, belonged to the realm of unreality, so only their total absence – or 'emptiness' – could in the end be described as real. Everything else that was, was not; and nothing that could be said about it referred to anything of substance at all.

The members of another schismatic sect that later ran foul of the Elders continued this line of philosophical exploration, while at the same time trying to bring back into place a rather more commonsense view of the world. These were the so-called *Pudgalavadins* or Personalists, who challenged the received canonical view that the 'self' (*pudgala*) was a fiction which had no place in ultimate reality.

The Personalists

The Personalists maintained instead that the self actually existed – not the sort of self, to be sure, that ignorant people constructed for themselves but one that nonetheless provided a sort of transcendental continuity for the events that 'happened' to an individual over a number of consecutive lives, up to and including Buddhahood.

In this the Personalists were – at least in part – reverting to the concepts of the *atman* (self) and of *brahman* (cosmic essence) that were contained in the Upanishads; and they had to perform a difficult balancing act to be able to accommodate Buddhist dogma concerning "the erroneous belief in the self". They were able to do this by asserting that the personality that survived transmigration on the road to *nirvana* was neither identical with the five *skandhas* that constituted what might be called the personhood of a particular living individual, nor was it different from them. Instead its relationship to them was as fire is to fuel, both identical and different at the same time. If a personality were indeed different from the *skandhas*, after all, it would have to be regarded as eternal and unconditional: if it were the same, it would be subject to annihilation. These alternatives, as they pointed out, were both heretical, for they flew in the face of Buddha's teaching.

The Personalists also used this notion of 'both-at-onceness' to characterize the relationship between the *dharmas* (the phenomenal world) and *nirvana*. Buddhist orthodoxy at the time, as represented by the Elders, held that *nirvana* was an utterly transcendent state, with no roots of any kind in the illusory realm of *samsara*. By contrast, the Personalists argued that if a person is neither the same as nor different from its components (as above), then its cessation must *also* be neither the same nor different. The concepts of the world of illusion and the final leaving of it thus bear a similar (fuel-fire) relationship to each other, just as the personality does to the *skandhas*.

All of this may now seem rather dry and remote, but what the Personalists were seeking was a renewed sense of the importance of life in the world. (They also argued that although both the person and the phenomena that 'happened' to it might be unreal, they nevertheless provided a framework onto which both knowledge and mutually comprehensible statements could be hung.) If the realm of the spiritual, after all, exists in an entirely different domain from that of the physical, the profane, then worldly activities can have no spiritual value, unless – and only unless – they contribute to escape from the one into the other. If spirituality, on the other hand, is somehow inherent in the world – as they argued – then worldly, secular activities such as raising a family or conducting scientific or philosophical enquiry can be said to have intrinsic worth. Buddhism, like Christianity, has seesawed between these two positions over the centuries but, like Christianity, it has by and large adopted the Middle Way between them, embracing neither the extreme other-wordliness of the Gnostics, for example, nor the extreme world-centredness of, say, orthodox Judaism.

The Personalists were to go on to become a powerful force

within Buddhism – in the seventh century AD, a traveller called Yuan Tsang estimated that over a quarter of all India's 250,000 monks were Personalists. Another schismatic sect, the so-called All-Is-Ists or *Sarvastivadins*, that appeared about fifty years after the Personalists, also became prominent. Led by a sage called Katyayaniputra, they maintained that things in the world, far from being altogether illusory and impermanent, do in fact exist – and not only in the present, but also in the past and future. They struck yet another blow, that is to say, for a commonsense view of the world and for ordinary experience, both of which appear – to the uninitiated at any rate – to unfold serially.

All-Is-Ists

The re-appraisal of the past and the future was the most significant heterodoxy within the schismatic philosophy of the All-Is-Ists, for this struck right at the heart of Buddhist meditational practices. Central to these practices was the concept of impermanence – each initiate was required to engrave the full significance of impermanence on his mind in order to be able to cancel out the anti-spiritual gravitational drag exerted by worldly things. He had to take an event, or *dharma*, and parse it out into its rise and fall – how it 'comes, becomes, and goes'. This inevitably drew him into questions about the nature of time, of course, and into a consideration of the status of the past and the future. Were both unreal? Did only the present truly exist? And if so, exactly how long did the present last? If it was only for an instant, the generally accepted view, then nothing in the world could exist for any longer: it had to be annihilated and re-created (just like present time) from instant to instant.

This particular All-Is-Ist view not only ran counter to

commonsense intuition – the way in which we collectively experience and negotiate the world – but it also produced considerable difficulties for the Buddhist doctrine of karmic effects. If an event or action in the past had instantaneously passed from the present and had ceased to exist, how could it possibly lead to a reward or punishment many years later? (This would require it to have an effect at a time when it was non-existent.) Furthermore, if both past and future events and actions were non-existent, how could we possibly either have knowledge of the past or be able to make predictions about the future, since both memory and prediction require the presence in the mind of an extant object of thought?

For all their appeal to ordinary experience, these All-Is-Ist views failed to find general acceptance. They were voted down at a Buddhist council held in about 250 BC (according to tradition) and the monks of the All-Is-Ists migrated away from the main body of the *Sangha* to the north and the west, where they established strong centres, particularly in Kashmir. From there, with the help of Indo-Greek kings such as Menander, who is said to have converted to Buddhism – and on the back of successive invasions from Bactria and Parthia – they spread out along the Silk Road between China and the West, before becoming a significant influence on the development of Buddhism in China. They also left behind them on the subcontinent an enduring legacy: the notion of a new type of spiritual hero which was to become of great importance in the *Mahayana*: the *bodhisattva*.

The *bodhisattva*, in contrast to the *arhant* and the (private, non-teaching and non-preaching) *pacheka* buddha – both of whom seek release from the cycle of rebirth for themselves alone – is a fully-achieved spirit who chooses to return again and again to the world of *samsara* in order to help others. It became necessary to practise what are called the six perfections when following the path of the *bodhisattva* (giving; morality; patience; vigour; meditation; and wisdom) and the six perfections are a still reverberating echo of All-Is-Ist doctrine.

This brief account of sects and rifts in the early history of the *Sangha* is necessarily schematic. In fact, Buddhist tradition identifies eighteen different schisms during the two-and-a-half centuries or so after the Buddha's death and it is likely that there have been many more – some caused by rivalry between monks, perhaps, some by genuine philosophical differences. It is best, I think, to imagine a period of often intense debate centering on such central issues as the relationship between the monks and laypeople; the degree to which *arhant*-ship was a fully achieved state or one that was subject to temptation and a fall from grace; the true nature of *nirvana*; the status of worldly experience; and the interrelationships between the concepts of death, determinism and *karma* and death, rebirth and time. There is little evidence of *ukases,* followed by acts of excommunication by some sort of central authority, being issued against heretics – except perhaps in the case of the All-Is-Ists. Instead it seems likely that 'homeless' monks of varying philosophical convictions interacted on a more or less reasonable level and that the debate was spread through the *Sangha* by the constant coming-and-going of mendicant initiates and of monks making pilgrimage or taking part in collective retreat.

The emergence of a new class of canonical literature in the third century BC – the *Abhidharma* – made it much more likely that there was indeed considerable philosophical debate of just this kind about the teachings of the Buddha. The *Abhidharma*, which means 'above or about the *Dharma*', is a systematic teasing-out of key themes and topics that are contained in the basic scriptures.

Composed in technical language rather than in the everyday demotic of the *Sutras*, it subjects these themes to rigorous analysis – as well as the experiences generated by meditation on them – and turns them into the building-blocks of an integrated philosophical system. The most celebrated body of *Abhidharma* literature was written down, like the *Vinaya* and the *Sutras*, in the first century BC, in what is now Sri Lanka – becoming 'the Third Basket' of the so-called Pali canon. (Since then it has been much added to by later texts and commentaries.) This version, however, is the legacy of one particular sect. The *Abhidharma* of earlier sects – written originally in Sanskrit – survives both in fragments and, in two Chinese translations, in its entirety. The *Abhidharma* phenomenon, in fact, provides ample evidence of wide-ranging – and competitive – philosophical speculation.

The Monks and the Laity

It is likely that the *Abhidharma*, the *Vinaya* and some of the more recondite passages in the *Sutras* were reserved for the monks' exclusive use from the start. Some of the *Sutras*, indeed, suggest that the laity should not be burdened with anything too metaphysical or complex. What, then, was the exact relationship of the laity to the monks it was required to support, in the early period? And what were the monks' responsibilities towards the laity?

As well as being distinguished by the colour of their dress – monks wore red or ochre robes and householders white – lay-people and initiated members of the early *Sangha* differed, as we have seen, in the spiritual possibilities open to them. If a man chose to remain as a householder and family man, it was generally assumed that he had accumulated insufficient merit in his past lives to be able to shake off the day-to-day world and join the elect. His only present religious duty, therefore, was to go about the task again – to accumulate enough merit to be able to take a step up the spiritual hierarchy after his next rebirth. This he could achieve by a variety of means, some ethical and some practical.

First of all he had to commit himself publicly to the Three Jewels (Buddha, the *Dharma* and the *Sangha*), as we have seen – although he was allowed to retain his ancestral beliefs and any other Brahminic practices and rituals that were appropriate to his caste. (The Buddha makes no exclusive demands on his followers.) He also had to observe the Five Precepts: that is, to refrain (as far as possible) from killing living things and to eschew stealing, inappropriate sexual behaviour, lying and drinking alcohol. On regular feast days he could also commit himself to a further three of the Precepts: that is, to fast after the pre-noon meal, to turn his back on all worldly amusements (singing, dancing, dramatic performances, etc.) and to wear neither perfumes nor ornaments. More merit could be earned from sleeping on a low (rather than a high) bed and refusing to handle gold or silver – and yet more from giving up sex entirely and exchanging his white robe for that of a novice monk.

The most important responsibility of the layman, however, was to be generous – especially to monks. This involved regular donations of food and drink, as well as such items as robes, medicines and sandals – it also meant gifts of land and buildings. The amount of merit earned by each act of generosity depended in part on the spiritual status of the recipient and so *arhants* were especially favoured – as, of course, was the memory of the Buddha himself. Although many of the early structures that were donated or built by Buddhist laymen were made out of wood – and have hence disappeared – traces survive of dwellings that were cut out of rock or made from fired brick at around the beginning of the second century BC. During this early period, *stupas* and *stupa*-halls also appear to have been erected within monasteries to enshrine relics of the Buddha and locally revered *arhants*. Attendance at these *stupas* and *stupa*-halls – and at the many shrines which continued to dot the local countryside – involved several actions including ritual circumambulation (walking around), prostration and offerings of flowers. These actions fell short of what we today would call worship, but they too generated merit.

The cynical might say that this system of merit-gathering worked largely to the benefit of the monks, for they were then allowed to concentrate selfishly on their own salvation, without having to concern themselves with bodily survival. However, the monks – at first living isolated lives on the outskirts of villages or else deep in the jungle, and then only gradually gathering in monasteries from which they re-emerged each year to lead the mendicant life – provided a kind of glue that held the wider community together, both socially and spiritually. The monks were sustained without having to work, but in return they preached the *Dharma* and instructed the laity in morality, the afterlife and salvation through self-forgetfulness. They were also a living example of the freedom and serenity that the laity could finally achieve if they committed themselves to live ethically. Over time, a vast body of literature grew up that proclaimed the virtues of the secular life, including both cautionary tales (*avadana*) and so-called Birth stories (*Jakata*) that recounted the adventures of the Buddha in his previous lives, both animal and human. In these stories, constant stress was laid on rebirth, the lingering effects of *karma* and the virtue of treating all living things with respect.

There were, of course, and this was also stressed, personal

rewards to be had in return for faith and commitment. Both laymen and laywomen, that is to say, were sure to become 'stream-winners' at least and have only happy rebirths. The householder who lived in accordance with Buddha's teaching was also guaranteed increase of wealth, reputation and public standing in life and a death that had both direction and meaning. Women were offered the additional prospect of rebirth among the Gods of Lovely Form, as long as they were sweet-natured and amenable, respected their husband's relatives and guests, made their homes into pleasant and well-run places and protected their husband's valuables.

There was, however, a further benefit that the monks brought to the lay community – this was a collective one, fed by a widespread belief that economic prosperity and freedom from epidemics, hunger and war could only be guaranteed by adepts who understood and could propitiate unseen occult forces. This had been – and remained to a degree – the responsibility of the Brahmin priesthood, but it increasingly devolved on to the more humble and democratic shoulders of the so-called sons of Shakyamuni, with their ascetic way of life, their daily rounds and their stories. All was well with the people, it came to be assumed, as long as they respected the monks and gave generously both to them and to their foundations. This attitude became state policy, in effect, during the reign of King Asoka in the third century BC, for a nation had taken the place of the people by then.

Asoka

In about 320 BC, a nobleman called Chandragupta Maurya succeeded to the throne of Magadha and set about the business of conquest. Within two decades he had achieved suzerainty over huge swathes of the Indian subcontinent, from Bengal to eastern Afghanistan and as far south as the Narmada river. By the time his grandson Asoka inherited the Magadhan empire some thirty years or so later, it stretched far beyond central India to the country of the Tamils in the far south. Asoka only had to bring Kalinga (modern Orissa) in the north-east of India to heel to become master of virtually the whole subcontinent.

Asoka's campaign against Kalinga, according to legend, was swift, brutal and successful, but he was so horrified by the carnage inflicted by his men that he began to turn away from the world. It was then that he had a chance encounter with a Buddhist monk called Nigrodha, who persuaded him to use his enormous power to promote peace and virtue throughout his territories, instead of violence. Asoka soon took up the study of the *Dharma*, became a Buddhist layman and gave up the royal pursuit of hunting, since it broke the principle of *ahimsa*. He made pilgrimage, so the story goes, to Bodghaya, the site of the Buddha's enlightenment and built *stupas* – both at Kusinagra, where his body was cremated, and at Sarnath, where he gave his first sermon. Asoka also ordered the enlargement of a *stupa* dedicated to a former Buddha called Kanakamuni and provided, in an inscription, the first evidence we have of the doctrine and cult of other Buddhas who had preceded Siddhartha into the world.

According to tradition, Asoka built eighty-four thousand *stupas* in all as part of a hugely ambitious building programme that included wells, roads, hospitals, dispensaries and monasteries and that stretched all over his empire. He went on religious tours and held discussions with holy men, so it is said, of every sect. He also arranged for exhortations to be carved in every territory on rocks and pillars, recommending the ethical life to his subjects: these were his famous Rock Edicts, the first recorded writing in history composed by a Buddhist layperson:

> Do not perform sacrifices or do anything else that might hurt animals. . . . Be generous to your friends . . . Do not get involved in quarrels and arguments . . . Try to be pure of heart, humble and faithful . . . Do not think only of your good points; remember also your faults as well and try to put them right. . .

There is no mention of the inner arcana of the Buddhist faith in any of the Edicts (twenty-one of them issued in two groups separated by a gap of thirteen years), nor are the Four Holy Truths, the Eightfold Path, Nirvana or the supramondane qualities of a Buddha referred to. Indeed there is little or no reference to either meditation or the acquisition of wisdom. These omissions may well have been deliberate, since Asoka's aim was to build a bridge between the state and all of its people, drawing them together into one ethical community no matter what their faith or sect. (Or they might also have been due, of course, to the fact that the monks denied the inner workings of the Buddhist system to laymen, however high their worldly status.) To Asoka, *dharma* seems to have meant respect for all life (*ahimsa*), loving kindness (*maitri*) and the first four of the All-Is-Ists' perfections: giving, morality, patience and vigour. He lived by these principles and as the first Buddhist king he ruled through them – and so opened up another front for the faith: the achievement of the *Dharma* under political patronage and within the structures of government.

Asoka tried to communicate this message to other rulers through special *Dharma*-emissaries. One of his edicts records that he sent envoys to preach the *Dharma* to the post-Alexandrian kingdoms of Egypt, Syria, Macedonia, Epirus and Cyrene (in northern Africa) in the middle of the third century BC. Although they had no traceable effect there were better results closer to home, for an inscription in Greek and Aramaic found in Kandahar, Afghanistan records Asoka's efforts to 'make men more pious', and concludes:

> Acting in this way, during their present life and in their future existence, they will live better and more happily in all things.

Asoka's spreading of the Buddhist message may also have helped in the later conversion of other monarchs of the post-Alexandrian age. Kings such as the Indo-Greek king Menander (Pali: Milinda) in the second century BC, whose debate with the monk Nagasena became, as *The Questions of King Milinda* (*Milinda-Panha*), a small jewel in the post-canonical literature; and the Scythian king Kaniska in north-west India, a century or so later. According to one tradition, it was under King Kaniska's aegis, in Kashmir, that a final Buddhist council on the subcontinent was held, to sort out once more the differences within the *Sangha*. Legend has it that a monastery was built at the site of the council and that five hundred monks sat down to engrave agreed commentaries on the scriptures on copper sheets. These sheets were then said to have been deposited in a specially-built *stupa* – although no trace of it has ever been found.

It was in what is now Sri Lanka, however, that Asoka's legacy most firmly took root. In about 240 BC, he despatched his son Mahinda and his daughter Sanghamitta to the island as missionaries and the result of their work is that Buddhism has flourished there longer than anywhere else. It soon became the state religion. In the words of Edward Conze in his authoritative *A Short History of Buddhism*:

Only Buddhists had a legitimate right to be kings and the island of Lanka was held to belong to the Buddha Himself, It was the king's duty to protect the Order of monks and great benefits accrued to the monasteries in the form of donations, prestige and protection from interference. The kings, although mostly laymen, were also the final judges in any dispute which might arise among the Buddhists. The monks in their turn generally helped the kings and won popular support for their wishes. This close connection of the Sangha with the state had its disadvantages. From the second century BC onwards it not only infused a spirit of nationalism into the Buddhism of Ceylon and made the monks prone to political intrigue, but it also led them to enthusiastically support the national wars of their kings. They assured king Dutta Gamani (107–77 BC) that the killing of many thousands of enemies was of no account, because as unbelievers they were really no more than animals. They accompanied the army of the same king, 'since the sight of bhikkhus is both blessing and protection for us', and the king himself had a relic of the Buddha put into his spear.

Theravadins

Of all the eighteen different sects or 'schools' of Buddhist thought that tradition records in the early period, this one, the Ceylonese 'school' – known as the Theravadins – is the only one that has survived. Gradually, one must suppose, the entire canon of Buddhist literature found its way to the island. There, at a council near the village of Matale, in the first century BC, it was rehearsed, revised and finally written down on palm leaves, which were then consigned by the writers to the three baskets of the *Vinaya*, the *Sutra* and the *Abhidharma*. The canon was written in Pali, an everyday dialect of Sanskrit, and it is the most complete version of Buddhist scriptures that we know, since the canons of other 'schools' have mostly been lost. It is from later practices of the Theravadins (geographically isolated, for the most part, from later developments in Buddhism on the subcontinent) that we can infer some of the festivals that early Buddhists must have celebrated: the coming of the New Year (mid-March or -April), for example, and the Offering to the Ancestors (the beginning of October), both of which roughly coincide with the Hindu calendar. Most important of all, of course, was the joint festival of the Birth and the Enlightenment of the Buddha, both of which events fell by tradition on the full-moon night of the month of Vaisakha (April–May). It continues to be celebrated today.

Sacred Places and Worship

Early Buddhist art, archaeological findings and continuing Theravada practice also provide us with a reasonably clear picture of the way in which Buddhism incorporated pre-existing customs and lore in this period. It shared its view of the world and its picture of life as an ever-turning Wheel with Brahmanism, of course. Some of its elements reach back further still, to the tree-spirit and serpent-cults, the fertility goddesses and the reliquary mounds of the invaders who arrived in the Indus Valley from the central European steppes. In the myth of the Buddha, Queen Maya gave birth to Siddartha under a sacred tree and she is characteristically depicted as standing beneath it in the traditional pose of a fertility goddess. The Buddha himself, it should be remembered, died between two trees and reached Enlightenment beneath another, the Bodhi Tree (*pipal* or *ficus religiosus*), veneration of which is an assimilation (and takeover) of a very much earlier cult-practice.

The Bodhi Tree, in fact, seems to have fulfilled for Buddhists the role a sacred tree played all over India as 'the fulfiller of wishes' and the bringer of all desires, in every settlement in which it found itself. Garlands of flowers were hung on its branches and offerings placed on the altar at its base, which was usually surrounded by a fence of wood and stone. Asoka is said to have become so obsessed with the original Bodi Tree at Bodghaya that his queen tried to have it destroyed and it was he, by tradition, who turned it into a place of pilgrimage and a shrine. He placed a carved stone seat (the so-called 'diamond seat') in front of the tree which, though empty, symbolized the eternal presence of the Buddha.

As we have seen, *stupas* were also built by Asoka and others, both in cave-buildings and in the open, and these too were derived from earlier funerary practices: they had been traditionally built over the cremated remains of holy men and kings. Within Buddhism, they became the most venerated of all monuments, not only presiding over the ashes and relics of the Buddha and his *arhants*, but also commemorating miracles, laying claim to sacred spots and honouring the merit of their building in the name of the Buddha and the *Dharma*. The dome of a *stupa* is traditionally built over either a circular or square base and was – and is – called 'the egg' (*anda*). It represents rebirth, the potential transformation of the human spirit, and it not only commemorates the Buddha's death but also his entry into *nirvana*. (This, *mutatis mutandis*, was similar to the original symbolism – now mostly lost – of the Christian Easter egg.) At the pinnacle of the egg-dome rises a stone umbrella, the symbol of the Buddha's status 'as spiritual royalty', to use the phrase employed by Robinson and Johnson in their *The Buddhist Religion*.

In early Buddhist sculpture, we see Buddhists – and even serpents and gods – gathered round a *stupa* or a Bodhi Tree, their hands folded together in front of them in the traditonal way, some kneeling, some carrying garlands. Offerings, mostly of flowers (particularly lotuses), are laid out on shrines and altars, hung from branches or draped over a *stupa*'s dome. There are, during this period, no actual representations of the Buddha himself. Instead, he is symbolized by a variety of sculpted images: an empty throne; a pair of footprints; a wheel; a lotus; a shrine with a turban on it; and a circle beneath a tree. The empty throne, recalling the 'diamond seat' at Bodghaya, is a recollection of his Enlightenment and the footprints, often engraved with representations of the wheel and the Three Jewels – as well as swastikas (symbols of well-being in Sanskrit) – are a reminder that he walked the world among humans and left behind him a Path to be followed. The wheel is both the Wheel of Life and an aide-mémoire of his First Sermon at Srinath and the turban is a symbol of the wealth and power that he left behind him when he 'went forth'. The lotus, the most beautiful and the most ubiquitous of these images, has a symbolism all of its own. Growing out of the constantly shifting waters of becoming, it rises up out of the mire of existence and transcends it, just as the Buddha does.

Why no images of the Buddha were carved in, or have survived from, this early period remains a matter of speculation. Perhaps, in contrast to the vivid and teeming pantheon of Hinduism, symbols alone were thought sufficient to evoke his presence. Perhaps his Enlightenment was regarded as too ineffable for him to be represented in human form. Whatever the reason, the huge variety of images that we associate with Buddhism in the present day had to wait for the development of the movement which finally threw the esoteric knowledge of the monks open to the wider community of the Buddha's lay followers – Mahayana, the 'Great Vehicle or Course'.

Chapter Six:

Mahayana

The early period of Buddhism, as we have seen, was largely dominated by senior monks, who saw themselves as the sole caretakers of the Buddha's word – as indeed they were, in a literal sense, given that written texts did not yet exist in any organized form. They used their control over the oral transmission of the scriptures, however, to take on a further role, that of gate-keepers. They denied laypeople access to the Buddha's direct teachings, and downplayed the role of the laity in general and women in particular, whether ordained or not. Although Buddha had pronounced that salvation was available to any man or woman, whatever his or her status, the *Sangha* soon came to be divided into four categories – women, householders, nuns and monks – each (except for monks, of course) subservient to the category above. Even though lip-service was still paid to the Buddha's pronouncement that a householder was capable of becoming an *arhant*, there is little mention of this ever happening in the early literature. As for women, very few, even the most distinguished nuns, were thought worthy of mention after the first generation, although the first of their number had been Buddha's own foster-mother and aunt. A notable exception, of course, was

Saghamitta, who took a cutting of the sacred Bodhi Tree with her on her joint mission to Ceylon with her brother. But then she was an emperor's daughter.

Echoes of Dissent

Bubbling away under this increasingly rigid order of things, though, we can still hear the echoes of dissent. Among the eighteen 'schools', there were several which questioned – and sometimes denied – the privileged status of the *arhants*. (What goes up can still come down, they said.) Others questioned the monks' insistence on the futility and unreliability of individual consciousness and argued for a more commonsense view of the world. There was a feeling abroad, it could be said, that monks who cleaved narrowly to the received words of the historical Buddha – and interpreted them for their own benefit – were increasingly out of touch with real life and with the aspirations of lay people, who wanted equal standing and equal access to the spiritual rewards the monks so jealously guarded.

In the period around the first century BC this feeling, most clearly expressed in the early doctrines of the *Mahasanghikas*, first became a drift, then a movement and finally a wind that spread throughout the subcontinent and blew away the cobwebs and conservatism of the old establishment. It seems to have originated in two main areas – the south and the northwest – where local populations were most exposed to outside influences, both philosophical and artistic. In the northwest, for instance, Buddhists lived cheek by jowl with Brahmins and Zoroastrians; Indo-Aryans rubbed shoulders with Persians and Greeks; and some scholars believe that the *Mahayana*, the Great Vehicle or Course that Buddhism took around the time of the birth of Christ, owes much to the religions and iconography of the Iranian and Mediterranean worlds.

It also owes a great deal, of course, to a comparatively new and increasingly available technology: that of the written word. Central to the *Mahayana* is a literature, written in Sanskrit, that added to and embellished the scriptures of the Pali Canon – *and presented itself as equally authoritative*. The impulse behind this literature – which Edward Conze calls 'one of the most magnificent outbursts of creative energy known to human history' – is plain: it was designed to rejuvenate Buddhism, to prevent it from ossifying and to adapt it to a new age and new social conditions. It belongs very much to its time. Yet, for all this, it is made up of *Sutras* that, for the most part, purport to be absolutely authentic: the teachings of Buddha himself.

The Mahayanan Viewpoint

This was justified to some degree by the *Mahayana* interpretation of the essential nature of Buddha. Following the *Mahasanghikas*, Mahayanists belittled the significance of the Buddha's appearance in history: Sakyamuni the man, they maintained, had simply been the creature of a transcendental Buddha, who exists through all eternity and in all places as the supreme embodiment of the truth, preaching the *Dharma* at all times and in myriad forms. This clearly meant that he could also reveal new aspects of the Law – the new 'expanded' *Sutras* – wherever and whenever he chose. Furthermore, through his inspiration or charisma – on which Mahayanists laid great stress – he could infuse thoughts into the minds of his devotees and sustain their strength in the *Dharma*. Since he is eternal and omnipresent, it was plainly possible for his overpowering influence to pervade the minds of individuals to such a degree that their utterances – made however long after his disappearance from the world – would have the same value as his earthly teachings.

This was not, in fact, a defence that early Mahayanists ever articulated, for by then, in a sense, the die had been cast – they had already plumped for a mythological explanation. The new texts, they announced, had indeed been preached by Sakyamuni during his lifetime. However, at about the same time that the monks were codifying what later became the Pali Canon, at the first cave-council at Rajaghra, they had been collected and authorized instead by a council of *Bodhisattvas* (Buddhas-to-be) on the mythical mountain of Vimalasvabhava. Afterwards, they had been miraculously preserved by the Naga serpent-kings in their underwater palaces, ready for release when the time was ripe. 'Five hundred years after the Buddha's Nirvana', as the second-century AD sage Nagarjuna put it, 'when the good law, after having gradually declined, was in great danger', they were finally released into the world to give new life to the faith.

It is not altogether surprising – given this explanation of the derivation of the texts – that they should have been greeted with a good deal of scepticism by those who became known derisively by the Mahayanists as followers of *Hinayana*, 'the Inferior Vehicle or Course': even though *Hinayana* was to remain the most influential element within the Indian *Sangha* for another five or six hundred years. Being a Hinayanist, in fact, came to mean two things – rejecting the authenticity of the Mahayanist *Sutras* and continuing to cleave to the path of the *arhant*. Both came under increasing attack in the developing Mahayanist literature. At first, it has to be said, there was little disparagement. In *The Small Perfection of Wisdom*, one of the early 'expanded' *Sutras*, the description of the Mahayanists' innovative new spiritual hero, the *bodhisattva*, is put into the mouths of great *arhants*. A little later on, however, in another *Sutra*, *arhants* are described as being at a dead end, imprisoned in a nursery form of *nirvana*. Even the worst of sinners has a better chance of true salvation, says the *Sutra*. By the time of the *Lotus Sutra*, written in about AD 200, there is more or less open warfare. The *Lotus Sutra* describes those who do not believe the 'expanded *Sutras*' to be the words of the Buddha as wicked, and says witheringly of the *arhants* that since there is after all only one *nirvana*, even they might just be able to achieve it one day.

The many schools of *Hinayana* Buddhism have today more or less disappeared – their sole survivors are the Theravadins of Sri Lanka and their offshoots. So what is it about Mahayanist beliefs that made – and continues to make – them so attractive? Since Buddhism is first and foremost a doctrine of salvation, why did its particular path to salvation prove so popular and, given its successful export to almost the whole of eastern Asia, so universally applicable?

The Central Doctrines of *Mahayana*

Mahayanan beliefs can be separated out - as Edward Conze does - into five different categories.

1. The *bodhisattva*, driven by altruism and continually reborn into the world by choice, takes the place of the spiritually individualistic *arhant* as the pathfinder and exemplar.

2. A new road to salvation is mapped out in which compassion ranks as high as wisdom – and along which progress is made in the early stages via the six 'perfections'.

3. Faith – for initiate and layman alike – is given a fresh importance by

the creation of a new pantheon of divine beings, to whom worship, veneration and propitiatory offerings can be made.

4. A new virtue, 'skill-in-means', the ability to bring out the spiritual potential of others, is given priority in the attributes of a saint – even over wisdom.

5. A new coherent account of the nature of reality is given which, by advancing such notions as 'Emptiness' and 'Suchness', provides map-reference points to the whereabouts and nature of the Infinite.

The Bodhisattva *Ideal*

The *Bodhisattva* – or Buddha-to-be – was a familar figure to ordinary laymen through the *Jataka*, the elaborate folk-tales which recounted the adventures in previous lives of the Buddha on the way to his Buddhahood.   The Mahayanists opened up this path to Enlightenment to the faithful, in effect, while downgrading the virtues of that taken by the *arhant* and the *pacceka buddha*. A *bodhisattva*, that is to say, is one who turns down the pursuit of salvation for himself alone and embraces instead the opportunity to return time and again to the world to help others. Anyone who aspires to this path first seeks to generate *Bodhicitta* or 'Wisdom-Heart'. This will ultimately allow him to preserve an Enlightened equanimity after rebirth amid the distractions and noise of the world of *samsara*, rather than pursuing Enlightenment through extinction and cessation, as the *arhant* and the *pacceka buddha* do.

Compassion and the Six Perfections

In the early period, it was the wisdom of the *arhants* – their complete understanding of the nature of life and of ultimate reality – that had been the paramount virtue. Wisdom, however, maintained the Mahayanists, could be, and was indeed being, turned to ends that were selfish. In fact, there was nothing in wisdom alone that required it to be used to help others. Only when it was combined with infinite compassion could the stain of selfishness – and, therefore, self-centredness – be avoided. As in the end the only truly unselfish entities were Buddhas – who were both all-wise and all-compassionate – theirs was the path to be followed in an unselfish quest for enlightenment. The way of the *bodhisattva* became known as 'the Buddha-Vehicle', a word that was more or less interchangeable with the word *Mahayana*.

Following it, however, was, and is, no easy task, for it requires a very precise balance – a marriage of equals, indeed – between wisdom and compassion. (It also requires countless lives and aeons of time.) Compassion – empathy with the suffering of the world and a desire to rescue all living things from it – is vital to the decision to keep on postponing entrance into the bliss of *nirvana* and to continue being reborn; and wisdom is essential to a deeper and deeper understanding, through successive lives, of the emptiness (*sanyata*) of all there is. Compassion is necessary if the *bodhisattva* is to identify with all living things and share their passions, as he must, even though wisdom reveals again and again that they, their passions and their travails are equally illusory and fictitious. Finally, the *bodhisattva*, who is only separated from Buddhahood in the end by his clinging and contaminating belief that he somehow remains a separate individual, has to learn to obliterate himself completely –

and for this too both compassion and wisdom are required. Compassion to enable the loss of self through sacrifice and service and wisdom to tear through the veils to ultimate reality and the 'own-ness' or 'is-ness' of all things.

According to Richard Robinson and Willard Johnson in their *The Buddhist Religion, A Historical Introduction*, the *bodhisattva* path begins

> with instruction from a Buddha, a bodhisattva or some other spiritual friend. Seeds of virtue are planted in the mind of the hearers, and from much hearing they come to perform good deeds, through which they acquire more and more roots of goodness. After many lives, thanks to the infused grace of the various teacher-saviours and the merit earned by responding to them, a person becomes able to to put forth the bodhicitta ('thought of enlightenment'). The two motives for this aspiration are one's own desire for bodhi and compassion for all living beings who suffer in samsara. Initially the motivation is both egotistic and altruistic, but along the path one realizes the sameness of self and others, and transcends the duality of purpose . . . 'Arousing the thought of enlightenment' is a decisive conversion experience with profound psychological effects. It is compared to a pearl, the ocean, sweet music, a shade-giving tree, a convenient bridge, soothing moonbeams, the sun's rays, a universal panacea, and an infallible elixir.

From this point of acceptance, through future aeons of time, the *bodhisattva* practises, and keeps to the path through the six perfections or *paramitas*, 'the methods by which we go to the

Beyond'. Each involves a virtue – giving, morality, patience, vigour, meditation and wisdom – which is practised to perfection when exercised without cost-counting, ulterior motives or self regard. Any merit earned in the process is reassigned to universal enlightenment and the spiritual welfare of other beings, rather than simply being held in a sort of individual bank account as a down-payment for future bliss.

The first perfection – giving (*dana*) – entails total and complete generosity of spirit, a willingness to give away every asset one has: material, intellectual, emotional, even life itself. The second perfection – morality (*sila*) – requires utter dedication to moral precepts, even in the face of worldly retribution and death. The third – patience (*ksanti*) – involves endurance in the face of hardship and avoidance of anger and forgiveness, but it also means meek acceptance of unpalatable, even at first sight incomprehensible, *Mahayana* doctrines such as that of the non-existence of all things, the fact that they neither arise nor cease.

Vigour (*virya*), the fourth perfection, represents the unflagging energy that the *bodhisattva* must perfect in order to pursue good works throughout the aeons and not be discouraged. Meditation (*dhyana*), the fifth perfection, is the ability to enter every kind of meditative trance and leave it again at will – without reaching towards whatever paradise it might offer. Wisdom (*prajna*), the last perfection, is the ability to understand the nature of all things and how they are related in the end: the unreality of their separate existence. It leads at its highest point, in the words of Conze, 'right into the Emptiness [*sunyata*] which is the highest reality'.

The doctrine of the six perfections, or *paramitas*, had first been promulgated by the heretical All-Is-Ists two or more centuries before, as we have seen. However, laity and monks alike were also familiar with it through the tales of the Buddha's previous lives in the *Jataka*. Born as a hare, for example – and having decided to practise the perfection of giving – the Bodhisattva was approached one day by the god Indra, disguised as a brahmin, who asked him for food. Having no alternative he offered himself, telling the brahmin to light a fire and cook him. In another life, he demonstrated his vigour by ceaselessly trying to find water when his caravan had run dry in the desert; and in yet another life, reborn as a mariner, he achieved great feats of navigation through wisdom, despite the fact that he had gone blind. Reborn into a further life as an ascetic, he ran foul of a ruler, who demanded to know what doctrine he now espoused. 'Patience', he said. After the ruler had instructed his executioner to flog the Bodhisattva, he asked again and got the same reply. Finally, the ruler had his hands and feet cut off, followed by his nose and ears, but the Bodhisattva still professed his patience and, so the story goes, felt no anger.

Folk-tales like this were moral lessons – they encouraged their listeners to follow the example of the Bodhisattva. After hearing such stories, the hearer perhaps felt that it was not too great a step to become a Bodhisattva himself: to follow his path.

The New Pantheon

Having achieved the six perfections – and having come face to face with the reality of Emptiness – the Mahayanist *bodhisattva* could now, if he chose, leave the world of suffering and enter *nirvana*. If he did this, though, it would mean the end of his mission, so he elects to remain in order to go through the last four of what came to be known in Mahayanist doctrine as the Ten Stages. At this point, however, although he is still in the world he no longer belongs to it. He has instead become a supernatural being with miraculous powers and 'sovereignty over the earth' – a 'celestial Bodhisattva' – and as such, of course, worthy of worship and veneration. The faithful soon turned to a host of Bodhisattvas – twenty-three of them mentioned in the *Lotus Sutra* – of whom a number are worth examining further:

Maitreya: Maitreya is the object of the earliest *bodhisattva* cult of all. He is first mentioned in a Pali *Sutra* as a Buddha-to-be who will finally arrive in the world and command an even greater following than Sakyamuni. Acknowledged by all Hinayana sects – and still regarded by Theravadins as the only true *bodhisattva* of the present age – he is both a living compassionate presence and, in his present birth, a god. He can thus be worshipped by Buddhists and theists alike.

Manjusri: Manjusri ('gentle or sweet glory'), another Bodhisattva at the tenth stage of his journey to Buddahood, is the personification of wisdom and eloquence. By performing certain actions, such as worshipping him, meditating on his representations and teachings and chanting – or even hearing – his name, various benefits accrue to his followers: from happy rebirths and guarantees of future enlightenment to an appearance of the Bodhisattva himself. He takes on the form of a poor man or orphan and appears before his devotees either in the real world or, if their sight is obstructed by bad *karma*, in their dreams.

Avalokitesvara: Avalokitesvara (probably 'the lord who looks down') is described in a third century *Sutra* as an omnipresent, omnipotent saviour-deity who can take on any guise – Buddha, *bodhisattva* or god – to help living things save themselves from the snares and perils of *samsara*. He also guards his devotees against lust, anger and folly. Usually represented as a bejewelled layman wearing a high crown and often carrying a lotus, he became revered in Tibet as the country's patron-protector, worshipped through his mantra, '*Om mani-padme hom*'. Later, in China, he took on the form of a woman and is now worshipped as a Madonna-like figure throughout east Asia, under a variety of names that echo his original Chinese ideogram, *Kuan-Yin*, or 'sound-regarder'.

Samantabhadra: Samantabhadra, in a late passage of the *Lotus Sutra*, is described as arriving in the world with an elaborate retinue to ask Sakyamuni to expound the *Sutra*, of which he became, in effect, the protector and guardian. He wards off human enemies and demons from the monks who keep the *Sutra*. Mounted on a white elephant with six tusks, he is present to jog their memory should they forget any of the words during its recitation. He will also provide inspiration in person and give talismanic spells to any devotee who follows a rigorous programme of worship by circumambulation.

Celestial Buddhas

In addition to Celestial Bodhisattvas, the Mahayanist pantheon also admitted a new class of Celestial Buddhas that derived, at least in part, from early and accepted teachings. It will be remembered that Sakyamuni discouraged his disciples from venerating him as a person, on the grounds that this kind of adoration was misdirected. 'Whoever sees me, sees the *Dharma*. Whoever sees the *Dharma*, sees me' he was reported to have said – that is, 'concentrate on the *Dharma*'. He also said, in the version of the *Diamond Sutra* quoted by Edward Conze:

Those who by my form did see me,
And those who followed me by voice,
Wrong the efforts they engaged in,
Me those people will not see!

From this arose the view that the Buddha in fact had two bodies: a physical body and a *Dharma*-body. His physical body, for all his wishes, became an object of veneration after his Enlightenment – it was given the thirty-two major marks of the superman and was reputed to give off rays in six colours, as well as a heady perfume. The 'real' Buddha, however, was thought to lie in his *Dharma*-body. By the time the *Mahasanghikas* pronounced that the Buddha was eternally active, both transcendent and immanent, in the world – and that he had created his physical body merely as a convenience – it seemed reasonable to assume that these 'conveniences' existed, like the *Dharma*, in all places and in all realms. In fact, there had to be Buddhas both in the past and in the future – and in every possible corner of existence. In a remarkable prefiguration of modern theories of alternative universes, early Mahayanans posited up to a billion different worlds: in at least a proportion of those worlds, a *Tathagata* – or 'one who has come or gone to the True', as Sakyamuni preferred to call himself – lives, teaches and embodies the *Dharma*.

These myriad 'Buddha-lands', as they were known, lay in all possible directions, and in many ways they were similar to the heavens of the gods, except that they remained, however delightful, a staging-post on the way to the ultimate goal of *nirvana* (which every inhabitant was ultimately guaranteed). They were not in any sense final resting-places (like the paradises, say, of Christianity and Islam), nor were all their denizens confined to them, for both Buddhas and *bodhisattvas* could appear at will anywhere else in any of the other worlds where living beings needed their help. Supernatural intervention, that is to say, was available to the faithful who asked for it.

Aksobhya: Aksobhya ('imperturbable') is the earliest mentioned of the Celestial Buddhas, inhabiting a Buddha-world to the East. He can be thought of as the patron and sponsor of angerlessness in his devotees. He is usually represented as blue, with a blue elephant, holding a pure diamond in his right hand and making the 'earth-witness' gesture with his left.

Amithaba: The origin of Amithaba ('infinite light') probably owes a good deal to Iranian sun worship. He has a Buddha-world in the West called Sukhavati ('happiness-having') – a land of eternal daylight suffused with the colours of the rainbow, where his devotees (later known in China as the Pure Land Sect) are offered an existence full of ease and pleasure. Even the worst sinner, if repentant, can still gain access as long as he has faith. In the seventh century, Chinese travellers recorded that Amithaba had many worshippers in India – he later became a major cult figure in the Far East, where he is known as Amito (China) and Amita (Japan). In literature he is often conflated (or confused) with another Celestial Buddha, Amitayus ('unlimited-lifespan'), who is almost certainly derived from the Iranian Zurvan Akaranak ('Unlimited Time'). Both Celestial Buddhas probably originated in the borderlands between India and Iran, where Buddhism had a strong presence (see below).

Vairocana: Vairocana ('shining out') came to be regarded as the *Dharma*-body of Sakyamuni. (The word was orginally an epithet applied to him.) Sun and light imagery played a major part in early accounts of Sakyamuni and his Enlightenment. His knowledge was light shone into the darkness of ignorance, he revealed himself with a light-shaft beaming from the eye of wisdom on his forehead and his Enlightenment coincided with daybreak. Vairocana only became popular as a Celestial Buddha in the seventh century, which was comparatively late, but he played a central role in the form of Buddhism that was to enter Japan two hundred years later. He was known in Japan as Dainichi, or 'Great Sun' and was seen as the 'Cosmic Buddha' who pervaded the entire universe. When Jesuit missionaries entered Japan in the sixteenth century, they used the word 'Dainichi' as a translation for their word 'God'.

'Skill-in-Means'

'Skill-in-means' (*upaya*) is the quality that a *bodisattva* acquires at the seventh stage of his path towards Buddahood after he has achieved perfection of wisdom. That is, when he fully understands the fact that nothing really exists except Emptiness, that the whole edifice of Buddhism – the Buddhas, the Bodhisattvas, the perfections, the stages – is a fiction designed to assist living things towards the one Ultimate Truth, which alone can liberate but about which nothing can be said which is not false and fleeting. Compassion alone under these circumstances would ordinarily be mute – wisdom alone would see the futility of all communication, but 'skill-in-means' supervenes over them and attempts to find the best way of bringing out the spiritual potential in others by appropriate statements and actions. The aspiring *bodhisattva* accepts that absolute truth is beyond thought and description, but also recognizes that there is such a thing as commonsense everyday truth which, although distorted, can still be manipulated to point the way. Ordinary language, for all its faults, is still a recourse for the *bodhisattva*, because the salvation of all things in the end depends on it.

The Nature of Reality

Mahayanan ontology is derived from that of the Mahasanghikans and it constitutes – as Conze says – the inner core of Mahayanan doctrine. The teachings, however, are complex, recondite and hard to summarize, partly because the nature of ultimate reality is unavailable to intellectual enquiry and remains beyond the reach of words, as is recognized in the texts themselves. All the teachings can do, therefore, is to point somewhere in the right direction – they cannot, in the nature of things, explain anything or say anything definitive. They are, to this extent, a series of signposts to a place that can never be found in this life, map-references to the whereabouts of the unknowable.

Early Buddhism had decreed that the *dharmas* – the psychological-cum- experiential particles which make up both the world and our perception of it – are characterized by impermanence, suffering and absence of self (no-self or *anatman*). Mahayanists, following the lead of the Mahasanghikans, delved deeper into this sub-atomic theory of reality and consciousness, as it were, and added a fourth characteristic: that of Emptiness. All *dharmas*, they said, were empty (*sunya*) and therefore basically indistinguishable from one another. They were both non-existent and one and the same.

This wasn't a particularly radical departure on the face of it, since Buddhist theory had always accepted the essential emptiness of the concept of self. This time around, however, it was a matter of emphasis. For by emphasizing and stressing Emptiness, Mahayanists were at the same time downplaying the central importance of the impermanence and suffering to which the world was systematically doomed – and from which monks had been encouraged to retreat. If all things were empty, after all, then aversion to the day to day world was empty too – and was no solution. If everything, indeed, was marked by an identical Emptiness, there was no relevant difference between the relative and the absolute, between *nirvana* and *samsara*, or between the *Buddhas* and *Bodhisattvas* and the men and women they guided. 'Own-beings' of any kind – with some sort of inherent, enduring and self-sustaining essence – simply did not exist anywhere at all. Intellectually they were fictions and emotionally they were the focus of obsessions and passions that enslaved and achieved nothing.

The Mahayanan concept of Emptiness further reduced any perceived imbalance that remained between the (spiritually privileged) monks and the laity. Also, because it implied emptiness of thoughts, it provided a new object of contemplation – that is, Emptiness itself – as a form of therapy that was effective both intellectually and emotionally. This did not imply or involve turning one's back on the world, in any sense, or denying that things in it have existence. On the contrary, it meant confronting the world and its sense-objects in their Suchness (*tathata*), 'such as they really are', without adding to them or subtracting anything from them at all. Suchness and Emptiness are, to the Mahayanan, interchangeable concepts and understanding this fully is the foundation of True Knowledge, in which all seeming oppositions – between subject and object, perceiver and perceived, affirmation and negation – are obliterated once and for all.

Beyond this point, of course, there was – according to Mahayanist doctrine – well, nothing: just Beyondness, the enveloping silence of the ineffable and unknowable. The nature of the path to it – depending as it did on the same-egg-twin concepts of Emptiness and Suchness – was to have a profound effect on religious life, however, as Robinson and Johnson point out in their *The Buddhist Religion: A Historical Introduction*:

> Monks in training who are ridden with feelings of guilt and shame because they have infringed the Vinaya are told to appease their guilt by meditation on its emptiness. This does not give them license to sin, but it liberates them from the burden of evil. The bodhisattva can work and play in the secular world without fear of contamination from sense objects, because he knows that intrinsically they are neither pure nor impure. He associates with merchants, kings, harlots, and drunkards without falling into avarice, arrogance, lust, or dissipation. He accepts and excels in the arts and sciences, welcoming them as good means to benefit and edify living beings. He recognizes the religious capacities of women, listening respectfully when they preach the Dharma, because he knows that maleness and femaleness are both empty.

Even in their abstruse ontology, then, the Mahayanists acted as a democratizing force within the *Sangha*, one that served gradually to erase the old embedded divisions. They also showed considerable elasticity, as we have seen, in their absorption of elements from the beliefs of other peoples and religions. These two characteristics of Buddhism's new broom, taken together, not only explain why it became the dominant school in India itself in the end, but also, perhaps, why it was supremely successful as an export.

Early Mahayanan Sects

During what might be called the middle period in the development of *Mahayana* doctrine – that is, in or about the second century AD – there appears to have been a huge change in Indian culture, a change that could perhaps be summed up as The Rise of the Individual. Not only was there a new confidence in ordinary people's ability to arrive at knowledge without the intercession of gods or saints, but there was also an effloresence of secular literature, poetry, fiction and social and historical observation. There were advances in science, new developments in logic, raised standards of debate and, above all, named authors. From then on, named initiates of the Mahayanist school – virtually all of them monks, it seems – began to produce treatises that relied increasingly on personal experience and rational argument. They still routinely invoked the *Sutras* as evidence, of course –and *Sutras* continued to be written to provide new evidence and proofs wherever necessary – but the practice of Buddhism from then on had a human direction and face. What Konze calls 'the unsystematic phase' in the building of *Mahayana* doctrine began to come to an end.

Nagarjuna

One of the first great *Mahayana* sages whom we know by name as a historical personage is Nagarjuna, a southern Indian philosopher of genius who, at the end of the second century AD, founded what came to be known as the Madhyamikha school, or 'the school of the Middle Way'. Nagarjuna had very little to say about trance, meditation and altered states of consciousness. Instead he brought a ferocious intellect to his exposition of Mahayanist doctrine, through which he more or less bludgeoned into submission non-Mahayanist assumptions about the nature of reality.

Nagarjuna – whose most famous work is the polemical *Middle Stanzas* (*Madhyamaka-karikas*) – is, in a sense, the Indian Socrates. Firstly, like Socrates, he professed no views of his own – instead, he used his opponents' arguments to demonstrate that their implications flew in the face of the very assumptions they were based on. Secondly, he ruthlessly used the tool of the dialectic to demolish pairs of opposites that were routinely used to describe reality: unity and diversity, permanence and annihilation, coming and going, etc. By demonstrating how these opposites ended up negating each other, he produced what has been called a theory of universal relativity – one that prefigured Einstein's – by showing the conflicting effects of points of view (the man on the moon, the man who points to it, the man on the spaceship rushing by, etc.). He deconstructed the world of perceived reality, announced that all statements about it were ultimately untenable and pointed the way to where ultimate truth had to be positioned – that is, in the middle (hence 'The Middle Way'), in a place without point of view or angle of vision, where the urgent interior cinema of thinking and identifying had been switched off.

Yogacarans

Another school that can be identified with known historical figures is known as *Yogacara* ('Yoga Practice') or *Vijnanavada* ('Teaching of Consciousness'), which flourished in northwest India in the fourth century AD, under the aegis of two brothers, Asanga and Vasubandhu. These adepts chose a different pathway towards the unknowable than that taken by Nagarjana and his followers: it was based on psychological rather than intellectual theory. In other words, they attempted to answer some fundamental questions about the mind and the way in which it constructs the illusory world: questions at the heart of Buddhist doctrine, which remained unresolved. If, for example, what we perceive as the world is a fleeting and impermanent mind-construct, by what processes exactly do we create and objectify it from moment to moment? If sense-impressions are as ephemeral as their objects, which of them actually apprehends each object and how exactly does the world – or rather our construction of it – present itself as continuous even though it is forever dying away? What exactly is memory? How does it work? Above all, perhaps, what is the 'it' that experiences absolute truth, when 'it' is finally free from the mind-constructed shackles of illusion?

They started from the position that everything, even the Absolute, can be described as Mind, Thought or Consciousness – hence the name of their central doctrine, *citta-matta* ('mind only' or 'nothing but consciousness'). To explain how this central principle 'created' the world, they posited the existence of a 'store' or 'foundation' consciousness, a version of Jung's 'collective unconscious' in which the seeds of potential phenomena are stored and from which they constantly pour out to be made manifest in perception. They equated this 'store consciousness' with what they called *tathagatagarbha*, or 'the womb of Enlightened Being-ness'. However, *Garbha* – the 'womb' part of the word – means not only the womb but also the womb's contents: the embryo or developing child. For them, 'store consciousness' was not only the place where the Enlightened Being was conceived and matured, but it was also the embryonic Buddha himself who inhabits the 'store consciousness' of each individual.

In essence, this theory stems from an earlier doctrine – that the effects of good and bad *karma* are transmitted between lives as seeds, which ripen and bear fruit later, at their appropriate time. In the writings of the Yogacarans, however, this concept was expanded to include not only the embryonic presence of Buddha (the divine) within each one of us but also the stock of good *dharmas* generated by the universal power of his radiance. If these were not present in consciousness, they argued, how could there exist any impulse towards the religious life? Why would anyone choose to reject *samsara* and take up the difficult road towards *nirvana*? No, the womb/embryo was present in every living being – pure in its nature and synonymous with Suchness. In ordinary and ignorant people, of course, it was smeared and sullied over by the contaminants of *samsara* – impurities even remained in *bodhisattvas*. Only in Buddhas was *tathagatagarbha* pure and unsullied, right through to its core.

The storage of good *dharmas* and Eternal Being-ness in consciousness is the Yogacarans' contribution to what we might today call the psychology of conscience or the impulse to good. However, the Yogacarans' concept of *tathagatagarbha* also had intensely practical consequences. Since it was 'store-consciousness' which was responsible for what was in effect a hallucinatory illness – the projection of the twin delusions of the world and our 'independent' psycho-physical engagement with it – a cure was clearly available. The cure lay in learning to penetrate beyond these yoked chimeras by way of trance and meditation, so that one could finally arrive at a state of pure consciousness that was stripped of content and beyond the fake 'I-it' duality of appearances. The path to this lay in and through what the Yogacarans called 'the three natures': the absolute; the relative; and the imaginary. The imaginary – mistaking a coiled rope for a snake, for example – had first to be cleansed little by little through meditation, like a series of stains, from the relative. Things in the world had to be seen and confronted as they really were, with nothing added or subtracted. At this point, the relative (the world seen for what it actually is) could be gradually pared away too, until nothing remained of it and 'an act of cognition which no longer apprehends an object' could be achieved. This state, pure consciousness, with neither thinker nor thought, was the ultimate goal of Yogacaran trance-medicine – and was where salvation lay.

The *Yogacara* (or *Vijnanavada*) school produced another refinement in Buddhist thinking, one related, in a sense, to its notion of 'the three natures' (the Madhyamikhans recognized only two). This was its doctrine of the Three Bodies of Buddha, a doctrine which was to achieve some importance later. It had earlier been proposed, of course, that the Buddha must have had two bodies – his 'apparition' or 'form' body, the *ad hoc* phantom sent by the real Buddha to do his work on earth and the *Dharma*-body or Absolute Truth: the *Mahayana*-proposed embodiment of *nirvana*. To these two bodies the Yogacarans added a third: the 'recompense' or 'enjoyment' body. This is the body, acquired in reward for his career as a *bodhisattva*, in which the Buddha shows himself to *bodhisattvas* and other superhumans when he preaches the *Dharma* to them in other realms. The Buddha Amitabha, for example, spreading joy and delight in his kingdom of Sukhavati, is portrayed as appearing to the *bodhhisattvas* in his 'enjoyment' body, while at the same time making his presence known to his devotees on earth in the 'apparition' version of himself.

The Spread of Mahayanism

We have already seen how King Asoka sent his own son and daughter as Buddhist missionaries to the island of Lanka. Tradition has it that more of his emissaries arrived in what is now Thailand to establish the religion there among its original inhabitants, the Mon people. Another early success story for Buddhism is likely to have been Nepal, for after all Buddha himself was born there, at Lumbini, and King Asoka is said to have visited his birthplace to erect an inscribed pillar.

(Another of his daughters is said to have married Nepal's king.) Although almost nothing is known of Nepal's early history, a legendary version of events has it that the Bodhisattva Manjusri came to Nepal from China, emptied the great lake which had filled the valley, founded the capital of Kathmandu and then installed as ruler King Dharmikhara, whom he had brought with him.

However, the most important area in the history of the development of Buddhism lay in the northwest of India, away from Nepal and the northeast, with its associations with Buddha, in a great sprawl of territory that today includes parts of Kashmir and the Punjab, Pakistan, Afghanistan, Iran and what was until recently Soviet Turkestan. At its heart was the province or district of Gandhara, centred around Purishupara (modern Peshawar), the first town of any size to greet the traveller making his way towards India after crossing the Khyber Pass. The whole area around Peshawar was one of the world's great crossroads and meeting places and early Buddhists – many of them the All-Is-Ists (*Sarvastivadins*), who had been voted down at the Council in about 250 BC and had migrated here – were exposed to influences from all over Asia and the Graeco-Roman world.

Important trade routes passed through the territory and so did conquering armies, as well as successive waves of nomadic tribes, from the time of the Aryans onwards. The army of Alexander the Great arrived in the fourth century BC, routing local Persian dynasts before finally downing arms in the Punjab, desperate for home. Some of Alexander's soldiers and generals, stayed on, however, and they were soon joined by other peoples: Scythians, Parthians, Kushans and Huns in search of pasturage, conquest or trade. It is not surprising that this northwestern entrepot of peoples and cultures became one of the main breeding-grounds of the supple, assimilative creed of

Mahayana, as well as the main springboard for Buddhism's remarkable journeys to the north and east.

None of this, of course, happened overnight. In fact the religion does not seem to have taken real root in the northwest until the time of King Asoka, who had lived as a Viceroy in the area as a young man. (He is said to have founded five hundred monasteries for the *arhants* and to have given the valley of Kashmir to the *Sangha*.) A century or so later, the religion was given another shot in the arm by the conversion of the Greek king Menander (or Milinda), whose power base lay in Bactria, a fertile region in northern Afganistan between the Oxus river and the mountains of the Hindu Kush. (His conversations with the monk Nagasena are recorded in the Pali text, the *Milinda-panha*). The Indo-Greek hegemony, though, did not last long, for it was soon supplanted by yet more invaders, this time Scythians and Parthians. It was not until another empire, that of the Kushans, began to take shape that Buddhist influence once again started to predominate.

The Kushans were a nomadic people who had originated in China. They had travelled a roundabout route – through central Asia to the Kabul valley in northern Afghanistan and then southwards into the low country of India, consolidating their rule along the way. The empire they established in the process stretched across the whole of northern India, eastward to Sinkiang (Chinese Turkestan) and westwards almost as far as the Aral Sea. Although they were at first hostile to Buddhism, the Kushans became both believers and enthusiastic builders of monasteries and *stupas* in the end, particularly under another convert, their first century AD king Kaniska. In fact, Kashmir, with its many *Sarvastivadins*, became an extremely important centre of Buddhist learning from Kaniska's time onwards. Most major Buddhist scholars whom we know by name seem to have spent some time there – from Asvagosa, the first century AD Sanskrit poet who wrote the first biography of Buddha, to Asanga, the chief philosopher of the Yogicaran school. In an essay produced in the late 1950s, 'Some Great Buddhists After Asoka', Bharat Sing Upadhyaya wrote (as quoted in John Snelling's *The Buddhist Handbook*):

> Kaniska's reign . . . marked a turning point in the history of Buddhism and Buddhist literature. It witnessed the rise of Mahayana Buddhism and the magnificent literary activity started by Parsva, Asvagosa, Vasumitra, and others . . . It was in this age that Pali gave place to Sanskrit [as the literary and liturgical language of Mahayana]. In the field of art, Gandhara sculptures developed and the figures of the Buddha and Bodhisattvas began to appear. It was during Kaniska's reign and largely through his efforts that Buddhism was successfully introduced into central and eastern Asia. There was ceaseless literary activity throughout his vast empire . . . A truly integrated Asian culture came into existence at this time, based as it was on the highest purposes of life for which Buddhism stood.

Even though the Kushan dynasty was later overthrown by the Sassanids, who were Zoroastrians from what is now Iran – and Buddhism lost its royal patronage – the religion continued to thrive in the territories of what had been the Kushan heartland. Some time between the third and fifth centuries BC, for example, the famous cave-monasteries at Bamiyan in northern Afghanistan were dug out and the standing Buddha that was carved there became the world's largest stone statue at 177 feet high – although it was recently destroyed by the Taliban. Kashmir – although it went through many ups and downs as ruler followed ruler – was to remain an important Buddhist stronghold for a further thousand years after the time of Kaniska.

Not so the area immediately around Peshawar, however, where Buddhism fell victim to the depradations of yet more invaders, the so-called White Huns – and to a gradual revival of Hinduism, encouraged by the princelings who had taken over the remnants of the Kushan empire. When the famous Chinese traveller Hsuan-sang passed through Peshawar in the seventh century AD, he found it to be a dismal and mostly uninhabited place. Almost all of the monasteries were ruined and deserted.

Buddhism in Central Asia: The Silk Road

By then, however, Buddhism had already moved on into Central Asia, carried along the trading routes of the great Silk Road which ran between China and the West. Today, this vast oblong of desert and mountains is deeply inhospitable but two thousand years ago, before the glaciers dried up, the climate was wetter. There was irrigation and agriculture and there were important oasis-settlements that were virtually small city-states, some of them dating from as early as the third century BC: Turfan, Kucha and Kashgar on the northern spur of the Road and Khotan on the southern spur,. Having started life, no doubt, as caravan halts, they were consolidated under the Chinese Han dynasty (206 BC – AD 220) and were soon home to an astonishing variety of peoples who spoke languages related to Sanskrit, Latin, Greek, Persian and even Celtic.

Some of these so-called Serindians, judging by the evidence of surviving frescoes, were fair-haired with blue or green eyes. Included in their number were Manichaeans, fire-worshippers and Nestorian

Christians: one fresco found in Turfan (modern Kao-chiang) seems to show a Palm Sunday procession. Within the last century, archaeologists have discovered that their languages were written down in a modified Indian script whereas their art was essentially Gandharan, with Graeco-Roman, Sassanid and Chinese influences. However, their literary and sacral language was Sanskrit and their chief religion was Buddhism.

What little we know of the Serindian (or Sino-Indian) culture, apart from the archaeological record, comes to us from Chinese foreign-policy documents and the written accounts of later Chinese travellers. The picture that emerges is of industrious, sophisticated and independent kingdoms, kept in balance by Chinese watchfulness and trade. (One of the kingdoms was almost certainly the 'people in the west' to whom the Han Emperor Wu sent an expedition in 139 BC to 'make an alliance'.) They produced silk, jade, taffeta, felt and woollen goods and the musicians and artists of Khotan were famous. During the period of the first known travellers, sometime around the third century AD, Khotan was home to five thousand Buddhist monks and acolytes who lived in a hundred different monasteries. Meditating *arhants* also lived in mountain-caves to the south, where their hair was cut regularly as a religious duty by monks from the city. Before it finally died away, Khotan was to become an important centre for *Mahayana* Buddhism, but the first accounts from eye-witnesses, dating from the third century, suggest that there was a balance of some sort between Hinayanans and Mahayanans. We know this because when a Chinese pilgrim arrived in about AD 260, looking for a more or less complete text of the *Perfection of Wisdom Sutras*, he was warned by Hinayanans not to take back with him a *Mahayana* manuscript that might corrupt the Chinese people!

Whatever the original balance of the two sects, though, in this and the other oasis-states, it was the teachings of the *Mahayana* that achieved dominance in Central Asia. This was almost certainly because Mahayanists were a great deal more flexible than their opponents in their interpretation of the scriptures. Hinayanists continued to live under the rigorous monastic discipline of the *Vinaya* (as they did in Kucha), which forbade the practice of medicine. They were also bound to withold the *Dharma* from the nomadic peoples of Central Asia, who characteristically drove herds and ate meat. Cleaving stolidly to the core of Buddha's teachings, they also failed to adapt themselves to local beliefs and practices – which, from what little we know, seem to have been enthusiastically embraced by local Mahayanists. For example, the monks in Tun-huang appear to have practised both medicine and Central Asian shamanism, judging from the accounts we have. They had a reputation for magic powers as well as clairvoyance and clairaudience.

Tun-huang (now known as Dunhuang), which lay at the Chinese end of the Silk Road before its bifurcation into two branches, may also provide another reason for the ultimate dominance of *Mahayana* as virtually the only form of Buddhism that was to take lasting root outside India – for it was also a translation centre. In the third century AD, under the leadership of Dharmaraksa, the so-called '*bodhisatta* of Tun-huang', many of the central documents of *Mahayana* were translated into Chinese (and perhaps other languages) including the *White Lotus of the True Dharma Sutra* and the *Perfection of Wisdom*. Another translation centre was established later on in Kucha, under a saintly sage called Kumajariva. Once again it was preoccupied with Mahayanist texts like the *Diamond Sutra* and the lay-directed *Vimalakirti-nirdesa*, the story of a rich householder whose compassion was so great that he chose to take, even as a layman, the path of the *bodhisattva*. It was said that monks were afraid to visit Vimalakirti, since he could always beat them in argument.

The sheer scale of this essentially Mayanist enterprise was not uncovered until almost a thousand years after every last trace of Buddhism and its art had been brutally erased by Muslim conquerors and after the faith had fallen back into the desert. In 1888, a British officer called Hamilton Bower bought an ancient Sanskrit medical text written in Brahmi characters while on a secret mission to Kucha. When news of this and other discoveries leaked out, virtually all the imperial powers sent archaeological expeditions to the area as quickly as they could. They not only found texts and manuscripts in a huge variety of languages but also statues and frescoes, which they hacked down from walls and packed off to the world's museums. The greatest discovery of all, though, fell to the British Sir Aurel Stein, for in Tunhuang he found over a thousand temples and shrine rooms carved into a cliff, a vast Buddhist monastic complex. He also found an astonishing cache of paintings on silk and, above all, a huge collection of manuscripts in a cave that had been sealed off in about the year 1000. There were texts in long lost languages, historical and financial documents, vernacular Chinese versions of Buddhist writings – and the oldest printed book in the world, published in AD 868: a Chinese translation of the *Diamond Sutra*.

China

In the first century AD – so the story goes – the Chinese Han Emperor Ming Ti dreamed of a giant man sixteen feet tall, sending out great waves of light. He despatched emissaries to the west in search of him and somewhere on their journey they met two *bodhisattvas* in the desert, who had with them a white horse, a picture of the Sakyamuni

Buddha and a copy of the *Sutra in Forty-Two Sections*, a still-extant summary of Buddhist doctrine infused with Mahayanist thought. They were invited by the emissaries to return with them to the Han capital of Loyang, where they began translating the *Sutra* into Chinese at what became known as the White Horse Temple, a site that still exists.

It is a charming story, but the reality is almost certainly a lot more prosaic. Buddhism entered China gradually through the constant comings and goings of the great Silk Road. Buddhists from Central Asia – musicians and artists from Khotan, artisans and merchants – travelled eastwards (as well as westwards) by stages, before finally taking up residence in the Han capital and a few other northern cities. There they formed small emigré communities which must sooner or later have welcomed and supported monks travelling east with the Silk Road's caravans. These saffron-robed figures cannot have had much early success with the indigenous population as proselytisers of the faith – what, after all, could any barbarian possibly teach a citizen of the 'country of the sublime at the world's centre'? Nonetheless, with time, the monks must ultimately have lost their curiosity value and have become a more or less familiar urban presence. The monks' predilection for magic might even have made the Chinese regard them as being closely related to their own shamans and wizards.

However the idea, for all this, that this small seedbed of monks and nuns would one day grow into a vast Chinese *Sangha* would have struck them as being frankly ludicrous. For not only were the Chinese notoriously xenophobic but they also practised a worldly ideology that was profoundly unsympathetic to the idea of individual liberation. This was Confucianism – derived from the sayings of Confucius, the sage from the sixth century BC – which proclaimed the ideal of a harmonious social order in which everyone, from the highest to the lowest, knew his or her place exactly. Within Confucianism, correct ritual was everything and every aspect of life was mediated by strict codes of behaviour. To deny the importance of these things, to be indifferent to both family and country, to be prepared to cut off all worldly ties in pursuit of some vaguely-defined spiritual objective – as Buddhists were -- was clearly the most shocking of heresies. Such behaviour served to undermine the bonds which held the Chinese state together under the Son of Heaven.

Taoism

There was, however, another Chinese tradition, one which resonated with the influx of Buddhist ideas: the tradition of Taoism. This was popularly believed to have been derived from the sayings of the Yellow Emperor, Huang Ti, who is said to have ruled from 2698–2597 BC, but it had been fully formulated and given shape by the sage Lao Tzu in his classic work, the *Tao Te Ching*. Taoists, unlike Confucianists, were hostile to the social world and its values, which they saw as dishonest and meaningless. Convention and slavish obedience, they taught, should be abandoned for simplicity and one-ness with the cosmos.

Their ideal was *wu-wei* ('non-doing' or 'non-action'), a totally spontaneous form of behaviour – unpremeditated and undirected, unconcerned with doing good deliberately – which we might translate as 'going with the flow' of the *Tao* (the 'Path' or 'Cosmic Way'). Being in harmony with the *Tao* meant being able to respond without forethought, when action was called for, to any and all circumstances in an appropriate way, since it both drew from and furthered the impersonality and supra-mondanity of the mode of the *Tao* in action and at work – *wu-wei*. There was within Taoism, moreover, a strong mystical and meditative tradition. One-ness with the *Tao* – which was Absolute and yet empty, according to Taoist philosopher Chuang Tzu – could be achieved through contemplative exercises.

It is not surprising, then – given this coincidence of doctrines – that the first translations of Buddhist texts into Chinese drew strongly on the ideas and vocabulary of Taoism. The Sanskrit word *marga* (or 'Path'), for example, was readily translated as *tao*, 'the way to be travelled'. Emptiness became *pen-wu* – the 'Original Non-Existence' of Lao Tzu; the 'Void Filled to the Brim' – which like a womb carries all existence within it. Even the Buddha became identified with the Taoists' 'Spirit in the Centre of Existence', or World Soul. Sometimes, early Buddhist treatises carried direct quotations from the *Tao Te Ching*, such as: 'The Holy Man's good works are mighty as Heaven and Earth, yet he is not humane' – thus equating the *bodhisattva*'s detached compassion with the workings of the *Tao*, which is indifferent to the individuals who pass along it. They even sometimes abandoned Buddhist orthodoxy in their anxiety to strike a chord with Taoists, as in this quotation, again from the *Tao Te Ching*: 'The body suffers destruction, but the soul undergoes no change. With its unchangingness it rides upon changes and thus passes through endless transformations.' Until the fifth century AD or so, many Chinese, indeed, seem to have considered Buddhism as simply another method of achieving the *Tao*. An early Chinese pamphlet even refers to Buddhism as being born out of 'the conversion of the Barbarians by Lao Tze'.

This Taoist form of Buddhism was widely spread abroad by the Mahayanist texts that were first chosen for translation into Chinese: notably *The Small Perfection of Wisdom Sutra* and the *Vimalakirti-nirdesa*, the story of the formidable layman who followed the *bodhisattva*-path. (The *Sukhavati-vyuha*, the account of the Celestial

Buddha Amithaba and Sukhavati, his Buddha-kingdom in the West, was also translated in the second century AD, though it was some three hundred years before his cult – Amito in Chinese – took hold.) The *Perfection of Wisdom* literature, with its teachings on the nature of perfect wisdom and emptiness, in fact proved especially popular – more and more of its *Sutras* were soon translated and so were technical handbooks on Buddhist-style meditation.

Central Asian Buddhism, in the gradual process of its sinification, not only acquired its first vocabulary from Taoism but also something of its suaveness and irreverence. (At an early stage, Buddhist monks became known in China for their urbanity and wit.) Furthermore, in tandem with Taoism, it benefited a good deal from the collapse of the Han empire (AD 220), and from the so-called Period of Disunity (220–589) that followed. With the coming of war and chaos – during which China was divided, first into three and then into two (northern and southern) kingdoms – the imperial social glue of Confucianism lost its adhesiveness. The aristocratic and artistic élite began to look elsewhere, that is to say, for their spiritual needs and the Buddhist message about a suffering and impermanence that can ultimately be escaped from was well suited, one can imagine, to the tenor of the times.

Buddhism also held out the prospect of a personal salvation, it should be remembered, which was an idea new to the Chinese. It had acquired shamanistic elements in Central Asia and its meditational techniques offered the possibility of acquiring supranormal powers. Its teachings, at the same time, were sophisticated and complex, which must have appealed to the Chinese literati, and it invited withdrawal from the world for the purposes of contemplation – a refuge devoutly to be wished in times of strife. In this period there appears for the first time what was to become a

Chinese-Buddhist archetype: the gentleman-scholar devotee surrounded only by nature.

Buddhism also had considerable appeal to two other important levels of Chinese society: the ruling classes and the ordinary peasants. The emperors of the various kingdoms – even of the northern one, the domain of the Mongolian invaders of the Northern Wei dynasty – saw Buddhism as either a way of positively undermining Confucianism (the northern view) or of keeping the population tractable and unwarlike (the southern view): or both. Buddhist monks were a lot more amenable, after all, than their Taoist equivalents, who were inclined to rebel against convention. Unlike the Taoists, who financed their own places of worship, Buddhists relied on donations from wealthy laymen and were thus less inclined to upset the *status quo*. Buddhists, above all, though, with their views about the killing of any living thing, were eminently peaceful – and peace, in a country often at war but without universal conscription, was highly desirable.

As to the masses, they were perhaps drawn first and foremost to the doctrine of the *bodhisattva*-path, which provided equal access to the most esoteric mysteries – even to the lowest of the low. (The *Vimalakirti-nirdesa* was, for this reason, one of Buddhism's most important recruiting tools.) In the enlarged Buddhist pantheon – in Celestial Bodhisattvas like Maitreya and Avalokitesvara and Celestial Buddhas like Amithaba and Aksobhya – they found objects of worship who offered encouragement, comfort and help in trouble. Furthermore, by supporting the *Sangha* they were assured of yet more benefits in future lives. It was generally believed in China that supporting the *Sangha* would greatly impress and influence the decisions of Yama, the God of the Underworld.

For all of these reasons, Buddhism soon ceased to be a fringe religion in China and became, in effect, the main stream. By the middle of the third century, a Chinese version of the *Vinaya* (monastic code) had been produced. A hundred years later, Chinese Buddhists were given official permission (in the eastern kingdom of the Chin rulers, at least) to enter monastic communities. In the south, Buddhist monks became important court advisers and counsellors and they received imperial patronage, even in the northern 'barbarian' kingdom of the Wei dynasty. Huge numbers of monasteries, temples, pagodas and *stupas* were built there and when a northern army finally conquered Chin and entered its capital at the beginning of the fifth century AD, its commander ordered his troops to protect and preserve all *Sangha* property, to erect Buddha images and to provide homes for all monks.

This was important, because the Chin capital, Chang-an, had become by then the most important centre for the translation of Buddhist texts in the whole of China and it was to become the birthplace of the first native Buddhist philosophers. The reason for this was that the great Central Asian sage and translator Kumarajiva had arrived there in about 401, after being carried off from Kucha by a Chinese general seventeen years before. He had been quickly appointed Director of Religious Instruction and a translation bureau had been set up for him, with, it was said, eight hundred assistants. With their help – and in what Arthur Waley describes as 'an infinitely agreeable' style – Kumarajiva set about translating or retranslating more than a hundred works, including the *Diamond Sutra* and the first versions of four important *Madhyamika* documents, which introduced the teachings of Nagarjuna to the Chinese.

Two of Kumarajiva's disciples were of equal importance in the ultimate development of Chinese Buddhism. The first of these was Seng-chao, who was said to have literally 'held the brush' for his master, since he had earlier been a copyist of Confucian and Taoist texts. Seng-chao, however, also produced a work of his own, *The Book of Chao (Chao Lun)*, in which he attempted to convey the Buddhist notion of emptiness through Chinese and Tao-derived versions of the oppositions that Nagarjuna had demolished in order to point the way. His book, rooted firmly in the Chinese language and concepts, represents the first thought-through indigenous Buddhist philosophical system that we know.

Another (younger) disciple of Kumarajiva was Tao Sheng, who seems to have been eminently practical for in one of his treatises he wrote (as quoted by Conze):

> Ever since the transmission of the scriptures eastward, their translators have encountered repeated obstacles, and many have been blocked by holding too narrowly to the text, with the result that few have been able to see the complete meaning. Let them forget the fish-trap and catch the fish. Then one may begin to talk with them about the Way.

Tao Sheng's practical nature might well have encouraged him to propose, in a treatise of his own, what was at the time an essentially new doctrine, that 'Buddhahood is achieved through instantaneous enlightenment'. He argued that since the absolute emptiness of Nirvana was totally different from all conditioned things, then the moment of Enlightenment also had to be quite different from everything that might have preceded it. All else was mere learning, confined as it was to the phenomenal world. Enlightenment, by contrast – being 'genuine' and 'permanent' rather than 'temporary' and therefore 'false' – could only be achieved all at once, in its totality, and not in any gradual, bit by bit way, 'for when the single enlightenment comes, all the myriad impediments are equally brought to an end'. Later in the fifth century AD, an official wrote of this doctrine, in witness to its practicality (again quoted by Conze):

> The people of China have a facility for comprehending Truth intuitively or 'mirroring' it, but difficulty in acquiring learning. Therefore they close themselves to the idea of accumulating learning, but open themselves to that of one final ultimate. The Hindus, on the other hand, have a facility for acquiring learning, but difficulty in comprehending Truth intuitively. Therefore they close themselves to the idea of instantaneous comprehension, but open themselves to that of gradual enlightenment.

Practical or not, though, Tao Sheng's doctrine later became of central importance in the development of Chinese, and later Japanese, Buddhism. It became the foundation of the so-called Chang school in China and found its expression in Japan (as we shall see) as Zen. It also marked the coming of age of Chinese Buddhism as an independently developing religion.

A number of sects or 'clans', it is true, continued to adhere to the philosophies of the Indian schools. *San-lun* derived from The Three Treatises school (*Madhyamika*) and Fa-hsiang owed its philosophy to The *Dharma*-Mark school (*Yogacara*) – the most famous member of which was the so-called Great Traveller, Hsuan-tsang, who made a sixteen-year pilgrimage to India, mostly on foot, and brought back with him over 600 Sanskrit manuscripts. But Chinese Buddhists were increasingly concerned with the adaptation of the Buddhist Canon to fit their own needs, language and forms of worship. In about 402, for example, an ex-Taoist called Hui Yuan helped to found what later became known as the Fellowship of the

White Lotus, which was dedicated to the worship of Amidhaba (Amito) and to rebirth in his Buddha-kingdom in the West. This was the nucleus of the later Pure-Land (*Ching-tu*) school, which continued to rely on the benign intercession of Amidhaba as the one way of reaching Nirvana. Amidhaba and the other Celestial Buddhas, together with all the Celestial Bodhisattvas with the exception of Maitreya were, it should be remembered, the creations and gifts of *Mahayana*.

Chapter Seven:

Tantra:
The Third Turning of the Wheel

Indian Origins

When the Chinese pilgrim Hsuan-tsang arrived in India in about AD 640, he recorded that only about forty per cent of the monks he encountered there belonged to the *Mahayana*. The rest, one must assume, were Hinayanists of one school or another, who were dedicated in their writings to commentaries and endless systematizations of their *Abhidharma* literature – and given more to piety than to either missionary work or spiritual innovation. Although, as another Chinese traveller later put it, the sects 'rest in their own places, and do not get themselves embroiled with one another', it is remarkable that in all the Hinayanist literature there is hardly a mention of the *Mahayana* at all. It is as if, for Hinayanists, Mahayanans had passed beyond the horizon of things that needed attending to – as if, with their 'extended' *Sutras* and their teeming celestial pantheon, they had gone beyond the pale of traditional orthodoxy into another realm entirely.

In a sense, of course, they had, and Hinayanists had been left behind by them simply to mark time, doing what they had always done – which was to keep the rules of the *Vinaya* and to consolidate the legacy of Sakyamuni as laid down in the *Sutras* and the *Abhidharma*. Over the years they had produced a vast literature out of these scriptures, covering every theme and detail that could possibly be dug up from them. They meticulously recorded the views of different teachers and to the popular Buddha-tales of the *Jataka* they added their own long accounts of the Buddha's virtues and his adventures in previous lives. (They also produced, in the *Buddhacarita* of the poet and playwright Asvaghosa, the first 'biography' of the Buddha ever written.) But by the beginning of the fifth century AD, their job was finished, The well of creativity had finally run dry – it was as though there was no more to be said. Vasubandhu, one of the last great commentarists and synthesizers of *Hinayana*, seemed somehow to sense this, for he finished his exhaustive work, the *Abhidharmakosa*, with the words:

> The times are come
> When flooded by the rising tide of ignorance
> Buddha's religion seems to breathe its last.

It did not breathe its last, of course. Although *Hinayana* produced little more original literature it continued in India for another 800 years and flourished for much longer in Ceylon, Burma and Thailand, as we shall see. However, a new wind had already begun to blow through *Mahayana* Buddhism, roused in the frontier lands of the northwest and the northeast and fed by both Brahminism and local occult practices. It was the last great contribution of the subcontinent's turbulent spiritual climate to Buddhist thought and it became known as *Tantra*.

Tantra

Tantra, like yoga and *bhakti* ('religious devotion'), is not in any sense exclusive to Buddhism. It is a recognizable part of the *ur*-spring of the Indian religious impulse surfacing, in various forms, in Jainism as well as Hinduism. Its adoption into the mainstream of Buddhist thought, therefore, should be considered as yet another opening-up of the faith to accommodate all of the subcontinent's peoples and religions into one mighty flow. It set out to achieve this, it could be said, by borrowing wholesale from them all, but then it too had been born out of the same spiritual aquifer. Sakyamuni had long before permitted his followers other forms of worship; and besides, the magic practices which Buddhism now incorporated remained pointing towards the ultimate goal of Enlightenment.

Edward Conze recognizes three phases in the development of Tantra:

> The first may be called Mantrayana [the 'Secret Mantra Vehicle' or 'Mantra Path']. It began in the fourth century, gained momentum after AD 500, and what it did was to enrich Buddhism by the appurtenances of magical tradition. In this way many mantras, mudras [ritual gestures of the hands], mandalas [ritual versions of magic-circle diagrams] and new deities were more or less unsystematically introduced into Buddhism. This was, after 750, followed by a systematization called the Vajrayana [the 'Diamond Vehicle' or 'Diamond Path'], which coordinated all previous teachings with a group of five Tathagatas ['Enlightened Beings']. In the course of time, further trends and systems made their appearance. Noteworthy among these is the Sabajayana, which, like the Chinese Chan school, stressed

> meditational practices and the cultivation of intuition,
> taught by riddles, paradoxes and concrete images, and
> avoided the fate of turning into a dead scholasticism by
> holding on to no rigidly defined tenets. [Finally,] in the
> tenth century, we have the Kalachakra, 'Wheel of Time',
> which is marked by the extent of its syncretism and by its
> emphasis on astrology.

Conze's first phase, *Mantrayana*, almost certainly had its roots in early Buddhism, for magic had been specifically allowed into the Pali Canon in the form of spells (*parittas*) against such dangers as snake-bite. From there it was but a short step – taken by *Mahayana Sutras* as early as 200 BC – to the introduction of spells in the form of repeatable verbal formulae that were said to represent the doctrine of the *Sutras* (*dharani*) and to the borrowing of auspicious and powerful magical syllables such as *Om* from Hinduism. Over time, a vast phantasmagoria of gods, spirits, daemons, ogres and terrifying spirits, drawn from indigenous cults, was added to this base – probably inspired, to a degree, by the visions of Yogicarans in their advanced meditative states. From Brahmanism came esoteric yoga practice, including *Hatha Yoga*, along with popular magical rituals, instructions for ceremonials, mantras and perhaps even sacrifices.

The most important of Buddhism's borrowings from the great spiritual pool of popular Indian religion, though, was that of the guru, prefigured in the *Bhagavad Gita*'s account of Krishna as the divine preceptor from whom knowledge of all mysteries comes. The new spiritual hero of this phase in Buddhist development, that is to say, was no longer the *bodhisattva* but the *siddha* – the 'magician', 'adept', or 'wonder-worker' – whose role it was to show his disciples (*chelas*) the Way. Although the ultimate goal still remained Buddhahood or

Enlightenment, it was no longer a goal that had to be put off for aeons and aeons – it could be achieved here ('in this very body') and now ('in the course of one single thought') under the instructions, and through the example of, the *siddha*-guru. With his help, all that had to be done was to transform the body and its attributes into those of a buddha, by means of special – and often secret – practices that involved processes and powers beyond the range of normal awareness.

One result of this new relationship between the *chela* and the *saddhu* was an inevitable decline in the authority of the monastic system, for individual *saddhus*, with their bands of submissive disciples, could easily dismiss as unnecessary the constraints of collective discipline. (Some of them, indeed, made mock of conventionally cloistered monks with wantonly heretical behaviour and teachings.)

Another result was the appearance of a wholly new kind of literature – Tantric handbooks (*Tantras*) – secret documents designed, not for the many, as the *Sutras* and *Sastras* ('treatises') had been, but only for a chosen initiated few. These not only covered meditational practices but they also included rituals which often (deliberately) flew in the face of standard Buddhist precepts and were given a new importance as sacraments. A vast majority of the *Tantras*, then, were written in so-called 'twilight speech', an ambiguous and mysterious form of language which clearly relied on individual interpretation by an adept. Substitution codes figure widely in 'twilight speech': semen, for example, is known as 'camphor', '*bhodhicitta*' or 'elixir'; male and female genitalia are 'thunderbolt' and 'lotus'; and sexual union is 'compassion'.

This disguising of secret practices almost certainly stems from the Yogacarans, whose founder Asanga, in one of his treatises, classified the various methods by which a hidden meaning could be conveyed. Opacity, imprecision and coding alike were seen by him as necessary, not only to keep out the uninitiated, the careless dabbler, but also to protect the teachings from contamination.

The erotic element in Tantra – of so much interest to the West – is perhaps best summed up by a remark in the *Hejavra Tantra*:

> Those who have 'means' are liberated from the bondage of 'becoming' through the very thing by which wicked people are bound. The world is bound by lust, and released by the same lust.

Before we explore this theme further, however, it may be useful to look at the background of Tantric symbolism and ritual against which it should be placed. Tibet, where *Tantra* was preserved in a relatively pure form until modern times, is the main source for our knowledge of these practices, although they have also survived in the so-called Shingon school in Japan.

The Tantric Pantheon

In some ways, *Tantra* can be seen as a response to adversity and the steady erosion of passing time: a renascence of Hinduism; a loss of direction; a slackening of support for the *Sangha*; or drift. The path of the *bodhisattva* – like that of the *arhant* earlier – had become overshadowed by the popular worship of the Celestial Bodhisattvas and Buddhas. The faith needed new protection from the inroads of the world and at the same time it also needed a new immediacy, a way of commanding attention among ordinary people, in order to turn them once more to Enlightenment.

Both protection and immediacy were provided by the magic of

a fresh pantheon of deities (*yidam*), both male and female, a pantheon which –although often borrowed from elsewhere – coincided with the supernatural beings encountered by the Yogacarans in trance. (From the doctrine of Emptiness, which held that there was no essential difference between *nirvana* and *samsara*, it followed that these trance-visions were no less real and actual than anything else in the world.) Some of them, like Tara and Avalokiteshvara, were seen as welcoming and beatific, and were represented as holding their hands up in benediction to the faithful. Others, although equally beneficent in their way, like the *vidyaraja* ('kings of the sacred lore' also known as 'protectors of the *Dharma*'), were presented as terrifying, 'wrathful', fierce fighters against Buddhism's enemies. This was also the role of the so-called 'Five Protectresses' – with Mahamayuri, the 'Great Pea-Hen', at their head. They were all pictured in much the same way – as snarling, fanged, enflamed avengers, often carrying skulls, daggers and severed heads.

With time, the pantheon increased to include further objects of cult worship that had evolved from, and were turned towards the needs of, three separate Buddhist groups. Those who practised advanced meditation turned to Cunda, Vasudhara and other goddesses; others, who pursued magical powers, looked towards the 'Queens of the Sacred Lore' and the *dakinis*, or 'sky-walkers'; and the masses were encouraged to worship particular goddesses to meet their different needs, such as guarantees of motherhood, immunity from smallpox or the protection from spiritual and physical danger provided by Tara (an early Celestial Bodhisattva). Later still – based on the model of the Hindu god Shiva, often depicted as having sex with his consort or *Shakti* – Buddhas and Bodhisattvas were given consorts of their own, (*Vidyas* and *Prajnas*) whose cult became one focus of erotic Tantrism.

Mantra

Mantras, as we have seen, are magical formulae, generally Sanskrit, the purpose of which was to protect the initiate against malign forces. In Tantric Buddhism, however, they also serve two other important and inseparable functions. The first function of a mantra is to evoke a deity, so that the initiate can become one with him or her, and the second function is to act as an object of meditation in itself, thereby enabling the initiate to gain insight or mental calm through repetition (although a mantra can also be visualized or written down). The most famous of all mantras, of course, is '*Om mani-padme hum*' ('*Om* in the lotus a jewel, hail!'), but there are many other celebrated examples, a number of them invoking and expressing oneness with particular goddesses. '*Om tare tuttare ture svaha*', for instance, although it is now not easily translatable, is a play on the name of the goddess Tara and '*Gate, gate, paragate, parasamgate, bodhi svaha*' ('Gone, gone, gone beyond, utterly gone beyond, enlightenment hail') enshrines and summons the goddess of Perfected Wisdom *(Prajna-paramita)* who, like Tara, was earlier worshipped as a Celestial Bodhisattva.

Other mantras, sometimes in short form, sometimes in long, affirm the truth of the doctrine of Emptiness: '*Om sunyata-jnana-vajra-svabhavatmako ham*' ('Om I am a self whose essence is the diamond knowledge of emptiness') – or the emptiness of both the self and the dharmas: '*Om svabhavasuddhah sarva-dharmah svabhavasuddho ham*' ('Om by essential nature all the dharmas are pure; by essential nature I am pure'). To their number should be added what are called Bija ('Seed') mantras, a vowel or consonant which embodies the essence of a particular Tantric deity. It can be visualized as a luminous form, from which the deity emerges.

Mandala

The mandala is a highly evolved version of the magic circle that has been familiar since prehistoric times as the marker-off of a sacred spot from the profanity of its surroundings. It is based – in part at least – on the form and architecture of early *stupas* which, with their railings separating sacred from profane ground, were also designed as material maps or enshrinements of the Buddhist cosmos. When representations of the Buddha became general in the first century AD, Buddha-images were characteristically placed at certain key points of the symbolic design of both the *stupa* and the courtyard surrounding it. The *stupa* was thus transformed, in a sense, into a three-dimensional version of the mandala – while the mandala represented in two dimensions the cosmology embodied in the *stupa*.

The mandala, then, is first of all a visual mnemonic of the way in which the Buddhist scheme of things revolves around the central hub of Mount Meru. It is also a model of the individual human being, in whom the drama of the universe is reproduced in microcosm around the heart-centre, where the mystery of ultimate reality (known as *Mahamudra*, 'the Great Seal') is located. More than that, with its four gaps or doors on its periphery, it is a representation of the spiritual journey each initiate undertakes once he or she has chosen to enter the Path – travelling through the concentric precincts of deities and demons in their labyrinthine. towered palaces towards the focal sanctum where the Supreme Being which guides him or her holds sway.

The particular genius of *Tantra* was, and is, that it transformed the creation of mandalas into a process that Robinson and Johnson call 'actualization'. A mandala, that is to say, was no longer merely regarded as a representation of the cosmic and human setting of the quest for enlightenment. It became the very arena in which that quest was conducted, a ritual space in which communication with gods and other worlds was made possible. With the help of the diagram in meditation, the initiate could become the Buddha at the centre of the mandala, could confront primordial fears and passions in the shape of demons and could summon up gods by the use of the syllable of the *Bija* mantra that constituted their occult principles. By this means, latent spiritual potentials buried deep in the psyche of the practitioner could be unlocked, and he could learn to travel in the Buddhic universe, far beyond the reach of *samsara*, dominating and dissolving its gravitational pull at will. This was, of course, a potentially dangerous enterprise, as is stressed again and again in traditional Tantric texts. Dabbling without proper instruction from a *siddha* could cause a burn-out like that of Icarus, who travelled ill-equipped and too near the sun. For this reason, the making of mandalas and the actualization of divinities are governed by strict rules and precisely-defined rituals in *Tantra*, as a protection again the psychic damage that could be carried forward into future lives.

Ritual Objects and Gestures in Tantra

Mudra, literally 'a seal' or 'symbol', is a traditional ritual gesture of the hands carrying a symbolic – both communicative and interiorized – meaning. In *Tantra*, different *mudras* relate to different aspects of a particular Tantric deity.

Tibetan *Tantra* also makes use of ritual objects – particularly the *ghanta*, or bell, which symbolizes the female principle of wisdom, and the *vajra* (literally 'the lord of stones'), a single or double sceptre derived from the thunderbolt wielded by the Hindu god Indra. The *vajra* represents 'skill-in-means' and the diamond-like quality –

uncuttable by any other substance but itself – of the *nirvana* or ultimate Emptiness that can only be arrived at through the marriage of 'skill-in-means' to (the bell of) wisdom. Other important objects in Tibetan ritual are the dagger (*phurba*), the skull-cap (symbolizing impermanence) and the thigh-bone trumpet.

The *Vajrayana*

Around AD 750, as we have seen, the myriad spiritual and magical elements which had been assimilated into Tantric Buddhism from Hinduism, from aboriginal and animist cults and from the esoteric doctrines of the Yogacaran school of *Mahayana*, were systematized by the *Vajrayana* (the 'Diamond Vehicle' or 'Path'). From this time on, all cosmic forces were grouped into five classes, each of them presided over by a *Tathagata* ('Enlightened Being' or *Dhyani-Buddha*) of their own. The Five classes comprised Vairocana, Aksobhya, Ratnasambhava, Amitabha and Amoghasiddhi, and between them they represented the five primary energies responsible for all creation. They were linked together by a dense web of interpenetrative symbolism, by an endless series of 'magical correspondences', as Conze puts it, of 'identifications, transformations and transfigurations', bringing together 'all the forces and facts of the universe'. He goes on:

> The body in particular is regarded as a microcosm, which embodies the entire universe and is the medium for realizing the truth, very largely by methods which form a part of what is nowadays known as Hathayoga in India. We hear much about parallelisms between the visible, the audible and the touchable, and everything is designed to unite the powers of mind, speech and body for the purpose of realizing the final state of completeness, or

enlightenment. The Vajrayana has been well defined as 'the art of living which enables us to utilize each activity of body, speech and mind as an aid on the Path to Liberation', and in this way it is astonishingly akin to the contemporary Chan school [in China]. The true meaning of Vajrayana teachings is, however, not always easy to ascertain, because here it has become a convention to clothe the highest into the form of the lowest, to make the most sacred appear as the most ordinary, the most transcendent as the most earthly, and the sanest knowledge is disguised by the most grotesque paradoxes. This is a deliberate shock therapy directed against the over-intellectualization of Buddhism at that time. The abundant sexual imagery in particular was intended to shock monkish prudery. Enlightenment, the result of a combination of wisdom and skill in means, is represented by the union of female and male in the ecstasy of love. Their becoming one in enlightenment is the highest indescribable happiness (mahasukha).

The erotic element in *Tantra* teaching was not, of course, merely shock treatment for prudish monks, a sort of all-out attack by heavy metaphor for, in the consorts given to Buddhas and Bodhisattvas the sexual symbolism of bell and sceptre, etc. the union of male and female in *Tantra* was central. Part of the early revolution in Mahayanist thinking had been the promotion of a marriage between wisdom and 'skill-in-means' as a necessary step towards enlightenment. Wisdom was soon conceived as a goddess, and *Tantra* raised 'skill-in-means' to the same status. It is from the union of these two divine beings in *Tantra* – physical as well as symbolic – that *bodhicitta* ('Wisdom-Heart'or thought of enlightenment) derives.

Tantra, that is to say, fuses spiritual with physical love in certain of its rituals, both in idea and in practice. In Tantric texts, the relationship with one's deity is compared to the four stages of a relationship between a man and a woman (looking, smiling, touching, having sex) and *bodhicitta* is seen as finally arising from the explosion of orgasm. Robinson and Johnson give an example of how the spiritual and the physical are related in this:

> In the mandala of Hejavra, the goddess Nairatmya ('No-self') stands for Wisdom, and Hejavra stands for means. When the mandala is acted out, the yogin impersonates Hejavra, and his consort takes the part of Nairatmya . . . The rites are practiced long and thoroughly in contemplation before they are actually performed. The yogin imagines the mandala and the goddess around the circle and mentally envisages the rites with himself as the deity. Having conjured up this vivid drama, he contemplates that these phenomena, like all others, are empty – that there is neither subject nor object, thought nor thinker . . .

. . . and then he plays his part

One tradition maintains that this sort of sexual ritual is only to be practised under certain very special and controlled circumstances – and then only by advanced practitioners who have already generated *bodhicitta*. Other texts deny this – erotic rites are recommended elsewhere for those who are driven by hostility and must cultivate compassion and loving kindness. It seems most likely in the end that eroticism in *Tantra* is simply a part of its general thrust (so to speak), which is to sacramentalize every sort of human activity and yoke it to the pursuit of enlightenment. No activity is to be forbidden, because all activities, of whatever kind, whether forbidden by Buddhist precept or not, are equally empty. This belief had been prefigured by Vimalakirti, the famous layman *bodhisattva*, in the *Sutra* that recounted his life. Many of his sayings, quoted by Robinson and Johnson, have a distinctly Tantric feel:

> Only for conceited men does the Buddha preach that separation from lewdness, anger and folly is liberation. For men without conceit, the Buddha preaches that lewdness, anger and folly are indeed liberation . . .

> The bodhisattva seems to proceed in precept-breaking, yet persists in pure morality. He seems to proceed in the passions, yet is always pure in mind. He seems to have wives and concubines, yet always keeps far away from the mud of the five lusts . . .

> Just as lotus flowers do not grow on a high plain of dry land but only where there is low, moist mire, even so, only in the mire of passions are there living beings to produce the Buddha-qualities.

The *Hejavra Tantra*, of a much later date, explains, in a sense, this paradox, when it says:

> The unknowing worldling who drinks strong poison is overpowered; he who has expelled delusion, with his mind on the truth, has dispelled it utterly. . . The expert in poison repels poison by that very poison, a little bit of which kills most people.

Use the passions, in other words, to kill the passions. As in Rabelais' Abbey of Thelema, do what you will shall be the whole of the law. Nothing is forbidden to a true seeker. What may be dangerous or tabu to ordinary people is available to an initiate – so long as he enters it under the guidance of his guru and within the sacred precincts of the mandala. If he crosses the boundaries of Buddhic precepts, it has to be done with a pure mind – and not for personal pleasure.

The second reason to believe that erotic magic lay somewhere close to the original heart of *Tantra* is that there were considerable efforts made to cleanse it of its physical elements at an early date. By around AD 800, that is to say, *Tantra* had become, in effect, an academic subject. At the great Buddhist university at Nalanda, and at other new centres set up in eastern India by the Pala kings of Bengal, scholars were writing commentaries, providing keys to 'twilight language' and explaining the symbolic meaning of objects and actions – making *Tantra*, in other words, respectable. If everything was mind, they argued, then mental exercise alone could perfectly reasonably take the place of any physical engagement.

As a result, many Tantric sects, it is said, gave up their attempts to sacralize, indulge in tabu behaviour and explore the farther reaches of human experience and instead turned to pure contemplation. (Some of them did not, and there are many references to various illicit practices in Tantric texts, including incest, drinking, cannibalism and eating the flesh of cows, elephants, horses and dogs.) For all this, though, in Tantric teaching the human body remained, and remains, a supremely important arena for the drama of the struggle for enlightenment. The male and female body, in the Tantric physiology, has four pyschic centres – the navel, the heart, the throat and the brain – which are connected by various channels (*nadi*) along which there are a number of special plexus points, or *chakras*. A so-called wind-energy – which can be interpreted as consciousness – circulates through this system, but in ordinary people, whose channels are knotted and blocked, it manifests itself in unregenerate passions like greed, rage and desire. It is the responsibility of the follower of the Path – using the tools of mandala and meditation (and perhaps also sex) – to gradually unblock the channels in order to allow the wind-energy free circulation. Once that has been done, he can, by psychic means, attempt to direct and dissolve the free-flowing energy into the infinitesimally small droplet (*bindu*) at the centre of his heart *chakra*. When this is achieved, all conceptual thought automatically ceases. He has arrived at the goal of goals – bliss (*Mahamudra*).

Tantra and *Mahayana* in Tibet

Tibet is the highest country in the world. It is sparsely populated and covers an area of a million and a half square miles. Originally inhabited by a warlike, nomadic people of Mongol origin, speaking what has been called Tibeto-Burman, it sat crowning Asia in 'splendid isolation' for a millennium and a half – at least in the view of the imperial West – before beginning to reveal itself to the outside world during the nineteenth century. The British were the first to take an interest in it, sending military expeditions and political agents there. They were soon followed – not only by representatives of the other great powers but also by an army of European occultists and American Theosophists, who claimed it variously as Shangri-La, 'the forbidden land of the snows', the home of the secrets of past civilizations and the dwelling-place of immortal sages in possession of lost spiritual knowledge.

These outré wisdom-seekers were wrong, of course. In the first place, Tibet was not forbidden, for the Jesuits had set up shop there some centuries earlier, nor had it always been isolated. During a period of expansion, it had absorbed ideas and influences from everywhere around it, from India and China, from Iran and Central Asia – even from the shamans of Siberia. What it was, though, was essentially feudal. It was a tribally-oriented version of medieval Europe or Japan, set in its ways, with a culture firmly rooted in ancient tradition. Preserved within it, free from any effects of modernization, was its central religion: a mixture of *Mahayana* and Tantric Buddhism. This had survived in a form very like that in which it had existed centuries before in the Buddhic motherland of India. After the Chinese invasion of Tibet and the diaspora of many of Tibet's people, including lamas (gurus), it is the form of Buddhism which is most widely encountered in the West.

The early history of Tibet need not detain us long. It seems to have been consolidated into a kingdom in the early seventh century AD, when it began a period of military conquest. Up to that point, its religion had been essentially animist, presided over by a spell-casting shamanic priesthood called the *bon-po*. Then, some time in the seventh century, a king called Songtsen Gampo – by tradition an incarnation of the Bodhisattva Avalokiteshvara – sent an emissary south to Kashmir to develop a Tibetan alphabet and script. A century or so later, another king, Trisong Detsen, ordered the translation of a number of Buddhist texts from Chinese and Indian sources and also invited the first monks into the country, among them a Tantric Indian wonder-worker called Padmasambhava. Padmasambhava, it is said, subdued and co-opted to Buddhism all the local gods and demons. He helped build Tibet's first monastic complex at Samye and founded the sect of the *Nyingmapa* (Ancient Ones), which still survives to this day.

This early period is marked by what seems to have been a bitter, and sometimes murderous struggle between Buddhism and the popular animism of the *bon-po*, backed by most of the king's court.

One event stands out, though – a Great Debate held in the presence of King Ralpachen at the Samye monastery, between 793 and 794 pitted Indian Buddhist pandits against a leader of the Chinese Chan school of instant enlightenment. (It is likely to have featured the sort of ritualized gestures and elaborate forms of address still used in debate by Tibetan lamas.) The Indian gradualists seem to have won the day in this drawn-out battle between the two traditions and thirty years later a special commission of Tibetan and Indian scholars began standardizing the translations of Buddhist texts from Sanskrit – from then on the language from which virtually all Tibetan texts were taken. Precise equivalents for Sanskrit technical terms were established for present and future use and the result is a literature that remains internally consistent – and remarkably faithful to Sanskrit originals – today.

It was not long, however, before the newly-established *Sangha* ran foul of court intrigues. Ralpachen was murdered and Buddhism was ruthlessly suppressed for over a hundred and fifty years, only being kept alive by refugee monks and wandering *yogin*. The kingdom fell into chaos and it was not until the establishment of more or less stable independent governments in western, eastern and central Tibet around the year 1000 that the faith was allowed to return. Tibetans – among them a celebrated translator and (later) builder of monasteries, Rinchen Sangpo – began to travel to India, either to collect texts, to study with Tantric masters and at Buddhist universities, or to sit at the feet of adepts in their hermitages: as a man called Marpa did in Bihar.

Famous Indian teachers, one of them a legend called Atisa, made the journey in the reverse direction – northwards across the formidable Himalaya mountains. Atisa created the system of chronology still in use in Tibet, which defines each year by its position in a sixty-year cycle. The cycle relies on the combination of five elements (earth, iron, water, wood and fire) with the twelve animals of the zodiac (dog, boar, mouse, ox, tiger, hare, dragon, serpent, horse, sheep, monkey and bird). Without Atisa's system, the writing of history – a later speciality among Tibetans, one of whom, Buston, wrote a definitive *History of Buddhism in India and Tibet* in the early fourteenth century – would have been more or less impossible.

With the help of this cross-fertilization of pilgrims and scholars, monasteries were soon restored; temples and new monasteries were built; and individual schools began to emerge, each favouring particular teachings and texts with their own special emphasis and style. At the same time, because of royal patronage, the *Sangha* as a whole became more and more wealthy and powerful and it was not long before it found itself at the core of the country's political life. By the time Buddhism was destroyed in India by the ruthless suppression of Muslim invaders, Tibet, in its fastness, had developed into a Buddhocracy in which the faith, the *Sangha* and the state had become one. Preserved in a time capsule, the Buddhism of medieval India survived with little or no alteration. Although there is a vast ancillary literature in the Tibetan language – commentaries, histories, biographies and verses – it contains almost nothing by way of new doctrine.

Instead, the received teachings were systematically analyzed and codified in the early period and by the fourteenth century – supervised by the remarkable historian Buston – they achieved their final, canonical form. There were two categories – the *Kangyur* (the *Vinaya*, *Sutras* and *Tantras*) and the *Tengyur* – made up of treatises, commentaries and various works on such related subjects as grammar, astrology and medicine. The *Kangyur* was first printed in Peking in 1411 and the whole Canon, all 330 or so volumes of it, was printed at Narthang in Tibet in the first half of the eighteenth century.

The Main Schools of Tibetan Buddhism

Kadampa ('Bound by Command'): This school – the first to have a clear and accepted historical origin – was founded by a lay disciple of the immigrant Indian teacher Atisa and it regarded a severe monastic discipline as a vital prerequisite for Tantric practice. The Dalai Lama has written about the members of this school, as quoted (in an amended form) in John Snelling's *The Buddhist Handbook*:

> Their trademark was this synthesis of various vehicles (yanas), as expressed by their saying, 'The external practice is moral discipline [i.e. Hinayanan obedience to the Vinaya]; the inner practice is the bodhi-mind [i.e. Mahayanan mysticism]; and practiced in secret, is the secret mantra [i.e. Vajrayanan Tantra].' In the Kadampa Order, these three were taken as interconnected, intersupportive aspects of training.

Sakya: This school, named for its principal monastery in southern Tibet, devolves from the teachings of Drogmi (992–1072), who spent many years studying *Tantra* in India: he translated one of the school's basic texts, the *Hejavra Tantra*. Another key text for the school is *The Way and Its Fruit (Lam-dre)*, by the ninth-century Indian adept Virupa, a conflation of Sutric and Tantric teaching into a course of training designed to produce Enlightenment in a single lifetime. Sakyapa clerics are permitted to marry and the headship of the school traditionally passes from uncle to nephew. (The forty-first *Sakya Trizin* now lives in exile.) Early heads of the school wielded considerable political power. One was appointed as the viceregent of the Mongol overlordship in Tibet in the thirteenth century and his nephew succeeded him as the prelate and plenipotentiary of Kublai Khan.

Subsequent Chinese claims to Tibet as a 'natural' part of China were based on this emperor-client relationship.

Kargyu ('Transmitted Command'): The line of this school is traced back to two Indian yogic adepts, Tilopa and Naropa. Marpa studied with Naropa, the Tibetan pilgrim and founder of the Kargyupa school; one of the school's most important texts is *The Six Yogas of Naropa*, which includes the yoga of the *bardo* (the intermediate state between death and rebirth) and mystic heat-yoga (*dumo*), a practical necessity for any seeker alone in his snow-bound hermitage. Marpa, on his return from India, refused to become a monk and had become instead an ordinary householder. He married a woman whom he called *Nairatmya* ('no-self'), and with whom he practiced erotic Hejavran *Tantra*. It is a feature of the Kargyu sect that it requires neither celibacy nor monkhood – even though it has built monasteries of its own.

Marpa's chief disciple and successor as head of the Kargyupa school, Milarepa, is the most popular saint and the greatest poet of Tibetan Buddhism. As a young man he practised black magic in order to take revenge on an uncle who had dispossessed his widowed mother. In terror however at the karmic repercussions of this, he became Marpa's devoted *chela*. For six years, Marpa put him through the spiritual wringer: for example, he forced him to build a tall tower, then knock it down and rebuild it time after time as an act of expiation. Finally, though, he granted him access to Buddhahood and from that time on, for the remaining thirty-nine years of his life, Milarepa lived as a hermit on the high Himalayas near the border with Nepal, wearing nothing but a cotton cloth and eating nothing but herbs (a diet that turned his skin green). His song-poems are full of the agonies and ecstasies of the ascetic life, the heady mountain atmosphere and the joy of the *Dharma*.

After the time of Milarepa's succession, the Kargyupa school split into four branches, one of which was introduced into Bhutan in the seventeenth century and remains the main form of Buddhism both there, in Ladakh and in other parts of the region. Another was much favoured by the Mongol and Ming emperors of China. But one further offshoot, the so-called Karma Kargyu school, is of special interest. This school had a considerable following in the eastern part of Tibet, from where the head of the order, the Karmapa (sometimes known as 'the Black Hat Lama'), would go on elaborate progresses through the country with a large armed guard. Successive Karmapas were appointed, not on any hereditary basis, but by means of a system unique to Tibet – one also found in a number of other schools. Before each Karmapa dies, that is to say, he leaves behind directions which, after an appropriate time, set up a search for a child in whom he – or rather his compassionate spirit – has been reborn. Such voluntary reincarnations are known as *tulku* and carry the title of *rinpoche* ('blessed one'). The sixteenth Karmapa, exiled to Sikkim in 1959, soon afterwards sent two 'blessed ones' to the West to spread the school's teachings: Chogyam Trungpa Rinpoche and Chuje Akong Rinpoche, who founded the first Tibetan Buddhist centre in Scotland.

Nyingma ('Old Ones'): Instituted, according to legend, by the wonder-worker Padmasambhava, 'Nyingma' was perhaps an umbrella term for all those who cleaved to, and carried through the dark years of chaos, the teachings and practices of the first monks to arrive in Tibet. The school was organized and given new life by Guru Choswang in the thirteenth century, when it began to build monasteries and gather together a new canon of its own, based on manuscripts, purportedly written by Padmasambhava, that it claimed to have discovered hidden in caves and other secret places. Since Padmasambhava was believed to be a manifestation of Avalokiteshvara –and the spiritual equal of the Sakyamuni Buddha – these were holy scriptures indeed. They were known as *termas* (treasures) and formed the second part of the Nyingmaka tradition, after *kamas* – the sayings of the original Indian masters. Many of the *termas* – for all the later suspicions about the convenience of their discovery – do seem in fact to be of considerable antiquity. One of them, the so-called *Tibetan Book of the Dead*, not only appears to record extremely ancient ideas about life after death but it also bears a strong similarity to Egyptian, Persian and early Christian writings on the subject.

Nyingmapa *lamas* never achieved the organized power of some of their rivals, largely because they were individualistic, typically married and working at a local level by providing magical services – exorcism, rain-making, divination, healing and so on – to ordinary Tibetans. Indeed, they took over many of the responsibilities, and some of the teachings, of the indigenous animist priesthood, the *bonpo*; and they never fully adopted repressive Buddhist morality. Instead, they lay stress on the central role played by the physical body and its passions in the search for enlightenment, arguing, as the Celestial Bodhisattva Samantabhadra does in one of their texts:

> Suchness, including yourself, is not intrinsically entangled - so why should you try to disentangle ourself? It is not intrinsically deluded – so why should you seek the truth apart from it?

Like the Chan school in China, they prefer intuitive insight to any carefully amassed knowledge; and like Indian Tantric masters of the early period, they follow a practice which consists, according to Conze, of:

1. the mental creation of tutelaries (*yidam*) with the help of
   mantras, visions and the 'sky walkers'.
2. the control of the occult body, with its arteries, semen,
   virility etc.
3. the realisation of the true nature of one's own mind.

They are also much preoccupied with the nature of death and rebirth
and distinguish six intermediate states between normal awareness and
the spiritual realm of *Nirvana*. Three of these are experienced by an
'ethereal' body in the interval between death and reconception, seen
as lasting forty-nine days – and offering the sort of visions recorded in
The Book of the Dead. Three others are experienced in the womb, in
controlled dreaming and in deep trance.

Claims have been made that Nyingma represents Buddhism in
its purest form. Indeed, in the shape of Dzogchen ('The Great
Perfection') – a form of Nyingmapa tantric teaching popular in the
West – it is seen as the essence of all other teachings, the basic core of
Buddhist practice, striking right to the heart of the primordial state of
being within us all.

Gelug ('Virtuous'): The key master of the Gelugpa sect – sometimes
known as 'The Yellow Hat Order' in the West – was the scholar and
reformer Tsongkhapa (1357–1419), also known as Je Rinpoche.
Tsongkhapa, who is identified with Manjushri, the Celestial Bodhisattva
of wisdom, was originally a member of the Kadampa school, but he soon
gained a huge reputation as an independent teacher. After winning
control of the central temple in Lhasa, he set up three monasteries near
the holy city where he instituted a curriculum of doctrinal studies
leading to the degree of *Geshe* ('spiritual friend'), a sort of doctorate of
philosophy. He set great store by the long and careful study of the *Sutras*

and of Indian masters such as Nagarjuna and Asanga; he was a champion of strict monastic discipline; and he condemned the use of worldly magic. The *Tantra*, he pronounced, should only be used for the pursuit of Enlightenment and in the sixteen volumes of his Collected Works he laid out the path to it as a series of graduated stages, either through the Mahayanist Six Perfections or through *Tantra*.

Tsongkhapa is important as a great synthesizer and re-energizer of the faith. He was, says Edward Conze, 'the last great thinker of the Buddhist world' and after his death he became the object of a religious cult of his own. His body was embalmed and enshrined in a *stupa* at one of his university-monasteries, Ganden, which was later invaded and violated by Chinese soldiers. The annual festival of Ngacho Chemno, when thousands of butter-lamps used to be burnt, is a commemoration of his death and he is also believed to have started the three-week-long 'Great Prayer' Festival, which used to be held annually in Lhasa immediately after the Tibetan New Year.

In the course of the fifteenth century, Gelugpa elders helped to stabilize the country over the long term by adopting the *tulku* system of succession. This was based on the old Mahayanan doctrine which held that Buddhas and Bodhisattvas could create phantom-bodies to do their work on earth (or in any other realm). The head of the Order, Gendrun-trup, was recognized as having been the creation of Avalokiteshvara. He was retrospectively declared the first Dalai (or 'Ocean') Lama and, from that time on, with the death of each Dalai Lama, a new child, conceived forty-nine days later, is searched for as the next phantom-body of the last patriarch-cum-Bodhisattva - all this being based on extremely complex rules laid down by the Congregation of Rites. His main palace in Lhasa, where he is educated under the direction of regents, is called Potala, after the dwelling-place of the Bodhisattva in southern India. A second, and historically rival, authority within the school is the reincarnating Panchen Lama, whose traditional home is the monastic complex of Tashilhunpo in southern Tibet.

Despite the occasional warring between the followers of the two Lamas, the theocratic *tulku* system prevented any jockeying – or worse – for supreme power, which soon became the prerogative of the Dalai Lamas of the school. The third Lama converted the Mongols for the second time, co-opting their gods and demons in the process, it is said, as protectors of the *Dharma*. The fourth was actually the grandson of the Mongol Khan; and the sixth, a great scholar, was installed by Gusri Khan as the virtual ruler of Tibet under Mongol protection in 1642. The new Manchu dynasty in China confirmed his position, and relied on him and his successors to keep Tibet peaceful and protective of its interests.

The system broke down once, during the rule of the sixth Dalai Lama, who was accused of degeneracy, perhaps because he tried to revive erotic *Tantra*. There was bitter infighting among the Gelugpa lamas, and a Mongol army had to intervene. After that time, though a delicate political balance was by and large maintained, with successive Dalai Lamas and their regents providing social stability and continuity and managing at the same time to keep the Chinese from meddling in the country's internal affairs and establishing a presence. In this way, conditions favouring the religious life were preserved; militarism was reduced to a minimum; animals were protected; and noise and unrest were suppressed. For 450 years Tibet became a Buddhocracy for Buddhism reached into every corner of Tibetan life, even if slowly but surely ossifying in the process. In 1885, a visitor reported that monks and nuns made up a fifth of the Tibetan population: There were seven hundred and sixty thousand of them in eighteen hundred monasteries.

It was only, in fact, with the coming of the twentieth century that life in Tibet began to change radically for the first time in centuries. The thirteenth Dalai Lama was forced to leave the country twice, first in 1904 (for Mongolia) after a massacre by a British expeditionary force, and secondly in 1910 (for India) when another army – this time Chinese – invaded. He returned in 1913 after the fall of the Manchu dynasty and between then and his death in 1933 he led Tibet through a period of more or less full independence, during which he did his best to prepare Tibetans for the coming onrush of the modern world. Inevitably, he was resisted by conservatives in the monastic community, who not only opposed change of any kind, but had no conception of what life was like beyond the country's borders. They found out in 1950, when the fourteenth Dalai Lama was still only fifteen and recently enthroned. For modernity arrived in Tibet with a vengeance in the shape of an occupying Chinese Communist army. Nine years later, during a general uprising against the Chinese, the Dalai Lama fled to India where, as a figure of great spiritual authority, he now lives in exile in the hill-station of Dharamsala.

Ways and Means in Tantric Buddhism

Of absolutely central importance to Tantric Buddhism is the relationship between the *siddha* (adept) and his *chela* (disciple or student). The *siddha* is sometimes referred to in Tantric texts as Buddhism's 'Fourth Jewel', being of equal importance to the 'Three Jewels' of Buddha, *Sangha* and *Dharma*. Tantric practices are said to be useless without his guidance and blessing, and the *chela* is required to give him absolute submission and devotion as the embodiment of Buddha. This has been compared to a patient placing himself obediently, when ill, in the hands of a skilled surgeon: but in traditional lamaism the process of 'giving up' went further. For whatever the *chela* owned was seen as the personal property of his *guru*.

Siddhas are by no means always monks. They came, and come, from any walk of life and caste. They do menial work and very often flout the conventions of more orthodox believers. Their status as outsiders highlights the fact that in *Vajrayana* every form of human activity is seen as an expression of Buddha nature and every situation as an opportunity to cultivate the enlightened mind. It is not the task of the *siddha* to reform his students but to show them that enlightened energy is already manifest in their make-up and behaviour, however neurotic and passion-contaminated they may be. Everything is capable of transformation: anger into intelligence, ignorance into equanimity, passion into compassion and loving kindness. Not even sexual desire and pleasure are seen as enemies of spirituality. As the sixth Dalai Lama said:

> If one's thoughts towards the Dharma were of the same intensity as those towards love, one would become a Buddha in this very body, in this very life.

The enemies of spirituality, in sex as everywhere else in human life, are the attachment and greed of the fictitious 'self' which puts personal gratification before the needs of others.

Tantric practices are usually classified under four headings – Action, Performance, Yoga and Highest (or Supreme) *Tantra* – which are designed to fit the different needs and abilities of individual seekers, who have to find the level appropriate to them. Even then, it is not for everyone to follow the Tantric path, despite the fact that it holds out the possibility of achieving Enlightenment within a single lifetime. Aspirants, first of all, should already have accumulated enough merit – through good works, moral restraint, patience and so on, in this and previous lives – to be able to control their passions and transform the experiences of everyday life, rather than retreat from them into asceticism in the Hinayana-Mahayanan manner. They should also have some skill in meditation, an understanding of Emptiness and, above all, a commitment to follow the path, not for selfish personal betterment, but for the benefit of others. Compassion must be their essential guiding light.

Their next step is to find – and make what is called 'dharmic connection' – with a *guru*. To teach the lower categories of *Tantra*, he (or she) does not have to be a fully enlightened practitioner, but he must have the expertise to be able to judge whether his *chela* is ready and has the necessary qualities to be able to follow the Tantric path. He must protect him from pitfalls and dangers along the way, and steer him towards those practices which will be most beneficial in his particular case.

Once the two-way commitment has been made between *chela* and *guru*, the *chela* will be initiated into the alternative reality of his chosen deity's *mandala* through the ceremony of the *abhisheka* ritual. This is a public event which is open to all believers, but to the serious Tantric inititiate it represents both a giving of collective permission and a gathering of power to be stored up for the way ahead. From this point on, he can receive teachings and begin to gather the provisions for the journey onward in the form of ethical behavour, purity, right thinking and correct motivation.

At the level of Action Tantra, he is now required to pay intense devotional respect to his chosen deity: to recite *mantras* and prayers, to make offerings and to perform *mudras* and acts of obeisance, including what is known as 'the hundred thousand prostrations'. At the same time – or at a later stage – he will practise Guru Yoga in order to strengthen his devotion to, and reliance on, his lama-guide as the incarnation of his deity. Closer and closer identification with both *guru* and deity will ultimately involve a direct transmission of the state of enlightened mind from teacher to student – and with it the final understanding that the search is not for something outside in the world, but for what is within.

It will also involve the ability to generate an alternative *mandala*-world, populated by deities, via mantras and meditation. In a typical visualization, the devotee envisions himself as the Buddha-deity at the heart of this *mandala*-realm, inhabiting a 'divine house' or interior castle much like that conjured in meditation by the medieval Spanish mystic, St. Teresa of Avila. In Highest Tantra, the initiate learns to summon the deity from the primal Emptiness of mind or from his essence distilled in the seed-syllable (*bija*), and so becomes ready for the final actualization stage, at which full identification and dissolution of self takes place.

Chapter Eight:

Buddhism Throughout the World

The Death of Buddhism in the Indian Heartland

The conventional wisdom is that Buddhism disappeared from India in around 1200 AD because of its ruthless suppression by Muslim invaders, who were determined to root out every last trace of what they saw as idolatry; and it is certainly true that the new Turkic conquerors burned down Buddhist monasteries and butchered Buddhist monks whenever and wherever they found them. The great university at Nalanda, for example, was razed in 1198. When a Tibetan pilgrim visited it thirty-seven years later, all he found was an old monk teaching Sanskrit grammar to a handful of students in the ruins.

This is by no means the whole of the story, though. For Hinduism and Jainism were also suppressed and with equal brutality – and yet both somehow managed to survive. In those parts of the country that were untouched by the Muslim invasion furthermore, in Nepal and south India, for example Buddhism also died away, although rather more slowly. The truth seems to be that Buddhism on the sub-continent, even before the conquest, was already played out as a spiritual force. It had lost its roots in the rural population; and it had come to rely more and more on royal and aristocratic patronage. Once that had been lost – and its social base had been destroyed – it no longer had much to offer ordinary people. Jainists, by contrast – less visible as targets than saffron-robed Buddhist monks – probably survived because there was continuing popular support for ascetics, especially among wealthy merchants. Brahminism, for its part - for all its own great temples and monasteries - remained part of the social fabric of every village, taking care, as it did, of all the rites Buddhism had ceded to it: those of the agricultural cycle, and of birth, marriage and death.

Two other factors, however, also played a role. The first was that, over the preceding centuries, there had been a gradual erosion of the lines that had separated Buddhism and Brahminic Hinduism. The Buddha and a number of Buddhist deities had been absorbed into the Hindu pantheon; the *Vedas* were formally taught at the Buddhist university at Nalanda; and Buddhist Tantras had their precise counterparts in Brahminic literature, which refer constantly to Mahayanan deities. The iconographies and mythologies of the two religions – even their teachings – had become more and more like each other. There were fewer and fewer creative disagreements between them. So it was easy enough for the under-appreciated Buddhist lay community simply to transfer its allegiance, without much discomfort, when hard times came.

The second factor was that Buddhism had never had any particular allegiance to place – the lamp of the *Dharma*, after all, could be lit and maintained anywhere. So while the less flexible and internationally-minded Brahminists and Jainists stood their ground at home, the Buddhist monks who survived the onslaught of militant Islam simply moved elsewhere: to Nepal, for example Tibet and China. On the Indian subcontinent, the wellspring of creative energy that had renewed Buddhism twice in the past had finally dried up. That energy now lay elsewhere.

Buddhism Beyond the Borders

By this time, of course, Buddhism was already well established in Southeast Asia, having been brought there by early Indian settlers and traders. Burma, for instance, which received its first Buddhist missionaries in the third century BC, seems from the first to have been dominated by the devout *Theravada* form of Buddhism, imported from Ceylon. Later though it fell under Mahayanist influence, and it seems to have been dominated in the ninth century AD by a powerful organization of *Vrijnaya* monks called Aris ('Aryans' or 'nobles') who practised *Tantra,* made use of spells and animal sacrifices and worshipped the Mahayanan pantheon.

Two hundred years later though a fresh supply of *Theravada* monks (and scriptures) were brought in from Ceylon by royal order and although the *Mahayana* influence persisted in art and literature for at least another four hundred years, *Theravada* Buddhism eventually took over completely in the 1490s as, in effect, the state religion. Pagan, until it was destroyed by the Mongols at the end of the thirteenth century, was the most important Buddhist centre in the country, said to have been home to 9,000 pagodas and temples (among them the famous Ananda Temple). In the fourteenth century, the celebrated 326-feet-high Shwedagon pagoda was built in Rangoon as a gigantic reliquary for some of the Buddha's hair.

Cambodia (now Kampuchea), Thailand and Laos followed more or less similar paths. Cambodia, on the main trade route between India and China, was already throughly Indianised by the fourth century AD; and under an Indian ruling house and priesthood it developed a syncretic religion in which *Mahayana* Buddhism and Brahminism played more or less equal parts. At the beginning of the ninth century, this was taken over by the newly unified Khmer kingdom at Angkor, with its capital and marvellous temples. But Theravada Buddhism once more supervened four hundred years later – just as the Thai and Lao people were beginning to form states of their own in the area – brought in by a missionary Burmese monk. It was ultimately accepted by the kings of all three peoples and became the state religion, with various lingering traces of Brahminism and indigenous cults. In Thailand, for example – which has produced some of the finest bronze images of the Buddha in history – the King is styled 'the protector of the *Dharma*' and Buddhism has infiltrated every corner of the nation's life. Yet, as in Burma (now Nyangmai), petitions are still made to local genii and tree spirits, rather than the Buddha.

In Indonesia – also more or less completely Indianised by the fifth century AD – Sumatra became Theravadan, while Java followed the early Cambodian pattern. Both Brahminism and Buddhism took hold there in forms that harmonized with pre-existing magical and animist practices – Brahminism in the form of Shiva-worship and Buddhism in its *Mahayana* form, with *Tantra* as the link between them. The Sailendra kings filled the island's central plain with beautifully sculpted temples: including Borobodur, the largest and most remarkable example in southern Asia. This great ninth-century monument, which boasts 27,000 square feet of carvings and over 500 stone Buddhas, is a giant *mandala*, representing both the Buddhic cosmos, centred around Mount Meru, and the spiritual journey taken from *samsara* towards *nirvana*. Present-day pilgrims, as in the past, climb upwards on a path that leads through a succession of five terraces. Reliefs depicting the life of Sakyamuni and stories from the

Jakata and *Mahayana* scriptures can be seen along the way. When the pilgrims finally arrive at the top terrace they encounter three ascending circles of *stupas*, with the *stupa* symbolizing both mountain and the apprehension of Emptiness rising in the middle.

Fifty years after Borobodur was built, another Sailendra king erected a further great temple nearby, this time to Shiva. (Both may in fact have been funerary monuments representing their different paths to salvation.) Increasingly in fact, as time went on, the distinctions between the two religions faded, and a cult of *Shiva-Buddha*, with strong magical and Tantric elements emerged , mostly dedicated to the redemption of the souls of the dead. This produced, in thirteenth-century Java, some of the most beautiful of all Buddhist sculptures, in which kings and queens were represented as Celestial Buddhas or the Perfection of Wisdom and so on. But it was largely suppressed in the fifteenth century, – as was *Theravada* in Sumatra by a fresh wave of Muslim conquerors .

In all of these Southeast Asian countries, Buddhism has survived in one form or another until the present day, although it was recently almost totally destroyed in Laos and Cambodia by the Pathet Lao and Khmer Rouge respectively. In Bali, and elsewhere in Indonesia, Buddhism is still manifest in surviving forms of mystic Hindu-Buddhism and can be felt in the popular appeasement of dead spirits and ancestor worship. In Burma, eighty per cent or so of the population remain Buddhist; and every layman becomes a novice for a while, receiving some education in the monasteries. In Thailand, where an even higher percentage of Thais are Buddhist, and there is a Buddhist king, the *wats* (monasteries) also play an important role in education and social cohesion; and *Theravada* has survived in an especially pure and ascetic form in the northeast of the country in the so-called Forest Tradition (much admired in the West). It is not surprising that Thai monks were repeatedly summoned back to the mother country of Ceylon during its long years of European rule, in order to re-seed and bring back to life the local *Theravada Sangha* whenever it showed signs of collapsing.

What none of these Southeast Asian countries were to produce, however, was any revivification of the Buddhist *Sangha* as a whole. The monks of the *Theravada* tradition continued to be concerned with maintaining orthodoxy and preserving the Buddha's teachings in as pure a form as possible, while those following *Mahayana* and *Tantra* proved only too successful at adapting themselves to purely local needs and practices. None of the monks, that is to say, produced any new speculative literature or brought about revolution in either doctrine or approach. Such innovation had to come from a place in which, finally free from constrictive Indian models, Buddhism could adapt into a new form that was expressive of the national character: China.

Chinese Forms of Buddhism

At the end of the sixth century AD, China was once more united into a single empire, first under the Sui dynasty (581–618) and then under the T'ang (618–907). Thus began what might be called the golden age of Buddhism in China. A number of clearly defined schools arose, nearly all of them of Indian origin and based upon intense study of particular Sanskrit texts, but becoming more and more Chinese in outlook and philosophical cast as time went by. Many of these subsequently ebbed away, in part because of the dissolution of the monasteries ordered (and later revoked) by imperial edict in 845, when Buddhist institutions were destroyed, their lands and wealth confiscated, and their monks and nuns ordered to return to secular life. By that time, however, a number of them had already been exported to Japan, where they were further developed. They are worth mentioning here.

The Mantra or Tantric School (Mi-Tsung) consisted of devotees of the *Mahavairocana* (or 'Great Brilliance') *Sutra,* and it was for a time highly favoured by eighth-century T'ang rulers because of its magic powers and occult control over cosmic forces. It was later supplanted at court by Tibetan *lamas* – who built the famous 'Lamaist Cathedral' in Peking – but it re-emerged in Japan as Shingon.

The Avatamsaka or 'Flower Wreath' School (Hua-Yen) focused on the *Avatamsaka Sutra*, one of the scriptures of the Yogacarans, claiming it to be the most uncompromising expression of the Buddha's teachings. Avatamsakans held that everything in the cosmos interpenetrated everything else, so everything and anything in it, even the smallest particle of dust, was an equal expression of the harmony of Totality. All things were One. Thus Oneness was in all things and all things were equally worthy as objects of meditation. The bias of the school was towards contemplation and aesthetic appreciation (unlike the interventionist Tantra School), and it greatly influenced the Chinese attitude to nature, inspiring many artists in China and later in Japan, where it was known as Kegon.

The T'ien-t'ai or White Lotus School (Fa-hua) was named after Mount T'ien-t'ai, the home of its most important early patriarch, Chih-i (538–597). It followed the Avatamsaka school by maintaining that the mundane and the spiritual were not separate, but one – although it arrived at this conclusion from a slightly different philosophical perspective. Its central scripture was the *White Lotus of the True Law*

Sutra, and it represents an attempt to synthesize and harmonize all *Mahayana* Buddhist doctrines. The idea of harmony (as against dissension and dissonance) was very dear to the Chinese.; by bringing order to seemingly contradictory teachings, stressing that the ineffable was omnipresent in ordinary life and allowing that every being in the world possessed the Buddha-nature, the school was not only popular with ordinary people but also with the ruling classes, who saw it as promoting social order. In its doctrine it gave practitioners plenty of leeway for individual choice; and, in its practice, it laid equal stress on concentration (*chi*) and insight (*kuan*), the flash of intuition that suddenly penetrates to the heart of Ultimate Reality. In the end, the T'ien-t'ai School in China became a victim of its own efforts to be all things to all men. It promoted a syncretization of Buddhism with Confucianism; and the neo-Confucianism that was the result destroyed it. It survived in Japan as Tendai.

The Pure Land School (Ching-t'u) was of a different order from any of the above; and even though it produced no great masters after the ninth century, it was to have a pervasive influence on developments within Chinese Buddhism long after that. The Pure Land had its roots in the notion – also widespread in India – that a degenerate period would set in a thousand or so years after the death of the Sakyamuni Buddha, one in which it would become increasingly difficult to achieve Enlightenment through personal effort alone. (Unmediated personal effort, indeed, could be regarded as egoistic and presumptuous.) Another source was the common early practice of meditative concentration upon the Celestial Buddhas of the ten directions, of whom Amithaba, the Buddha of the Pure Land or Western Paradise (Sukhavati), was one. The main scriptural focus for the School was a first century AD Sanskrit text, the *Sukhavativyuha*, which claimed to tell Amithaba's story. One of the things it recorded was that as the Bodhisattva Dharmakara, inconceivable numbers of aeons ago, Amithaba had made forty-eight vows, including one that promised that anyone who called on his name would be saved. He had later become the Buddha Amithaba and, in keeping with his earlier vows, he had established the Pure Land or Western Paradise for those who invoked him.

In the Pure Land School, therefore, meditation took second place to the *mantra*-like repetition of the Buddha's name (*O-mi-to-fo*), and devotion to Amithaba took every form: sculpture, painting, hymns and the constant reproduction of the *Smaller* and *Larger Sukhavativyuha Sutras*. And because the veneration of Amithaba coincided, roughly speaking, with the popular Taoist notion of a spirit or spirits who kept a record of everyone's actions – and adjusted the length of their lives or granted them immortality accordingly – Pure Land had many Taoist converts. The first Pure Land master, T'an-luan (476–542) had been a Taoist himself, as we have seen, and he further widened access to the Amithaba cult by declaring that even the worst of sinners, except those who had blasphemed against the *Dharma*, could be reborn in the Western Paradise. All they had to have was faith.

The Pure Land School, then, was anything but élitist. It was both practical and democratic; and though, in its later development, it came to stress morality, meditation and scholarship as important further vehicles towards salvation, it continued to appeal to all classes in society with its message about the worth of every individual, wrapped – whatever his caste or position – in the boundless love of Amithaba. In its heyday it attracted everyone from emperors to slaves, including scholars, artists, soldiers, peasants, women, monks and novices; and though it was later condemned as being 'vulgar' and 'foreign' by *comme-il-faut* neo-Confucians, its influence remained, being transmitted into Japan in the form of the Jodo and Jodo Shin sub-schools. Although Pure Land also introduced a cult of the Indian Celestial Bodhisattva Avalokiteshvara – transformed ultimately into a female deity called Kuanyin – 'no native Chinese god', in the words of Robinson and Johnson in their *The Buddhist Religion*, 'has ever commanded the universal worship that [Amito] has received'.

Ch'an

All of the schools discussed above, particularly T'ien-t'ai and Pure Land, represented the adaptation of Buddhist ideas and doctrines to a specifically Chinese environment, both spiritual and social. None of them, though, had the lasting impact of a further school, the Dhyana (or 'Meditation') School, which was known in Chinese as Ch'an (Korean: *Son*; Japanese: *Zen*). Ch'an, in fact, represents the last great turn of the wheel in the development of Buddhist thought after *Abhidharma, Mahayana* and *Tantra* and it gave a new kind of saint to Buddhism, who was the successor of the *arhant*, the *bodhisattva* and the *siddha*: the *roshi* (or Ch'an 'master').

Ch'an represented a sort of back-to-basics movement within the Buddhist establishment. It held that all the paraphernalia of Chinese monastic practice and doctrine (the lectures on philosophy; the constant reading of the *Sutras* and commentaries; the codes of behaviour; the devotional rituals; the use of images; the constant pressure to perform good works; and so on) ran the risk of obscuring, rather than pointing the way to, Enlightenment – the one and only true goal. What it proposed was a radical simplification of the means used to achieve what remained the heart of the matter – the direct insight which had transformed Sakyamuni into the Buddha under the Bodhi tree. It announced that salvation could not be achieved through the study of books; it had to be practically realized. It brought the discipline of meditation, that's to say, right back centre-stage.

In doing so, Ch'an claimed to be part of a special transmission that was 'outside the scriptures', beyond words and writing, a transmission that had originally come from the Sakyamuni Buddha himself. On one occasion, thousands of people went to hear him preach at Vulture Mountain and for some time he sat before them in silence. Then he held up a flower. Only one person there, a seeker called Mahakashyapa understood what he meant – that words were no substitute for the living organism – and at that moment he intuited the whole essence of Buddha's teaching. The first transmission between mind and mind, acknowledged by Sakyamuni and Mahakashyapa with a complicit smile, had taken place.

This transmission from mind to mind and from master to student had then continued in India, according to Ch'an traditions, until it was brought to China by its twenty-eighth recipient, a south Indian monk called Bodhidharma, in about AD 470. Bodhidharma was said to have spent nine years contemplating a wall after his arrival and even to have cut off his eyelids so that his gaze would not falter. At some point, however, he found time to meet the pious Emperor Wu of Liang. Their conversation, in the version given by Jane Hope and Borin Van Loon in *Buddha for Beginners*, is fairly typical of Ch'an exchanges:

> 'From the beginning of my reign I have built many temples, translated numerous scriptures and supported the monastic life. What merits have I earned?'
> 'None'.
> 'Why?'
> 'All these are inferior deeds. A true deed of merit comes straight from the heart and is not concerned with worldly achievements.'

'Then what is your holy doctrine all about?'

'Vast emptiness, nothing holy'.

'Then who are you?'

'I don't know'.

Bodhidharma, who is conventionally pictured as a wild, exophthalmic and bushy-bearded barbarian, became the legendary First Patriarch of the Ch'an school, and he passed the robe (and the transmission) on to his disciple, Hui-k'o – although not before Hui-k'o had been severely tested. When he first asked for teaching, Bodhidharma made him stand outside in the snow until the drifts came up to his knees. Finally, desperate to demonstrate his earnestness, Hui-k'o, according to the story, cut off one of his arms with his sword. At last the master was impressed, and ushered him in.

'My soul isn't at peace', Hui-k'o is supposed to have said. 'Please pacify it, master'.

'Bring your soul here and I'll pacify it for you', replied Bodhidharma.

'I've been looking for it for years but haven't been able to find a trace of it'.

'There!' said Bodhidharma with a gesture. 'It's pacified once and for all!'

Bodhidharma had obviously absorbed from the *Tao* some of its earthiness and irreverent humour, and his successors, from Hui-k'o onwards, seem to have taught an ascetic form of Tao-Buddhism. It is not, in fact, until the time of the Fifth Patriarch, that Ch'an as an independent school of thought begins to come into focus – even through via what may be later propoganda. A tale records that the Patriarch announced that before he died he would pass on his mantle to the disciple who could write a verse that best expressed the true nature of Enlightenment. One of them, a sophisticated and learned monk called Shen-hsui (608?–708), his chief disciple, wrote:

> The body is the Bhodi tree,
> The mind is like a bright mirror in a stand.
> Take care to wipe it constantly
> And allow no dust to cling.

But another disciple, an ex-woodcutter and lowly monastery menial called Hui-neng (638–713), thought he could do better. He wrote, in a kind of gloss:

> Fundamentally the Bodhi tree does not exist;
> The bright mirror also has no stand.
> Since everything is primordially empty,
> What is there for dust to cling to?

The story goes that when the Patriarch read this he interviewed Hui-neng at the dead of night, recognized that he had been truly awoken to Enlightenment, and passed on his robe to him in secret. This not only broke every rule of monastic law but it also officially, so to speak, downgraded book-learning in favour of direct apprehension. (Ch'an later came to dismiss the complex cosmological and psychological theories of other schools as 'rubbish' and 'useless furniture'.) More than that, because Shen-hsui was identified with the so-called northern school of Ch'an, which held that Enlightenment could only be gradually achieved by purification and strenuous practice (the constant wiping of the mirror), it was abandoned by mainstream Ch'an in favour of the teachings of the southern school, represented by Hui-neng. A central belief of the latter school was that since all beings were already part of the emptiness of Buddha-nature, they therefore did not need purifying. Enlightenment could be achieved in a single instant.

The whole story of the competition between Hui-neng and Shen-hsui may well have been a later confection of the victorious southern school. But it also contains another element that was very important to the development of Ch'an – the interview, at the dead of night, between the Patriarch and Hui-neng. Interviews like this, between master and disciple, became a crucial adjunct to meditation and more or less standard practice in Ch'an, the aim of which was 'to cultivate no-thought' without self-assertion, striving or, indeed, deliberate purpose – the ground-base onto which Enlightenment could be encouraged to supervene. Such interviews enabled the master to check on a disciple's spiritual progress in general. But they also provided an opportunity to provoke insight or awareness (Chinese: *wu*; Japanese: *satori*) – a shift to a higher level of understanding which was sometimes equated with Enlightenment itself. Robinson and Johnson, in their *The Buddhist Religion*, explain the process:

> Dialogs that occur in these private encounters form a substantial part of later Ch'an literature. They are terse, often witty, sometimes bizarre and obscure. The master usually had a lot of students, and only two or three short periods a day were set aside for interviews, so the chance was precious. In addition, the student's hopes and fears were usually keyed up by long waiting and intense striving, so that the meeting had the sudden death quality of a duel. The master diagnoses the student's problem and treats it. Sometimes he simply explains or advises. Sometimes he provokes, shocks, or otherwise manipulates the student.

> The Ch'an strategy is to catch a person at the critical
> moment and do the appropriate thing that triggers
> awakening. Chan masters similarly treat each case as sui
> generis, acting and expecting responses with spontaneity
> and without preconceptions or premeditation.

Any and all means were appropriate in this 'treatment', including
suddenly beating the students with a stick, slapping their faces or
tweaking their noses, or making rude or inconsequential noises. But
one of the most powerful tools was what came to be called the *kung-
an* (Japanese: *koan*). The *kung-an* (roughly speaking, 'legal
precedent or authority') was in practice a riddle or seemingly
nonsensical remark, usually connected with a saying or action of one
of the Ch'an masters. (A variety of these *kung-ans* were collected in
Sayings of the Ancient Worthies.) Some are more or less
comprehensible, as in this story of Pai-chang and his student Ling-yu,
also recorded in Robinson and Johnson:

> When Ling-yu was twenty-three, he came to Pai-chang,
> who recognized his talent and took him as an attendant.
> One day the master said, 'Who's there?'
> 'It's Ling-yu.'
> 'Poke and see whether there's still some fire in the stove.'
> Ling-yu poked around and said, 'There's no fire.'
> Pai-chang got up, went to the stove, poked quite a bit,
> managed to stir up a small glow, and said to his pupil, 'Isn't
> this fire?' Ling-yu was awakened, knelt down, and bowed
> in gratitude to the master.

Pai-chang was not only telling Ling-yu that he wasn't striving hard
enough. He was also pointing towards the nature of ultimate reality,

the direct experience of the unextinguished – and inextinguishable – fire within.

Other *kung-ans* made less immediate sense – as this, recorded as an interview between Hui-neng and one of his disciples, shows. The disciple asked Hui-neng: 'How do I get rid of ignorance?'

'Cease running after things', he replied. 'Stop thinking about what is right and wrong. Just see, at this very moment, what your original face was like before your mother and father were born.'

Another *kung-an*, quoted in Conze, takes the form of a three-line stanza:

> In the square pool there is a turtle-nosed serpent.
> Ridiculous indeed when you come to think of it!
> Who pulled out the serpent's head?

The purpose of the *kung-an*, however absurd, was to point the way towards ultimate reality. This was in the end inexpressible, but Ch'an masters were not content with simply saying this by evolving methods of what Conze calls 'stating it through a non-statement'. Put another way, we are so accustomed to the existence of rational answers to our questions that we must be put through the shock of facing the fact that there is no answer at all to this central question. The whole intellectual apparatus of mind has to be violently short-circuited if we are to find our own answer and experience reality directly. The beauty of the language of *kung-an* – known as 'strange words and stranger actions' – is that it is not remotely scholastic. Instead, it is an acting-out and an off-the-cuff invocation of objects in the world that is designed to jolt or deflect the mind of an individual student in the right direction. It is, if you like, the Buddha-mind of the master speaking directly, beyond the power of any mere words, to the Buddha-mind that inhabits his pupil.

As a result of this – because each interview, each jolt and deflection, was so to speak tailor-made – we know little of Ch'an teaching practice as a whole since its masters, distrusting words as another kind of attachment, wrote little down. Indeed, beyond sermons, some hymns and collections of cryptic sayings and anecdotes, there is little that can be described as Ch'an literature at all. This raises a number of questions, both about the status of the masters and about the very nature of Ch'an Enlightenment.

It is natural to suppose that the Ch'an master, like the Tibetan *siddha*, was regarded as the very embodiment of Buddha by his disciples. The Ch'an Patriarchs, indeed, are referred to as 'venerable Buddhas' and a collection of sermons by the (perhaps mythical) Hui-neng is deliberately entitled a *Sutra*, a word usually reserved for the Sakyamuni Buddha's teachings. What their realization as Buddhas consisted in, though, is a very much harder question to answer. For the word for Enlightenment in Ch'an texts is not the word *pu-ti*, applied to Sakyamuni's Enlightenment, but once again *wu* ('insight' or 'awareness'); and it seems to have consisted in the simple cessation of all ambition, all striving – much closer to Taoist ideals than those of traditional Buddhism.

Meditation is central to this achievement in Ch'an, in that it produces in initiates via constant introspection an inner potentiatiy: a state of 'being in thought, yet devoid of thought', a state in which the mind 'stops dashing hither and thither'. Then comes the moment of 'sudden' enlightenment, in which this 'inner potentiality' breaks through into ordinary consciousness and all doubts and problems instantaneously drop away. From this point on, the enlightened initiate continues to engage fully with the world, but he is no longer completely of it. He exists in an eternal present, beyond birth, death, space and time. In the words of Hai-yun: 'To eat all day yet not to swallow a grain of rice; to walk all day yet not tread an inch of ground; to have no distinction during that time between object and subject; and to be inseparable from things all day long, yet not be deluded by them – this is to be the man who is at ease in himself.'

The approach to Ch'an Enlightenment, in other words, may involve complex and arduous preparation, but its achievement is simplicity itself. It can be achieved anywhere, as one contemporary Buddhist has put it: 'working in the fields, cooking rice, hearing one's name called, a slap, a kick!' There is no essential difference between the sacred and the profane, as Ch'an monastic practice had already established in the eighth century. (Po-Chang, also known as Huai-hai, had decreed that Ch'an monks, unlike others, should work. 'A day without work', he announced, 'is a day without food'.) Enlightenment was therefore fully open to lay people, like the peasant P'ang, on whom a *haiku*, a seventeen-syllable Japanese poem, is said to have been based: 'How wonderful, how miraculous! I fetch wood, I carry water'. His actual words are recorded as: 'Spirit-like understanding and divine functioning *lies* in carrying water and chopping wood.'

In this, as in many other things, there are similarities between Ch'an and earlier Taoism. The *Tao* sage, also, was very much of this world. He practised trance meditation and he expected his disciples to learn by intuition from him through wordless teachings and occasional sudden attacks. Furthermore, the image of the dusty mirror, invoked by Shen-hsiu and Hui-neng, occurs a thousand years earlier in Lao Tse and Chuang Tsu. There is also in Ch'an much of the *Tao*'s sometimes grotesque irreverence and humour, something hitherto unknown in Buddhism. For example, a particular Ch'an master simply burned a wooden statue of the Buddha when he was cold, arguing that it was only a piece of wood, after all, not a relic. Another master announced that Buddha ought to be killed if he ever got in the way – he was merely another form of attachment. Yet another, when asked 'What is the Buddha?' was given to replying 'What is not the Buddha?', 'I never knew him' or 'Wait until there *is* one, then I'll tell you'. In Ch'an, just as in *Tao*, there is little talk of enlightenment as an escape from the world. For fully engaging in life is the path to immortality. In the words of another Ch'an master: 'Only do ordinary things with no special effort: relieve your bowels, pass water, wear your clothes, eat your food and, when tired, lie down! Simple fellows will laugh at you, but the wise will understand.'

Perhaps because of this resonance with the very Chineseness of Taoism – and because Ch'an monks and nuns were willing to work – Ch'an, along with the Pure Land school, survived the ninth-century dissolution of the monasteries relatively unscathed. Five different sub-schools began to appear at around that time, with different styles of teaching and meditational practice. But only two of them were to last – the Tsao-tung (Japanese: Soto) and the Lin-Chi (Japanese: Rinzai) schools. The Tsao-tung school favoured sitting in silent meditation and its founder proposed five steps towards ultimate awareness, based on the Chinese Book of Changes. The Lin-Chi school rejected this kind of meditation (and the study of the *Sutras*) as a way of simply hiding from the world. It was vehemently anti-rationalist; it continued to use the disruptive methods of shout and stick; and it awarded virtually mantric status to the use of meditation on a chosen *kung-an* as an opener of the door to awareness. One of its masters told his students: 'Just steadily go on with your *kung-an* every moment of your life! Whether walking or sitting, let your attention be fixed on it without interruption. When you begin to find it entirely devoid of flavour, the final moment is approaching: do not let it slip out of your grasp! When all of a sudden something flashes out in your mind, its light will illuminate the entire universe.'

Illuminate or no, the *kung-an* tradition – as is clear from these words – somewhere along the way lost its intense creativity. It was no longer a kind of tailor-made spiritual ad-libbing. It had come to rely on set texts. From the beginning of the Sung dynasty (960–1279), this kind of standardization and the ossification of old methods set in all over the *Sangha*. There was also a rise in neo-Confucianism, which was by now equipped with a sophisticated new metaphysic, much of it borrowed from Ch'an. Because of what came to be called 'the persecution', Buddhism had lost its powerful economic base; and with the establishment of a new dynasty and the arrival of peace, the intellectual élite was now more inclined to enter the imperial bureaucracy, where Confucianism ruled – as it did in the educational system – than they were to enter a monastery.

Buddhism in general, therefore, lost its intellectual edge; and because there was no longer any meaningful contact with India and Tibet, due to Muslim invasions, there was no fresh fertilization from outside of either theory or practice. Instead, the different schools began, in effect, to grow together. Some Ch'an practitioners, like the Pure Land societies, took to chanting the name of Amidharba. Pure Land societies awarded the status of a *kung-an* to this chanting and Confucianism absorbed the Tsao-tung practice of quiet meditation into their own 'quiet-sitting' (ching-tso). At the same time, the Buddhist *Sangha* lost prestige because it was controlled by the state and, having no central authority (like a pope and cardinals), could be easily kept in line. This control involved periodic confiscations of wealth and land and forced defrockings of monks and nuns. But it also involved the state selling off certificates of ordination, when times were hard, to whoever could pay the price – even criminals on the run from justice. It is hard not to see the transfiguration of the Buddha-to-Be Maitreya into the so-called 'Hemp-Sack Monk', which happened at this time, as almost an enshrinement of this loss of status. For Pu-tai, known also as the 'Laughing Buddha', is on the face of it a cheeky pot-bellied hedonist – hardly a celebration of spiritual or other-wordly values.

For all this, the Sung period was in many ways a golden age for the Ch'an school. It had a profound influence on cultural life and the arts, particularly on painting. (Many Ch'an monks were among the painters of the period and the simplicity, naturalness and spontaneity of Chinese watercolour and some forms of calligraphy can be said to represent a Ch'an ideal.) Ch'an was also much favoured at court, and many new monasteries were built, which subsequently became important social and cultural centres. In the process, though, Ch'an became more worldly and, in Buddhic terms, infected by impermanence. All over the Sangha, in fact, the period of decline and decadence which Sakamuni had predicted as inevitably stemming from initial creativity, set in. There was a revival under the Ming dynasty, but the only effect in the long run was that the two most original and lasting expressions of Chinese Buddhism, Pure Land and Ch'an, became one. The only hint of revolutionary thinking now came from secret messianic societies that claimed Buddhist connections and took Buddhist names – from which stems the legend of the so-called *kung-fu* monks.

Under the Manchu dynasty, just as with the Ming, Buddhism was tolerated. However, state patronage was given to a rigid form of neo-Confucianism which constantly propagandized against all forms of the faith. Then, in the mid-nineteenth century, when the Chinese empire began to unravel, the T'ai-p'ing rebellion (1850–1864) virtually destroyed Buddhism's monastic base. The rebels, who professed a sort of Christianity, sacked sixteen provinces, destroyed 600 cities and burned thousands of temples and monasteries to the ground. A range of Buddhist organizations were set up in response – Buddhist schools were founded and attempts were made to promote a world fellowship of Buddhists. With the final collapse of the Manchu dynasty, and the arrival of a nationalist government, there was a brief period of relative religious freedom. In 1930 there were still said to be in China 738,000 Buddhist monks and nuns and 267,000 temples.

When the Communists took over the mainland in 1949, though, the Buddhist clergy were quickly denounced as parasites. Their land was confiscated and they were either forced back into secular life or imprisoned and/or brainwashed. The *Sangha* was soon put under the aegis of a Chinese Buddhist Association, which was controlled – like the Orthodox Church in Russia – by the Communist secret police. During the Great Cultural Revolution (1965–1975) that followed, Red Guards went on the rampage and destroyed thousands of surviving Buddhist buildings and monuments, along with all the relics of China's past that they could get their hands on. Now, with the coming of runaway capitalism to China, the omens for Chinese Buddhism continue to look poor.

Chinese Buddhism Abroad

Vietnam and Korea

The same is true for what were once Chinese dependencies: Vietnam and Korea. The northern part of what we now call Vietnam was, for centuries, a province of the Chinese empire. It was also where the Vietnamese people arose, before sweeping south to occupy the whole region. Much earlier, Indian settlers had brought a form of *Theravada* with them to the south, which still survives on the Cambodian border; and this seems to have been followed by the sort of Shiva-Buddhism found in Indonesia. Eventually, though, it was the Ch'an school, which had arrived in the north in the sixth century, that came to dominate the entire country. (Northern Ch'an is unique in that its twenty-eighth patriarch was a Ch'an nun.) Later, a version of Pure Land became popular at village level and, as in China, the distinction between Pure Land and Ch'an began to disappear – though Ch'an remained a powerful influence on the way in which Vietnamese culture developed. In fact, Buddhism remained more or less central to Vietnamese life until French colonialists brought in Roman Catholic missionaries and western-style education. The Vietnam War, the American-backed puppet governments of south Vietnam, and the ultimately victorious Communists of the north did the rest. Between them they managed to undermine and damage the Vietnamese *Sangha* irreparably.

As for Korea, Buddhism seems to have arrived in what were then the Three Kingdoms sometime in the fourth century AD – after which it gradually spread throughout the whole peninsula. By the sixth century it was well enough established to be able to send missionaries to Japan, along with Buddhist statues and texts. The main early schools in Korea were similar to those in China, but when Buddhism was made the state religion in the seventh century the appearance of Ch'an, with its volatile mix of simplicity and iconoclasm, gave them new competition and life. There followed a golden period for Buddhism in Korea, in which members of the royal family often became monks and nuns, and huge sums were spent on building, publishing projects, art and elaborate ceremonies. Buddhist *bonzes*, most of them Ch'an (Korean: Son), controlled the government for long periods of time and Buddhism was rapturously taken up by the common people, who brought to it the sort of magic practices – divination, rain-making, the raising of spirits, etc. – that it had acquired elsewhere.

At the end of the fourteenth century, though, Buddhism in Korea also went into a rapid decline. A new dynasty, the Yi, took power and it favoured, not Buddhism, but the sort of orthodox Confucianism that had taken hold in China under the Ming. Buddhism was eventually disestablished, its land confiscated and its monasteries and convents closed. It survived away from the cities to some extent, and when the Japanese took control of the country (1910–1945), there was a modest revival which saw Buddhism finally united into a single sect. After the defeat of the Japanese, however, land reform took away much of the *Sangha*'s income and although this was soon replaced with state grants in the south, in the north it dealt Buddhism a mortal blow. In today's South Korea Buddhists remain active. But in the North –as in Vietnam and China – land reform, the War and ultimate Communist control have put paid to any fresh revival.

Japan

When Buddhism arrived in Japan in the sixth century AD – by means of missionaries from Korea – the country was in the process of creating a central state out of loose federations of clans. At first it was permitted a grudging toehold, but as more Korean monks began to appear it started to be seen not only as the representative of a higher civilization but also as the guardian of occult powers, through which it could protect against disease and bring good luck and social harmony. Buddhism was soon adopted therefore, by the emerging empire, as an instrument of state, rather than as a bringer of individual salvation.

During the seventh century, temples and monasteries were built under the aegis of a series of devout emperors. Monks were ordained and ceremonies were funded out of the public purse. Buddhism proved adept at assimilating the deities or spirits (*kami*) of indigenous Shinto; and it soon became, in effect, the official Religion and Civilization Department of the imperial court. Tradition has it that the Empress Suiko became a devout Buddhist nun and that her nephew, Prince Shotuku, who lectured on the *Sutras* himself, wrote the first 'constitution' of the country under the direction of Buddhist monks. He is still known as the founder of Japanese Buddhism.

The faith was no doubt helped in Japan by the fact that Confucianists made poor missionaries: they did not like to travel or proselytize among 'barbarians'. But, for whatever reason, Buddhism became the main conduit for the wholesale importation into Japan of Chinese architecture, technology and literary and artistic forms. Buddhism may have largely been the preferred religion of the intellectual élite – at least at first – but it helped shape the culture of the entire country. (It is said that the only original cultural or technological artefact that Japan exported back to mainland China was the folding fan.)

In time, ordained Japanese monks went on pilgrimage to China, and the early Buddhist sects that appeared in Japan seem to have depended on who their teachers were. Groups of monks – largely gentlemen-scholars – gathered around particular texts and only one of the groups (*Hosso*, based on *Fa-hsiang* teachings) survived to become a fully-developed school. It wasn't in fact until the time of the building of the capital at Nara in the eighth century that a Chinese philosophical system rose to any prominence. This was the Hua-yen school, known as Kegon in Japan, which equated the emperor with the Celestial Buddha Vairocana and Japanese society as a whole with the Hua-yen *Dharma*-realm, in which everything interpenetrated everything else via a seamless web of connection. This vision of the Japanese world that was created by and centred on the emperor/Buddha proved so effective in making the link between individuals and their collective fealty to the state that a colossal bronze image of Vairocana was erected in Nara's Eastern Great Temple in 752, where it remains today.

In general, though, the doctrines promoted by the different schools were less important than the generic state Buddhism that was set up in the provinces by imperial edict and the lasting effect on Japanese culture that it had. Knowledge of Chinese spread through translation of the *Sutras,* and the making of cult objects stimulated virtually every art and craft, from sculpture to papermaking. Monks introduced geomancy, astronomy and calendars to the country. They not only served as scribes and clerks in the developing Japanese bureaucracy but also as engineers: building irrigation systems, bridges and roads. They encouraged public bathing and cremation, as in China, and even made the first maps. So powerful did the Nara monks become that at the end of the seventh century the capital was shifted to Heia (now Kyoto) to rusticate them. From then on the focus of Buddhism shifted from metropolitan centres to monastery-settlements in the mountains.

Monasteries in the Mountains

One of these monastery-powerhouses was on Mount Hiei, northwest of Kyoto, which became the main centre for a *Tantra*-influenced form of the Chinese T'ien-t'ai school (known as Tendai). This had been brought to Japan by a Japanese monk called Saicho or Dengyo-daishi ('Great Master Who Transmitted the Teaching'), who kept his monks in mountain seclusion while they underwent a rigorous twelve-year course of study and meditation. At its height, the temple complex of the Mount Hiei community contained 3,000 buildings – among them halls set aside for the Pure-Land chanting of Amidhaba's name (*Amida*) and fully 30,000 monks. From its ranks came the founders of almost all the new schools which followed in later centuries.

Another powerful centre was the monastery settlement on

Mount Koya, which became the headquarters of the Japanese version of the Mantra or Tantric School, Shingon (Chinese: *Chen-yen*, 'Truth-Word'). Shingon, with its emphasis on *mantras, mudras, mandalas* and contemplation, was brought to Japan by an aristocratic monk called Kukai or Kobo-daishi ('Great Master Who Propagated the *Dharma*'), who was much favoured by the imperial court for his occult powers and skill in rain-making. Kukai was also a prolific writer and sculptor, an educationalist, a promoter of the arts and a skilled calligrapher – he is said to have invented the cursive syllabary of forty-seven signs in which, with the sometime addition of Chinese characters, the language is written and he remains perhaps the most celebrated scholar-teacher in Japanese history. Under his rule, disciples flocked to Mount Koya for instruction and many of them followed the path of the early ascetics, living alone or in groups in the forests (as they also did on Mount Hiei). Followers of Shingon still maintain that Kukai is not dead, but is merely waiting on Mount Koya to rise up again with the coming into the world of the Buddha-to-be, Maitreya.

During the so-called Heian period (794–1184), there seems to have been considerable cross-fertilization between these and other sects. Tendai, for example, took over much of Shingon's esotericism; Shingon adopted Tendai Amidist invocations; and the Nara and the mountain monks not only came to set great store on the arts but also on elaborate rituals, chanting and ceremony (the ground-base for the later emergence of Noh drama.) But there was also intense competition both between the sects and between individual monasteries. Armies of mercenaries led by warrior monks (*sohei*) regularly attacked and burned down rival institutions. From time to time they even invaded the capital to assert their political will.

Often paid a kind of tribute money (or rental on the faith) by their provincial offshoots, the monastic institutions had become major centres of wealth and power by the end of the Heian period. The monks were still largely drawn from the élite: many of them were aristocrats and therefore no strangers either to earthly pride or the arts of war. Towards the end of the era, Amidism, with its *Nembutsu* (*Namu-Amida-butsu*) chant, began to spread among ordinary people, but for the most part Heian Buddhism remained a very exclusive affair.

In the era that followed, the so-called Kamakura period (1185–1333), this was to change for ever. For it was a period of crisis, when Japan was threatened by Mongolian invasion and disrupted at the same time by internal disunity, marked by a shift in power between the capital and the provinces. A disaffected new class had appeared, that's to say, made up of *samurai* (warriors) and provincial landowners, and although it was nominally Buddhist it was reluctant to support either an esoteric faith or an emperor in some distant capital. The result was the establishment of a new centre of power in Kamakura in 1185, in the form of a Shogunate (or military government), and a new democratization of Japanese Buddhism. For the new class, which needed popular support, succeeded in bridging the yawning gap that had existed between the old aristocracy and the peasantry. High Japanese culture was diffused across every class in the country; and Buddhism in the process became a distinctively Japanese coloration for the first time.

New Sects and Schools

Times of anxiety and violent change do not generally favour the pursuit of abstruse philosophy or the systematic deferment of gratification; and both the laity and a number of Buddhist monks seem to have felt this equally. For following the lead of early Amidist missionaries, two new popular devotional schools were quickly established by disaffected monks schooled at Mount Hiei. The first was Jodo-shu ('Pure Land'), founded by a learned Tendai monk called Honen (1133–1212), who had become convinced that enlightenment, given the nature of the times, could no longer be reached through personal effort (*jiriki*) alone. It now required the supernatural intercession of Amida, whose name had to be ceaselessly invoked through the *Nembutsu*. Honen preached that even the greatest sinner could be reborn in the Western Paradise by this means, so long as he had faith, avoided sin and not only paid due respect not only to Amida but also to the other Buddhas and the *Sutras*. Pure-Land Buddhism soon found favour with both court and commoner, and it still exists as a school today, although a later modification of its central teaching proclaimed that rebirth in the Pure Land involved a change of mind and condition rather than translation to another cosmic region.

The second school, founded by ex-Tendai monk Shinran (1173–1262), was Jodo Shinsu, or 'True Pure Land' which threw the net of Amidism even wider. No personal effort at all was either needed or recommended in Jodo Shinsu. All that was necessary was to take up Amida's gift in a state of faith, and after that the fate of the individual lay in the Buddha's beneficent hands. Shinran abandoned monastic rule and married a young aristocrat, as if to demonstrate that living in the everyday world was as redeemable a condition as any other. Indeed, he argued that as he had become a sinner he was more likely to gain access to the Western Paradise, because he had given up self-help and the path of merit and had literally nowhere else to turn. His teachings made salvation easily accessible to ordinary people, among whom he spent the rest of his life – and he remains much revered today.

A third devotional sect, with a difference, was founded by yet another monk from Mount Hiei, Nichiren Shonin (1222–1282). The son of a humble fisherman, Nichiren had become as frustrated as Honen and Shinran with the ineffectiveness of the monastic regime, but he chose a different path. He maintained that the *Lotus Sutra* was the essential and pure *summa* of Buddhism and that men and women could achieve the Enlightenment of Sakyamuni Buddha by merely invoking it with the words *Namu-myoho-renge-kyo* ('Homage to the Lotus Sutra'). Enlightenment was not deferred as in Pure Land, but obtainable right now – they would become embodiments of paradise. Not to take this step, he preached, would be to deny the whole country its manifest destiny as an earthly and inviolable Buddha-land, from which the *Dharma* – and all things Japanese – would go out to conquer the world. It meant that apocalypse – at first in the shape of a Mongol invasion – would surely come.

Nichiren's role, as he saw it, was to cure the country of its social and political disorders by uniting it under the banner of the *Lotus Sutra* and rooting out all the other schools which had led to the poisoning of the Japanese state and soul. He denounced Shingon and the Amidist schools for worshipping Vairocana and Amida rather than the Sakyamuni Buddha and Zen for paying attention to the historical Buddha rather than the eternal Buddha of the *Sutra*. He was a zealot, uncompromising and virulent. '*Nembutsu* is hell', he said, 'the Zen are devils; Shingon is a national ruin; and the Risshu are traitors to the country.' He was twice exiled for these views, but persecution only made him more messianic. Conze says of him drily: 'On this occasion [i.e. in the figure of Nichiren] Buddhism had evolved its very antithesis out of itself.' Neverthless Nichiren came to be widely admired for his stubborn grit and – when Mongol fleets did invade (only to be beaten back) – for his gifts as a prophet. His brand of nationalistic Buddhism, if that is what it is, remains highly influential today.

Zen

The most important of the schools that Nichiren attacked – and more important to Japanese history, in the end, than any of the devotional schools, including his own – was Zen (Chinese: Ch'an) which had probably been brought to Japan in the seventh century, but did not become popular until the beginning of the Kamukara period, when it emerged as the most significant alternative to the populism of the devotional cults.

Devotees of Zen believed that although the times might be difficult and degenerate, Enlightenment was still open to those who dared to concentrate every personal resource available on its attainment. Stripped of all ritual and doctrinal study, Zen was down to earth and practical and it stressed exactly what the devotional sects denied: self-power. For this reason, it appealed greatly to the *samurai*, who constantly lived under the shadow of death and needed to see the way they lived, not as a dead end but as something they could control as part of a general spiritual development. Thus Buddhism, in its Zen form, contributed hugely to *Bushido*, the 'Way of the Warrior', for it enabled the *samurai* to confront death calmly and it transformed their skills into adaptations of Buddhist ritual and contemplation: true martial arts such as Zen archery, judo and kendo. The goal in these arts, in the words of Robinson and Johnson:

> is to realize a perfect fusion of aesthetic perception and noumenal awareness, of stillness and motion, utility and grace, conformity and spontaneity.

By invoking a form of action beyond thought, the Zen *samurai* could learn to act, even in war, in perfect harmony with the spirit of the moment and escape from concern for his own personal safety into another (and impersonal) realm.

There are two main surviving schools in the Japanese version of Chinese Ch'an – the Lin-chi and the T'sao-tung, known as Rinzai and Soto respectively. Rinzai was brought to Japan in the late twelfth century by a monk called Eisai (1141–1215) who, after running foul of Tendai influence at the Kyoto court, eventually set up his first temple in Kamakura and forged the alliance with the warrior class that became Zen's most important social foundation. He also wrote a nationalist tract called *Propagate Zen, Protect the Country*. Soto, which is in general more quietist – hence the expression 'Rinzai is for the general; Soto is for the farmer' – was founded by Dogen (1200–1253), who may first have studied Zen under Eisai's successor. An aristocrat who had became a monk at thirteen after being orphaned, he subsequently spent four years in China, and on his return, like Eisai, he turned his back on the capital and settled in a small rural temple in an eastern province. But he attracted so many disciples there – who had perhaps read his chief work, *The Eye of the True Law*, written in Japanese – that he had to move several times. He finally settled in a mountain temple, Eihei-ji, not far from Kamakura, which remains one of the two most important centres of his school today.

The difference between Rinzai and Soto was, and remains, largely one of emphasis. Both maintained the importance of *zazen* ('sitting-cross-legged meditation') as a pure religious exercise, although in Soto, which incorporated the belief that man was already enlightened from birth, to be in *zazen* was actually to be in the enlightened state, giving thanks to the Buddha. *Zazen* in Rinzai was much more purposive; and in general the school was more militant and aggressive, continuing to make use of the shout-and-stick approach and the *koan* (the Chinese *kung-an*). Rinzai, furthermore, rejected the study of the *Sutras* as useless, but was tolerant of worldly ambition, while Soto tended to encourage book-learning and preached abandonment of fame and fortune. Today, even these differences, never great, have by and large been eroded. In the words of Wilson Ross in *his Hinduism, Buddhism, Zen*:

> In the Rinzai sect we find the dynamic character of the daring koan experiment and of lightning-like enlightenment, while the Soto School is characterised by a preference for silent sitting in zazen and the quiet deeds of everyday life. It appears [however] . . . that adherence to one sect or the other is determined largely by the spiritual bent of the monks, who are inherently suited to one tradition or the other and pursue enlightenment in a way appropriate to their character. Thus one can find in the temples of the Soto sect men of brilliant wit and dynamic character who devote themelves to the koan exercises, while on the other hand certain Rinzai monks of subdued character can scarcely be distinguished from Soto disciples.

The differences, then, between the two Zen Schools should perhaps not be stressed too much. What cannot be overemphasized, however, is the contribution that they made between them to Japanese culture. At the end of the Kamakura period, and through the age of the Ashikaga Shoguns (1335–1573) that followed, Zen monks produced huge numbers of texts in Japanese; they opened schools, devised new methods of accounting and conducted widespread trade with China. Much more importantly, however, Zen doctrine itself – with its emphasis on concrete action rather than speculative thought – came to permeate almost every aspect of the national character. A Zen-derived code of behaviour took hold, as described by Edward Conze:

Part Two: Buddhism after Buddha

> Actions must be simple, and yet have depth – and 'simple
> elegance' (wabi or sabi) became the accepted ideal of
> conduct.

Wabi (or *sabi*) was a central principle carried over through Zen into every form of human expression. It was exemplified in the tea ceremony (*cha-no yu*) that was systematized by Zen masters in the sixteenth century. (Tea was said to have been first brought to Japan by Ch'an masters as an aid to meditation.) But it found expression too, in garden and house design, calligraphy, ink painting, sculpture, pottery, music, Noh theatre and even the art of flower-arranging (*ikebana*). All these arts, at their core, are imbued with a profoundly Buddhist sentiment that combines the awareness of transiency, aloneness (no-self), compassion for living things and an understanding that the Buddha-nature is everywhere in the here and now – Enlightenment and the mundane natural world are one. This sentiment finds its best expression, perhaps, in the seventeen-syllable *haiku*, some of which were written as 'farewell songs' by Zen masters facing death:

> Fifty-three years
> This clumsy ox has managed,
> Now barefoot stalks
> The Void - What nonsense!

> Life's as we
> Find it - death too
> A parting poem?
> Why insist?

Perhaps the most famous of all *haikus*, however, was written by a Zen layman, Japan's greatest poet, Matsuo Basho, in the seventeenth century:

On this road
With no traveller
Autumn night falls.

Autumn night did fall, in a sense, on Japanese Buddhism at the end of
the Ashikaga period. For a warlord named Nobunaga (1534–1582)
ruthlessly set about the pacification and reunification of Japan – and
for this the great monasteries, being independent and often fortified
centres of power, had to be destroyed. He razed the temples and
libraries on Mount Hiei to the ground, slaughtering most of its 20,000
monks; and his successor Hyegashi did the same to the Shingon
headquarters at Negoro. Zen, which had never fortified its
monasteries, survived – many of its temples can still be seen in Kyoto.
But when unification was finally achieved in 1603 – and the Tokugawa
Shogunate was set up at Edo (modern Tokyo) – it too paid a heavy
price. For the Shogunate, which ruled Japan for over 250 years, closed
the country to foreigners and imposed an internal authoritarian
régime which stifled all innovation. New teachings and practices were
simply forbidden, as was the opening of new temples and schools.
Doctrinal disputes were decided by the state, which favoured rigid
orthodoxy, not to mention an austere and feudal Confucianism. At the
same time, in order to combat the spread of Christianity, the entire
population was required to register at an existing temple with the
result that Buddhism was increasingly seen as merely the religious arm
of the central power.

There were, for all this a few bright spots. A new form of
simplified Zen called Obaka arrived from China through the open port
of Nagasaki, along with new Chinese styles of ritual, architecture and
clothing. A number of inspirational figures also appeared on the home
front, among them Hakuin Zenji (1685–1768), a much-revered monk

who reformed Rinzai Zen, restored the use of *koan* and laid down the template for the development of Zen down to the present day. It was Hakuin who coined the famous koan of 'The Sound of One Hand Clapping,' described by Paul Reps in his book *Zen Flesh, Zen Bones*, although used, perhaps as a set text, by another master:

> The master of Kennin Temple was Mokurai, Silent Thunder. He had a little protegé named Toyo who was only twelve years old. Toyo saw the older disciples visit the master's room each morning and evening to receive instructions in sanzen, or personal guidance, in which they were given koans to stop mind-wandering.
>
> Toyo wished to do sanzen also. 'Wait a while' said Mokurai. 'You are too young'.
>
> But the child insisted, so the teacher finally consented.
>
> In the evening little Toyo went at the proper time to the threshold of Mokurai's sanzen room. He struck the gong to announce his presence, bowed respectfully three times outside the door, and went to sit before the master in respectful silence.
>
> 'You can hear the sound of two hands when they clap together', said Mokurai. 'Now show me the sound of one hand'.
>
> Toyo bowed and went to his room to consider this problem. From his window he could hear the music of the geishas. 'Ah, I have it!' he proclaimed.

The next evening, when his teacher asked him to illustrate the sound of one hand, Toyo began to play the music of the geishas.

'No. no', said Mokurai. 'That will never do. That is not the sound of one hand. You've not got it at all'.

Thinking that such music might interrupt, Toyo moved his abode to a quiet place. He meditated again. 'What can the sound of one hand be?' He happened to hear some water dripping. 'I have it', imagined Toyo.

When he next appeared before his teacher, Toyo imitated dripping water.

'What is that?' asked Mokurai. 'That is the sound of dripping water, but not the sound of one hand. Try again'.

In vain Toyo meditated to hear the sound of one hand. He heard the sighing of the wind. But the sound was rejected. He heard the cry of an owl. This was also refused. The sound of one hand was not the locusts.

For more than ten times Toyo visited Mokurai with different sounds. All were wrong. For almost a year he pondered what the sound of one hand might be.

At last little Toyo entered true meditation and transcended all sounds. 'I could collect no more', he explained later, 'so I reached the soundless sound'.

Toyo had realized the sound of one hand.

Buddhism's Struggle for Survival

In 1868 – partly under pressure from the West and partly inspired by a Shinto nationalism hostile to Buddhism – a coup-d'état finally restored the imperial régime. Shinto became the state religion, the Meiji Emperor was given the status of a god, and Buddhism was disendowed – its land expropriated and its temples either closed or destroyed. Paradoxically, however, this seemed to give the faith a new lease of life, for Buddhist schools and universities were established once the persecution had diminished and contacts were made with other Buddhist countries and with the West. New editions of Pali, Sanskrit, Tibetan and Chinese texts were produced.

Buddhism retained its popularity among ordinary people, meanwhile – although in the 1920s and 1930s it was Nichiren, with its nationalist message of Japan as a promised Buddha-land destined to spread the *Dharma* abroad, that came to the fore. Though almost all Buddhist schools acquiesced in the Japanese conquests of Manchuria and Korea and condoned Japan's entry into World War II, it was Nichiren that set the brutal overall tone.

After the War, the American occupying forces' 'land reforms' brought financial ruin to the monasteries and led to a widespread revival of Nichiren among the laity. Perhaps forty per cent of all those who call themselves Buddhists in Japan today are members of Rissho Kosei-kai and Soka Gakkai, two of the many so-called 'New Religions' – both of them lay offshoots of Nichiren. In some ways they resemble American organizations like the Kiwanis or the Shriners, in that they offer practical support for their members and stress both wordly success and involvement with social issues. (They are also very careful to stress that their ultimate aim is world peace.) Conze says of them somewhat drily:

> This is one of Buddhism's more successful attempts to
> come to terms with the 'American Century'. One may
> well doubt whether capitalism has been any more kind to
> the Buddhists than communism.

In the meantime, the traditional schools have still managed to preserve an impressive roster of temples, clergy and lay followers, for they too have regenerated themselves, to a degree, in response to the modern world. (Jodo-shu and Jodo Shinsu, for example, still have considerable followings.) Serious meditation, however, has on the whole become neglected. Zen meditation halls, though open to the laity, are ill attended – which may explain why so many Zen *roshi*, particularly, have come to the West in search of fallower ground, following in the footsteps of the first able interpreter of Zen in the West, Dr. D.T. Suzuki.

Afterword:

The Present

There is a melancholy note that has sounded out from within Buddhism, almost from its beginnings. This plangency is variously expressed: 'Everything is impermanent, even the power of the Buddha's example'; 'We live in a degenerate age in which self-effort is no longer enough to achieve awareness'; and, especially, 'The Buddha's teachings will lose their efficacy after two-and-a-half thousand years and it will take many thousands more before the Buddha-to-Be, Maitreya, appears in the world to renew them . . .'

The 2,500th anniversary of the Sakyamuni Buddha was, in fact, celebrated in India in the 1950s; and shortly thereafter the young Dalai Lama fled from Tibet, as a Chinese army set about ruthlessly destroying every last trace of *Vajrayana* Buddhism. The earlier pessimism suddenly seemed to be completely justified; the prediction was fully accurate. Everywhere the light of the *Dharma* was being extinguished. The shamanic Buddhism of Outer Mongolia had already been destroyed by Soviet Communism. In China, Buddhism had been denounced as parasitic and its monks and nuns had been defrocked or imprisoned or worse. In Japan, the faith had been undermined by American occupation and popular forms of Buddhism were emerging which bypassed the whole monastic tradition, and were only really Buddhist in name.

Worse was yet to come. Following the path of North Korea, Buddhism was virtually eliminated in Vietnam, Laos and Cambodia, the victim, in equal parts, of two branches of materialism: American capitalism-in-arms and Marxist-Leninism. Burma fell to a heavy-handed dictatorship. In Thailand, Buddhist monks were co-opted into an anti-communist campaign – some were even seen blessing American tanks. The only bright spot seemed to be the conversion to Buddhism of huge numbers of lowest-caste Indian 'Untouchables' – called by Mahatma Gandhi the *Harijan*, or 'Children of God' – although that had largely been a political decision, taken by their leaders.

There is no inherent reason for the endurance of any religion. Mithraism and Manichaeanism – extremely powerful in their day – both disappeared, after all. Christianity vanished from its Eastern heartland under Muslim occupation and, in this century, Confucianism has ceased to be a religion. It is always possible for the book to be closed and for us to say: 'Ah yes, Buddhism – a very beautiful religion indeed. A doctrine of salvation even older than Christianity, yet completely unmarked by violence, religious wars, inquisitions, crusades or the burning of witches. It flourished in some of the most remarkable periods in human history and it left behind it astonishing buildings and works of art, a vast literature and an extremely sophisticated and dense metaphysics – which we no longer understand.'

And yet Buddhism has proved itself remarkably adaptable over its (now) more than 2,500 years. From *Sutras* to *Hinayana* to *Mahayana* to *Tantra* to *Zen*, it has consistently found ways to accommodate a new environment or altered social conditions, without losing sight of its central aim of Enlightenment, or the road to it via compassion. It continues to maintain: 'Right beliefs, right knowledge, right conduct' – a central message with which few could argue. Also, being a doctrine without a creator god, it continues to be extremely tolerant of other forms of worship.

It is true that Buddhism has so far been ill-equipped to withstand the inroads of materialism and scientific rationalism (from which Christianity, too, has taken a bludgeoning). Its traditions of pacifism and acceptance have precluded any fighting back. Yet in the past it has taken five or six hundred years for it to emerge each time in a new accommodative form – so by that reckoning another of its creative transformations is soon due. One prophecy has it that after being played out in the East it will appear once more, newly energized, in 'the land of the red-faced people' – which many have assumed to mean the West. And indeed there are signs that more and more urbanists and professionals in the West, dissatisfied with the loss of the magical and spiritual in their lives, are already turning to Buddhism – just as the early town-dwellers in India did during the Sakyamuni Buddha's earthly mission.

So far the Western approach to Buddhism has been fairly haphazard and scattergun. Individuals have tended to cherry-pick for what suits them in available schools, without approaching the central mystery of awareness in any disciplined way. Buddhist monks and adepts living in the West as exiles from their native countries have equally - with some notable exceptions like Dr. Suzuki - found it difficult to adapt the Buddhist message, and themselves, to Western life. But the ground has already been laid. For Western philosophers from Schopenhauer onwards – and psychologists like Jung – have found important resonances for their ideas within Buddhism. Physicists, too, like Fritjof Kapra, have begun to mine Buddhist metaphysics for its understanding of the nature of reality. Many of the central texts have been translated, just as they were in China before the characteristic forms of Chinese Buddhism appeared. Westerners have travelled east to study in monasteries, as the founders of the Japanese schools did in China. Buddhist missionaries have appeared in the West, as they did once in Central Asia and Tibet. Comparative scholars have done their work. All that remains, perhaps, is for time to pass, time that will allow for consolidation and for a fresh – and perhaps characteristically Western – pathway to Enlightenment to unfold.

Bibliography

Batchelor, Stephen, *The Jewel in the Lotus: A Guide to the Buddhist Traditions of Tibet*, Wisdom Publications, 1987.

Carus, Paul, *The Gospels of Buddha*, Oneworld, 1994.

Connolly, Holly and Peter, *Buddhism*, Stanley Thones, 1992.

Conze, Edward, Buddhism: *Its Essence and Development*, Cassirer, 1960.

Conze, Edward, *A Short History of Buddhism*, Oneworld, 1993.

Erricker, Clive, *Buddhism*, Hodder and Stoughton, 1995.

Gelsin, Rupert, *The Foundations of Buddhism*, Oxford University Press, 1998

Hope, Jane and Van Loon, Borin, *Buddha For Beginners*, Icon Books, 1994.

Humphreys, Christopher, *A Popular Dictionary of Buddhism*, Curzon Press, 1975.

Bibliography

Ikeda, Daisaku, *The Living Buddha*, Weatherhill, 1995.

Ling, Trevor, *The Buddha*, Penguin Books, 1973.

Pagels, Elaine, *The Gnostic Gospels*, Weidenfeld & Nicholson, 1979.

Palmer, Martin, *Elements of Taoism*, Element Books, 1991.

Rahula, Walpola, *What the Buddha Taught*, Wisdom Books, 1985.

Reps, Paul, *Zen Flesh, Zen Bones*, Pelican Books, 1972.

Robinson, Richard H. and Johnson, Willard L., *The Buddhist Religion, A Historical Introduction*, Wadsworth Publishing, Third Edition, 1982.

Scott, David and Doubleday, Tony, *Elements of Zen*, Element Books, 1992.

Snelling, John, *The Buddhist Handbook: A Complete Guide to Buddhist Teaching and Practice*, Century Hutchinson, 1987.

Snelling, John, *Elements of Buddhism*, Element Books, 1990.

Stokes, Gillian, *Buddha: A Beginner's Guide*, Hodder & Stoughton Educational, 2000.

Thomas, Edward J., *The Life of the Buddha*, Kegan Paul, 1949.

Watts, Alan, *The Way of Zen*, Penguin Books, 1962.

Index

Index

Index

'Great Seal' (*Mahamudra*) 167

gurus 162, 187

H

harmlessness (*ahimsa*) 22, 114

Hejevra Tantra 178, 179

Hinayana 124, 125, 148, 159

Hinduism 15 – 20, 117, 164, 189

History of Buddhism in India and Tibet 176

Hua-yen school 213 – 14

Hui Yuan 157 – 8

I

ignorance 73, 74, 75, 76

impermanence (*samsara*) 56, 60 – 1, 65 – 6, 106 – 7, 136

Indonesia 192

Indra 20, 129, 168

Infinite 126

J

Jains 21 – 2, 31, 189, 190

Japan 134, 157, 164, 195, 212 – 26

K

Kadampa 177 – 8

Kargyu 178 – 80

karma 19, 36, 58, 64, 67 – 72, 87, 112, 141

knowledge 104, 137

Korea 210, 211 – 12, 230

Kushans 144, 145, 146

L

laity (*upasakas*) 43 – 4, 91, 93, 94, 108 – 13, 122

lamas 181

Laos 191, 193, 230

M

Mahamaya (Maya), mother of Buddha 26 – 7, 118

Mahapajapati 27, 46, 47

Mahasanghikas 103 – 4, 122, 123, 132, 135

Mahayana 'The Great Vehicle or Course' 103, 104, 108, 120, 122 – 58, 191

    and celestial *bodhisattvas* and

        Buddhas 130 – 4

    in China 150 – 8

    doctrines of 125 – 6

    and the nature of reality 135 – 8

    schools 138 – 46

    spead of 143 – 50

Maitreya 130, 215

mandala 166 – 7, 170 – 1, 187, 188

Manjusri 131

mantras 161, 165 – 6, 187

Mantrayana 161, 162

Mara 33 – 7, 52

meditation 205 – 6

meditation (*dhyana*) 18, 32, 36, 69, 85, 129

    in the Ch'an School 198 – 9, 205 – 6

mental discipline (*samahdi*) 57, 85

mental formations 64

merits 110 – 11, 186

Middle Way 33, 41, 56, 59, 84

Index

mind 63, 73, 140

missionaries 115, 116

monasteries 46 – 7, 102, 214, 215

monastic rules 45, 91 – 3, 99 – 101

monks and nuns 43 – 7, 90 – 4, 109 – 13, 121

    in China 154 – 5

    in Japan 213 – 19

morality (*sila*) 47, 57 – 8, 68 – 71, 83 – 5, 128

mudras 187

Muslim invasions 189, 208

N

Nagarjuna 139, 140, 155

Name and Form 73

Nepal 143, 189, 190

nirvana 40, 58, 79 – 82, 81 – 2, 105

Nyingma 180 – 2

O

ordination 44, 45, 90 – 1

P

pacceka buddhas 90, 126

Pali canon 25, 109, 117, 123, 162

paranirvana 52, 54

patience (*ksanti*) 128

perception (*skandhas*) 42, 44, 64

Personalists (*Pudgalavadins*) 104 – 6

pre-Buddhist cults 117 – 18

Pure Land School 134, 158, 196 – 8, 207, 211, 217

Q

Questions of King Milinda 115

R

Rahula, son of Buddha 28, 30, 46

Rains Retreats 46

rebirth 19, 22, 36, 66 – 72, 74, 76, 77, 112

restlessness 88

Rig Veda 17

Rinzai 220, 221, 224

ritual objects 168

Rock Edicts 114

roshi (Ch'an master) 198

'royal discipline' (*raja-yoga*) 31 – 2

S

sacred places 117 – 20

sacrificial rituals 21, 22

saddhu (wandering holy man) 30, 163

Saghamitta 121 – 2

saints (*arhants*) 43, 89 – 90, 102 – 3, 111, 124

Sakya 178

Sakyamuni see Buddha

salvation 59, 153

Samantabhadra 131 – 2

Sangharaskshita 48

Sanskrit 17

Sanskrit literature 122 – 3, 145, 149

Sayings of the Ancient Worthies 203

schisms 101 – 8

schools of Buddhism 102 – 8, 116 – 17, 122

    in China 194 – 210

    in Japan 212 – 17

Index

Managing Business Risk

THE POWER OF APPLIED EXPERTISE

In an increasingly complex world, competence alone is rarely enough to provide a winning edge. You need both leading edge insight and the hands-on expertise to be able to make your insights count.

DNV has been in the business of managing risk since 1864. Our team of engineers, consultants and analysts combine to provide deep, cross-functional expertise. Talk to us and learn how you can leverage the power of applied expertise.

Classification • Verification • Technology qualification • Safety, health and environmental risk management • Enterprise risk management • Asset risk management

www.dnv.com

MANAGING RISK DNV

NINTH EDITION

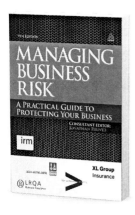

Managing Business Risk

A practical guide to protecting your business

Consultant editor:
Jonathan Reuvid

KoganPage

LONDON PHILADELPHIA NEW DELHI

First published in Great Britain and the United States in 2003 by Kogan Page Limited

Second edition 2005
Third edition 2006
Fourth edition 2007
Fifth edition 2008
Sixth edition 2009
Seventh edition 2010
Eighth edition 2012
Ninth edition 2013

120 Pentonville Road	1518 Walnut Street, Suite 1100	4737/23 Ansari Road
London N1 9JN	Philadelphia PA 19102	Daryaganj
United Kingdom	USA	New Delhi 110002
www.koganpage.com		India

© Kogan Page and individual contributors, 2003, 2005, 2006, 2007, 2008, 2009, 2010, 2012, 2013

The right of Kogan Page and individual contributors to be identified as the author of this work has been asserted by them in accordance with the Copyright, Designs and Patents Act 1988.

ISBN 978 0 7494 6684 8
E-ISBN 978 0 7494 6685 5

British Library Cataloguing-in-Publication Data

A CIP record for this book is available from the British Library.

Library of Congress Cataloging-in-Publication Data

Managing business risk : a practical guide to protecting your business / [consultant editor] Jonathan Reuvid. -- 9th ed.
    p. cm.
  ISBN 978-0-7494-6684-8 – ISBN 978-0-7494-6685-5 1. Risk management. I. Reuvid, Jonathan.
HD61.M26 2013
658.15′5–dc23
                    2012037098

Typeset by Saxon Graphics Ltd, Derby
Print production managed by Jellyfish
Printed and bound by CPI Group (UK) Ltd, Croydon, CR0 4YY

CONTENTS

4.5   **Thailand: manageable business risk** 205

Eric Lynn, mylifeQs

4.6   **South-East Asia: managing risk regionally through delegation** 213

Stephen Gill, Stephen Gill Associates

FOREWORD

The world will not evolve past its current state of crisis by using the same thinking that created the situation.

Albert Einstein

As I write this foreword, the chairman and chief executive officer of Barclays Bank have just resigned in the wake of accusations that the bank colluded with others to fix inter-bank lending rates. With the bank losing both its reputation and its market value, the word on everyone's lips is *culture*.

This follows on the heels of recent governance, control and risk management failures at Olympus in Japan, where the president and CEO discovered corruption driven by an inappropriate risk culture, and BP's Gulf of Mexico and Texas City disasters, where again the firm's culture was held ultimately accountable for loss of life and massive environmental contamination.

Such recent failures underpin earlier risk culture failures at Enron, WorldCom, Parmalat, Woolworth and elsewhere.

So why else is risk culture so important? All organizations need to take risks if they are going to achieve their objectives. The prevailing risk culture within an organization, or parts of an organization, can make it significantly better or worse at managing risk. Risk culture has a significant impact on an organization's capability successfully to take strategic risk and deliver on performance promises. Organizations with inappropriate risk cultures will find themselves allowing activities that are totally at odds with stated policies and procedures, or operating completely outside these policies. An inappropriate risk culture means not only that certain individuals or teams will undertake these activities but that the rest of the organization ignores, condones or does not see what is going on. At best this hampers the achievement of strategic, tactical and operational objectives. At worst it will lead to serious reputational and financial damage.

Problems with risk culture are frequently found at the root of organizational scandals and collapses. Following the global financial crisis, the Walker report into corporate governance of UK banks concluded: 'The principal emphasis is in many areas on behaviour and culture, and the aim has been to avoid proposals that risk attracting box-ticking conformity as a distraction from, and alternative to, much more important (though often much more difficult) substantive behavioural change.' The Baker report into BP's Texas City explosion in 2005 concluded that deficiencies in leadership, competence, communications and culture led to the circumstances that caused the deaths of 15 people.

Risk culture is not always about taking too much risk: the challenge is that certain cultures may be so good at developing and implementing formal processes and frameworks that they stifle the risk taking necessary for successful innovation. The erstwhile film maker, Eastman Kodak was a leading brand for over one hundred years, yet its strategic failure to reinvent itself and exploit digital technology led to a descent into Chapter 11 bankruptcy in 2012. Its culture meant it avoided risky decisions, in exchange for a focus on procedures and policies that maintained the status quo. By contrast, the Danish toy maker LEGO has used its positive embedded risk culture to reinforce its market positioning and business success.

In other situations, cultures can make it virtually impossible to embed the risk attitudes and behaviours that guide appropriate action outside of rules and policies, ultimately leading to uncontrolled risk taking. The causes of the global financial crisis include a considerable element of such behaviour.

We live in a world which continues to change rapidly, particularly with the global move from a West-centred to an East-centred economy. A good understanding of culture, and specifically how culture differs by race, religion and nationality, is therefore a key business competency. Changing patterns of work and the use of newer technologies such as social networking media, coupled with increasingly reduced product development life cycles, add to volatility in today's organizations. All these elements conspire to mean that, whilst formal risk management codes and processes remain important, increasingly it is the people element in risk management that makes the difference between merely competent and truly great companies.

The Institute of Risk Management has recently published guidance to boards in this key area of risk management, addressing:

- lack of board direction in respect of the desired risk culture;
- lack of clear understanding of the current culture;
- lack of clarity over how to embed enterprise risk management.

The guidance follows a similar guidance paper last year on risk appetite and tolerance, another vitally important risk topic for boards to consider.

With over 4,000 members in over 100 countries, the IRM is the leading educational body for the enterprise risk management profession. Our approach to consultation papers mirrors that which we recommend to risk professionals in business, namely working with colleagues from across all the professions to develop practical, workable solutions. We believe strongly in the need to balance leading academic business school approaches with practical 'hands-on' tools and techniques: indeed, all of our certified qualifications and short courses are designed with this in mind.

Steve Fowler
Chief Executive
Institute of Risk Management

CONTRIBUTORS' NOTES

Geert Aalbers is Control Risks' General Manager for Brazil and Director of Corporate Investigations in Latin America. As a senior member of the corporate investigations department and the company's management team, Geert frequently works alongside leading law firms to support clients with complex investigations into fraud, corruption and other integrity breaches. He also works closely with specialist practitioners advising global clients on operational risk management challenges, particularly related to political, integrity and security risks.

Before joining Control Risks, Geert was Chief Financial Officer of Makro Venezuela, a subsidiary of Netherlands based SHV Group and a Director at consultancy Roland Berger. Geert graduated *cum laude* in corporate law from Erasmus University in Rotterdam where he completed a European Masters in Law and Economics, having finalized with a thesis at Oxford University. He holds an Executive MBA from Business School São Paulo where he is currently a lecturer in Corporate Risk Management. He sits on the International Bar Association's Expert Panel for Anti-Corruption and is a member of the Association of Certified Fraud Examiners.

Chietigj Bajpaee is an associate fellow at Vivekananda International Foundation, a New Delhi-based public policy think-tank. He has worked with several political risk consultancies and public policy think tanks, including Control Risks, IHS Global Insight, the Centre for Strategic and International Studies and International Institute for Strategic Studies. He completed his graduate and undergraduate studies at the London School of Economics and Wesleyan and Oxford Universities and is a doctoral candidate at King's College, London. He has lived in India, China, the United Kingdom and the United States.

Ben Cattaneo is a manager, Accenture Risk Management and works within Accenture's Cross-Industry and Resources team. Based in London, Ben possesses over 12 years' experience helping clients assess, quantify and manage political risk, design and implement enterprise risk management (ERM) programmes and manage acute crises. He combines deep risk management expertise with strategy and change management skills to help clients become and remain high-performing businesses.

Timothy Copnell is an Associate Partner at KPMG and the founder of KPMG's Audit Committee Institute – a body established ten years ago to work with audit committee members and help enhance their awareness, commitment and ability to implement effective audit committee processes. Timothy provides both training and risk and corporate governance advice to individual boards, board sub-committees and non-executive directors in both the private and public sectors. He is a past winner of the 'Accountant of the Year' award for his work with audit committees.

Sverre Danielsen is Head of Financial Solutions at the Risk Management and Corporate Responsibility Practice of DNV KEMA.

Dr oec HSG Mukadder Erdoenmez is Regional Casualty Manager for XL's Upper Middle Market operation and responsible for the Casualty book for mid-sized customers. In addition to his Underwriting role, Mukadder is accountable for the strategic projects of the unit on a worldwide basis (excluding the United States). Previous to his underwriting role he has over ten years' experience in strategic consulting within XL and several consulting companies.

XL was formed in 1986 in response to the unmet risk management needs of 68 of the world's largest companies. Today, XL Insurance provides industrial, commercial and professional services to firms around the world. Offering a wide range of insurance products, XL Insurance is a solution-oriented underwriter supporting clients with technical expertise, flexibility and responsiveness.

Paul Eccles Is a Partner and Head of Insurance at Shoosmiths. Paul works for corporate clients and insurers alike in the field of Insurance services including policy disputes, Employers ad Public Liability, Product Liability and Industrial Disease as well as assisting corporate, commercial, banking and real estate clients on insurance related issues arising from transactional work.

Thomas Favaro is Control Risks' Analyst for the Mercosur countries (Brazil, Argentina, Paraguay and Uruguay). As a member of the global risk management department, he provides political, operational and security risk analysis for subscription services as well as undertaking tailored services for clients operating in the region. Prior to joining Control Risks, Thomaz worked as Assistant Editor of Foreign News at *Veja*, Brazil's largest weekly news magazine, and as a freelance correspondent for several media outlets in Buenos Aires and London. He holds an MSc on Comparative Politics of Latin America from the London School of Economics and a BA in journalism from the Univsarsity of São Paulo.

Carlo Gallo is an independent political risk analyst, with particular expertise on Russia and the FSU. Until April 2012 he was Control Risks' lead political, operational and security risk analyst for Russia and other parts of the FSU. In that capacity, Carlo has helped many FTSE 100 companies understand and mitigate their exposure to political, regulatory, integrity, supply chain, criminal and security risks in the region. His work included dozens of substantial, in depth, written reports spanning the oil and gas, banking, retail, healthcare and automotive sectors in Russia. Before joining Control Risks In late 2005, Carlo developed an academic background, including a highly commended PhD in Russian politics from the LSE, and lecturing and research positions at top UK universities. He has extensive media experience, including TV interviews with the BBC, Bloomberg, CNBC, CNN and with printed media.

Allan Gifford is a Principal in DNV KEMA's Enterprise Risk Management Practice with experience designing, implementing and assessing enterprise-wide risk management frameworks for organizations globally. He is a member of the Institute of Risk Management and Institute of Operational Risk.

DNV KEMA Energy & Sustainability, with more than 2,300 experts in over 30 countries around the world, is committed to driving the global transition toward a safe, reliable, efficient and clean energy future. With a heritage of nearly 150 years, the company specializes in providing world-class, innovative solutions in the field of business and technical consultancy, testing, inspections and certification, risk management and verification. As an objective and impartial knowledge-based company, DNV KEMA advises and supports organizations along the energy value chain: producers, suppliers and end-users of energy and equipment manufacturers, as well as government bodies, corporations and non-government organizations. DNV KEMA Energy & Sustainability is part of DNV, a global provider of services for managing risk with more than 10,000 employees in over 100 countries. For more information on DNV KEMA Energy & Sustainability, visit www.dnvkema.com.

Stephen Gill is a an experienced business manager and company director with a strong engineering background, and with much of his experience gained at senior management or board level.

Stephen's active involvement in Asia began several years ago after being brought in to manage a failing joint venture company in Shanghai; he has experienced at first-hand the highs and lows of business in Asia and, more recently, South East Asia and Asia Pacific. Currently based in Singapore and the United Kingdom, he is developing and managing the Southeast Asia and Asia Pacific operation for an international engineering group.

Stephen is a regular contributor to business and technical magazines and books, as well as a conference speaker. He has an MBA from Loughborough University and and LLM (Business Law) from De Montfort University. In 2011, Stephen Gill Associates received the prestigious ACR News 'Consultant of the Year' Award.

Cor Groenveld is the Global Head of Food Supply Chain Services at Lloyd's Register Quality Assurance (LRQA). He has a degree in Food Technology and spent ten years in the food industry before joining LRQA. His background includes being a Quality Assurance Manager, working in product development and production as well as logistics in the confectionery and convenience food industry. Before taking on his current role, Cor has been an assessor manager, lead auditor, trainer and service developer at LRQA.

Cor's other relevant activities include: Chairman of the Board of the Foundation for Food Safety (owner of the FSSC 22000 certification scheme); Representative of the Independent Organization for Certification (IIOC) in the Food Safety Working Group of the European Accreditation Committee; and Member of the ISO working group for Food and Food Safety standards ISO 22000), the Food Committee of the Dutch Normalization Committee (NEN) and the Technical Committeee of the Global Food Safety Initiative (GFSI).

Gunnar Hauland PhD is a Principal Specialist at DNV KEMA's Energy & Sustainability Practice.

Chris Hodge is Director of Corporate Governance at the Financial Reporting Council. Chris is responsible for the UK Corporate Governance Code which sets government standards for companies listed in the United Kingdom, and for related guidance to boards on topics such as risk management and internal control and the role of audit committees.

The Financial Reporting Council is the United Kingdom's independent regulator responsible for promoting high quality corporate governance and reporting to foster investment.

Simon King is a Principal in DNV's Risk Management & Corporate Responsibility Practice. An enterprise risk management professional with 15 years' experience, he has delivered assurance to boards of listed companies and public interest bodies, led the development of risk management frameworks and been responsible for the strategic planning and delivery of assurance over the effectiveness of internal control and good corporate governance practices. He is a Chartered Accountant and trainer for the Institute of Risk Management's Fundamentals of Risk Management Course.

Jocelyn Kirkwood is the Professional Support Lawyer for Shoosmiths' National Commercial litigation team. Based in the Birmingham office, Jocelyn has over 10 years' commercial litigation experience acting for corporate clients in business critical, high-value, complex multi-national disputes,

Hans Laessøe MSc is the LEGO Group head and Senior Director on Strategic Risk Management – a function he established in 2007. He has more than 30 years' of LEGO Group experience from a number of areas, which provides him with a strong business insight and network to drive the task of strategic risk management. Hans is a founding member of a Danish ERM network as well as an executive member of the European Council of Risk Management and a Specialist member of the IRM. He is also a member of RIMS where he serves at the 'Strategic Risk Management Council'. The LEGO Group and Hans Laessøe have won multiple European awards for the risk management approach implemented, and he has authored or co-authored articles in international magazines plus speaking engagements at international risk management conferences.

The LEGO Group is the third largest toy manufacturer in the world in terms of sales with its headquarters in Billund, Denmark. Based on the LEGO brick, its portfolio encompasses some 25 product lines sold in more than 130 countries. Worldwide, LEGO Group today has 10,000 employees. LEGO toys are produced in plants in Denmark, Czech Republic, Hungary and Mexico. The company remains family owned and the third generation owner serves as deputy chairman of the board on which the fourth generation owner also serves.

Eric Lehmann is Senior Manager, Risk Management and works within Accenture's Cross-Industry and Resources team. Based in London, Eric has more than 13 years' of experience advising multinationals on identifying and managing risks as well as improving their risk management capability. He has worked particularly on integrating new standards in the management of supply chain risks for a number of industries. Eric combines deep risk management expertise with strategy and change management skills to help clients become and remain high-performing businesses.

Irvine Lauder is the Internal Auditor at WMSNT Limited. He has long-term experience in internal auditing a large, national audit firm and prior to that within a large local authority.

Eric Lynn is a Leadership Coach, Cultural Integration and Change Consultant with a reputation for asking powerful questions which engage people in organisations to achieve meaningful results. He founded his first training company in the late 1980s and since the mid-1990s has consulted on a range of high-profile international projects and corporate acquisitions with a focus on getting leaders to really work together. Educated in the UK, Eric has been based in Germany for the majority of his professional life and now lives in Berlin following an 8 year sojourn in Asia (Thailand, India, Nepal, New Zealand). mylifeQs offers Change Management and Personal Development Coaching services for corporations and individuals. The change focus: integration for international management teams and projects, as well as conflict resolution and mediation. The coaching focus: personal leadership, leadership, reorientation. Eric has also developed a unique affordable online self-coaching programme (30-Days Self-Coaching) which can be accessed via the website.

Kevin McCavish is a Partner and Head of Shoosmiths National Employment Law Team. He advises on all areas of employment law from redundancies and contractual variations to sale and purchase of businesses and senior executive severances. As a former barrister, Kevin has considerable contentious employment law experience and regularly represents clients in employment tribunal proceedings dealing with issues varying from unfair dismissal and redundancy claims to lengthy and complex discrimination cases.

Kevin regularly provides in-house training on employment law/ practices/ procedures to clients/ HR managers and lectured at Cardiff Law school, the University of Wales. He also appeared on Legal Network Television. Kevin co-authored the Tolleys and Butterworths books: *Termination of Employment*, *Employment Law* and *Working Time*. He also edited Croner's *Employment Law and the European Union* and was appointed to their editorial board. Kevin is ranked as 'a Leading Lawyer' and 'Highly Recommended' in the Legal 500 and; Tier 1 in Chambers.

Peter Maggs, CBE, has been Chief Executive of WMSNT Limited since 2008. He was previously at British Forces Post Office, where he was also Chief Executive, prior to which he held a number of Directors' appointments at the Ministry of Defence (MoD).

WMSNT Limited is a charitable company that exists to improve the quality of life of people living in the UK's West Midlands region who find it difficult or impossible to use conventional public transport, by providing effective and efficient door-to-door, fully accessible bus services.

Dr Morten Bremer Mærli is a Principal Specialist at DNV KEMA W, working in particular on security risk management. A nuclear physicist by training, Morten has hands-on expertise on Material Protection Control and Accounting practises in Europe and North-West Russia. His doctoral thesis assesses the risk of nuclear terrorism and control, verification and transparency as threat-reducing strategies.

Amanda Morrison is a Partner at KPMG. Whilst her background was initially in Audit, she has spent the latter part of her career specialising in risk management. She is currently the Deputy Risk Management Partner for KPMG in the UK and as such part of her role is to advise KPMG on its own internal risk management processes. She is also responsible for leading the enterprise risk management services that KPMG provides to its clients.

Stephan Peters is co-founder and CEO of Deposix, a leading worldwide software escrow firm. During his more than 20 years' of professional experience in the IT industry, he handled a wide range of software licensing and intellectual property concerns for his clients at Accenture and Booz & Company. Additionally, Stephan was involved in several technology startups, among others as a co-founder of WebToGo, a wireless ISP based in Munich. Stephan holds an MBA from Columbia Business School New York and is a frequent speaker and contributor to technology and business publications.

Rachel Reeves is an Associate in the Corporate department of Shoosmiths. Her areas of expertise in corporate advice include share buy backs, reductions of capital and shareholder issues, acquisitions and disposals (share and business sales and purchases) for UK and overseas clients. Rachel also deals in private equity work, acting for management teams and private equity houses.

Jonathan Reuvid has more than 25 years' experience of joint venture development and start-ups in China. An Oxford MA with a degree in Politics, Philosophy and Economics he worked first as an economist for the French national oil company, Total, before moving into financial services and consultancy. He joined a Fortune 500 US multinational in 1978, where he became Director of European Operations before engaging with China in the mid-1980s for clients and on his own behalf. In 1989 he started a third career as a writer and editor of business books for Kogan Page and has more than 80 editions of 35 titles to his name, including eight editions of *Managing Business Risk*, three editions of *The Handbook of International Trade*, five editions of *Doing Business with China*, two editions of *Business Insights: China* and investment guides to each of the European states that became EU members in 2004 and more recently Morocco. He is a founder director of a conference management company, specializing in business areas such as advanced patent management strategies and infrastructure investment.

Steven Shackleford is a professional and university academic, as well as a practitioner in Risk Management, Accounting and Internal Audit. He worked as Risk Consultant in WMSNT Limited.

WMSNT Limited is a charity that exists to improve the quality of life of people living in the UK's West Midlands region who find it difficult or impossible to use conventional public transport, by providing an effective and efficient door-to-door, fully accessible bus service.

Martin Sutherland joined Detica in 1986, gained a seat at the UK Board in 2002, became a Managing Director in 2008 and now runs Detica's business within BAE

Systems sitting on the Programmes and Support Board. Martin started his career with Detica as a technical and business consultant, focused on secure Government programmes. He provided commercial and technical advice into a significant UK procurement of US defence capability, as well as a number of secure programmes relating to the Regulation of Investigatory Powers Act (RIPA). He advanced to take account management responsibility for a number of secure Government clients, before standing up in a cross market Security Practice in 2000. After becoming Director in 2002, Martin took on a portfolio of Public Sector clients with remit to grow revenues outside of Detica's traditional secure Government footprint. He spent a year standing up Detica's NetReveal software product business before taking on his most recent role as Managing Director, leading Detica's integration into BAE Systems. He also has responsibility for supporting BAE Systems' Global Security initiative.

Prior to joining Detica, Martin started his career in technical and business consulting (now Accenture) and British Telecom. He holds a MA in Physics from Oxford University and an MSc (Distinction) in Remote Sensing from Imperial and UCL, London University.

INTRODUCTION

F or this 9th edition of *Managing Business Risk* the contents are grouped rather differently into four parts rather than the five parts of the previous edition. Part 1 explores priority risk topics on which boardroom focus is necessary in the current challenging times. In Part 2 the emphasis shifts to operational risk topics that head the attention list of many risk managers. Part 3 is a collection of chapters on risk issues of concern to specific industries, while Part 4 reprises the final two parts of the last edition with overviews of business risk in key emerging markets where EU companies are looking for new growth opportunities to balance stagnation in their own territories.

In the first chapter of the book, Chris Hodge of the Financial Reporting Council summarizes conclusions drawn from a series of meetings with directors of more than 40 UK listed companies, revealing the heightened boardroom focus on risk in the wake of the 2007 financial crisis and the preceding series of international corporate crashes. This chapter sets the tone for Part 1, which includes a series of three chapters by Allan Gifford and Simon King of DNV KEMA on the myth and reality of risk appetite, asset integrity and the upside issues of risk management. These are interspersed by chapters from Ben Cattaneo of Accenture Risk Management on the foundations of capital risk management, Paul Eccles, Rachel Reeves and Jocelyn Kirkwood of Shoosmiths on the liability of parent companies for subsidiaries' actions, and Timothy Copnell of KPMG on recent developments in corporate governance.

Part 2 opens with chapters on risk-based security as a fundamental of operational risk management by Morten Bremer Maerli of DNV KEMA and on the use of scenarios in preparing for uncertainty in which Hans Læssøe of The LEGO Group relates his company's experience of this approach. In the final chapter from Det Norske Veritas (DNV) Gunnar Hauland and Sverre Danielsen apply the experience of safety-critical industries to the management of financial risk in finance. Eric E Lehmann of Accenture writes next on new standards in supply chain risk management, followed by Stephan Peters of Deposix Software Escrow explaining how software escrow can be deployed to manage both risk and new opportunities. In the final chapter of Part 2, Steven Shackleford, Peter Maggs and Irvine Lauder of WMSNT detail their approach to managing risk economically in organizations with limited resources based on application in the charity sector.

Part 3 consists of four chapters on the application of risk management in specific sectors, followed by a more general chapter on current risks arising from TUPE or the resignation of employees without notice, written by Kevin McCavish of Shoosmiths. The first four are chapters on cyber-security risk by Nick Wilding of BAE Systems Detica, on risk management in the life sciences industry by Mukadder Erdönmez of XL Group, on independent assessment and certification in the food industry by Cor Groenveld of Lloyd's Register Quality Assurance (LRQA), and on distance learning opportunities and risks by Eric Lynn of mylifeQs.

Risk assessment of opportunities in emerging markets is reviewed in Part 4. This time, the BRIC markets are addressed in the order where the balance between opportunity and risk is perceived to be strongest. The chapter on Brazil, where Geert Aalbers and Thomaz Favaro of Control Risks expand their previous assessment, comes first. The second chapter is a reasoned update of my last overview of China, taking into account domestic political events and the depressing effect of the Eurozone crisis on its economy. Russia comes next, in Carlo Gallo's revision of his 2011 chapter, followed by Chietigj Bajpaee of the Vivekananda International Foundation detailing why the business environment of India remains disappointing, with no significant improvement in the past year. Thailand, where risks are considered manageable, is selected as an addition to our emerging markets list and is assessed by Eric Lynn of mylifeQs based on his recent experience of living and working there. In the final chapter of this edition, Stephen Gill of Stephen Gill Associates returns to his overview of South-East Asia and adds his comments on how risk can be managed throughout the region through delegation.

Across the spectrum of key industries, the 'elephant in the room' absent from the pages of this edition is the range of corporate governance risks of greatest concern to managers and their clients in the banking sector that have emerged since 2007 and have continued to surface dramatically in 2012. Indeed, there are so many now in the UK and internationally that there is ample content for a companion book on risk management issues in banking alone. Certainly, we shall be including a separate section on risk management in banking or, more broadly, the financial services sector in the next edition of this book.

Once again, I offer my sincere thanks and those of the publisher for author contributions, many through their organizations that are active members of the Institute of Risk Management (IRM). Some of these contributors have also participated as front cover sponsors or advertisers in this edition; several are regular supporters. We are especially grateful for their support, which is essential to the funding of the book. I add my personal thanks to Steve Fowler, the IRM's chief executive, as a stalwart supporter of the book through its many editions. As always, comment from readers is welcome, as are suggestions for the 'hot' topics to be addressed in the 2013 edition, for which we shall be starting to prepare the outline in January.

Jonathan Reuvid
London

PART ONE
Boardroom focus on risk issues

Risk recognition in the boardroom and its management

CHRIS HODGE, FINANCIAL REPORTING COUNCIL

Introduction

The crisis in the UK banking sector in 2007 to 2009 sent shock waves through boardrooms in all sectors of the economy. Companies that had taken it for granted that liquid markets would ensure that credit was always available found their assumptions being challenged. A significant risk had materialized that would not have appeared on the risk registers of many, if any, major companies.

This event, combined with a number of high-profile cases such as the Deepwater Horizon oil spill and a recognition that in some sectors traditional business models are becoming obsolete, has prompted company boards to reassess their approach to identifying and managing risks. Many now concede that they had taken their eye off the ball. Risk tended to be delegated to committees or management rather than be seen as a matter for the board itself. The result was 'bottom-up'-only systems that failed to address strategic or external risks that had the potential to do irreparable damage to the company's performance or reputation and therefore to its future prospects.

In 2011 the Financial Reporting Council (FRC) held a series of meetings to learn more about how boards were approaching their responsibilities for risk in challenging economic times and rapidly changing markets. Participants from over 40 major UK listed companies – including chairmen, executive and non-executive directors and heads of risk and internal audit – discussed the issues involved in assessing and managing risk. It was apparent from these discussions that there has been a step change in boards' focus on risk in the last few years, at least in the companies that we spoke to.

There were a number of recurring themes in these discussions, including:

- the importance of being clear about the respective roles of the board, board committees and management, and about the company's attitude to risk;

- the changing nature of risk, and therefore of risk management, with much more emphasis being placed on scenario planning and crisis management than might have been the case previously;
- the challenge of managing the flow of information to and from the board, and embedding the right risk and control culture throughout the organization; and
- for publicly listed companies, the challenge of reporting meaningfully to shareholders on the risks faced and how they were being mitigated.

The rest of this chapter summarizes the main points to emerge from these discussions. The FRC believes that the insights gained about the issues boards are facing, and the way they are addressing them, may be helpful to other companies in thinking about their own approach to risk.

The role of the board

Participants identified a number of different elements to the board's responsibilities for risk. They included:

- determining the company's approach to risk;
- setting and instilling the right culture throughout the organization;
- identifying the risks inherent in the company's business model and strategy, including risks from external factors;
- monitoring the company's exposure to risk and the key risks that could undermine its strategy, reputation or long-term viability;
- overseeing the effectiveness of management's mitigation processes and controls; and
- ensuring the company has effective crisis management systems.

It was important for the board to have a clear understanding of the company's overall exposure to risk, and how this might change as a result of changes in the strategy and operating environment. It was also important for boards, when developing the strategy, to agree their appetite or tolerance for individual key risks. At its simplest, this could be done by articulating what types of risk were acceptable and what were not.

Many participants emphasized that greater awareness of risk did not necessarily mean that boards were less willing to take risks. Rather, it meant that they ought to have a better understanding of the nature and extent of the risks involved in pursuing their strategy, with the result that risks were taken on consciously not unconsciously and were monitored more effectively as a consequence.

The role of board committees

Board committees were used to ensure that the board received good-quality advice and information and to enhance the quality of oversight, not as a substitute for board discussion or decision making. The committee structure through which this support was provided varied between companies. It was considered that ensuring there was an effective relationship between different board committees, and between the committees and the board, was probably more important than the exact committee structure.

Many felt that the complexity of the business and nature of the company's product should be the determining factors in selecting a committee structure. For many companies, responsibility rested with the audit committee. Separate board committees to deal with particular types of risk were more common among companies in sectors where they were exposed to significant safety, environmental or regulatory risks. Examples included compliance committees dealing with risks associated with product regulation and corporate responsibility committees dealing with ethical, environmental and safety issues, as well as risk committees in banks.

Separate committees could help if the audit committee was already heavily loaded, or if a different set of skills was needed to deal with specific risks. On the other hand, having an additional committee might create confusion about responsibilities and/or lead to risk being compartmentalized, although this could be overcome by, for example, ensuring some common membership or by holding joint meetings at least once a year.

The role of management

The role of management was to implement board policies on risk and control using effective processes and procedures. Management needed to understand the business and its risks and ensure that there was trust, openness and transparency between themselves and the board.

There was also general agreement that the ownership and day-to-day oversight and management of individual risks were rightly the responsibility of executive and line management, rather than the board, although the board needed to assure itself that these responsibilities were being carried out effectively. This could be done, for example, by ensuring that responsibility and accountability for managing specific risks were clearly allocated to individuals at all levels of the organization, and through direct contact between board members and those responsible for key risks.

Management was also responsible for identifying emerging operational risks and bringing them to the attention of the board where appropriate, and for ensuring the quality of the information that went to the board. Companies used different structures to ensure this was done effectively. Some companies, for example, had established executive committees to scrutinize the detailed risk reports from around the organization, and to ensure consistency in the information provided to the board and board committees.

The changing nature of risk

Many participants in the meetings felt that the role of the board in *identifying* risks differed for different categories of risk, with the board having particular responsibility for identifying risks linked to the strategy, or resulting from external developments such as economic or regulatory change, or changes in the market. These were characterized as 'top-down' risks, and contrasted to 'bottom-up' operational risks that it was the responsibility of management to identify and, where appropriate, bring to the attention of the board.

However, these distinctions did not hold when it came to the board's responsibility for *managing* risk. Some operational risks were just as capable of damaging the long-term viability or reputation of the company as strategic risks. In its oversight capacity the board needed to focus on those risks capable of causing most damage to the company if they materialized, regardless of how they were classified. While greater awareness of so-called 'black swan' risks was necessary, this ought not to be at the expense of addressing more 'traditional' risks.

There was evidence that boards were spending more time than previously considering key risks, both at board meetings and outside (for example, at strategy away-days). It was important that it was a proper discussion not a form-filling exercise. The value came from the discussion, which could help the board identify priorities and better appreciate potential outcomes.

The form these discussions took varied. For example, some boards would start with a blank sheet of paper, while others involved presentations from management or others, including external experts. Others looked back over the previous 12 months to identify what had caught them unawares or why they had missed their targets. Participants felt it was important for boards to challenge received wisdom and ask themselves what would be the worst thing that could happen, and to consider the cumulative impact and disruptive effect of a number of significant risks materializing at the same time.

Reputational risk was not considered a separate category, but a consequence of failure to manage other risks successfully. However, it had grown in importance, not least because the 'velocity' of risk had greatly increased. It was considered that the 'grace period' that a company had to deal with a problem before it became reputationally, and consequently financially, damaging had been greatly reduced. News of failures or problems often now had an almost instantaneous impact. Reasons given for this included developments in media and communications, including social networking, and a general mistrust of large corporations.

For these reasons, and given the inherently unpredictable nature of many risks, many participants emphasized the importance of ensuring that flexible crisis management and disaster recovery systems and business continuity plans were in place alongside control systems. In crisis situations, the chairman and chief executive had crucial roles to play which needed to be defined and agreed in advance. Getting the internal and external communication right was almost as important as dealing with the source of the problem.

The quality and use of information

Managing the flow of information to the board was considered one of the most difficult challenges by many participants. If the information was too detailed it would not help the board focus on the key issues. If it was too high-level the board might not understand the assumptions that had been made about the extent of the risk or the effectiveness of mitigation, and it could provide them with false assurance.

There was also a danger that too much reliance might be placed on models and 'traffic-light' systems that themselves made a number of assumptions that could be incorrect. These assumptions needed to be explicit, and it was important for the board and committees to indicate to management what information they needed to do their job effectively.

It was widely agreed that a focus only on 'net risk' after mitigation could be dangerous. Such an approach tended to obscure the true extent of the company's potential exposure and the interconnected nature of the risks being taken by the company. It was important that boards had a view of the risks before the application of risk mitigation policies ('gross risk'), in order to understand and challenge assumptions about the effectiveness of those policies.

Many participants mentioned the difficulty of judging when the board should be alerted to a particular risk, and how to ensure the board was made aware of an emerging risk in a timely fashion while avoiding a situation where absolutely everything was reported. The chairman and other board members needed to be involved in deciding the level at which the triggers that determined when a risk was escalated up the organization were set. Some companies had attempted to address this issue by drawing up lists of emerging risks that were presented to the board alongside the more conventional risk registers. But there might also be cultural issues to be addressed.

Sources of assurance

Effective risk oversight required a clear line of sight and accountability through the organization. There was no single correct approach, but clarity was essential.

There were a number of sources of assurance on which the board could draw. Many boards and committees now held regular meetings with managers from across the company to discuss the risks for which they were responsible and how the risks were being managed. The frequency and nature of these meetings varied, but the direct contact and accountability were felt to be important by board and committee members. As part of their management assurance process, some companies had introduced requirements for managers to self-certify as to the effectiveness of the controls related to the risks for which they were responsible.

This was in addition to independent assurance provided by the internal audit or risk management functions, which continued to play an important role. They did so by providing objective assurance to the board and committees and by challenging and/or providing advice to line management. Many participants felt that it was important that these functions reported directly to the board, or a board committee, in order to ensure that their objectivity and independence were not compromised.

Some of the companies participating in the meetings had developed 'assurance maps' that identified the different sources of assurance around key risks and controls. Those who used such maps felt they helped to focus discussion at the board and in board committees, and to identify gaps that might need to be filled by internal or external sources of assurance.

Risk and control culture

Many participants highlighted the importance of embedding the right culture throughout the company, alongside any improvements in systems and processes. There was particular emphasis on the need for openness throughout the organization.

This would enable management and staff to escalate concerns in a timely manner without fear.

It was essential that boards led by example and set the tone at the top in order to influence the behaviour of management and staff. This required leadership in particular from the chairman and chief executive, who needed to be seen to live the values they espoused. This had been attempted in different ways, for example by the use of values statements and codes of conduct, and by being clear about any risks or practices for which there was zero tolerance. Everyone in the organization needed to understand the boundaries within which they could operate and the actions they personally had to take.

It was recognized that the risk and control culture was one of the issues on which it was most difficult for boards to get assurance. The risk management and internal audit functions could play an important role, as could reports from and discussions with senior management, but some directors felt that there was no substitute for going on to the 'shop floor' and seeing for themselves. It was otherwise very difficult to judge whether risk awareness was truly embedded or whether it was seen as a compliance exercise.

The importance of ensuring that incentives were aligned with the company's strategy and risk appetite or tolerance in order to promote an appropriate culture was widely recognized. One common approach was to ensure that responsibility for managing specific risks was clearly allocated to individuals at all levels of the organization, and that their performance was measured and reflected in how they were rewarded.

Reporting to shareholders

Investors who participated in the meetings felt that there was scope for considerable improvement in reporting on risk and internal control. None of them found the tendency to produce long lists of risks useful, and felt that boards should focus especially on strategically significant risks.

Companies were understandably wary about disclosing commercially sensitive information or information that might bring about the very risks the company was seeking to avoid. Reporting on the company's risk appetite was felt to be difficult, as risk appetite was not constant but varied over time and depended on market conditions, if it could be defined at all. The same could be said about the company's overall exposure to risk. However, it was accepted that there was a need to find ways of conveying more useful information.

Suggestions for improving reporting included:

- linking reporting on risk and internal controls to discussion of the company's strategy and business model;
- explaining changes in the company's risk exposure over the previous 12 months; and
- disclosing how key risks were being mitigated.

Risk appetite: cut through the hype

ALLAN GIFFORD, DNV KEMA

Introduction

Although the term 'risk appetite' has been around for a number of years, deliberations are still taking place and documents being produced that discuss its application and purpose, with many varied ideas on what represents good practice.

It is apparent that risk appetite is not an easy concept for many organizations, in different sectors, to understand and implement. The profile of risk appetite has been given more prominence in recent times as a result of major risk events such as the global financial crisis and a large number of natural disasters. Indeed, risk appetite is now explicitly an integral part of corporate governance requirements in both the private and the public sector.

There is plenty of opinion, yet very little formal guidance. Many different definitions are used; some are popular and widely recognized. This chapter will discuss the concept of risk appetite and offer some approaches.

The challenges

There are probably only a few overarching challenges when it comes to understanding risk appetite, yet they have a wide range of implications:

1 Who cares? Different stakeholders will have different needs and expectations with regard to an organization's risk appetite.

2 It is not a single, fixed concept. There is no 'one size fits all'. There might even be a range of appetites for different risks, and these may well change over time.

3 Risk appetite should be developed in the context of the organization's risk management capability. The Institute of Risk Management defines risk management capability as a function of capacity and maturity; this is explored later in the chapter.

4 There are differing levels of risk appetite in an organization, depending on whether you are a project manager, business unit leader, board member and so on.

THE POWER TO HANDLE THE COMPLEXITY OF RISK

Swift and dramatic changes in business public scrutiny: managing risk has never

Through our extensive, worldwide experience in risk management within the offshore energy and maritime industries, we understand risk at all levels from the detailed technical through to long-term

Classification • Verification • Technology qualification • Safety, health and environmental risk management • Enterprise risk management • Asset risk management • Sustainability & innovation • Corporate responsibility

www.dnv.com

conditions, stricter regulations, intense been more critical – and more complex.

business strategy. We transfer our knowledge to other industry sectors too, thereby helping all types of organisations to handle the complexity of risk.

MANAGING RISK

5 Risk appetite should be integrated into the control culture of an organization. You would not wish to take *any* risk without some thought to how you might control it. You should be motivated to make *complete* decisions that are in accordance with your appetite for risk.

Definitions and terms

TABLE 1.2.1 Some popular definitions of risk appetite

Source	Definition
Institute of Risk Management	The amount of risk that an organization is willing to seek or accept in the pursuit of its long-term objectives.
ISO Guide 73	Amount and type of risk that an organization is willing to pursue or retain.
BS 31100	Amount and type of risk that an organization is prepared to seek, accept or tolerate.
HM Treasury	The amount of risk that is judged to be tolerable and justifiable.
Institute of Operational Risk	The operational risk [an organization] is prepared to tolerate.
Institute of Internal Auditors	The level of risk that an organization is willing to accept.
Basel	The broad-based amount of risk a company or other entity is willing to accept in pursuit of its mission or vision.
Business Continuity Institute	The willingness of an organization to accept a defined level of risk in order to conduct its business cost-effectively.

Table 1.2.1 refers to some of the more popular and widely recognized definitions of risk appetite. The following are of note:

● The Institute of Risk Management published guidance on risk appetite in 2011 (referred to later in this chapter).

● BS 31100, published before ISO 31000, introduced the word 'seek' into its definition of risk appetite.

● In 2011 HM Treasury and the Cabinet Office published a code of governance for UK central government departments that places responsibility for setting risk appetite directly with the board.

● ISO 31000 doesn't define appetite, preferring to refer to risk attitude ('organization's approach to assess and eventually pursue, retain, take or turn away from risk').

● A 2009 survey by the Association of Insurance and Risk Managers in Commerce (AIRMIC) found that 78 per cent of organizations surveyed had developed their own definition of risk appetite.

- The UK Corporate Governance Code, published in June 2010, requires all UK listed companies to report on how they have applied the main principles of the Code. One such requirement obliges the board to 'determine the nature and extent of the significant risks it is willing to take in achieving its strategic objectives'.

So it is clear that there is no single, fixed, agreed concept. Nor, in fact, should there be. Essentially, risk appetite is about risk taking within 'acceptable' limits (with the challenge being in how clearly an organization can articulate what it finds acceptable). A review of the logic behind each of the definitions suggests that the common factor in all these descriptions is the attempt to influence important decisions taken inside organizations, to get people thinking effectively about risk when making decisions, and to aid the achievement of objectives through risk management.

Interestingly though, there seems to be a divergence of opinion between whether risk appetite should be calculated *before* strategic objectives are considered and whether appetite is decided *arising from* the strategy.

'Risk appetite', 'risk attitude', 'risk tolerance ', 'acceptance risk' and 'risk capacity', among others, are all terms used interchangeably (and perhaps inconsistently), in different contexts and for different purposes, by risk practitioners to describe in one way or another the concept of risk appetite.

As shown in Figure 1.2.1, the aspects that matter and can be better defined, understood and adjusted are the:

- risk capacity;
- risk tolerance;
- risk measures.

In general, we discuss the fact that the risk appetite of an organization is the collective activities, actions and decisions that are made or generated by a combination of the risk capacity, tolerance and measures. Arguably the risk appetite therefore becomes a state of being, rather than a statement. It becomes part of the paradigm of the organization, rather than a mandate. It is both the driver of and the manifestation of the culture and resources and the way decisions are made. Consciously or subconsciously, the risk appetite is demonstrated in the behaviours of organization leaders, and will influence decisions across the whole risk management life cycle, such as:

- the risk process, eg its structure, level of detail, bureaucracy;
- the framework, eg the time, support and effort that go into integrating risk management into other activities, how risk reporting is used, and how risk information is used in decision making;
- the investment, eg budget, knowledge skills and awareness training, or the 'tools' that people have to manage risk(s).

Risk appetite is more than a number; it is a view, perception, vision, aspiration or emotion. An organization might claim that it welcomes risk; after all, risk and reward are usually strongly correlated. Therefore the important task is to understand and manage or control the risks adequately. Another organization might claim to be risk averse, cautious and careful, and seek to avoid or reduce risks as far as possible and

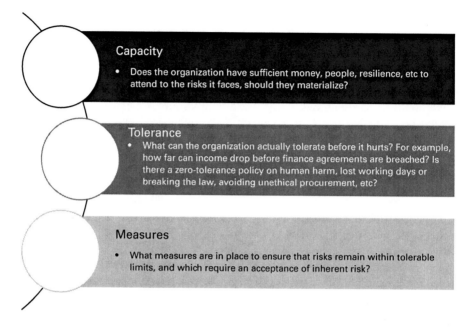

FIGURE 1.2.1 Aspects of risk appetite

as often as possible. This type of organization will accept that in doing so the rewards might be compromised, but that a stable, less volatile performance will result.

Appetite versus tolerance

The Institute of Risk Management's 2011 guidance note on risk appetite states: 'We believe that while risk appetite is about the pursuit of risk, risk tolerance is about what you can allow the organisation to deal with.' It expresses this through the illustrations summarized in Figure 1.2.2.

Figure 1.2.2a depicts expected business performance over time. In practice, performance is subject to risks that, if they materialize, could result in a range of performance (Figure 1.2.2b). This gives the potential risk 'universe' (Figure 1.2.2c). It is clear that line AC is not desirable. However, it is not necessarily obvious that line AD also might not be desirable; extreme success might itself produce additional risks. Consequently there are some outcomes (negative or positive) for which there is no tolerance. This is the area outside of the triangle AXY (Figure 1.2.2d).

The appetite for risk, however, is likely to be shown by a narrower band of performance outcomes, depicted in the triangle AMN (Figure 1.2.2e). So tolerance becomes about absolute values, eg 'We will not expose more than x per cent of our capital to losses.' Risk tolerance statements become lines in the sand beyond which the organization will not proceed without board approval (although, of course, the board may grant it), whereas risk appetite becomes about what the board wants to do.

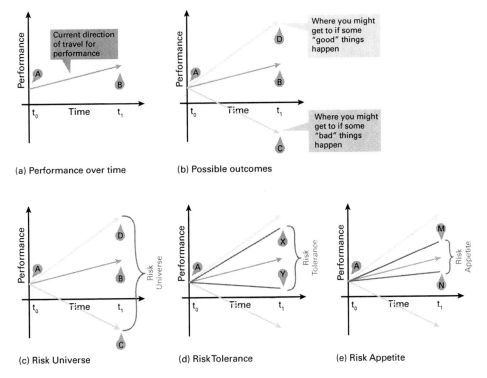

(a) Performance over time

(b) Possible outcomes

(c) Risk Universe

(d) Risk Tolerance

(e) Risk Appetite

FIGURE 1.2.2 Appetite versus tolerance
SOURCE: IRM.

Designing a risk appetite

There are a number of aspects to consider when designing a risk appetite, as illustrated in Figure 1.2.3.

The IRM's guidance paper offers a selection of 'building blocks' in developing a framework for risk appetite. Firstly, it proposes that risk appetite should be established within the context of the risk capability of the organization. This is the combined function of the organization's risk capacity (its ability to carry risks) and the risk management maturity to manage them.

Furthermore, risk appetite may be set at differing levels within the organization. The guidance paper acknowledges that this 'allocation' of risk appetite across the organization represents one of the biggest challenges.

Risk appetite must be understood in terms of the control culture. The framework encourages consideration of the propensity to take risk alongside the propensity to exercise control. It promotes the idea that the strategic level of an organization is proportionately more about taking risk than exercising control, while at the operational level the proportions are broadly reversed (of course, the extent of this differs from one organization to another).

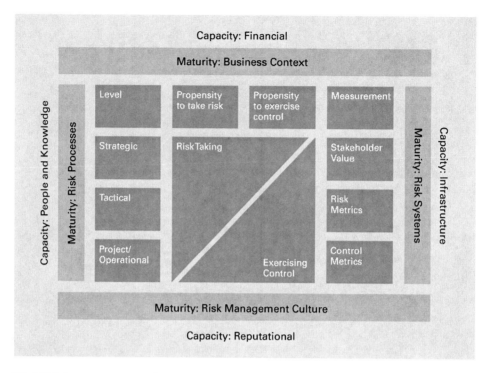

FIGURE 1.2.3 IRM framework for risk appetite
SOURCE: IRM.

Finally, the framework envisages measures of risk appetite, for stakeholder groups, and for risks and controls.

Expressing risk appetite

Risk appetite can be expressed and calculated in a number of ways. Some of the techniques widely used include:

1 *Setting a boundary on a probability and impact matrix.* This is the most widespread approach adopted by organizations. The benefit of this approach is that it can be applied across an organization and at all levels. It uses standard risk assessment terminology that individuals should already be familiar with, which makes it easy to communicate and therefore embed. It helps integrate the appetite with the control culture of the organization. A limitation to this approach, though, is that it can promote a negative view of risk, with actions taken only where risk exposures exceed a tolerance threshold line (unless the risk appetite matrix is also used to monitor upside risk).

2 *Limits or targets for key indicators.* This method of expressing risk appetite is arguably the simplest form. Indicators are expressed in any one of three categories: key risk indicators; key control indicators; and key performance indicators. The advantage of this method, similarly to the risk matrix, is that it can be used at all levels within an organization's hierarchy.

3 *Qualitative statements.* Most organizations include qualitative statements as part of their formal risk appetite approach. Such statements might include, for example:

  – 'We have a zero tolerance for deaths due to service.'
  – 'We have zero tolerance of regulatory breaches.'
  – 'We will at all times attempt to avoid negative press coverage.'
  – 'We are committed to protecting the environment.'
  – 'We will not take risks that affect the quality of customer service.'

Such qualitative statements can be very useful, as they can help to fill in the gaps of an organization's appetite for risk by expressing certain attitudes or philosophies that cannot be articulated numerically. Moreover, they can be applied to risks that are difficult to quantify effectively, as well as being easy to understand and communicate.

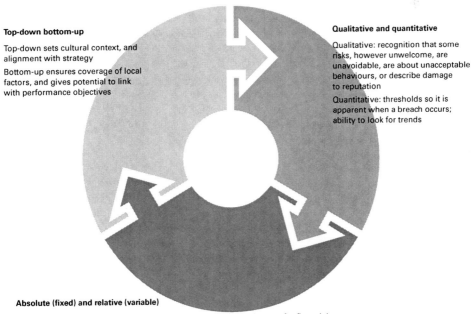

Top-down bottom-up

Top-down sets cultural context, and alignment with strategy

Bottom-up ensures coverage of local factors, and gives potential to link with performance objectives

Qualitative and quantitative

Qualitative: recognition that some risks, however unwelcome, are unavoidable, are about unacceptable behaviours, or describe damage to reputation

Quantitative: thresholds so it is apparent when a breach occurs; ability to look for trends

Absolute (fixed) and relative (variable)

Qualitative: zero tolerance for breaking the law (absolute), or tolerance for financial crime expressed not in value but in comparison with a peer group (relative)

Quantitative: monetary values, volumes, times (absolute), or losses as a proportion of profit, ratio of complaints to active customers, or project overrun as percentage of plan (relative)

FIGURE 1.2.4 Ways of expressing risk appetite

4 *Economic capital measures (balance-sheet-based expressions).* These set a level of buffer capital to help absorb unexpected loss, or allocate capital to specific business units or activities or specific risks. They express the balance an organization wants to achieve between its ability to absorb losses by holding capital and its desire to invest this capital in order to generate a positive return. Alternatively an economic capital measure might represent a hurdle rate for a project.

5 *Profit and loss measures (eg tolerable level of loss).* Popular within privately owned and publicly listed companies, these measures define a limit of negative impact on profit, perhaps expressed as a monetary amount or a percentage deviation from budget.

The Institute of Operational Risk (2009) provides guidance on the various considerations when setting risk appetite. It proposes that there are three broad considerations, illustrated in Figure 1.2.4.

Using risk appetite as the basis for risk control

Risk appetite can be used as a means of helping to decide when controls (or improvements to current controls) are required, ie when the risk exposure is outside the risk appetite area.

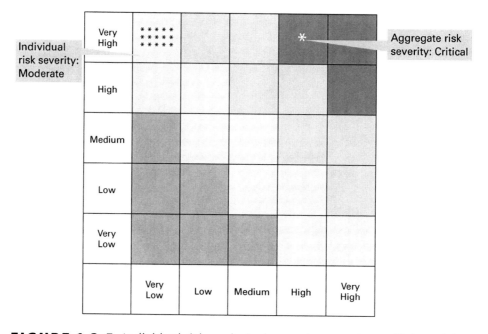

FIGURE 1.2.5 Individual risk analysis does not guarantee sufficient risk control

However, exercise caution if the risk analysis has been qualitative and the risks have been plotted individually on a risk map. In Figure 1.2.5 each individual risk has a risk severity of moderate; hence only cost-efficient risk control seems to be required. This might lead to a false sense of security, as the aggregate effect of these risks occurring might require a different approach to risk control.

Benefits

An important aspect of risk appetite is its role in supporting an organization's risk management activities. Notably, by determining its appetite for risk, an organization should have a clearer picture of its risk management objectives.

This means that the risk management function will better understand the specific risk events to which the organization needs to reduce (or improve) its exposure, and the risk categories that need more or less attention. It will also allow for more effective and efficient allocation of (risk management) resources, whether process- or people-based, by targeting them where they are needed most.

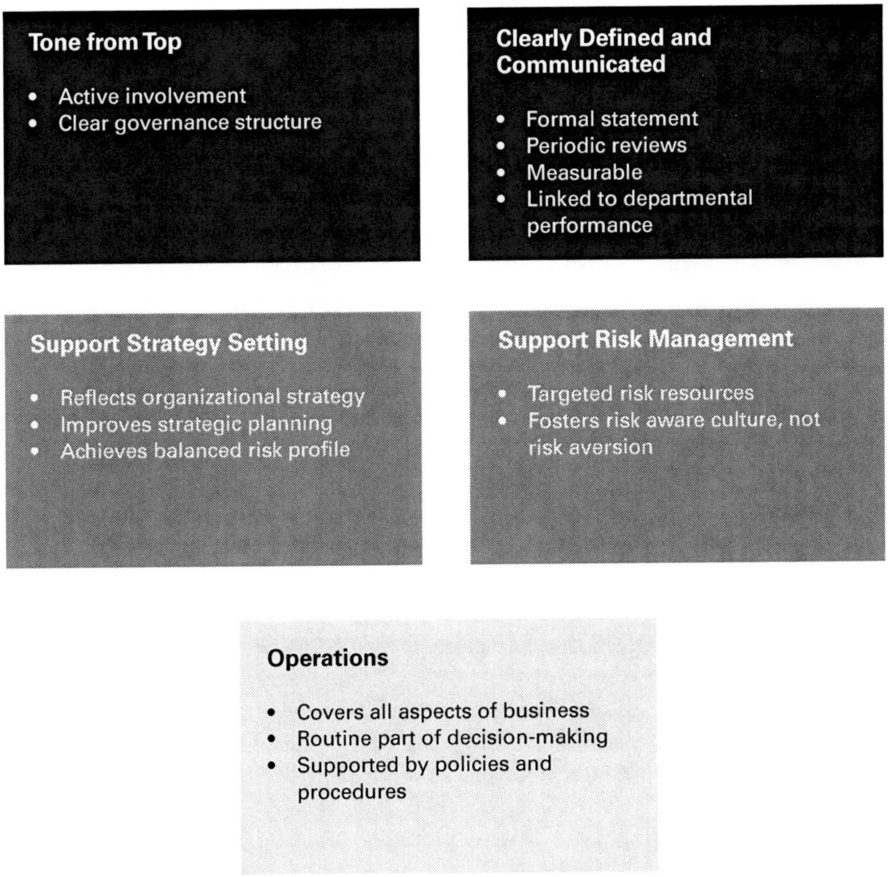

Tone from Top

- Active involvement
- Clear governance structure

Clearly Defined and Communicated

- Formal statement
- Periodic reviews
- Measurable
- Linked to departmental performance

Support Strategy Setting

- Reflects organizational strategy
- Improves strategic planning
- Achieves balanced risk profile

Support Risk Management

- Targeted risk resources
- Fosters risk aware culture, not risk aversion

Operations

- Covers all aspects of business
- Routine part of decision-making
- Supported by policies and procedures

FIGURE 1.2.6 Key attributes of risk appetite

Formally determining risk appetite should also help improve buy-in for risk management activities by highlighting the consequences of not maintaining appropriate levels of risk exposure. Moreover, if the organization's risk appetite is communicated effectively, it should promote a healthy, risk-aware culture.

All in all, risk appetite can be a complex subject that can be (and is) problematic for organizations. There are a number of key attributes of best-practice risk appetite, defined in Figure 1.2.6.

Clearly defined and communicated, risk appetite improves a board's or leadership team's risk oversight and its ability to communicate with stakeholders. Having a clear picture of your stakeholders' appetite for risk will help to set your own appetite in a manner that achieves the best balance.

A risk appetite provides a better understanding of the organization's risk categories and risk events to which it needs to reduce its exposure (or for which it is 'on appetite') or to which it should increase its exposure. This produces a better allocation of risk management resources, and may lead to more efficient decision making.

As an input to (or output of) strategy setting, a definition of risk appetite helps to make considerations and decisions around both strategic and operational performance, thereby thinking short-, medium- and long-term. It will help an organization to make decisions that support organizational success, and avoid making decisions that either expose the organization or are too conservative.

In conclusion, I would like to offer some 'top tips' for embarking upon your risk appetite journey:

1 *Decide your risk appetite statement.* It will be unique. Have the discussion around the details and principles of *your* risk management activity, and *your* appetite for risk, to help risk management become part of decision making and general management of performance.

2 *Decide on qualitative and quantitative measures.* Qualitative statements, if communicated and visible, might help create a deeper and more informed understanding of risk appetite.

3 *Think short-term and long-term.* Measure and track your appetite for different categories of risk.

4 *Incorporate risk appetite into existing activities.* Ensure risk appetite is not viewed as a compliance activity but rather as a key enabler of decision making. Use internal papers or proposals for annual budgets, change projects, infrastructure development, etc to address the effect of uncertainty on objectives and departmental and corporate risk appetites. Educate people on your risk appetite.

5 *Develop leading indicators that will prompt reconsideration of your risk appetite.* Once the appetite has been developed and implemented, the importance of effective communication and monitoring of it becomes critical. There is little point going to the time, trouble and expense of determining your appetite for risk if this is not subsequently cascaded to all of your decision makers, who, having been appropriately trained, can then understand the 'limits' within which they should be operating (note: decision makers might include important contractors or suppliers). Similarly there is no point in going to the trouble of determining your appetite for risk if you do not then monitor and measure the

state of your actual risk profile and the extent to which it deviates from your ideal risk position. Moreover, you should attempt to identify leading indicators that allow you to address any potential breaches of your appetite before they actually occur. It is essential to gather sufficient leading indicator data to allow management to take pre-emptive action before appetite is exceeded or limits are breached. It is of less value to report passively at the end of the period that appetite has been exceeded. Of course, for this to be effective, appropriate escalation procedures need to be in place to report promptly on risks that deviate from the risk appetite. While such a process is often easy to create, organizations can face significant challenges in implementing escalation processes, especially where the cultural norm might be to avoid uncertainty or cover up or suppress 'bad' news. Ensuring the successful development of risk appetite, therefore, needs to be actively endorsed by decision makers and not driven solely by the risk management team.

References

Institute of Operational Risk (IOR) (2009) *Operational Risk Sound Practice Guidance: Risk appetite*, IOR, London

Institute of Risk Management (IRM) (2011) *Risk Appetite and Tolerance Guidance Paper*, IRM, London

Capital project risk management: foundations to mastery

BEN CATTANEO, ACCENTURE RISK MANAGEMENT

The future growth of many organizations and industries – including infrastructure, energy, utilities, mining and chemicals – depends upon the successful implementation of increasingly large capital expenditure programmes. After a period of under-investment – exacerbated by the economic crisis that began in 2008 – companies in these industries are undertaking significant projects. A leading energy company recently declared a record $32.7 billion capital expenditure budget for 2012, while another announced a $15 billion infrastructure development plan for North America alone.

The International Energy Agency estimates that $1 trillion per year in new investments will be required from now until 2030. The Organisation for Economic Co-operation and Development (OECD) estimates that, by 2030, combined annual infrastructure investment requirements will represent 2.5 per cent of the world's gross domestic product (GDP). When electricity generation and energy-related infrastructure investments in oil, gas and coal are included, the annual share of GDP rises to approximately 3.5 per cent.[1] Many of these initiatives will be driven by the need to replenish proven and probable (2P) reserves and find new sources of cash flow, as existing sources of production are now entering their twilight years. There is also a global shortage of refining capacity.

While capital projects have always involved large expenditures with often long payback periods, these dynamics are increasing project complexity. Companies are undertaking increasingly large and complex projects in new geographies, working with new partners (for instance, partnerships between international oil companies and national oil companies from emerging markets) and utilizing new technologies. All of these factors increase complexity and add risk to already difficult undertakings.

Capital projects are becoming more exposed to intricate and interrelated risks, including:

- *Regulatory.* Changing regulatory regimes pose numerous new risks and requirements, particularly in the oil and gas industry, for example new environmental regulations for the coal seam gas (CSG) industry put in place in various countries or changing tax and royalty regimes.

- *Geopolitical.* Volatile political conditions in a number of geographical areas, including the Middle East, North Africa, Nigeria, Venezuela and Russia, create the potential for government interference, 'resource nationalism', civil unrest and related challenges.

- *Technical.* New and at times untested technologies may not function as planned, especially in remote locations or under severe geological or climatic conditions (eg oil and gas exploration in Arctic waters off Baffin Island and Greenland); and, for some kinds of projects such as nuclear power plants, the required skills may be in extremely short supply, since few such projects have been attempted in recent years. New technology can also create uncertainty around safety management.

- *Supplier and contractor.* The availability, competence, financial health (eg solvency), safety performance and increasing costs of contractors pose multiple challenges; companies are experimenting with risk-sharing arrangements with contractors and exploring other options to reduce supply chain complexity.

- *Governance.* New partners and new governance models such as non-operated joint ventures present consortium members with differing standards and approaches to risk.

- *Financial.* Companies have been subject to increased volatility in commodity costs and prices along with more traditional exposures, for instance swings in foreign currency spreads, counterparty credit risks and increases in the cost of insurance and options available.

- *Reputational.* The 'not in my backyard' or NIMBY syndrome can delay or prevent capital projects from getting started. At the same time the involvement of numerous stakeholders[2] presents ongoing risks to project viability. This area of risk can also create asymmetries; for instance, a reputational issue in one geographical area can have global repercussions on company investments elsewhere (eg through enhanced regulatory or community scrutiny following an environmental or social incident). 'Social licence to operate', the support of the people who live and work in the area of impact and influence of a project, is progressively becoming a necessary aspect of any capital investment.

These risks are real and the stakes are high. In the current economic environment, there is a strong need to ensure that returns on capital employed for such projects are optimized. However, senior energy industry executives estimate that over 40 per cent of oil and gas capital projects are delayed (McKenna and Wilczynski, 2006), with the average estimated at 12 months (Goldman Sachs, 2008). This results in the erosion of net present value (NPV) while affecting portfolio performance and the effectiveness of capital.

Capital project risk management is, at a minimum, a way to improve project performance to time, budget and schedule. When it is embedded throughout an organization, it can form the core of capital effectiveness and therefore be a source of competitive advantage.

Capital project risk management and its benefits

Capital project risk management simply refers to the identification, analysis, treatment and communication of uncertainties to the objectives of both individual capital projects and project portfolios.

Through effective capital risk project management, organizations can ensure that:

- projects are completed on time and within budget;
- cost overruns and delays are minimized, improving the NPV of investment portfolios;
- cash flow volatility is minimized;
- decision-making capability is increased through greater understanding of risk exposures;
- earnings at risk are constrained within a predictable profitability envelope; and
- share prices are maximized, as markets reward the company for consistent delivery on completion promises.

We have identified four key foundational principles that are necessary to manage the risks associated with capital projects effectively. When these are in place, companies are in a position to ensure that capital project risk management is a core element of capital effectiveness and high performance.

The four foundations

Foundation one: Run capital projects like a business

It is important for those accountable and responsible for the delivery of capital projects to think and act like business owners, not just project managers. While large capital projects involve many moving parts, they all entrust project managers as stewards of the company's capital.

The leadership team should consider measuring success in terms of time to operation and the financial importance of this to the business. This implies making sure their project is integrated with, and transparent to, the company's business from the very beginning. In risk management terms, this means that risk tolerances and appetites for the project need to reflect those of the organizations involved.

Three important ways in which an organization can move from a project-only to a business mentality are:

1 *Align risk management with strategy and project delivery.* Too often, risk management is viewed as a menu item to be ticked off by project teams. This happens when risk management objectives do not reflect strategic project objectives. This leads to risk management proceeding with a compliance rather than a performance mindset, and execution suffers. This can be overcome by ensuring that:

   - A project's risk profile is aligned to the company's overall risk appetite and driven by the project strategy. The project profile should also be visible and transparent to the project team.

- Company risk appetite and tolerance are reflected in the criteria used in risk management, which will help clarify how risks are managed. In fact, examining risk criteria is often a good litmus test of whether or not risk and strategy are linked. If companies can 'see themselves' in the risk criteria and methodology used, this is often a signal that the risk criteria and methodology accurately reflect the strategy. Conversely, if the risk criteria and methodology appear 'generic' or applicable to 'any old project', this is often an indication that they don't and should therefore be reconsidered.

2 *Get the organization right.* Project organization is a significant factor in performance. Risks are minimized when:

- Incentives of team members do not create excessive or unnecessary risk taking (for instance, we have found that, on poorly performing projects, those shaping the project at the early stages can have incentives to get through stage gates too quickly, thereby creating greater risks in later stages). A risk-focused review of incentives within a project team can reveal where and how performance targets can create wider, unintended project risks.

- A risk culture is instilled across the organization. This means that risk-focused behaviours are emphasized, incorporated into performance objectives and measured, which assists in ensuring that risk management is not seen simply as the purview of risk managers and is embedded within the organization. This should include effective risk management training and communication.

- Governance and reporting structures provide clear visibility of top risks to senior management and decision makers. Good risk analytics and reporting can assist, providing company leadership with sufficient line of sight into key risks.

3 *Manage suppliers effectively.* Suppliers capable of handling large, complex capital projects have undergone significant consolidation in recent years, and companies can no longer dictate terms on major projects. Finding and securing the contracting support needed to complete such projects has become a significant undertaking in and of itself. We find that companies that manage capital project risks effectively often develop relationships with key suppliers that extend from project to project, or that link multiple projects, giving suppliers the opportunity to spread their own risk and to allocate resources and expertise more efficiently.

The number and type of suppliers involved in any project can similarly be complex. Companies that manage capital projects well are able to ensure that the risks that these numerous relationships can create are assessed and managed. For example, some contractors may come into close contact with local communities during the construction phase of a project, effectively representing the operating company. If the risks these interactions can pose are not identified and managed, projects can become susceptible to community-led opposition, reputational damage or related problems. We find that companies that maintain visibility and ownership of the web of supplier relationships they possess reduce project risk.

Foundation two: Align project partners

Where projects involve multiple partners, risk appetites, tolerance and corresponding processes and approaches to be deployed throughout the project should be defined and agreed. This should involve all partners not only approving these, but subsequently embedding the risk management approach within the project's operating model:

1 *Get the governance right.* Upfront investment to achieve alignment on risk management is crucial. It will protect the project later on, as it makes decision making more efficient and transparent. It is alarmingly easy for key risks and issues to slip through governance cracks and wind up with no owners. When this happens, the likelihood of risks occurring dramatically increases.

   For projects run by a consortium of companies, a governance framework should be established on three levels:

   – An internal governance structure is essential for communication and decision making. The internal structure helps the company maintain discipline, keeping the project on time and on budget.

   – A project-wide governance framework can help determine which levels of risk are acceptable to all partners, as well as how such risks are identified, reported and managed.

   – Companies need to agree on principles to monitor and assess risks. The introduction of key risk indicators (KRIs) supports the necessary level of transparency and visibility. In addition it helps measure the effectiveness of management strategies in reducing risk exposures.

2 *Put an extra focus on non-operated joint ventures (NOJVs).* NOJVs are challenging for obvious reasons – companies do not have managerial control of the project. This, however, is not an excuse for the joint venture partners to ignore risks or leave the project to the operators alone. Companies should:

   – incorporate risk monitoring on NOJV projects;

   – use influencing strategies where risk levels appear to be deviating from the tolerances or expanding beyond the approved risk envelope;

   – agree on dispute resolution mechanisms alongside the establishment of the NOJV so that, when the inevitable disagreements arise, they can be resolved quickly and effectively.

Foundation three: Manage 'above-ground', 'non-technical' risks in capital projects

Many delays in capital projects are the result of regulatory (eg permitting complexity), stakeholder (eg loss of social licence to operate, labour issues, environmental scrutiny), political (eg expropriation, political violence) and reputational (eg NIMBYism) risk. For example, 'resource nationalism' stemming from government actions to raise taxes or royalties or carry out cash flow expropriation can significantly affect project economics. Such actions often occur after significant capital is sunk into projects. In many cases, these kinds of risks are beyond the core expertise of the project leadership and consequently may not receive the treatment that they warrant.

To ensure that capital projects are managed effectively consider the following:

- *Measure non-technical risks.* Non-technical risks are often not managed because they are not measured. Some companies employ subject matter experts to explore risk areas that are outside the core competency of the company and project team (eg experts on a particular country's politics or on local community dynamics). Companies similarly have methodologies to manage social and environmental performance. However, high performers go beyond this by measuring these risks using core commercial metrics. For instance, they may use Bayesian analysis to incorporate these risks into project NPV calculations. Similarly, some companies use organization network analysis to model the impact of different risk types. We find that, when non-technical risks are measured in the same way as more traditional risks, they are managed more effectively. For example, these types of analyses can reveal that it makes sense for a company to slow down the early phases of a project to conduct stakeholder consultation and partnering. This can create an approach that achieves buy-in from key stakeholders and avoids project delays from protests or court orders later.

- *Ensure accountability and decision-making authority around non-technical risks.* With effective measurement, it is easier to assign accountability for non-technical risks. It is crucial that those responsible for specific areas have a 'seat at the table' of project decision making. For example, a director of community relations on a project should have sufficient resources and authority within the project governance structure. This will help ensure that project delivery is not unnecessarily compromised by a lack of understanding of these types of risk.

Foundation four: Use strategic objectives to define quantitative approaches

All capital project teams should quantify and stress-test their risk exposures using techniques such as Monte Carlo simulation and other financial risk management tools that can be applied to capital projects. These might include modelling techniques used in other areas of finance, such as derivatives trading. Some companies, for example, use value at risk (VaR) to assess the economic impact of commodity price risk on their projects. However, quantitative techniques should always be focused on delivering value to decision makers and planners, not as an end in themselves. As a consequence, project strategy should define quantitative approaches, not the other way around.

To maximize the benefits of quantitative techniques, companies should bear two critical considerations in mind:

- *Ensure modelling approaches and results are understood by decision makers.* Quantitative models are useless unless decision makers can understand and use the results they produce. Critically, they need to understand both the advantages and the limitations of the results that models produce. This can be accomplished when:
  - quantitative models employed follow the strategic imperatives of decision makers (for instance, if the company has a focus on cash flow, then it should consider a cash-flow-at-risk modelling approach rather than a model that tests predominantly earnings or capital metrics);

- – the assumptions of quantitative models are clearly communicated and understood;
- – the hypotheses and incoming data of models are defined and shared by every individual involved in the evaluation;
- – simulation results are understood by decision makers.

- *Use models to stress-test risk exposures.* Many companies use databases of historical project costs and schedules to estimate the cost and duration of planned projects. However, relying on historical data alone can provide a false sense of security. Historical data are not available for many types of capital projects (particularly those in new geographical areas or employing new technology). Historical approaches can also underestimate volatility of prices, costs, or the probability of 'extreme events'. Conversely, stress testing allows management to understand the effect of an extreme event on the project, helping management identify flaws and gaps in the risk measurement methodology. When accurate data and appropriate computational tools are available, stress testing can be an effective technique for assessing the consequences and impact of risk events. By identifying risk factors (for example, extreme cost spikes or pricing events) and creating and assessing scenarios, companies can see which actions may be necessary to reduce the exposure and manage the risk profile. In addition they should evaluate whether the mechanisms and resources are in place to take these actions.

Mastery – capital project risk management to drive capital effectiveness

Once an organization is able to apply the four foundational principles effectively and consistently across a number of projects, it will be in a position to utilize risk management to contribute to greater capital effectiveness. Figure 1.3.1 provides a capital risk management maturity model.

Mastery of capital project risk management involves the following elements:

- *Post-performance appraisals – learning from mistakes.* Developing a knowledge management system around project performance can help organizations achieve high performance. Too often, mistakes get repeated, while the knowledge of the individual who contributed to good performance remains bottled up within the company or, worse, departs to a competitor.

- *Aggregation of risk profiles across portfolios.* If companies are able to assess project risks accurately and aggregate these into portfolios to evaluate the risk profiles, it will help them understand where and how capital is underutilized and where additional opportunities may reside. This can include using a common set of risk typologies found across different project types.

- *On-time delivery management.* Once a company develops a level of confidence around its ability to measure and manage capital project risk, it will be in a better position to estimate and disclose project completion dates more accurately to investors – and then deliver on those promises. Doing so can create a share price premium and reduce the cost of capital.

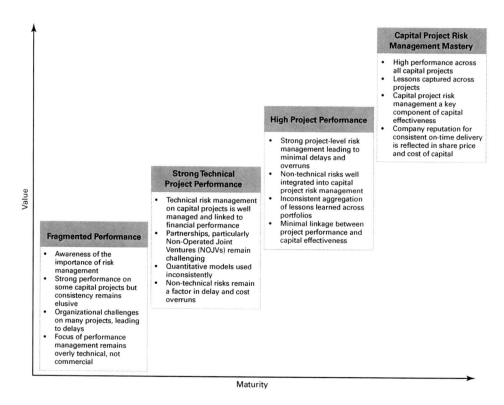

Value

Maturity

Fragmented Performance
- Awareness of the importance of risk management
- Strong performance on some capital projects but consistency remains elusive
- Organizational challenges on many projects, leading to delays
- Focus of performance management remains overly technical, not commercial

Strong Technical Project Performance
- Technical risk management on capital projects is well managed and linked to financial performance
- Partnerships, particularly Non-Operated Joint Ventures (NOJVs) remain challenging
- Quantitative models used inconsistently
- Non-technical risks remain a factor in delay and cost overruns

High Project Performance
- Strong project-level risk management leading to minimal delays and overruns
- Non-technical risks well integrated into capital project risk management
- Inconsistent aggregation of lessons learned across portfolios
- Minimal linkage between project performance and capital effectiveness

Capital Project Risk Management Mastery
- High performance across all capital projects
- Lessons captured across projects
- Capital project risk management a key component of capital effectiveness
- Company reputation for consistent on-time delivery is reflected in share price and cost of capital

FIGURE 1.3.1 Capital project risk management maturity framework

- *Asymmetry management.* One of the least understood aspects of capital projects is how reputational risk can defy the size of a project. For instance, an environmental issue in one project can have repercussions on how regulators view the company in other geographical areas. Aggregation of risk across portfolios should include the modelling of reputation risk and its linkage across projects.

Capital projects are an increasingly important yet challenging aspect of companies' future growth and profitability. Those companies that master effective capital project risk management will create enduring and significant value for their shareholders.

Copyright and disclaimer

the accuracy and completeness of the information in this document and for any acts or omissions made based on such information. Accenture does not provide legal, regulatory, audit or tax advice. Readers are responsible for obtaining such advice from their own legal counsel or other licensed professional.

Notes

1 Organisation for Economic Co-operation and Development, http://www.oecd.org/dataoecd/24/1/39996026.pdf.

2 Stakeholders can include the general public, local communities, governments, environmental groups, workers' councils and labour unions.

Sources and references

Accenture (2011) *Charting a New Course in Capital Projects in Australian Mining and Energy*, Accenture

Accenture (2012) *Capital Projects in a High Risk World: A best practices perspective*, Accenture

Goldman Sachs (2008) *190 Projects to Change the World*, Goldman Sachs, New York

McKenna, MG and Wilczynski, H (2006) *Capital Project Execution in the Oil and Gas Industry*, Booz Allen, New York

Asset integrity risk management

ALLAN GIFFORD, DNV KEMA

Introduction

This chapter provides a risk-based approach and framework for asset integrity management throughout an organization and across systems. Furthermore, it proposes a basis for making decisions and provides a coherent way to communicate asset integrity.

Definition: asset integrity

Within this chapter asset integrity is defined as the asset's ability to fulfil its intended function throughout its operating life, ensuring a safe and reliable operation. It is an outcome of technical and organizational efforts in design, construction and operation.

The information presented is oriented around an oil and gas installation, but you may be able to draw parallels with other asset types. It is derived from good practice within organizations that are required to achieve structured evidence of sound asset integrity management. It is also based on international standards for management systems and risk management such as ISO 9001, 'Quality management systems', and ISO 31000, 'Risk management – principles and guidance'.

Overall approach to asset integrity management

The operator of an asset has to both meet high performance goals and satisfy stringent regulations in health, safety and environment. This can be achieved by ensuring that asset integrity management is based on the following four main components:

1 life cycle approach;
2 risk management;

3 barrier management;

4 management system.

Life cycle approach

Asset integrity is the ability of the asset to fulfil its intended function throughout its planned operating life. A system progresses throughout its life cycle as the result of actions, performed and managed by people in the organization, using work processes for execution of these actions.[1] Hence asset integrity management should take into account the whole life cycle of the asset, starting with design and ending with abandonment.

In this chapter, asset integrity is further defined as including three elements: design integrity, technical integrity and operational integrity. The life cycle phases of an asset and where these apply are illustrated in Figure 1.4.1.

The operation phase is 'business as usual' and is typically carried out by the base organization. Design, fabrication and installation, modification and lifetime extension, decommissioning and abandonment, however, are usually carried out as projects. Maintenance activities may also be carried out as a project.

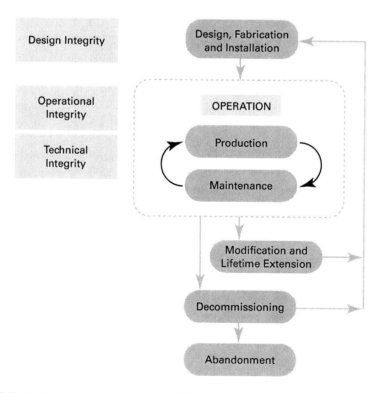

FIGURE 1.4.1 Asset integrity in different phases of the life cycle of an asset

The life cycle phases for an asset are outlined in Table 1.4.1.

TABLE 1.4.1 Life cycle phases for as asset

Design, fabrication and installation (DFI)	Design integrity is established by ensuring that facilities, systems and equipment are designed, modified or redesigned according to defined criteria of reliability, availability, maintainability and safety, and fabricated and installed in accordance with governing standards, meeting specified operating requirements.[1]
Production	Production typically includes start-up and shutdown activities, operation control and monitoring activities to ensure that critical fluid parameters are kept within the specified design limits, flow assurance, production planning and production optimization. Operational integrity is achieved by proper planning, preparation and execution of activities to ensure efficient operational performance of the facility within a predefined and qualified operational envelope. Operational integrity ensures appropriate staffing, competence and decision-making data to operate the asset as intended throughout its life cycle.
Maintenance	The purpose of the maintenance process is to sustain the capability of the system to provide a service. The process monitors the system's capability to deliver services, records problems for analyses, takes corrective and preventive actions, and confirms restored capability. Maintenance activities typically include developing and carrying out preventive maintenance programmes, condition monitoring programmes, condition testing programmes, condition assessment programmes and condition-based maintenance. Technical integrity is achieved by proper planning, preparation and execution of maintenance activities to ensure the facility's physical condition.
Modification and lifetime extension	Modification is any alteration to the facility that changes the original design envelope. A modification should follow the same processes as during the DFI of the facility. As systems reach the end of their design life, there may still be a need to operate the systems for longer than anticipated. Lifetime extension has to be systematically planned and implemented in a similar way as the DFI processes.
Decommissioning and abandonment	Decommissioning includes a set of activities associated with taking a facility, or part of it, temporarily out of service. Decommissioning should be planned and prepared properly. Abandonment comprises the activities associated with taking the system or part of it permanently out of operation. An abandoned system is not intended to be returned to operation.

NOTE: 1 Design integrity is also established during modifications and lifetime extension.

Risk management

One key element of an effective management system is a systematic approach to the identification of hazards and the assessment of the associated risks in order to provide information on the need for risk reduction measures.

The backbone of efficient asset integrity management should be a sound risk management process ensuring that all relevant risks related to a safe and reliable operation are identified and managed. The risk management process outlined in this chapter is aligned with ISO 31000, 'Risk management – principles and guidance'. The main elements in the risk management process are illustrated in Figure 1.4.2.

The asset integrity risk management process provides important data and information to both the production and the maintenance processes. Risk assessments should be used as the guiding principle for production and maintenance decisions.

Risk-based decisions should be taken against defined criteria. The definition of the criteria should be in accordance with overall company policy for health, safety and the environment, production and cost. The criteria should be properly defined and communicated.

The risk assessment effort should be tailored to the level and source of risk. Risk assessment techniques should be chosen based on needs and available data. Good guidance is provided in ISO 31010, 'Risk management – risk assessment techniques', and ISO 17776, 'Petroleum and natural gas industries – offshore production installations – guidelines on tools and techniques for hazard identification and risk assessment'.

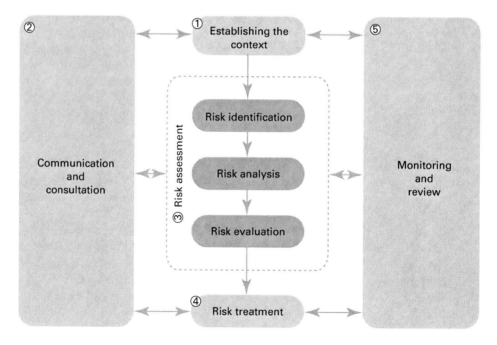

FIGURE 1.4.2 The overall risk management process for asset integrity management

The identification of hazards and the evaluation of risk should be undertaken by personnel who are both skilled in the techniques involved and knowledgeable about design, operation and maintenance of the asset and its condition.

Barrier management

Safety barriers are an important part of asset integrity management. International regulations such as the Seveso II Directive and the Machinery Directive, and industry standards such as ISO, IEC and NORSOK focus on safety barriers as important means to reduce the risk of major accidents.

Definition: barriers

A functional grouping of safeguards and controls selected to prevent the realization of a hazard. Each barrier typically includes a mix of plant (equipment), process (documented and 'custom and practice') and people (personal skills and their application). The selected combination of these ensures the barrier is suitable, sufficient and available to deliver its expected risk reduction.

A document stating the strategies and principles for design, operation and maintenance of barriers should be established. The purpose of this document is to give a common understanding of requirements for the individual barriers, including the connection between risk and hazard assessments and requirements for, and relating to, the barriers.

Different types of barriers

There are different types of barriers, typically consisting of:

- Technical elements such as gas detectors, signals to carbon capture readiness (CCR) and alarm, hardware and software.
- Operational elements such as maintenance and operational activities, modifications, management of change and deviation handling. These operational elements are all *active* elements executed by personnel to fulfil the barrier function.
- Organizational elements such as planning, competence, communication, work practice and procedures. The organizational elements are all *passive* elements to ensure and manage the operational elements.

Passive barriers are often a combination of physical and human or operational elements, while active barrier systems are often based on a combination of technical and human or operational elements.

Some barriers are permanent, while others may be temporary. Permanent barriers are implemented as an integrated part of the whole operational life cycle, while temporary barriers are used only in a specified time period, often during specific activities or conditions, eg maintenance.

For oil and gas assets, barriers can be categorized as:

- *prevention:* primary containment, process control, primary and secondary structure;
- *detection:* control room alarms, fire, gas or leakage detection;
- *control and mitigation:* equipment orientation and spacing, secondary containment and drainage, blow-down systems, fire protection and suppression;
- *emergency response:* local alarms, escape and evacuation, emergency communications, emergency power.

By having a structured and risk-based approach towards which type of barriers to choose, the number of barriers for an asset can be held at a manageable level.

Bow tie model

Recognizing continual changes due to, for example, equipment deterioration, temporary safeguard bypasses, operational changes, maintenance lapses, individual and team competences etc, we must accept that no barrier is 100 per cent effective. Hence multiple barriers are used to manage the risk of major accidents.

A good way to understand the need for barriers is to use the 'bow tie' model. This indicates how barriers can both reduce the threats from a hazard (preventive barriers) and limit the consequences if the hazard is realized (reactive barriers). Figure 1.4.3 illustrates this model.

The left-hand side of the bow tie is constructed from a causal analysis and involves the causes of the failure or undesired event and the controls associated with each cause. The right-hand side of the bow tie is constructed from the consequence analysis detailing mitigating controls and recovery preparedness measures. The centre of the bow tie is commonly referred to as the 'top event'. The left-hand side of the bow tie strongly resembles a traditional fault tree, whereas the right-hand side forms an event tree.

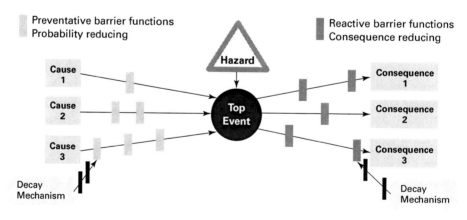

FIGURE 1.4.3 The bow tie model

Performance standards for barriers

A specific set of barriers should be defined, each with its own set of performance standards, as in the box below, detailing the performance requirements for the technical, operational or organizational elements and its expected performance in terms of functionality, availability, reliability and survivability.

Definition: performance standard

A measurable statement, expressed in qualitative or quantitative terms, of the performance required of a system, item of equipment, person or procedure, and that is relied upon as the basis for managing a hazard.

Source: OGP (2008).

Performance standards determine equipment design specifications and set requirements for maintenance and testing throughout the asset's life cycle.

Input to the requirements are rules and regulations, standards (eg API, NORSOK, IEC), and classification and assumptions from risk and safety analyses (human factor analysis, QRA, safety case, RBI, Hazop, SIL). Fulfilment of functional requirements needs to be operationalized to ensure a proper barrier management system; hence all barriers need to be maintained and their availability and effectiveness regularly verified.

Barrier monitoring and follow-up

Assurance processes should be put in place to confirm that the barriers remain fit for purpose. This requires operational controls and limits, maintenance, inspection and testing plans, performance records, audits and reviews.

Performance indicators should be linked to the barriers. The barrier indicators should be proactive, motivate for action, and provide necessary information for decision makers about where and how to act. Based on the performance indicators, the actual condition or level of compliance of the barriers should be assessed in a continuous timeframe process. A multidiscipline approach where experienced personnel evaluate and document the status of barriers based on a variety of information sources and performance indicators is recommended. The bow tie model can be a useful tool to communicate the status and availability or effectiveness of barriers.

Management system

The success of asset integrity management depends on the effectiveness of the management system providing the foundations and arrangements that will embed it throughout the organization and across systems. A structured, consistent and coherent asset integrity management system of policies, processes and procedures should be established.

Here we present an overall, generic framework for an asset integrity management system and outline the work processes and resource needs.

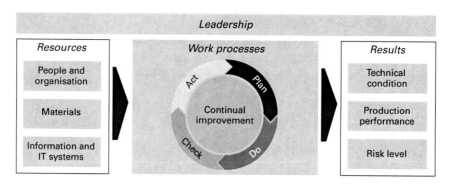

FIGURE 1.4.4 Framework for an asset integrity management system

Framework

An asset integrity management system is a framework of control and coordination, containing a number of discrete elements and important relationships. It should be seen as an integrated, cross-functional way of ensuring that all activities are aligned to the delivery of the organization's objectives and that processes of continual improvement are followed.

The asset integrity management system should be based on the methodology known as 'Plan, Do, Check, Act'. The whole management system as well as each work process should be designed according to this methodology to ensure continual improvement.

Figure 1.4.4 outlines an overall framework for an asset integrity management system. It shows the key elements that need to be in place to ensure efficient asset integrity management. Resources are the necessary input to be able to carry out the defined work processes that generate results according to the company's policies and objectives.

Resources

Asset integrity management takes input from people and organization, materials, and information and IT systems.

People and organization

To achieve asset integrity the organization needs competent people working collectively towards common goals. Hence ensuring suitable competency, defining roles and responsibilities and giving the human component proper consideration are essential.

Human factors are important to ensure asset integrity. We need to consider how individuals interact with each other, facilities, equipment and management systems. This interaction is influenced by both the working environment and the culture of the people involved. It is important that tasks are designed in consistence with the knowledge, skills and physical capabilities of the person or team.

Task schedules should take account of any physical conditions that increase fatigue and error rates such as restricted access, temperature or humidity extremes, or a noisy, damp or contaminated work environment.

The safety culture of the organization is also a key contributor. Lack of focus on human factors and safety culture may lead to a decline in work quality, omissions, or faulty decision making.

Appropriate supervision should be provided to guide asset integrity activities, to encourage good performance and positive behaviour, and to correct and/or discipline poor performance and wrong behaviour. Senior managers should ensure that the performance of staff is actively managed through performance appraisal, rewards and recognition in accordance with asset integrity.

An organizational structure should be in place with clearly defined roles and responsibilities for all relevant personnel involved in asset integrity management. Due consideration should be given to interfaces with production and other main work processes. The roles and responsibilities for each position need to be defined in the job description. The job description should include the competency required of the person in that position.

The following examples of roles or functions are typical for an asset integrity management organization:

- *technician:* responds to operational alarms;
- *technical authority:* develops and defines suitable barriers and performance standards;
- *asset supervisor:* ensures that operations are within the defined envelope;
- *asset manager:* provides leadership and ensures a suitable budget and competent resources to monitor.

Senior managers should be able to secure the necessary personnel to achieve their specified asset integrity objectives. This requires a structured overview of the competence available in the organization, as defined in the box below, combined with the needed competence identified for asset integrity management.

Definition: competence

Application of knowledge, skills and behaviours in performance. Hence competence includes a behavioural element, ie the ability to apply personal skills and knowledge in typical workplace situations.

Competence is a combination of knowledge, skills and behaviour, developed through education, appropriate training and experience. Competency for a role or function or a team should be managed by the following four steps:

- Identify the required competences.
- Define training needs and provide relevant training.

- Evaluate the training outcome.
- Maintain competence.

Key tasks associated with asset integrity management should be defined for each role or function. This should be followed by determining the range of knowledge, skills and behaviour to execute these tasks successfully. In addition, competences that are a prerequisite for filling the role should be identified.

The organization should have a training system in place for asset integrity management personnel to develop the required competence of individuals. Asset integrity training should fill an identified need, based on an analysis of existing competence, role requirements, training objectives and employee aspirations. All new personnel working with asset integrity management should receive a job induction.

Internal training may include classroom instruction, practical exercises, field experience and on-the-job training.

Processes should be in place to review periodically which competences are required for each role or function, as this may change because of changes in technology, reorganization, facility size etc. Furthermore, personal competences should periodically be assessed to identify needs for refresher training.

Management system

The level of detail and the degree of formal documentation of the system elements need to be proportionate to the criticality and complexity of the assets being managed, and to the business and asset integrity objectives to be achieved. Furthermore, the management system should be sensitive to the influence of all stakeholders and the environment. These influences are likely to change over the life cycle of the asset, and the management system should be robust to potential changes.

An asset integrity management system typically includes the main elements related to 'Plan, Do, Check, Act' listed in Table 1.4.2.

Based on the overall framework outlined in Table 1.4.2, this chapter proposes a set of management, core and supporting work processes necessary to deliver efficient and effective asset integrity management. These processes are shown in Figure 1.4.5.

Work processes usually consist of a set of activities or tasks that need to be defined. The activities should be supported by procedures and detailed work instructions when relevant to instruct people how to perform a specific task.

Work procedures and instructions should be defined with input from experts within the relevant field of asset integrity management and should be evaluated annually or after significant changes. The procedures and instructions should be easily available to all relevant personnel.

TABLE 1.4.2 Plan, Do, Check, Act

Plan	Define objectives that commit the organization to a safe, reliable and efficient level of performance. Develop asset integrity strategies. Long-term planning. Annual and short-term planning. Budgeting.
Do	Execute maintenance work, including work permits, risk assessments, preventive and corrective maintenance activities, inspections, monitoring and testing. Execute verification of the quality of the work, when relevant.
Check	Report system and equipment conditions, including collection and quality assurance of maintenance data, and presenting these in the form of defined indicators. Carry out analysis of historical maintenance data and unwanted incidents related to maintenance. Ensure lessons learned. Plan and carry out asset integrity management system audits.
Act	Evaluate and implement actions based on conducted analyses, lessons learned, audits and other information sources. Monitor the effect of implemented improvement actions. Ensure commitment from senior management.

The work processes in the framework are divided into three types of processes: management processes, core processes and support processes. Each of the work processes is described in more detail below.

Management processes

The management processes should provide leadership and translate the organization's overall objectives into policies, objectives and plans for asset integrity management. Furthermore, the management processes should include systematic evaluation and follow-up of asset performance on an overall level.

Set company direction for asset integrity

Senior managers need to have sufficient awareness and understanding of asset integrity management, and asset integrity should be prioritized and funded accordingly. The objective of this process is to define and communicate the company's policies, objectives, strategies and long-term plans and programmes for asset integrity management.

Senior managers should develop and endorse an asset integrity policy to guide asset integrity activities throughout the organization. Yearly asset integrity objectives should be set to guide the organization in the application of the policy. Objectives should be consistent with the organization's commitment to continual

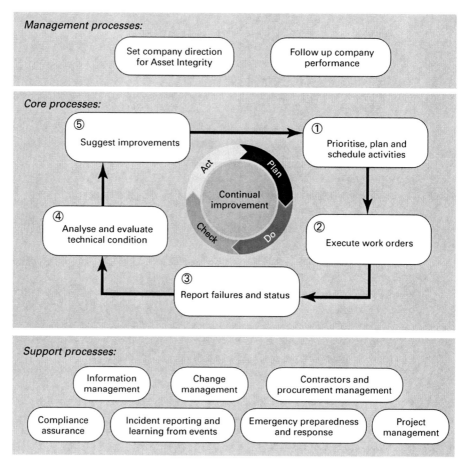

FIGURE 1.4.5 Asset integrity management work processes necessary to deliver efficient and effective asset integrity management and ensure continual improvement

improvement and should be quantified where practicable. Objectives should be appropriately communicated to stakeholders in the context of their relationship with asset integrity management.

Production and maintenance activities should be properly planned, taking into account the interaction between the activities, forecasting and optimization. A long-term, single asset integrity programme should be prepared for the organization based on the information of each system or item of equipment. The purpose of the programme is to control all risks associated with degradation of equipment. Hence the asset integrity programme should be established using applicable risk assessment and analysis methods.

The asset integrity programme should include maintenance activities such as calendar-based activities, inspections, condition monitoring and testing, and should define activities and maintenance intervals for equipment. It should be periodically revised and updated to reflect changes in the operating environment. The evaluation should be based on historical data and experience.

Effective planning will ensure that asset integrity objectives are achieved on time, to the desired quality and in budget. Senior managers should mobilize the combined resources available to the organization towards achieving the asset integrity policy and objectives. This includes obtaining the necessary people, allocating these among the required activities, as well as motivating individuals to contribute towards the collective objectives. It also includes creating a positive, open and trusting culture with effective communication lines in which asset integrity can operate.

Follow up company performance

Asset performance should systematically be measured and reviewed against the asset integrity objectives set.

Data and information from condition monitoring, reported failures, non-conformities, audits, key performance indicator reporting etc should be used to evaluate past experiences and performance, and plan improvement initiatives for future asset integrity operations, ensuring continuous improvement of asset integrity management in the organization.

The organization should have an activity tracking system for capturing and close-down of activities. Senior managers should frequently review the progress of activities in relation to plans, utilizing the activity tracking system, and should report and communicate this progress in accordance with stakeholder expectations and asset capacity.

Key performance indicators (KPIs) should be defined to review progress against the asset integrity programme and support the overall objectives of asset integrity management.

Audits of the asset integrity management system should be carried out on at least an annual basis. An audit programme should be in place to review and verify the effectiveness of all aspects of asset integrity management. Non-conformities, areas for improvement and corrective actions identified during an audit should be reported to the senior management.

Top management should, at intervals that it determines, carry out management reviews of the asset integrity management system to ensure its continuing suitability, adequacy and effectiveness. The management review process should ensure that the necessary information is collected to allow management to carry out the evaluation.

Core processes

Prioritize, plan and schedule activities

A short-term or annual maintenance plan should be developed covering both preventive and corrective maintenance. It should be aligned with the asset integrity management programme. A maintenance plan is a structured set of tasks that include the activities, resources and time required to carry out maintenance. Criteria for prioritization should be defined, and a method for prioritizing maintenance should be in place.

Based on the short-term maintenance plan, work orders should be generated in, for example, a computerized maintenance system. The work orders require that detailed planning should be carried out, including order material, personnel and tools for the activity.

Prioritization of corrective maintenance should be done based on the risk the failure represents, described as consequence and impact of failure.

Preventive maintenance should in principle be executed according to the given maintenance plan. Backlog related to the plan should be prioritized based on risk, ie probability and consequence of failure.

Report failure and status

Monitoring and reviewing asset integrity performance (Check, Act) is as important as developing and implementing asset integrity management plans (Plan, Do).

The organization should establish procedures to monitor and measure the performance of the asset integrity management system. It should also establish procedures to monitor and measure the technical conditions of the asset as appropriate. The procedures should provide for both qualitative and quantitative measures.

Asset integrity monitoring should be fact-based and could include the following:

- KPIs;
- barrier performance standard verification;
- audit findings;
- incident investigation;
- benchmarking and lessons learned.

ISO 14224, 'Petroleum, petrochemical and natural gas industries – collection and exchange of reliability and maintenance data for equipment', defines information recommended to be reported related to maintenance activities. Table 1.4.3 lists some examples from ISO 14224.

TABLE 1.4.3 Examples of reporting of maintenance data

Preventive maintenance	Corrective maintenance
Condition of equipment before maintenance work	Failure mode
Person hours for activity	Failure cause
Start and finish time	Failure mechanisms
	Equipment down time
	Spare parts used
	Person hours for activity
	Start and finish time of repair

Analyse and evaluate technical condition, and suggest improvements

Based on reported maintenance data, the effectiveness of the asset integrity management system should be evaluated systematically.

KPIs should be used to evaluate asset integrity performance against stated objectives. Both 'lagging' and 'leading' indicators should be defined. Typically, lagging indicators are generated by a process of reactive monitoring indicating facts about past events, while leading indicators are the outcome of active monitoring that indicates future value or direction of performance.

Proactive measures of performance monitor compliance with the asset integrity management plans, operational control criteria and applicable regulatory and other asset integrity management requirements.

Reactive measures of performance and condition monitor asset-related deteriorations, failures, incidents, non-conformances and other historical evidence of deficient asset integrity management performance.

ISO 14224 gives examples of KPIs.

Analyses should be carried out of historical maintenance data, and unwanted incidents related to maintenance as a basis for identifying areas of improvement. This may include trend analysis, root cause failure analysis etc.

The analysis process should include evaluation of the asset integrity management system effectiveness, ie to what extent the asset integrity programme is handling risks and performance requirements for individual systems. Identified improvement actions should be implemented, and the effect should be monitored.

Support processes

The support processes provide essential support to the core processes to ensure an efficient execution and consistency of asset integrity management across the organization's functions and work processes.

Information management

The organization should have a system in place to effectively manage and control all documentation, data and information relating to asset integrity management. Documents, data and information include, but are not limited to, the equipment or tag register, drawings and design details, historical maintenance data, maintenance task descriptions and spares lists.

The system should identify the documents, data and information requiring periodical review, revision and approval by authorized personnel. Documentation, data and information should be readily available for relevant users and decision makers.

The information management system should be maintained for the whole life cycle of the asset.

Change management

Organizational and engineering changes affecting the integrity of the asset should be subject to a structured analysis of how the change may affect asset integrity.

A management of change procedure should be established that addresses the continuous safe and reliable operation of the asset. The procedure should include identification, authorization, evaluation, implementation, documentation and verification of the change.

Processes to ensure documentation of changes and necessary updating of asset integrity management system documentation and technical information should be in place. Changes should be communicated effectively to all involved parties.

Contractors and procurement

In many organizations contractors perform a substantial role in managing asset integrity. Management of contractors could be a key element of the organization's ability to achieve its asset integrity management objectives.

A pre-qualification process should be in place for contractors providing asset-integrity-related services. During the pre-qualification process, contractors should provide the organization with proof that they are able to comply with the organization's asset integrity policy and asset integrity management system. Contractors should be evaluated and selected according to predefined selection criteria.

The asset integrity policy should be incorporated into the requirements of each contract as appropriate in order to align the contractor's objectives with the overall policy. The contract should be a basis for developing bridging documents between the management systems, including asset integrity management, of both the company and the contractor.

The contract should describe the contractor's obligation to notify findings, report and share information to ensure that all relevant data and documentation for managing asset integrity is made available to the company.

For the duration of the contract, means should be in place to follow up the contractor. These should as a minimum include:

- appropriate arrangements for contract supervision;
- ongoing assessment of contractor performance through the period of the contract;
- appropriate verification of the quality of work carried out by contractors to confirm that it meets the contract terms and is to a suitable standard.

Compliance assurance

The organization should have a system in place that identifies regulations, codes and standards relevant for asset integrity management. The system should determine the requirements on the organization to comply with the identified regulations, codes and standards, assess their impact on how asset integrity is managed in the organization, and communicate these requirements to the necessary personnel working in asset integrity.

The compliance assurance system should identify updates in relevant regulations, codes and standards and inform senior management when these changes affect the organization's asset integrity policy.

Emergency preparedness and response

The organization should establish appropriate systems and plans to identify potential incidents and emergency situations, and to prevent and mitigate the consequences that can be associated with them.

Emergency preparedness is closely related to the risk management process. The emergency preparedness for an asset should be based on relevant major accident risks that are identified through risk assessments.

Plans and procedures should include information on the provision and maintenance of any identified equipment or system that could be required during incidents and emergency situations. This may include, for example, emergency pumps, generators, temporary shelters, access to back-up information etc.

The relevant major accident risks might change because of degradation, failure or modification. The asset integrity management organization continuously receives information based on inspections, monitoring and assessment activities and is also often responsible for initiating modification projects. This organization therefore plays a vital role in ensuring that a suitable emergency response is available for the asset.

It is challenging to maintain awareness of major accident risks because of their low occurrence. Frequent and structured training and plans for testing or drills based on major accident scenarios should be in place to ensure that a suitable emergency response is available and to maintain awareness within the organization.

Incident reporting and learning from events

The organization should establish processes for the handling and investigation of failures, incidents and non-conformities and associated incident reporting and learning from events with assets, asset systems and the asset management system. The processes should define responsibility and authority for:

- investigating failures, incidents and non-conformities to determine their root cause;
- evaluation of the need for implementation of changes to the involved assets, processes and procedures;
- communicating as appropriate to relevant stakeholders the results of investigations and identified actions.

Project management

The asset integrity management organization often initiates projects. Such projects could be asset modifications, maintenance operations, lifetime extensions etc. All activities organized as projects should follow a defined framework for project management.

Project management is the application of knowledge, skills, tools and techniques to project activities to meet project requirements. Managing a project typically includes: addressing and meeting stakeholder requirements, expectations and needs; and balancing competing project constraints.

Project managers should have sufficient training and knowledge of the processes required to carry out projects within project constraints successfully.

The link and alignment of asset risk management with ISO 31000

The backbone of efficient asset integrity management should be a sound risk management process ensuring that all relevant risks related to safety and reliability are identified and managed. Risk management is a continuous activity that reflects the changes in the operating environment and the need to monitor and maintain the performance of the resources allocated.

What we propose in this chapter adopts and embraces the concepts, framework and guidance encapsulated in ISO 31000, as illustrated in Figure 1.4.6:

- that, for risk management to be effective, an organization should comply with various overarching principles;

- that the success of risk management will depend upon the effectiveness of a management framework providing the foundations and arrangements that will embed risk management at all levels; and

- that a risk management process should be an integral part of management, embedded in the culture and practices, and tailored to the business processes.

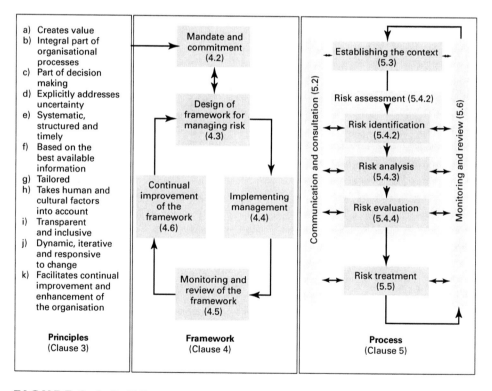

FIGURE 1.4.6 ISO 31000

Through the risk management process, senior managers ensure that there is a systematic approach to the identification of asset integrity threats and to the assessment of the associated risks, in order to provide information on the need for risk reduction measures and to reduce major accident risks.

The intention of using a risk-based approach is that the asset integrity activities are selected and scheduled on the basis of their ability explicitly to measure and manage threats and ensure that associated risks are kept within acceptable limits.

Senior managers must ensure that employees have a good awareness of risk at all times. A team approach to process and task risk evaluation will drive a strong culture in the organization.

Note

1 ISO 15288, 'Systems and software engineering – system life cycle processes', second edition 2008, section 5.2.1.

Reference

OGP (2008) *Asset Integrity: The key to managing major incident risks*, Report no. 415, December, OGP, London

Piercing the corporate veil: liability of parent companies for the actions of their subsidiaries

PAUL ECCLES, RACHEL REEVES AND JOCELYN KIRKWOOD, SHOOSMITHS

The principles of the corporate veil

A fundamental principle of English law is that a company is considered to be a separate legal entity that is distinct from its shareholders. This can sometimes be referred to as a company having its own 'personality'.

In a group structure a parent and its subsidiary companies are separate legal entities in their own right, in terms of their rights as well as their liabilities. In essence, the acts or omissions of one company should not cause repercussions for another by reason of a corporate relationship.

Traditionally, the courts of England and Wales have respected this separation in both tort and contract cases. In limited circumstances the courts will disregard the concept of a separate legal personality and 'pierce (or lift) the corporate veil', although it is not sufficient simply to point to ownership, control or interests of justice to dislodge the doctrine.

Piercing the veil refers to a situation whereby the court is satisfied that the parent and the subsidiary should be regarded as a single legal entity, for example where:

- the subsidiary is a 'shell' of the parent; or
- there is some form of impropriety and use of the corporate structure resulting in a deliberate attempt to avoid liability; or

- it is required by statute; or
- the parent is considered to owe a duty of care to a claimant.

In such circumstances, it can be possible to pursue the parent company for the liabilities of the subsidiary.

When a claim might be made against a parent company instead of its subsidiary

It may not be possible to make a claim against a subsidiary company because either there is insufficient cover or funds in place or the subsidiary no longer exists. This is particularly true in uncertain economic times, when an increasing number of companies are being wound up or entering administration. Where a subsidiary company no longer exists or is insolvent, a claimant may look to the parent to be responsible for the liabilities of its subsidiaries.

A long-awaited Court of Appeal decision could have considerable implications for businesses, concerning the well-established principle that a parent company, as a separate legal entity from its subsidiaries, could not be held responsible for the subsidiaries' failings or liability.

The Court of Appeal has confirmed in *Chandler* v *Cape Plc* [2012] EWCA Civ 525 that there *are* circumstances when a parent company can be held liable for the health and safety of the employees of its subsidiary – where it had assumed a duty of care to advise and failed to ensure that steps were taken.

The circumstances in which a court can impose an assumption or attachment of responsibility on a parent company include:

- where the business of the parent and subsidiary are essentially the same;
- where the parent had, or ought to have had, superior knowledge on some relevant aspect of health and safety in the particular industry;
- where the parent company knew, or ought to have known, that the subsidiary's system of work was unsafe; and
- where the parent knew, or ought to have foreseen, that the subsidiary, or its employees, would rely on using that superior knowledge for the employees' protection.

The Court of Appeal also provided guidance that it will look at the wider relationship between the companies. For example, if the parent has a practice of intervening with the trading operations of the subsidiary on production issues, the court can infer a sufficient link between the companies for the purposes of health and safety responsibilities.

Piercing the veil?

The Court of Appeal in *Chandler* 'emphatically rejects any suggestion that it is in any way concerned with what is usually referred to as piercing the corporate veil'. The court further stated that 'a subsidiary and its company are separate entities. There is no imposition or assumption of responsibility by reason only that a company is the parent company of another company. The question is simply whether the parent company actions amounted to a direct duty to the subsidiaries' employees.'

The overriding message must be that, if there is any degree to which a parent has some relevant or superior knowledge of health and safety in a particular industry, coupled with knowledge that a subsidiary's system of work is unsafe, and that it is foreseeable that the subsidiary or its employees would rely on the parent's superior knowledge, then it is not necessary to show that the parent is intervening in the running of the subsidiary.

On the facts of the *Chandler* case it is highly relevant that Cape had employed medical and other officers responsible for safety issues for itself and the subsidiary.

In essence, the corporate veil in these circumstances *is* pierced, but only on the basis of an existing concept of assumption of responsibility – *Caparo Industries* v *Dickman 1990* – by its actions or knowledge. No doubt there will be cases that follow this and cases that are capable of being distinguished.

Cause for concern?

It should be borne in mind that there has been no indication that the decision should be applied generally to parent and subsidiary companies. The decision is more likely to be of particular concern to those that operate in industries where the health and safety of employees could be easily compromised or where there are potential environmental risks or liabilities, such as mining, oil and gas, energy or industrial cleaning.

Parental responsibility

Group companies are set up in various ways. The relationship between the parent and subsidiary company can vary depending on the type of structure and the driving forces behind the organization of the group.

There should be a clear distinction between the parent and subsidiary companies, and any practices and procedures that blur the lines of separation should be considered.

Acquisition and joint ventures

Due diligence is an essential part of the acquisition or joint venture (JV) process. Parent companies should scrutinize the information available to establish how closely the parent company and its new subsidiary will be linked. The closer the links, the easier it will be to trace liability up the corporate structure to the parent.

The following is a non-exhaustive checklist of the issues that parent companies should consider when acquiring a subsidiary:

- Review the structure of the group and establish where the subsidiary sits within it.
- Consider where board-level decisions are made, together with the structure of the board. Who is going to be on the board of the subsidiary post-acquisition? How far will the parent company intervene in the decision making of the subsidiary?

The number of hats worn by the same people will determine the ease with which liability can be traced to the parent company.

- Look at employee contracts. Where are employees contracted to work? If there are employees from the subsidiary who are going to work at the parent company or vice versa, it is important to set out clearly who their employer is and the extent of their role within the subsidiary.

- The articles of association should be scrutinized to establish what policies and procedures are in place about decision making within the group structure. Does the parent make the decision?

- In addition, the articles of the subsidiary company must be reviewed to establish whether or not an internal delegation policy exists. The more distinct the policies and procedures between the parent and subsidiary companies, the less likely liability ties could be established to the parent.

- Check the proposed accounting system for the parent and subsidiary companies. The closer the accounts are linked, the harder it is to argue corporate separation.

- Consider obtaining an indemnity from the seller of the subsidiary against unpaid taxes or potential liabilities arising pre-acquisition.

- Finally, check who it is that you are contracting with: the group, the parent or the subsidiary.

The key to establishing liability is determining who the ultimate decision maker is. Broadly, to avoid tracing liability back to a parent company, decision making and corporate and accounting structures between parent and subsidiary should be distinct.

Private equity

When a private equity house invests in a company, it is likely to work alongside the management team to increase the profitability of the business with a future sale or exit in mind. The investors often look to keep a tight rein on the investee company or group in order to protect the 'value' of the investment.

Whilst it is understandable that investors will want to protect their investment, there is a fine line between overseeing the decisions that are made and actually taking control of the day-to-day running of the subsidiary company's business – whether through intervention in the subsidiary's operations or in relation to funding issues.

Owing to the nature of an investment, and the protections an investor would require, it is advisable to make clear to a private equity house the risk of blurring the lines of separation, although the nature and business of the company should be considered when assessing the level of risk.

Public limited companies

Public limited companies (PLCs) are required to comply with additional corporate governance including, amongst others, the UK Corporate Governance Code. A PLC will often form committees dealing with matters such as remuneration or audit.

In addition, areas such as health and safety compliance may be delegated to a committee, which can make decisions that affect the entire group, potentially resulting in subsidiary companies surrendering some or all of their individual controls. Consideration should be given as to whether these procedures and governance create a risk of parent liability.

Practical steps to protect or reduce a parent company's liability to its subsidiary – the corporate angle

There are some practical steps that can be taken by parent companies to minimize the risk of any assumed responsibility:

- Consider whether the implementation of group-wide governance is appropriate and/or whether it goes too far as to control of the affairs of subsidiary companies.
- Consider the roles and responsibilities of the directors and managers.
- Consider the composition of the board. Where directors of a parent and subsidiary company are the same, they should make clear when they are making decisions on behalf of the parent and the subsidiary. This should be clearly recorded in the records of the relevant company, but may also extend further to the location of the meeting itself – if the locations of the parent and subsidiary are different.
- Plan ahead and consider whether having close links between the parent and subsidiary company is necessary. It may not be necessary for the board of the parent company to control the subsidiary's operating function.
- Ensure that subsidiary companies have their own policies and practices that allow them to operate adequately as separate entities.
- Assess the risk. It may be that the sector in which your business operates is unlikely to give rise to any assumption of liability issues.
- Where risks are being identified, a 'risk register' in respect of the subsidiary's business operations should be maintained to ensure appropriate measures are implemented.
- Consideration should always be given to the directors' potential liability under the Companies Act 2006.
- The implications of being classed as a shadow director should also be considered by a parent company. The actions of a parent company, in controlling or directing a subsidiary company, could amount to the parent being a shadow director.

Corporate manslaughter

In addition to employers' liability insurance, companies must be mindful of the offence of corporate manslaughter under the Corporate Manslaughter and Corporate Homicide Act 2007. The offence is triggered by a failing of senior management.

Parent companies need to be careful that their actual managing is not exercising such control that they have neutralized the subsidiary's own board of management and assumed control. That could then mean that the parent company comes within the definition of senior management contribution. The result would be that the parent company would be liable instead of the subsidiary, because it could be said that the parent company is managing the subsidiary's affairs rather than there being any degree of independence.

Bribery Act

Under section 7 of the Bribery Act 2010 a 'relevant commercial organisation' will be capable of being prosecuted if a person associated with the company bribes another person with the intention of obtaining or retaining a commercial advantage whilst conducting business for that company.

Even if it can be proven that the subsidiary was performing services for the parent company, the offence will be committed only if the subsidiary intended to obtain or retain a commercial advantage as above. In the absence of proof of intent, liability will not attach to the parent company. This is the case even if the parent company indirectly benefited from the bribe.

Whilst it is clear that a subsidiary can be entirely independent and responsible for its own actions, the wording of the Ministry of Justice guidance makes it clear that the parent company could be liable if the subsidiary is not independently managed. To avoid liability the parent company would need to demonstrate independence and show that the subsidiary is not merely a puppet of the parent through decision making and its implementation.

Practical steps to protect or reduce a parent company's liability to its subsidiary – the insurance angle

Parent companies should review their existing claims portfolios with insurers to ensure that their employers' liability cover does in fact cover any potential liability.

Other potential danger zones to look for from an insurance angle are indicated by the following questions:

- Is there sufficient cover in place?
- Does the parent carry a large deductible?
- Does the potential for such an argument in existing cases you have give rise to a 'circumstance', which might give rise to a claim triggering claims notification provisions in insurance policies? Indeed, is there an actual claim triggering notice provisions?
- Does this raise any potential non-disclosure issues for the parent company when renewing policies?

- What is the financial impact on premiums for your existing claims portfolios?

If in any doubt, discuss the issues immediately with brokers and insurers alike.

Summary

The decision in *Chandler* potentially has far-reaching consequences for UK companies and multinational companies. While the facts of the Chandler case were very specific, the ruling may encourage further claims to be brought against parent companies. However, in all cases the nature of the business of the group should be taken into account when assessing the level of risk of an assumption of liability.

As a consequence of *Chandler*, parent companies should take a look at how closely they are tied to their subsidiaries through the level of their involvement. It may be that changes have to be made to the way decisions are made throughout the group and policies implemented to govern the subsidiary and, mindful of the facts in *Chandler*, to protect the health and safety of employees.

Practical steps should be implemented to ensure that companies are not taken by surprise when disaster strikes. This risk may be considered greater when a UK company has subsidiaries in the developing world, where there is a less rigorous regulatory framework and/or a greater potential for liability. After all, prevention is better than cure!

A new dawn for board oversight

AMANDA MORRISON, KPMG LLP

There continues to be an intense focus on risk. This is not surprising given the continuing economic uncertainty and increasing regulatory pressure, both in the UK and internationally, to address the fallout from the financial crisis. A ballet of 'black swan' events – high-impact, low-probability events such as the near nuclear crisis caused by the 2011 Japanese earthquake – has highlighted concerns about traditional risk management approaches and the need for boards to plan for the unforeseen. But it is not just the 'black swans' that are keeping boards occupied. In an increasingly unstable world there is a myriad of known threats that could have a massive impact on the sustainability of today's businesses – an unstable Middle East, economic fragility in southern Europe, rising utility prices and the potential collapse of a major bank to underscore just a few crises on the horizon.

The reputational damage of failing to manage risk properly is also now a major threat. As a result, many companies are reassessing their risk management processes and, in particular, the role played by the board (and audit committee) in providing effective risk oversight.

Corporate governance developments

While much of the regulatory focus continues to be on the banks and broader financial services sector, the current debate on risk will have an impact on all market sectors. In the UK, the Financial Reporting Council (FRC)'s revised UK Corporate Governance Code now includes a 'main principle', setting out that the board is responsible for determining the nature and extent of the significant risks it is willing to take to achieve its strategic objectives, and a 'provision', recommending that the board, at least annually, carry out a review of the risk management system and report to shareholders that they have done so. To help understand what this means in practice, the FRC has held a number of meetings to better appreciate how boards are approaching their 'risk and control' responsibilities under the UK Corporate Governance Code. Participants from over 40 major listed companies – including chairmen, executive and non-executive directors and heads of risk and internal audit – have participated in these meetings, and the conclusions have been pulled together in a new FRC paper, 'Boards and risk: a summary of discussions with companies, investors and advisors'.

One of the main conclusions is that, while the existing guidance, 'Internal control: revised guidance for directors' (the Turnbull Guidance), is still broadly fit for purpose, some changes are needed to reflect the role of the board as articulated in the latest version of the Code. It was the FRC's intention to carry out a limited review of this guidance in the second half of 2012.

Risk management is also on the European Commission's regulatory agenda. The latest proposals for a Corporate Governance Framework for European Companies set out that the board is the body responsible for reviewing and approving the company's approach to risk, and that it should report it meaningfully to shareholders as far as possible without disclosing information that might damage the company, for example in relation to competitors. In a separate series of European Commission initiatives aimed at financial institutions, there are proposals to mandate board risk committees, require some sort of risk control declaration addressing the adequacy of internal control (something that sounds suspiciously close to the US Sarbanes–Oxley Act), and set out a new role for external auditors with respect to risk-related financial information.

Has it all gone horribly wrong?

At the beginning of the millennium, risk management was a new tool enthusiastically embraced as a panacea to help guard against all corporate ills. Fast-forward a decade and we are still regularly seeing major organizations (in both the financial and the non-financial sector) fail or having some other disaster or scandal that suggests that the risk management processes weren't really doing the job at all. So what is happening? Is enterprise risk management as a concept really discredited?

The answer is an emphatic 'No'. Rather, what we are experiencing is that the world is changing at an unprecedented speed, and in many organizations their risk management processes are simply failing to evolve to keep up with this pace of change.

So what should boards be thinking about doing to ensure that their risk processes are fit for purpose and working as intended in today's world? Typically there are six key questions that boards should be asking:

- What are we trying to achieve?
- Who is doing what?
- Has enterprise risk management been properly embedded into our business processes?
- Have we considered our risk appetite?
- Do we view risks in isolation?
- Have we factored scenario planning into our risk management processes?

What are we trying to achieve?

Before considering how the board oversees the risk management activities, the board should first consider the goals and objectives of its oversight effort. What should the board seek to accomplish in its oversight role? Is it about ensuring that expected risks are commensurate with expected rewards, that the system in place to manage risk is appropriate given the strategy, that the risk management system operates to inform the board of the major risks facing the company, or that an appropriate culture of risk awareness exists throughout the company? In most companies, the board will be answering 'Yes' to all of these questions.

Do we understand who is doing what?

There has been extensive debate about the pros and cons of establishing board-level risk committees, as well as about the role of audit committees in providing risk oversight. Indeed, guidance and regulation flowing from the FSA and EC suggest that risk committees are now de rigueur for financial institutions.

In the non-financial sector, more and more boards are coming to the conclusion that it is unlikely that any committee – including a risk committee – has the time, resources or expertise to assume full responsibility for risk oversight. In fact, more and more boards are recognizing that risk oversight is a 'team sport' involving the full board and all of its standing committees. Just as every player on the team needs to understand their role, the challenge for every board is to ensure proper alignment and coordination of the risk oversight responsibilities and activities of its various standing committees.

The FRC paper 'Boards and risk: a summary of discussions with companies, investors and advisors' draws attention to this point and notes that the responsibility for reviewing a company's risk management system might be delegated to board committees, but this does not detract from the board's responsibility for risk decision taking.

Different board committee structures may be appropriate to different companies, and risk committees should not generally be imposed on all companies. The exact dividing line between the audit committee and the board and between the audit and risk committees will differ from company to company, but the essential requirement is clarity of role and purpose.

In assessing its committee structure, a board should also consider whether there is a need for a separate committee to oversee an area of risk that might pose a particular concern for the business. For example, some boards have formed finance committees to focus on mergers and acquisitions and financing; and many technology companies have technology or science committees to review priorities and investments for research and development. Despite the benefits of these committees, a complex committee structure with too many committees may pose its own risk: a fragmented committee structure with no one seeing the 'big picture'.

Has risk management been properly embedded into our business processes?

A common failing is that many companies see risk management as merely an exercise that should be conducted once a year and then put aside to gather dust until the annual cycle of refreshing the risk map starts again!

Outside of this cycle there is typically no monitoring by the business of the KPIs around the key risks, no management reporting on the effectiveness of controls over key risks, no horizon scanning for new and emerging risks and certainly no reference to risk when key decisions are being taken. Is it any wonder then that in today's fast-changing world this approach to risk management should be doomed to failure?

Have we considered our risk appetite?

A fundamental element for managing risk in today's world is having a clear definition of risk appetite that is both directly linked to an organization's strategic objectives and also properly promulgated across the business. However, outside of the financial sector many organizations still struggle to define in a meaningful way how much risk they are willing to take on.

The FRC paper 'Boards and risk: a summary of discussions with companies, investors and advisors' notes that, owing to the difficulty in quantifying many of the risks facing a company and the limited ability to mitigate some external risks, it is not always necessary, or even possible, for the board to arrive at a single aggregate risk appetite for the company as a whole.

Nevertheless, it is really important that organizations clearly define their risk appetite – even if it is expressed around individual risks – so that those making decisions or monitoring key risk exposures have a clear reference point against which to do so.

Do we view risks in isolation?

Another important factor is to ensure that the interconnectivity or dependencies between various risks affecting a company are properly considered. Most risks will have consequential impacts on other risks the company faces. Take a very simple example: the impact for a manufacturing company of an accidental chemical leak into the water supply would be more than just monetary (eg fines, clean-up costs). In all likelihood this risk would also have an impact on its reputational risk (eg through adverse press publicity, impact on share price, potential loss of key customers), its regulatory risk (eg potentially greater environmental regulatory scrutiny) and even its employee-related risks (eg staff morale, the impact on its ability to attract high-quality new recruits etc).

The FRC paper 'Boards and risk: a summary of discussions with companies, investors and advisors' also stresses the importance of interconnectivity and notes that many participants reported that, while risk had historically been looked at in isolation, there was increasing awareness that risks were sometimes interconnected and sequential, and of the cumulative impact and disruptive effect of a number of significant risks materializing at the same time.

Have we factored scenario planning into our risk management processes?

Finally, given the speed of change in the many external factors that have an impact on today's business it's vitally important for companies to build into their overall risk management approach some scenario planning to address how they would respond to given scenarios. Techniques such as reverse stress testing are also beginning to be adopted outside the financial sector and, at the very least, boards should be challenging received wisdom and asking what would be the worst thing that could happen.

In conclusion, the world continues to change at a phenomenal speed, so the way in which boards manage risk needs to move on from the traditional risk management approach that was embraced so passionately over a decade ago.

Companies now need dynamic strategies and processes for how they manage risk that are alert to the changing world in which they operate and the 'once in a lifetime' events that of late seem to have a horrible habit of occurring much more frequently. Most importantly, today's risk management systems need to be agile enough to facilitate the right people in the business getting the right risk information to be able to make the right decisions at the right time!

Positive risk: the upside issues

SIMON KING, DNV KEMA

Introduction

The upside of risk has received considerable attention in recent years and has now secured a place in the vocabulary of today's professional risk managers. However, it has yet to receive an active place in many risk management frameworks.

Risk management is traditionally viewed by practitioners as the means of understanding and protecting against the potential obstacles to success. Irrespective of the particular framework we follow, or are influenced by, we all broadly accept that risk is 'the effect of uncertainty on objectives'[1] and recognize that outcomes 'can be positive and/or negative'.[2] The challenge is that some organizations are more willing to hear risk managers talk about preventing worse outcomes while the business and strategy managers focus on achieving better outcomes.

Risk managers have been discussing positive risk for some time now, yet there is little publicly available evidence around what is actually happening in organizations. The likely reasons for this include:

- Risk is still largely viewed as relating to downside outcomes, particularly in the 'operational' risk management community (and reinforced by the focus on risk management after the recent financial crisis).
- Organizations seem to find it difficult to introduce easy and understandable ways to apply the concept of positive risk to their existing risk management frameworks (or if they do they are not talking about it publicly).
- In all but the most entrepreneurial environments culture tends towards 'protecting' and 'assuring' rather than seeking opportunity.
- The performance of management and leadership teams is measured against success criteria. It is easier for a risk management process to identify and manage the hindrances to success than find and exploit enablers to succeed.

This chapter considers the concept of 'positive risk' and looks at the challenges and issues inherent in its practical application. Our intention is to help you decide whether, how and what you might want to do differently:

- Does it require you to take a fundamentally different focus?

- What can you do to show your organizations the benefits of looking at positive risk and the value you can add?
- Should you worry if the focus of your risk management efforts appears to be on downside rather than upside?

Organizational challenges

Organizations that expose their employees to hazard-rich working environments routinely do their best to protect them from harm. There will be a robust and often industry-standard approach to identifying and responding to the risks present, with the aim of minimizing their occurrence. For such organizations 'positive' or 'upside' risk can be a difficult concept, as it goes against the traditional and cultural approach to risk management and its focus on mitigating threats, albeit that operational risk is accepted.

Similarly, organizations that have a strong culture of working towards published performance targets might find it challenging to establish processes that divert attention towards non-core areas of activity.

In times of ongoing economic uncertainty risk managers in all organizations, as well as their executives, should want to explore the benefits of different strategies and how more can be achieved, possibly with fewer resources.

Management reporting systems make available a range of information about progress towards targets that helps to inform decisions about where to place resources, and to manage expectations and likely sources of uncertainty in the future. Some of this information is already explicitly related to risk and uncertainty, and it often takes only a little effort to represent it as forward looking, supporting innovation and helping to seize opportunities through better-informed decision making. For organizations with high-risk operating environments this can mean that a change in mindset is required first.

Perhaps it is the more 'strategic'- or 'corporate'-level initiatives that offer the opportunity for risk management to focus on the 'upside'. If this is the case, do we need a whole new approach to talk about positive risk, or do we just need to think differently? We must, however, be careful not to treat this too theoretically, as we would run the risk of disengaging people if we cannot keep this simple.

How do we see positive risk?

One pragmatic view is that upside is achieved by default, when managing downside risk(s) prevents loss or harm through the reduction in impact or likelihood (or both) of a negative risk materializing. For example, if an organization has an objective of having a safe and productive workforce, while this might more usually be presented in a negative frame of aiming to have zero injuries, the risks and controls that address this might be the same whichever way the objective is presented; however, one seems more upbeat.

This view can be reinforced with the application of risk assessment techniques such as cause-and-effect analysis or bow tie analysis.[3] Cause-and-effect analysis provides a structured pictorial display of a list of causes of a specific effect. The effect may be positive (eg an objective) or negative (eg a problem), depending on context. The cause-and-effect analysis identifies contributory factors to wanted as well as unwanted effects. Putting a positive focus on an issue, perhaps in terms of the desired change, can encourage greater ownership, participation and fresh thinking so that we identify the things that we positively need to happen rather than only things that typically go wrong.

Bow ties are a useful method for providing an analysis of the barriers (or controls) that should prevent causes leading to unwanted consequences. Where factors might cause escalation, barriers to escalation can also be represented. However, bow ties can also be used for positive consequences, mapping 'controls' that stimulate the generation of the event.

We can argue that if our risk identification is effective we will identify positive risks. If a 'risk' is the 'effect of uncertainty on objectives',[4] and 'an effect is a deviation from the expected – positive and/or negative',[5] then a thorough risk identification will by default identify potential upside risks. What often happens next, however, is that organizations analyse the risks (causes, sources, consequences and likelihoods) with an orientation towards downside, even if this relates to not doing the positive things. We often see impact scales that refer to a negative impact on measures such as a financial value (cost, revenue and profit), human factors (health, safety and welfare), organizational aims (shareholder value and corporate social responsibility) or brand and reputation (including stakeholder opinion).

ISO 31000 incorporates the concept of understanding the upside of the risk ('Risk analysis involves consideration of the causes and sources of risk, their positive and negative consequences, and the likelihood that those consequences can occur'[6]), but we don't see much analysis of the positive consequences of a risk, were it to materialize. Do we need to add a positive orientation to our risk identification, workshops, analyses etc? Could we also ask 'What events would create a better-than-expected outcome?' Could we produce a register that includes positive outcome risks (effects of uncertainty on objectives), for which actions can be planned and taken to make them more likely to occur or produce bigger, more positive consequences?

At this point we can start to see a link with risk appetite. The focus on avoiding or reducing downside is also how risk appetite is often articulated. Generally, risk appetite is expressed in terms of 'tolerance' or 'acceptability' (both of which imply a downside effect), or indicators that are expressed numerically and in terms of boundaries or limits (and usually about the avoidance of, or reduction in, negative incidents).

However, it may be appropriate to set a positive or opportunity risk appetite that will provide guidance around the level up to which risk can be sought. This approach will be familiar within financial market and credit risk environments. It is also inherent in the nature of organizational strategy setting where decisions are taken as to the acceptability (often to financial stakeholders) of the levels of uncertainty around desired outcomes. However, there is no reason why a positive risk appetite shouldn't form a structured part of the risk management framework too. It will help risk management to become more aligned with strategy by encouraging discussions around what activities or opportunities can be pursued that otherwise might have been sidelined.

The above is all summarized by the Institute of Risk Management (Hopkin, 2010), which recognizes a range of interpretations of the upside of risk management, including:

- fewer disruptions to normal operations and greater operational efficiency, resulting in less downside risk;
- the ability to seize an opportunity denied to competitors because a better-informed view is taken of the management of risks;
- deliberately identifying during the risk assessment events that will be positive and actively deciding how to manage those events;
- opportunity management, whereby a detailed evaluation is undertaken of new business opportunities before deciding to take the opportunity;
- achieving a positive outcome from a situation that could have gone wrong without good judgement or risk management; and
- achieving compliance and risk assurance in difficult circumstances as an unintended or automatic consequence of good risk management.

Have we been seeing negative risk as inherent in an organization or its existing activities or having an impact on us as a result of third parties' acts of omission or commission? Would it help if we saw positive risk as needing to be identified in situations, strategies and plans that we initiate or seek out ourselves?

Positive risk terminology

Is the risk management profession over-complicating the topic? Do we believe that upside risks are something different to downside risks and therefore require different, separate thinking or effort to identify and manage? Have we made things too complicated by trying to define them?

People generally agree that failings in the management of risk of different types contributed to the financial crisis. Is good risk management not simply a part of good business management? If this is the case it would be of no surprise that the topic of positive risk suffers from ambiguity. Is the positive outcome of risk or risk management anything more than the result of effective organizational decision making and tactical delivery?

Ignoring the external definitions, does an organization need to be clear what positive risk is for itself, in order to embed methods for using it? Naturally, once organizations produce internal definitions of positive risk, then its application becomes bespoke and what one organization does might not be transferable to another. Do we need to worry about defining it or do we just need to more fully consider the positive and negative outcomes of the uncertainty we face?

Different labels are applied to the topic, including:

- positive risk;
- upside risk; and
- opportunity risk.

We propose that positive risk and upside risk are synonymous. They both seem to relate to a state, condition or 'property' that a risk possesses (ie it might have a positive effect on objectives) or to a consequential happening (ie the risk produced or will produce a positive effect, perhaps unplanned).

Opportunity risk, however, is more related to a deliberate act by an organization, ie the organization has undertaken an opportunity assessment of some kind, or identified a business opportunity it wishes to seek or exploit, or a change it wants to implement in order to realize defined benefits. In these cases, the organization should require its risk management process to influence the go/no go decision and, if it is 'go', then to help the opportunity be successfully realized. In this sense opportunity risk management is deeply embedded in general business management; the opportunity might be a new product launch, a cost-saving or efficiency-improving initiative, a merger or acquisition, and so on. The risk team in this instance should be a part of the opportunity project team.

Ironically though, whether dealing with opportunity risk, positive risk or upside risk, the response is to apply the classic risk management process – identify, analyse, evaluate, treat (including seek and exploit) – in order to mitigate negative outcomes and enable positive ones to happen. The choice of label used will largely be influenced by what is acceptable to the organization and aligned with existing (risk) management terminology.

We need to help our organizations understand whether positive risk, for them, would be:

- a state that is being described, ie the advantage that arises from a risk, which we then seek to exploit (eg worsening economic conditions produce a more competitive environment among suppliers, pushing our own purchasing costs down);

- positive happenings or outcomes, simply arising as a result of our existing actions (eg fire prevention activity, which raises fire safety awareness and protection and reduces the number of fires); or

- something that is aimed for, ie an outcome deliberately created, manipulated, manufactured or sought, which might not otherwise have existed (eg the introduction of new terms and conditions to a workforce that allow it to be more flexibly managed, thus reducing costs and improving customer service).

This clarity is important, as it helps us understand how we can adapt our typical approach to better identify ways to demonstrate a different approach to risk management.

A final note on terminology comes from PAS 200:2011 (BSI Group, 2011): 'A well-managed crisis can demonstrate the positive qualities of an organization and enhance its general reputation.' Therefore we must not forget that for many organizations the existence and application of risk management, per se, have a positive effect, whether for pure risk management process and procedure, crisis management and business continuity, or compliance.

Reinforcing the paradigm of downside risk

It is fair to say that most management teams orient their (risk management) behaviour around avoiding the 'bad things'. By default, this approach surely removes obstacles to success. No risk manager would be criticized for taking this type of action. Unfortunately, this behaviour alone ignores the identification of equally important opportunities that may help achieve better performance.

Generally, risk appetite statements are created to protect the performance and success measures against which management teams are targeted and often rewarded. Therefore, while it is possible to understand the contribution that 'upside' can have, it is intuitively easier to protect against downside.

Think like an entrepreneur?

To entrepreneurs, risk is the potential downside of a significantly larger potential upside. It is the draw of the upside that makes the investment worth the risk. But even in public sector organizations tough economic times or challenging conditions can bring about entrepreneurial behaviours. People see opportunity (for savings, improvements, change), which itself will require investment (money, time, resources). This could manifest itself with the ultimate goal being the desired upside, and the 'risks' being the barriers, which in this sense are to be overcome, whereas barriers otherwise protect us from the sources of risk and its impact.

The extent to which the goal is articulated as the positive benefit to be achieved is determined by the attitude towards risk management, for example the activity that will have successfully ceased and whose costs are, therefore, avoided.

What we can do in practice

In order to better accommodate, or even only to recognize, the upside of risk in organizational management frameworks, we do need to adjust existing processes and procedures. If this has not yet happened it may be why many organizations are yet to be (or feel) well enough equipped to manage this topic.

We suggest trying the following.

1 *Positive differences.* Systematically review corporate performance to identify examples of where current risk management practices have made a difference to the outcomes achieved

2 *Articulation of the risk.* Think about using terms such as 'ability to...', 'increase in...', 'be ahead of...' in risk descriptions. Adopt a different approach to articulating risk, such as 'Because of X, Y happens, resulting in Z', and provide training or practice time for those who will be doing this.

3 *Scoring.* The upside effect of an event might have a different quantum of impact from a downside effect. It may be easier to measure the size of the lost or missed

opportunities (with a negative risk mindset) using a reverse matrix, although this might not always work. If this is the means to score (some) positive risks then be prepared to use a separate scale or a separate matrix.

4 *Different mitigation techniques.* Mitigation for downside risks typically involves the four Ts (tolerate, treat, transfer, terminate), yet for upside we might think about behaviours such as seek, pursue, capture or enhance.

5 *Definitions and terminology.* We expect non-risk professionals to be engaged with the risk management framework. We need to make it easy for them to understand and embrace it. Something that is an academic or theoretical headache is unlikely to engage colleagues. Think carefully about how you define upside risk, and who needs to know this.

6 *Rewards and incentives.* Organizations tend to be rewarded for meeting objectives or success criteria. Therefore managers often take a 'protective' approach to managing risk, looking for ways of preventing downside rather than proactively seeking upside. Find and share examples (see 1 above) of where risk has created positive effects to encourage others to understand how upside can be achieved.

7 *Cultural awareness.* If the organization currently seeks to minimize hazard risks and has well-established and robust safety management processes, bringing positive risk into the risk management framework might need to be incremental and initially require the involvement of a selected, discrete group of colleagues.

8 *Integration with existing frameworks.* There is no need to create a whole new work stream around positive risk. Reviewing existing performance management initiatives for successes and recognizing these better (through minutes, publicizing results, retelling the story etc) help drive a realization that this was actually positive risk management and act as encouragement and a confidence builder to pursue other opportunities.

Notes

1 ISO 31000, 'Risk management – principles and guidelines'.
2 ISO 31000.
3 ISO 31010, 'Risk management – risk assessment techniques'.
4 ISO 31000 and ISO Guide 73.
5 ISO 31000 and ISO Guide 73.
6 ISO 31000.

References

BSI Group (2011) *PAS 200:2011: Crisis management – guidance and good practice*, BSI, London
Hopkin, P (2010) *Fundamentals of Risk Management*, Kogan Page/Institute of Risk Management, London

PART TWO
Approaches to operational risk management

Risk-based security

Dr MORTEN BREMER MAERLI, DNV KEMA

Security is never as visible as when it fails.

The world is seeing new security risk environments and dynamics, from hackerism to state-run 'cyber-wars', fraud and industrial espionage. Globalization has eased mobility of crime and terrorism. Rapid technological development has increased system interconnections, complexities and interdependencies, and a convergence between previously disjointed security functions. In parallel, high-profile events have boosted security risk awareness. 'Securitization', or the use of extraordinary means in the name of security, has become part of the political tool box.

Inevitably, security has become a business issue; either as an opportunity, where companies exploit general security trends and market demands, or as a precautionary and protective means towards own buriness activity in order to create comparative advantages. Security impacts on businesses and organizations can be devastating, yet all too often businesses willingly seem to neglect credible security risks. Security risks may be perceived as less likely or less important; the neglect may stem from failure to appreciate asset values, threats and vulnerabilities, or simply from organizations being unsure how to manage security risks effectively and proportionally.

This chapter aims at providing a platform for understanding the characteristics of security risks and risk-based security. In the following, some considerations on security methodologies and security concepts are provided.[1] It is shown that security is indeed different from safety. For security risk reduction, identification of vulnerabilities may be more important than focusing on threats; once identified, vulnerabilities can be managed. Threats on the other hand are uncertain and fluctuating.

Characteristics of security risks

Security is different. Whereas security risks stem from intentional malicious and normally planned acts that are brought about by people, safety incidents find their origin in accidents and mishaps. For security assessments, it becomes important to understand how intentions relate to particular assets in need of protection. Correlations of possible intentions, goals and targets help in identifying threats. The scope of credible threats may be narrowed by considering the likely motives of possible perpetrators to determine whether they will result in specific assets being targeted (Baybutt, 2002).

Threats must hence be assessed on the basis of asset characteristics (see Table 2.1.1) and how well the use of these assets meets the perpetrator's motivations and intentions. This is even more the case with rational (calculating) adversaries: the target chosen, the means applied and the time and location of the attack could be tailored to optimize desired outputs. Safety risks will involve neither targeting nor any damage optimization. Likewise, whilst security risks could emanate from security glitches, safety events are never the result of any 'opportunities' – rather the consequence of mishaps.

Risk responses are likely to differ accordingly, and so are the tools and the expertise needed for security risk assessments.

Risk-based security assessment: DNV methodology

1   Asset analysis. A structured and detailed review of the assets, including an evaluation of:
     –   how critical the assets are to the operator;
     –   how attractive the assets may be to a perpetrator.

2   Threat analysis. Identification and documentation of potential threats (espionage, terrorism, theft and sabotage) associated with the critical and/or attractive assets. The analysis serves as a framework for establishing threat levels.

3   Vulnerability analysis. Identification and documentation of any vulnerability in the security system that can be exploited by a perpetrator:
     –   addresses both technical aspects and human factors;
     –   assesses the system's ability to deter, detect, delay and deny perpetrators.

4   Risk analysis. Combines the threat and vulnerability analysis, and estimates the risk accompanying each scenario that has been developed and prioritized. It includes the dynamic characteristic of a perpetrator.

5   Cost-effectiveness analysis. Identification and documentation of options to reduce the risk in a cost-effective manner:
     –   supports decision making;
     –   reduces ad hoc implementations of security measures.

TABLE 2.1.1 Security risks and safety risks compared

	Security risk	Safety risk
Trigger	Gain or desire to harm	Breakages, errors, failures
Trait	Purposeful	Accidental
Initiator	Person	Person or nature
Origin	External, possibly with insider(s)	Internal, possibly external
Tailored	Yes	No
Damage maximizing	Possibly	No
Discriminatory	Possibly	No

Components of security risks

Protective measures against various threats have been central to all societies throughout time. Missing or inadequate protection could introduce vulnerabilities, thus exposing valuable assets. Asset owners could face losses or direct or indirect damage. Associated risks may be expressed as a combination of the threat to a particular asset and the vulnerability of the asset to the threat. This is illustrated in Figure 2.1.1.

Assets

Assets are items of value from the perspective of the organization or a potential adversary. An organization has numerous assets that warrant protection. An asset may be rare, valuable or otherwise hard to replace, or may cause an unacceptable delay in mission execution if lost. Assets may also be defined as the resources by which the organization derives value (Landoll, 2006, p 30). People, information, competence etc are included in this definition.

The identification and ranking of assets are a necessary precursor to understanding the overall risk to those assets. The enumeration and valuing of the assets present help to scope and guide the security assessment (Landoll, 2006, p 30). This exercise, however, should to the extent possible also be done from a perpetrator's perspective – in other words, what possible adversaries may find to be an attractive target (and why).

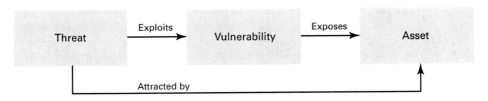

FIGURE 2.1.1 Risk as a threat that exploits a vulnerability that exposes an asset

Threats

A threat is any action with the potential to cause harm in the form of death, injury, destruction, disclosure, interruption of operations or loss of reputation. As part of the threat assessment, possible perpetrators should be identified, allowing for an assessment of the capabilities needed to perform an attack, and whether this seems reasonable to establish. A thorough analysis of the business environment facilitates the identification of threats (Graves, 2006, p 4).

A threat evaluation requires the analysis of the potential threat actions. Threat analysis defines the level or degree of the threats against an asset by evaluating the intent and capability of those who may carry them out. The process involves gathering historical data about hostile events and evaluating which information is relevant in assessing the threats against the asset.

Threats are determined by who wants to achieve what, by what means and with what target in mind. An actual threat does not occur until someone has both the will and the ability to carry out an attack. If the assets fail to arouse any interest amongst potential perpetrators, the risk is negligible irrespective of any skills and expertise that may prevail. Likewise, even dedicated attackers pose no risk without the necessary capacities.

Why and to what extent those posing threats are attracted to the assets depend on the assets' characteristics. To terrorists, assets with a significant damage potential could be particularly attractive targets. Thieves will typically look at the profit potential associated with valuables. In industrial espionage, information is the (valuable) target. Prospects of larger profits or larger impacts could increase perpetrators' risk appetite.

An actual attack, however, will depend on the perpetrators' own assumptions about their abilities in the face of security measures at selected targets, as well as other practical challenges they may foresee. Facilities with a strong security appearance, ie facilities that are seemingly well protected, could be less attractive than poorly secured targets. Such 'cost-effect' assessments by the perpetrators will determine the target's attractiveness, and thus the likelihood of the target being attacked.

What is to be attacked, when and where are, in other words, up to the perpetrators. Because the attack is carried out deliberately, this also gives perpetrators the opportunity to influence the outcome (consequences). The choice of the time and place of the attack will affect who and how many people are affected. Perpetrators may also introduce barriers that prevent a proper response.

Vulnerability

Vulnerability can be understood as the factors that reduce or limit the ability to withstand attacks against targets containing or sustaining the assets. Examples may range from unlocked doors to disloyal employees (so-called insiders).[2] To potential perpetrators, modern lifestyles and demands provide a target-rich environment. Protecting them all is neither feasible nor desirable. The respective organizations potentially at risk, however, do have incentives to minimize any harm (physical, financial, reputational etc) to themselves and the surroundings and to protect assets.

Incentives may be internally driven or externally pushed, eg national or international compliance demands. In both cases, there is a proven, documented ability to manage variations (sometimes unpredictable variations) in the operating environment with minimal damage, alteration or loss of functionality.

A beneficial approach for security risk assessments may be for the security auditors to 'change side'. Security staff should then try to think and perform like potential perpetrators and look for security weaknesses and vulnerabilities. In addition, a cost–benefit analysis from the point of view of the perpetrators should be attempted, in order to understand their prioritizations. Response systems within organizations may hence be put closer to the real tests.

Reduction of security risk

Any security risk mitigation involves dealing with determined and presumably capable actors who will explore and exploit opportunities to reach their goals. Further, they will potentially try to circumvent risk-mitigating measures put in place. Hence, while security personnel and others engage in proactive risk *mitigation*, perpetrators may be seen as engaging in proactive risk *generation*.

Malicious acts follow their own logic, based on perpetrator motivations, opportunities and constraints. Accordingly, security measures may have to deal with a range of different perpetrator characteristics, such as their varying levels of expertise and skills for carrying out their unlawful and undesired actions. Possible sanctions, moreover, could make cunning perpetrators less risk prone and hence more conservative. As targets may be determined to be too strong, so perpetrators' well-proven tactics may be maintained and applied elsewhere.

Risk develops in the interplay between assets, threats and vulnerabilities; remove the assets and the risk is removed. Without threats, the asset may well be very vulnerable yet not at risk. Finally, with no vulnerability, even large-scale threats pose no risk. Figure 2.1.2 illustrates this point.

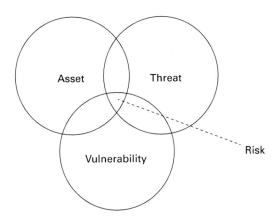

FIGURE 2.1.2 Risk, asset, threat and vulnerability

The risk of losing critical objects or assets can therefore be reduced in three ways: the threat can be countered directly or indirectly, vulnerabilities can be identified and eliminated, or assets and objects can be removed, relocated or consolidated. Sound security practices should consider, and possibly include, all the elements – to varying degrees.

Asset reduction

Assets can be consolidated to reduce security costs. However, completely removing or reducing the assets is rarely an option. Assets are valuable to their owners and are usually present for a reason. A hedging strategy may be to reduce the value of assets that are compromised or stolen; examples include encrypted hard drives or the colouring of stolen money. This makes assets of possible interest to perpetrators less attractive.

Threat reduction

Monitoring threats may provide important signs of an impending attack or indications of particularly vulnerable industries. But threats may also remain undetected. Traditional trend analyses will be of particularly limited relevance to highly innovative perpetrators. In general, understanding the threat component is the most challenging and uncertain part of risk assessments.

Vulnerability reduction

Vulnerabilities will always be present. Like threats, vulnerabilities may be difficult to deal with. However, vulnerabilities rest with the owner of the assets, allowing for interventions once the vulnerabilities are detected. Threat-specific scenarios make it possible to identify vulnerabilities by analysing the security controls (technical, human and organizational) put in place to protect the assets.

Conclusion

Lack of security could be bad for business. Theft, sabotage, espionage or terrorism may be aimed specifically at those assets that an organization most wants to protect. Effects could be devastatingly harmful. In a security context, understanding vulnerabilities is particularly important. Where threats are uncertain and fluctuating, vulnerabilities – if identified – may be the key to cost-effective risk reduction. Security vulnerability exercises could hence be a viable support to crisis and emergency exercises – measures that primarily aim at responding when the damage has already occurred.

Paying for prevention is often demanding. However, done wisely – ie in a risk-based manner – measures for security risk reduction could be amongst the more secure investments. Security is never as visible as when it fails.

Notes

1 The following text builds on 'Risk-based security management: concepts and overview', DNV Technical Report 2008-2101, as well as 'Risk-based security and security risk reduction', a DNV background note for the Norwegian 22 July Commission. Henrik Fonahn provided useful comments during the preparation of the chapter.

2 Often security systems are designed to deter, detect, deny, protect and delay an external adversary. Few systems are designed to address the insider threat. The insider threat stems from trusted individuals who steal, distribute, sabotage, destroy or release critical assets or key assets like information. The insider threat may also include personnel being manipulated or threatened by, or working in collusion with, external adversaries. An insider has a significant advantage over external people with respect to carrying out a malicious act. The insider can bypass physical and technical security measures designed to prevent unauthorized access because he or she has been granted authorized access to what is considered the most valuable assets. Accordingly, the insider is considered by most security experts to be the most dangerous threat to any organization – authorized persons involved in non-authorized activities.

References

Baybutt, Paul (2002) Assessing risks from threats to process institutions: threat and vulnerability analysis, *Process Safety Progress*, **21** (4), pp. 269–75

Graves, Gregory Howard (2006) Analytical foundations of physical security system assessment, PhD dissertation, Texas A&M University, August

Landoll, Douglas J (2006) *The Security Risk Assessment Handbook*, Auerbach Publications, Boca Raton, FL

Preparing for uncertainty: using scenarios

HANS LÆSSØE, THE LEGO GROUP

Introduction

Large parts of enterprise risk management (ERM) are based on day-to-day operations such as the handling of minor disruptions, employee health and safety, currency fluctuation and the like. For most of these it is 'easy' to use experience and present-day conditions to identify the risks that need to be embedded and handled in the ERM process.

For strategic risks this risk identification is significantly more difficult to do coherently for two reasons. First, strategies are focused on a farther time horizon, leading to significant uncertainty as to what the future may hold. Second, strategies may divert the business from the known path and hence include assumptions related to less-known territory. Hence, if risk (and opportunity) assessment is based on the current insight and imagination of relevant people, this may not be adequate to cover the real uncertainties pertaining to the strategy.

At the LEGO Group, we realized this some years ago and decided to make an effort to enhance our risk and opportunity identification process by use of strategic scenarios.

The first approach

To do this, a small team of insightful people were collected to define how to optimize risk and opportunity identification – and the use of scenarios was quickly established as the basic approach.

After some discussion (and frustration), the team found that a best-practice approach was to base these scenarios on a 'cross' between two key uncertainties, as shown in Figure 2.2.1. The important challenge is to find the best possible uncertainty drivers.

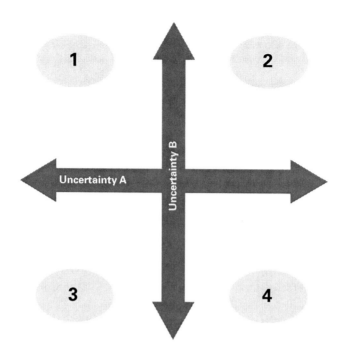

FIGURE 2.2.1 The scenario cross

When we did this in 2008, we found, based on 12 mega-trends prepared by the World Economic Forum and other material, that the two most relevant drivers would be:

- *Consumer market growth.* At one end it was assumed that the consumer market during the next 5–10 years would see growth, most likely driven by Asian and BRIC markets. At the other end it was assumed that an actual decline would materialize owing to continued financial strain and liquidity scarcity.

- *Strategic direction.* At one end it was assumed that the current strategic direction of the LEGO Group would be relevant for the coming horizon – and potentially only need minor evolutionary changes – whereas the other end assumed that a dramatic change of direction would be needed.

This led to four scenarios, which were then described in detail both from a STEEP (social, technological, economic, environmental, political) approach and on a business system approach looking at consumers, customers, competitors and business system.

These four scenarios were then presented to top management (approximately 30 people), who were split into four groups, each focusing on one scenario and discussing 'What will it take to make the LEGO Group successful in a future that looks like this scenario?'

The outcome of these discussions was shared and documented and served as input to the upcoming strategic planning process. Subsequently, the strategies were defined, and this may to some extent have been based on the awareness created by the half-day scenario session. However, we have no specific documentation of this.

The benefit of this process was that it drove good discussions – whereas the tangible business impact is hard(er) to justify – and the scenario team ended up concluding that the process had not had the impact we wished for and had expected, given the (significant) amount of work that had gone into preparing these scenarios.

An after-action review disclosed a set of weaknesses:

- As the scenarios were predefined and described by a team of 'experts', they gained only limited buy-in from the management team who were to use them.
- The generic nature of the uncertainties chosen meant that the scenarios may have been relevant for an overall discussion of the LEGO Group strategic direction, but were useless when defining more explicit strategies, for example entering new markets.
- The detailed description of each scenario led to a perception of these as being predictions, and hence hampered 'out of the box' thinking.

In short, the process had to be revised to be useful.

Defining 'scenarios version 2'

In spite of the above shortcomings, we still believed scenario thinking was a strong tool for identifying risks and opportunities and driving managers to 'think the unthinkable' and be bold in assessing potential changes in the world.

So we started out by addressing the shortcomings, focusing first and foremost on the purpose of using strategic scenarios, which was defined as 'support management to think the unthinkable and identify risks and opportunities not visible when basing planning on present-day paradigms'.

Hence, it was *not* the purpose to try to predict the future – a 'mission impossible' – but to prepare a basis for a future that might change and be different from the one we expect or plan for.

Then we looked at the process and found that, efficient as it might be to have specialists define the scenarios, this reduces buy-in and application. Hence we needed a process in which management was directly involved in defining the scenarios they used.

Then we addressed the approach, and attempted alternatives derived for example from strategy consultants, but here we found that the cross of two key uncertainties was probably the best approach to defining relevant and different scenarios.

Finally, we found that it was important that management could apply the uncertainties most relevant to the specific strategy in question. For instance, if you are in the process of defining a strategy for IT development, it has little or no impact whether the consumer market is increasing or decreasing.

Preparing for the scenario process

The fact that managers have to be involved in choosing key uncertainties does not mean that we have to start from a blank sheet of paper, and we defined some preparatory work that was brought to the process to increase both efficiency and effectiveness:

- A clear process and agenda for the scenario session were defined in five sequential steps as described below.
- A wide set of uncertainties were predefined (some shown in Figure 2.2.2). These served to expand the imagination of the managers, as well as speeding up the process of defining the 'best' uncertainties upon which to build the scenarios.
- Predefined tools or templates effectively collected data and findings during the process (as shown in Figure 2.2.4).

With these elements in place, members of the strategic risk management team were called upon to facilitate and drive the process as a part of defining and/or testing an explicit strategy.

Furthermore a prioritization tool was needed. The process identified a set of issues in terms of risks and opportunities, not all of which would lead to action, as this would resemble betting on every horse in the race.

We have defined a tool to identify generic strategic responses, the PAPA model, illustrated in Figure 2.2.3 and based on assessments of: likelihood of happening (low or high); and speed of materialization (slow or fast).

Issues that are not expected to materialize and, if they do, will do so slowly enough for us to be able to act upon them in time are parked.

Issues that are likely to happen, slowly, are adapted to. For the LEGO Group this encompasses, for example, changes in demographics, children's play patterns, consumer behaviour etc.

A		B
Consumers become uniform or global, as they are all affected by the same news, films, stories, music etc.	Consumers	Consumers become individualistic and wish every product to be customized or personalized.
Legislation becomes focused on developing global growth and hence predictable and 'easier' for companies to operate worldwide.	Legislation	Driven by, for example, fiscal constraints, legislation becomes local and focuses on improving short-term national competitiveness.
Retail remains based in stores located close to the consumer.	Retail	Retailing becomes a 'thing of the past' as a significant share of sales moves to globally based e-tailing or m-tailing.
The technological development is continuous and predictable.	Technology	The technological development is erratic and provides quantum leap changes.

FIGURE 2.2.2 Potential uncertainty drivers

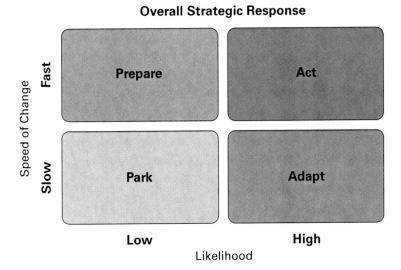

FIGURE 2.2.3 The PAPA prioritization model

Issues that are not likely to happen but, if they do, will have a disruptive character are those we need to be prepared for. These are the strategic risks and opportunities in essence, the issues where predefined contingency plans and/or mitigation plans are called for. These may be issues such as trade barriers, changes in competitive landscape or the like.

Issues that we 'know' will materialize (high likelihood), and will happen fast, need to be acted upon and embedded in the strategy for this to be successful. For the LEGO Group this includes issues related to, for example, 'connectivity', ie children's use of the internet, mobile phones, social networks or the like – almost whatever we imagine. We add these to the strategy, assuming that otherwise we will be caught unprepared.

It is noted that the parameter of 'impact' is not included, as it is assumed that all identified issues will have a significant enough impact for them to be listed in the first place.

Preparing for the future: the process

The 'prepare for uncertainty' process is conducted through a four-hour session, where a team of managers is assembled to discuss a specific strategy. This is done either as an input provider to the strategy, and hence before it is even drafted, or as a test of the resilience of the defined strategy, and hence after it has been drafted but prior to its finalization and approval.

1 The 'owner' presents the target and scope of the strategy, and this is documented in the defined template. This serves to clarify the purpose of the session.

2 The team is then presented with a range of plausible uncertainties (like the ones shown in Figure 2.2.2) and discusses these. The objective of this part is to identify the two most impactful uncertainties for the strategy. The team is inspired and allowed to define new uncertainties if it wishes to do so.

At the end of this step, two key uncertainties are identified, and it is validated that the team assesses that both extremes of each uncertainty are plausible, and that the uncertainties to a large extent are mutually independent. Hence, if the team assesses that one extreme is not really plausible, either the description of this is altered or the team is requested to find another uncertainty driver.

3 The two uncertainties are crossed (as shown in Figure 2.2.1), and four distinctly different scenarios (corners) appear. These are then described by the team, supported by the process facilitators.

   – A few base characteristics are described. These should be clear and relevant to the team and serve as scenario differentiators.

   – Based on these, a few key success factors are defined in terms of 'what it will take to succeed'.

   – Finally, using the 'insights' of the descriptions, the scenario is given a catchy or cartoonish name for easy identification.

This is repeated for each of the four scenarios – and insights from one scenario may invoke the team to adjust or sharpen the description of other scenarios. The outcome is a set of clearly defined and distinctly different, yet plausible, 'images' of a potential future.

4 Now the team looks at the strategy, and may address this by means of a business system model (as done in Figure 2.2.4) or may choose some other approach to 'come around' the strategy systematically. The team identifies issues in terms of risks and opportunities, based on the scenarios. For the individual issue, it does not matter which scenario drives this, as they are all defined to be plausible and given due consideration. These issues are then documented in the tool to provide a full listing of risks and uncertainties pertaining to the strategy in question. Our experience shows us that only a few of the identified issues are 'act' issues that need to be embedded in the strategy, and a rather large group of issues ends up being 'parked'.

5 Then the issues list is addressed in terms of the PAPA model, and each issue is prioritized accordingly. At this point in time, we do not put effort into deciding what to do about the specific issue, but may assign an owner to each, explicitly the 'act' issues.

The session is then finalized, and the management team has a set of defined and explicit issues to address when defining or finalizing the strategy.

Strategy Name **LEGO e-commerce strategy. How do we make e-commerce a business channel**

Delivery speed is driving consumer value

The consumer becomes increasing global and uniform

1

The Indy 500	Scenario Name
• Massive sales on "hit" products Characteristics
• High volatility on volumes
• High risk of a global launch failure
• Capacity utilization is low
• Strong launch testing Key Success Factors
• Strong standards and platforms
• Flexible equipment
• Strong consumer feedback capture

2

The Americas Cup	Scenario Name
• Volume volatility Characteristics
• Single piece production
• Local sourcing or air-lifting
• Millions of consumers and product varieties
• Flexible platform Key Success Factors
• Strong logistics
• Local sourcing when possible
• Strong base of evergreen components

The consumer wants individual products at any time

The McDonalds World	Scenario Name
• Massive volatility on hit products Characteristics
• High capacity utilization
• Global delivery system are warehousing
• Simplicity drives cost down
• Flow of components anywhere Key Success Factors
• Low cost operations
• Capacity planning
• Planning and inventory handling

The Hong Kong Tailor	Scenario Name
• Limited volatility on volumes Characteristics
• Enormous variety in product range
• 1001 Chinese/Asian competitors
• Pressure on "good enough" quality
• Strong mix of investment & standards with low cost finalization
• End-product adaptability
• Standard and platforms Key Success Factors

3

4

(lowest) costs to serve drives consumer value

Scenario Consequences / Impact / "So What"		PAPA Prioritization
Concept, Product & Marketing Development	Stronger launch testing and follow-up system	Act
	Design for adjustability	Adapt
	Comprehensive and simple component platform	Act
	...	.
Supply Value Chain	Enhanced forecasting capability	Adapt
	Balanced capacity utilization	Park
	Low cost flexible end-product delivery system	Park
	Late dedication	Plan
Sales & Marketing	Strong internet based marketing vehicles	Adapt
	Use of social media marketing	Adapt
	M-commerce strategy to be defined	Park
	...	.
Customers (ie retailers)	The demise of the traditional toy store	Park
	Support brick and mortar trade experiences	Park
	Variable pricing structures	Adapt
	...	.
Consumers	Close monitoring of trend development	Act
	M-commerce trend to be monitored	Adapt
	...	.
	...	.
Other, including "infrastructure"	Extremely close distribution liaison	Plan
	Potentially dispersed warehouse setup	Plan
	Use of a portfolio of distributors	Park
	...	.

FIGURE 2.2.4 Illustrative case study

Preparing for the future: the value

The value of the process is demonstrated in terms of the food for thought defined for and by the team, as well as by those issues that would not have been identified if and when the strategy had been discussed based on a present-day paradigm. Furthermore, the process is reasonably fast, and (at least within the LEGO Group) it serves as a selling point that the process is actually good professional fun.

A success has many sources, and hence the explicit business value of the above approach is not measured in terms of having successful strategies, as these will naturally be claimed to be based on the decisions and efforts made by the organization. Instead the value is more implicitly measured by the extent to which the strategic risk management team is requested to facilitate the process, and do this again within the same organizational unit.

The ideas of globalization have moved into standard operating procedure, where even smaller companies outsource specific parts of their value creation to low-cost vendors. After the financial crisis, we are now in a 'new normal' where the competitiveness of a company is not defined by its ability to save money, but by its manoeuvrability, ie the ability to spot the need for change sufficiently early, and the capacity to change accordingly. Perhaps this is not precisely risk management by nature, but it is certainly supported by risk management processes and concepts such as early warning metrics, contingency plans etc.

The 'prepare for uncertainty' process is designed to drive a more informed and open-minded discussion prior to decisions being made on how and where to move in the future.

Operational risk in finance: lessons learned from safety-critical industries

GUNNAR HAULAND AND SVERRE DANIELSEN, DNV

Operational risk lies embedded in all activities in a company and it includes human and organizational factors, factors that do not easily fit into existing quantitative models and tools. This chapter argues that there are key lessons for the finance industry to be learned from the management of operational risk in safety-critical industries. There is a need to acknowledge that operational risk management must address the interaction between human, technical and organizational factors. Furthermore, there is a need to establish governance equivalent to a safety management system. Finally, there is a need to benefit from having a management system for operational risk, by nourishing an organizational culture that is actually living it.

Safety-critical industries, especially aviation, have evolved from emphasizing technical factors to addressing a systems perspective on safety. This evolution is driven both by regulatory compliance and by the financial and reputational losses associated with accidents.

In order to get accident statistics down to an acceptable level within aviation, it is necessary to go beyond the immediate causes and address how technical, human and organizational factors interact to produce accidents. Proper management of operational risk requires the finance industry to follow the same path.

The evolution of a systems perspective on safety

The evolution of a systems perspective is revealed when looking at accident investigations throughout history. When the technology is perceived as mature, accident investigators look for additional factors to address in order to reduce the number of accidents. A systems perspective simply means taking one step back and looking at any system in a wider context than the strictly technical parts that make up the system. It means addressing the interaction between technical, human and organizational factors as well as the operational context.

When looking at accident investigations within the aviation industry, we can see an evolution from a narrow technical focus to the modern systems perspective applied today:

- The de Havilland Comet, the first jet airliner, flew for the first time in 1949. In 1954 two such aircraft simply fell apart during flight. The Comet disasters were addressed from a technical perspective, uncovering the problem of metal fatigue. As time went by, and technology became more mature, accident investigators started to include supplementary factors in their reports.

- The investigation of the Tenerife runway collision in 1977, the most serious accident in aviation history, emphasized human errors and team work as explanatory factors for the first time. It demonstrated, for example, that respect for authority means that colleagues may not speak up about perceived dangers. Today, such problems are addressed in team resource management training.

- The 1989 crash of a Fokker Fellowship airliner at Dryden, Ontario, brought about a major shift in the industry's attitude to safety. The Canadian Ministry of Transportation rejected an accident report that blamed the experienced captain for not removing snow and ice from the wings before take-off. A new report clearly showed how a range of organizational dilemmas forced the crew to take sub-standard decisions. It was no longer sufficient to blame individuals. It was now required that the underlying factors that shape performance should be addressed.

Today, accident investigations within mature safety-critical industries will address multiple interacting contributing causes, including human and organizational factors. The finance industry, in contrast, has a long way to go before reaching its Dryden, moving on from blaming individuals as the main explanatory factor, and starting to look for system failures. Operational failures within finance are often blamed on a single failure mode (often human or technical), without addressing underlying performance-shaping factors. Regulators in the finance industry are not challenging this view as was done in the Dryden case.

What is human error?

A modern systems perspective on safety implies the acknowledgement that human error is inevitable. All professionals in all industries commit errors during operations. In fact, errors are part of our human nature. Careful selection, repeated training and long operational experience will not change this fact.

It is not a solution to remove human errors by eliminating humans from the loop. Instead, the objective is to design systems in such a way that we keep the benefits of having humans in the loop, but reduce the consequences of the inevitable human errors. This basic acknowledgement is fully integrated in mature safety work.

Within the aviation industry, the important distinction between intended and unintended human errors is recognized. The risk picture does not change by getting rid of employees who commit errors, unless we are talking about employees with evil intentions (such as fraud or sabotage). In finance it seems that individuals violating procedures but generating good profits may be seen as high performers. At the same time, the same violation followed by a significant loss is easily categorized as fraudulent.

Controls as barriers

James Reason, a psychology professor at Manchester University, developed the so-called Swiss cheese model: an organization may have a series of barriers against failure, each of which (like a slice of Swiss cheese) has holes in it. Accidents or losses occur when the holes line up.

A barrier can be a physical installation that stops energy, such as an engine firewall, or it can also be a procedure or an organizational mechanism designed (a priori) to stop the development of an unwanted event. The flaws in each barrier mean that there is a need for redundant barriers. Introducing new barriers usually also introduces a need to analyse whether the new barrier itself adds to the risk picture. This iterative process is part of the continuous improvement process.

Controls are the conceptual equivalent to safety barriers. Controls are constructed to prevent failures from developing into incidents such as losses, exactly as barriers do in the Reason model. New controls are typically put in place after an incident investigation or a risk analysis. Carrying out controls is one of the main purposes of the middle- and back-office functions in a financial organization, and must be based on an understanding of a systems perspective and the nature of human errors.

The financial sector can also learn from the safety management approach of safety-critical industries. The safety management system is part of company governance, and it describes all the things you must do to maintain and continuously improve the safety of operations in accordance with defined goals. Thus a safety management system defines topics like overall safety objectives, policies, risk appetite, safety organization and processes, ownership, approaches and tools.

The cornerstone of any safety management system, or an equivalent operational risk management system, is to enable the organization to learn. Organizational learning is the systematic reflection on possible improvement possibilities in an organization, with the goal of avoiding similar types of mistake or accident striking again. The aviation industry leads the field in learning from accidents, as well as learning from potential loss incidents. Organizational learning requires some form of learning process, generically described as a management loop.

Learning from incident registration and investigation

A management loop for organizational learning requires three main components:

- The company must possess an easy-to-use and available reporting tool that allows stakeholders to report both incidents and worries about possible incidents. This should include an escalation mechanism in the organization, bringing reports to the attention of relevant managers.

- The reports should pass through a feedback system so that the employee who generated the report will receive feedback. Finally, they should pass to an analysis group. Reported incidents must be registered for statistical purposes, and bigger incidents and potential losses must be investigated with respect to underlying causes. Such analyses must result in relevant mitigating actions, which should be followed up to verify implementation and validate that risks are mitigated as intended.

- There must be a dedicated part of the organization that runs these learning processes in order to avoid building up a pile of data that is never used. The output should be a contribution to the total risk picture and associated mitigating actions, typically the construction of new barriers. Thus a new control could be the result of such a learning loop.

Learning from risk analyses

Typically, new financial products have to go through a product approval process before deal capture. Similarly, in European air traffic management, Eurocontrol requires air navigation service providers to do a risk analysis of all changes to the air traffic management system before going live with the system change. Such a risk analysis typically includes an analysis of how the overall functions can fail, a more detailed analysis of the potential hazards and the associated risk categorization, a listing of requirements that may reduce the risk, and finally a verification and validation process of the requirements to see if they actually mitigate the risk as intended.

One important key to capture a systems perspective in such an analysis is the breakdown of functions and tasks before the actual identification of hazards and the classification of risks. A combination of process mapping, scenario analyses and hierarchical task analysis can be set up to address the complex interactions directly. This can be done also for the life cycle of a new financial product, enabling a risk analysis of how hazards that directly relate to the interactions can fail.

This is typically done in semi-quantitative analyses where the classification of risk is relative. In order to address the complexity of interactions, subject matter experts usually evaluate the risk in facilitated meetings. Such a relative evaluation of risk is often sufficient when making risk-based decisions, such as when comparing alternative profit opportunities.

The quality of such workshops or meetings is crucial. With a lack of historical data, there must be good mechanisms for supporting creativity in the discussion of probability. The level of abstraction is key: not asking yes/no questions, but helping an elaboration process in the group as the basis for analysis, assigning probability and consequence classes that are relative to each other (but without absolute acceptance criteria).

Having the very best of management systems is not enough if they do nothing but collect dust on a shelf. The management system must be used, ie addressing organizational culture.

Organizational culture

Safety culture was first addressed as an explanatory factor in accident investigations after the Chernobyl nuclear disaster in 1986. Although a safety management system was in place, the inadequate safety culture contributed to the disaster. The term is now used in many mature safety-critical industries.

Similar types of companies can perform differently as a result of cultural factors. The organizational culture also affects the management of operational risk and eventually business performance. Thus organizational culture must be measured and managed as part of the management of operational risk.

The factors that traditionally make up safety culture, or rather the aspects of organizational culture that are assumed to affect safety, are generic. These factors can easily be applied to the management of operational risk in finance. Within the social sciences, typical definitions of organizational culture address the shared values (beliefs) and norms (accepted behaviour) in an organization. Culture expresses a relationship between individuals, 'the way we do things around here'. The good, and bad, property of culture is that it is continuously reinforcing itself. New employees quickly learn what type of behaviour is acceptable. For example, if it is acceptable, and maybe even expected, to 'double when in trouble' (exceeding your limits), then this is part of the culture that needs to be managed.

The culture improvement framework used by DNV includes structure and collaboration in a somewhat wider definition of organizational culture: for example, addressing how the structure affects the practices in an organization, such as how reporting lines themselves may influence the quantity and quality of reporting. Collaboration is about the within-silo and cross-silo processes: how employees collaborate formally and in informal networks. Thus shared values and norms, structure and collaboration are the three main ingredients in this framework.

Culture can be managed through proper diagnosis measuring the relevant culture factors, developing effective improvement actions based on this diagnosis, implementing these improvement actions, and sustaining the culture through continuous follow-up and re-measurements. As is the case for any such change process, a solid buy-in at all levels in the organization is essential for success. The business case must be clear from the perspective of all stakeholders, because culture improvement cannot be outsourced to somebody else. All individual employees have to improve and share their improvements.

Table 2.3.1 gives a quick overview of common culture factors.

TABLE 2.3.1 Common culture factors

Competence	This topic addresses how well the mechanisms for establishing and maintaining competence in the organization are working. Competence is both theoretical knowledge and practical skills. Competence can be formalized, or a result of experience, including tacit knowledge (knowledge that you do not explicitly know that you have). The ideal is that competence is related to business objectives, including the competence needed to manage the operational risk. Cross-disciplinary competence is needed in order to address operational risk, applying a mix of qualitative and quantitative methods. It is also crucial for middle- and back-office functions, carrying out controls and approving new products, to fully understand the business processes in the front office.
Collaboration	This topic addresses the coordination processes taking place within and between silos in order to collaborate towards common goals. The collaboration could be formally defined or take place in informal networks. The ideal is that employees know enough about each other's tasks to work towards the common goals for the organization. This is a particular challenge between silos that, in the worst case, may not even trust each other. Establishing transparency, eg through mutual knowledge about each other's tasks, can contribute to more effective collaboration between silos.
Managing conflicting goals	Controls and profit generation can be conflicting goals, which must be balanced. The objective is not to dictate specific individual behaviours, but to benefit from individual problem solving and at the same time make sure that all individuals pull in the same direction. When these goals are in conflict, production must be reduced, stopped or changed until the conflict has ended. The ideal is to manage such conflicting goals at a high level in the organization by establishing guidance and clearly communicating this to all stakeholders. The guidance must be understood, accepted and followed by all employees. Furthermore, employees must know that the management supports them when prioritizing safety or controls, rather than continuing a hazardous operation perceived to lie outside the company risk appetite. The proper management of conflicting goals is therefore very much a leadership responsibility.
The management role	The chief executive and senior management play a crucial role in ensuring sufficient buy-in for all stakeholders throughout the organization.

Compliance	Organizations that perform safety-critical operations often have many procedures to ensure the appropriate level of safety in these operations. There is often variation in the employees' compliance with such procedures. The ideal is that procedures function as a help for employees to reach the overall goal in a safe manner, and not as an obstacle to performance. Procedures must therefore be relevant for the objective, updated and available at the workplace. Employees must have the competence needed to follow the procedure. The rationale underlying the procedures must be understood and accepted.
Incentives	Incentives can be defined formally, such as bonuses coupled with key performance indicators, or they can be informal incentive systems: who attracts more respect from their colleagues and their line managers? The ideal is that both formal and informal incentive systems pull in the same direction and that they support the risk management in an organization.
Organizational learning	When evaluating culture, it is the extent to which learning systems are successfully used that is the issue. One key source is to learn from previous incidents. All elements making up the learning loop must be used by all in accordance with the intention of continuous improvement. Ownership at all levels in the reporting process must be defined. It must be possible to see what happened to a report once it has been filed. The ideal is that the organization, as part of the organizational culture, establishes and maintains a good reporting culture. It is crucial that the concept of blame is taken out of this equation. The act of reporting should be rewarded. Organizational learning is also about using the results from various types of risk analyses and revisions to improve existing systems and processes. In safety-critical industries, such learning is also based on what the organization does well.
Creative worrying	This is a kind of professional worry where all employees proactively function as risk managers. All employees need to see the relationship between their function and risk management. Improvement suggestions resulting from such creative worry must be included in the organizational learning loop.
Error tolerance	Given that human errors are inevitable, the design of systems in an organization must be forgiving towards these errors. This means that the organization can benefit from having humans in the loop, but at the same time avoid the consequences of the human errors that will take place when using systems. It must also be acknowledged that human errors can be a symptom of an organizational error; organizational factors can force the operative employees to make sub-standard decisions. Such designs avoid deterministic single failures and aim for design principles such as redundancy, flexibility and adaptability.

We need to take into consideration that many of these culture topics are not directly observable. Furthermore, employees may not be able, or willing, to tell you about their culture. We therefore need to use multiple methods to put together inferences of the overall culture and sub-cultures in an organization.

Conclusion

The financial industry first needs to acknowledge the positive contribution that operational risk management has on sustainable generation of profit. There are also several key lessons from safety-critical industries that the industry can incorporate:

- Financial institutions need to take a systems perspective when addressing operational risk. This includes an understanding of the nature of human errors, looking beyond the immediate causes, and applying the concept of barriers.
- Although holding capital is necessary, one should not pretend that all aspects of operational risk can be forced into one model in order accurately to calculate the capital needed to cover losses. Instead, multiple methods and techniques must be used as the basis for establishing the total risk picture.
- There is a need to emphasize that risk management by nature is proactive in reducing the probability of incidents. This comes in addition to reducing the consequence if the risk event were to occur.
- The organization can learn from various sources, not only records of previous mistakes and losses, but also from various types of risk analyses.
- At the forefront of safety theory today is also the idea that organizations should learn from things that go well. After all, things that go wrong are often the very same things that most often go well but under slightly different circumstances.
- It is a key lesson that risk management requires companies to develop and maintain governance and tools, and also to manage the associated organizational culture.

The main argument in this chapter has been that the finance industry should learn from safety-critical industries how to manage operational risk. The framework, methods and tools are there, waiting to be applied.

Managing risks in the supply chain: reaching new standards

ERIC E LEHMANN, ACCENTURE

Introduction

Preventing supply chain interruptions is undoubtedly one of the central purposes of supply chain management; indeed, most supply chain managers would say that they spend too much of their time managing risk issues, ranging from delivery delays to product quality issues. While traditional supply chain risk management has allowed corporations to deal with the most well-known supply chain concerns, recent events have shown that more specific and more sophisticated risk management methods are essential to better protect globalized supply chains.

Recent events – including the Japanese earthquake and tsunami, the floods in Thailand and the ash clouds caused by the 2010 Icelandic volcano eruption – have demonstrated how far the consequences of such risks can extend. The incurred losses were a warning to C-level executives across the globe about how exposed their supply chains can be. The Japanese earthquake severely affected global electronics production and led to extended business disruptions for the automotive industry. The Thai flooding created significant shortages in the hard disk drive market that generated hundreds of millions of dollars of losses for well-known electronics manufacturers.

Aside from these headline events, however, the nature of supply chain risks is constantly changing. New risks and new vulnerabilities require close attention from management. Counterfeited products, for example, have entered supply chains in greater numbers and can inflict lasting damage on a company's product quality and reputation. Original equipment manufacturers seeking to ensure the continuity of their operations have increasing concerns about supplier solvency at times of high volatility in financial markets or currencies. The financial crisis that emerged in 2008 has shown how reduced access to credit can have an impact on the less financially stable companies and create headaches for supply chain managers.

Current supply chain fragilities are not just related to emerging risks; they are as much a result of supply and network design strategies as they are driven by a limited integration of risk management into supply chain management.

In light of these and other concerns, companies recognize the need for a more formal management of supply chain risks. They need to rethink their operative model to define an optimum balance between financial efficiency and control over the supply chain.

Current business models are more vulnerable to supply chain risks

The continuing focus on operational efficiency and cost optimization has been a strategic priority over the last few decades, helping corporations lower the cost of manufacturing through outsourcing, offshoring and other practices. Cost reduction efforts, however, often outweighed other strategic priorities. Companies that once kept back-up inventory and manufacturing facilities in place may have exposed themselves to additional risk as they concentrated on working with fewer redundancies.

New supply chain models generate new risks

The Kaizen model has become the basis for the lean strategies that have become so popular globally. Key components of this model include just-in-time or even just-in-sequence production, with minimal in-process inventories, geographic and operational concentration of assembly and parts production, and a high level of subcontracting. While lean management has provided significant advantages in terms of cost reduction and increased manufacturing efficiency, it also increases risk velocity and impact.

For many companies, make-or-buy decisions have been decided in favour of buying, not making. While this reduces manufacturing overhead, companies lose oversight of key governance and management strategies and introduce unknown risks into the supply chain. Periodic risk rebalancing is essential.

Globalization of supply chains as a risk factor

Many companies switched from local suppliers to low-cost and often distant suppliers on the basis of cost optimization, without considering the cost of risks caused by this strategic change. Larger companies now buy from smaller suppliers in very remote areas of the globe. The extended supply chain now has many additional points of potential failure, requiring new approaches to risk management. Companies face longer logistics lead times, as well as new and unfamiliar risk profiles encompassing natural disasters, epidemics, and social, political or monetary instability.

A global supply chain also increases risks related to supply chain integrity, compliance and quality control. Relationships with remote partners are subject to differences in business and cultural practices. Such risks are difficult to forecast and monitor, creating gaps in the risk management capability for most companies. Realizing the systemic nature of supply chain risks, some companies are reviewing their purchasing strategies and practices, and rethinking the way they are doing business.

Because risk is a key factor of financial performance, the absence of qualitative and quantitative valuation can affect overall desired business outcomes. Improving the understanding, valuation and management of those systemic risks will provide a clear contribution to decreasing the cost of risks for each transaction.

The challenges with classical risk management and risk transfer strategies

Classic risk management methods have proved inefficient in addressing these new supply chain risks. Many companies are operating with insufficient insurance coverage of key risks. Insurers do not always understand rapidly evolving supply chain risks; it is easier, from an underwriting perspective, to insure a company's own facility than it is to insure against disruptions related to multi-tiered suppliers in multiple, far-flung locations.

In recent years, property and casualty insurers have significantly improved the scope of underwriting services to cover supply chain disruptions. They are now providing business interruption insurance for disruptions occurring at a supplier's facilities, although with coverage constraints that reduce the efficiency of risk transfer. Risk coverage is provided by most insurers for named suppliers or facilities only and does not cover the whole network of suppliers and subcontractors. Coverage limits are also usually low and not adequate to sufficiently insure against a larger part of the risk exposure, leaving a significant part of the risk uninsured. Partial coverage, as much as self-insurance, can prove costly, especially in the event of a loss. This makes the actual identification and management of supply chain risks even more important.

Another traditional challenge for risk management is related to the fact that risk managers are not typically in a position to influence strategic and operational business decisions; owing to the structural separation between a traditionally more risk-reporting-focused function and operational decision making, they are more often than not called in after the fact rather than during the planning process, while risk management requires more operational integration.

In fact, most companies do not have a risk function in the supply chain that would review risk appetite and risk tolerance through the supply chain to take action to address specific risks that the company could not bear. While traditional risk reporting – focused on collecting and prioritizing risk reports from operations to inform senior managers – is useful for corporate governance purposes, it is mostly inadequate to develop proactive risk management and prevention strategies.

While one might wonder why there is no further integration of risk management into operations, the low frequency of larger supply chain disruptions and the efficient management of experienced supply chain professionals are probably the most likely reasons. The natural tendency to assume that events that have not happened in the past are not likely to happen in the future should not prevent corporations from upgrading their risk management practices to meet new standards. Better practices undoubtedly contribute to helping corporations achieve their business goals.

Improving the management of risks in the supply chain

There are a number of effective approaches to dealing with new types and levels of supply chain risk. One of the most important principles for organizations to bear in mind is to start with increasing the visibility of inherent risks; it is impossible to plan for and difficult to manage risks that have not been envisioned. Unforeseen events of recent years have shown that limited risk scenario analysis and planning lead to gaps in the risk management framework.

Among the tools available for charting risk are:

- *Scenario planning.* Scenario planning is a key step in improving supply chain risk management. It examines the underlying factors affecting the supply chain, including political, logistical and technological dimensions, as well as global economic factors. As part of scenario planning, probability modelling can help identify unknown risks and develop contingency plans for business continuity.

- *Financial quantification and modelling.* These tools work on several levels, first as an operational decision-making tool (many software vendors have developed solutions specifically for supply chain modelling) and also as a strategic risk management tool.

- *Ongoing measurement of risks.* Close attention to changes in key performance indicators (KPIs) along with detailed risk reporting and monitoring can provide valuable insight and early warning of new conditions.

- *Improving the 'traceability' of the supply chain.* More and more organizations are following key deliverables through the entire supply chain and identifying risks not only among top-tier suppliers but among lower-tier suppliers and their subcontractors.

With a clearer understanding of the risks facing the organization – and the potential financial, operational and reputational consequences of those risks – it is much easier to address the question of how to integrate risk management into business operations and ensure its effectiveness. Key steps include:

1 *Look at the whole, not just the parts.* Companies tend to look at risk in individual parts such as procurement, logistics, distribution or manufacturing. Most risks, however, should be managed across the supply chain network. Because of the systemic nature of supply chain risks, a problem in one area can easily affect the entire supply chain and the entire organization. Such risks must be identified, managed and communicated throughout the network.

   The assessment process may begin with a look at all suppliers, including third-party vendors and counterparties. The operational and financial risk profile of each vendor should be inventoried, and the vendor's own risk management processes should be identified.

   Similarly, all risks can be measured by their impact, not only within their own function, but across the company and all the way to the customers. Measurements of risk should incorporate reputational and market share impacts that can have lasting effects on a corporation's business. In order to be able to aggregate risks, sophisticated supply chain management software is increasingly required in order to measure interdependencies within the entire value chain, and help quantify financially what are the most effective options to manage or mitigate risk.

2 *Review the governance of the organization's risks.* The risk function is too often focused on reporting risks that are well known within operating units, with less ability to ensure that the scope of risks under consideration is adequate and includes less frequent risks that could have a much higher impact. These risks encompass the entire supply chain and include business continuity, creditworthiness of suppliers, currency risk, commodity volatility, supply chain integrity, political risks and a number of other operational risks. A holistic approach to risk management with a clearer focus on identifying and preventing risks, rather than reporting, is essential to moving risk management from a risk response function to risk anticipation and prevention.

Ideally, the risk management structure and capability should match the company's risk appetite, and be sized to reflect how much risk the organization is willing to take. This implies a clear quantification of the risk appetite as well as operational vulnerabilities in order to define the adequate structure and depth of risk management. The company that strives for maximum efficiency should have highly efficient and integrated risk management to reflect this larger risk appetite.

3 *Review current operating models.* The adequate range and scope of risk management changes can only be achieved through an in-depth analysis of the risk embedded into a company's operating model, and through an additional review of all procedures and controls intended to manage those risks. Typical steps are a systematic review of the supply chain risk inventory, the identification of critical single points of failure in the organization, and the end-to-end quantification of the financial impact those key risks can generate. As painstaking as it seems, this process is key to defining how to improve risk management practices, systems and related governance.

Some companies are, for example, re-examining the benefits of global versus local processes to determine which operations should be centralized and which should be managed locally. A comprehensive procurement review may, in some cases, point the way toward bringing some suppliers back onshore or adjusting the risk management framework to concentrate on clearly identified risks, while considering key issues such as currency fluctuations or rising transport costs.

4 *Integrate risk management into operations planning and management, in terms of both functions and workflow.* Typically, the risk function is 'headquarters centred' and less likely to provide input into the daily decision-making process for operations, including procurement, manufacturing, supply chain and logistics. To change this, a risk management function that contributes to the strategic, sales and operational planning processes would factor in key risks in the decision-making process. This newly designed risk management function in the supply chain can contribute to improving the risk management capability in the current organizational set-up but can also ensure that the right amount of risk management flows into key supply chain decisions.

Leading car manufacturers are currently reviewing their operating model for risk purposes, aiming to increase the standardization of non-differentiated parts, together with an increase of multiple sourcing strategies. While there is a cost associated with these changes, most corporations will be able to achieve overall cost savings while reducing current and future risks in their supply chain.

5 *Use a financial modelling capability for the supply chain.* Because management of the supply chain is increasingly complex, using advanced supply chain modelling tools is essential for scenario planning as well as supply chain design and risk quantification. This capability can in particular achieve the following:

- Gauge the financial impact of supply volatility on supply chain economics.
- Analyse the impact of product and service demand volatility.
- Measure the impact that launching a new product or entering a new market can have on long-term production capacity.
- Quantify the cost of operational disruptions.
- Balance the distribution of risk between the company and its customer, suppliers and joint venture partners.
- Use financial products to mitigate procurement, manufacturing and distribution risks.

6 *Improve risk reporting and monitoring.* Risk management is benefiting from performance management systems that help monitor key performance indicators to identify problems and take corrective measures quickly. Dashboards and scoring models are increasingly becoming a risk manager's tool for areas such as supplier solvency or supplier quality management. Real-time risk monitoring capabilities used in combination with mapping software are also providing supply chain managers with techniques to track key supply chain flows from supplier locations to manufacturing facilities through to final customers. Such tools speed response in the case of numerous unplanned events, such as political conflict or natural catastrophes. Based upon our experience and research in the space, companies with the most dependent supply chains such as electronics or high-tech manufacturers have for the most part already integrated these tools into their standard supply chain management practices.

Taking risk management live

The increased understanding of how vulnerable supply chains are has strengthened the case for companies to enhance their risk management practices and systems. Most corporations have also realized that the cost of effective risk management is significantly lower than the cost of dealing with supply chain disruptions. Proactive prevention measures pay for themselves many times over. In the context of heightened pressures on operating costs and the need to improve business efficiency permanently, the risk function will play a key role in identifying the best opportunities to rebalance operational efficiency with risk management. This is a key step in avoiding unnecessary vulnerability in the operating model.

The trend is clear. Leading manufacturers that previously focused almost solely on efficiency as the primary metric of success are now actively changing their supply chain business models to incorporate risk-based and cost-effective supply chain management to balance the overall definition of success. Companies need to consider reviewing their own business models and identify how best to raise their capability for managing supply chain risks. This can, at times of great uncertainty and volatility, prove to be a key differentiator and a source of competitive advantage.

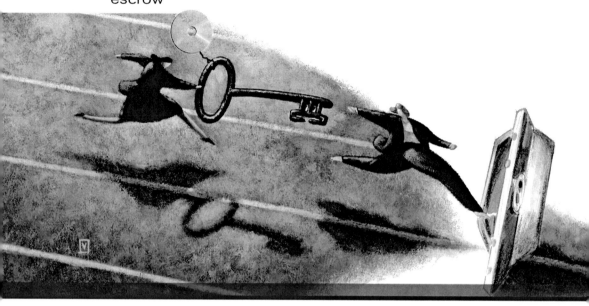

Software and Cloud escrow: an effective tool for managing risk and new business opportunities

STEPHAN PETERS, DEPOSIX SOFTWARE ESCROW GMBH

Introduction

Observant readers who are not yet so familiar with escrow may ask themselves: 'How can something that supposedly mitigates risks at the same time enable new business opportunities?' This question drills right down to the heart of this particular tool, which always serves two parties and at the same time offers both the benefit of risk mitigation and the benefit of new business opportunity. This chapter, in plain words, will describe how escrow works for software, for technology and – with regard to the increasing significance of cloud computing – also for SaaS.[1] All forms of escrow can offer significant benefits, in particular in light of the continuing recent financial crisis.

So in what real-life situation could escrow offer real business benefits? We have all heard about cases in which the financial or other difficulties of a supplier have severely affected the ordering customer. Typical examples refer to original equipment manufacturers (OEMs) and analyse the supply chains of, for example, the automotive or pharmaceutical industry. In most of these examples, the failure of the supplier of a specific component is critical to the following process chain. The stories typically describe in great detail how long the whole production and output of the OEM were halted for and how this caused huge financial losses. 'That's old hat', you might say. 'OEMs have been addressing the issue for a long time. And we all know that commonly promoted risk strategies to avoid such a situation are optimizing inventory management and multi-sourcing.' You are right – so long as it applies to OEMs and physical goods in the production chain. But what about non-physical value chains without the option of stockpiling? Or when the goods are specialized software or other technology for which multi-sourcing does not make sense or is not even available? In such a case, software or technology escrow is the solution for all the parties involved. Please read on.

What can go wrong: negative examples and risky situations

Imagine a large licensee like a bank that had commissioned some very complex and important software, eg its central credit-scoring tool, from an external developer. The development, including specifications, all necessary testing, debugging and the international pilots, had been lengthy and costly. Now that the bank is ready to reap the first benefits from its investment, the licensor goes bankrupt owing to some other big project and is wound up. The licensor is therefore no longer able to deliver the agreed maintenance support (continued roll-out, prolonged bug fixing and development of additional functionalities). Even though the bank would have the internal know-how and resources to take over these tasks from the licensor, it does not have the means to do so since it does not own a copy of the underlying software source code. The bank would face the tough decision of either continuing to use its central scoring tool 'as is' or starting all over again by looking for a new supplier.

In a slightly modified example, a large licensee works closely together with the licensor and has the know-how, resources and a complete copy of the source code plus the development environment available. This time, though, the trustee appointed to the licensee under insolvency proceedings intervenes and forbids the usage of the source code by the bank because of a missing licence for continued development. Here the bank would face the option of negotiating from a weak position with the trustee for additional licence fees, to use the software 'as is' (as above) or to start all over again.

In a further example, a medium-sized fashion company licenses a system for its store management from an external licensor that originally developed the software and also made individual adaptations for the licensee. Then the licensor gets bought by a main competitor of the fashion company. In addition to the very irritating 'know-how drain' to the competitor, which can now access parts of its particular know-how, the licensee also depends on this competitor to provide future maintenance for its store management system – or else face the known options of as-is usage or starting over again.

As a fourth example, we consider a venture capital (VC) company that has to close down one of its portfolio companies owing to its failure to be economically viable. Nevertheless, the start-up had developed some very valuable software technology, which unfortunately had not been secured. Since the team of developers is upset about the close-down and refuses to help the investor further, the source code of the technology is inevitably lost. Any potential partial recovery of the original investment in the start-up by exploiting the technology at hand has gone astray. In an even worse scenario, the team of developers takes along the source code of the VC's technology and founds another company with a similar focus that then continues to exploit the market momentum that had been created with the original investor's money. Any attempt by the investor to stop that 'unfriendly' exploitation is doomed to fail owing to a lack of proper documentation of the technology in question.

And, last but not least, a case in point for cloud computing and cloud escrow: in January 2010 salesforce.com, a major SaaS provider for customer relationship management (CRM) services in the market, suffered from a widespread outage as a result of a system failure in its data centre that disabled both normal operations and back-up systems (Raphael, 2011). Hence most of its 68,000 clients had to manage more than one hour's down time, resulting in an interruption of business processes and inaccessible customer data. Although in that case the problem had been resolved relatively soon after it occurred, companies that outsource software or services and, for example, their proprietary customer data to the cloud can get into serious trouble if they are not hedged against discontinued service or potential data loss.

These examples could be extended easily to various other industries, markets or fields of technology, in particular against the background of the recent economic turmoil, which spilt from the real estate market to banking and subsequently to various other industries and countries, in particular in the European Union. All the instances described above have one thing in common: the risk could have been mitigated significantly or even avoided altogether by using a professional escrow agreement tailored to the specific situation.

What can go right – positive examples and opportunities gained

This time a young and agile but small software development company is challenging a more established competitor. The incumbent's software products are mature and known to work but outdated from a technological point of view and lack leading-edge functionality. The young developer faces the typical concerns of potential licensees on the reliability and financial viability of the company, its current size and a missing track record. At the same time, the licensor strives to protect its leading edge and keeps the technology (ie the source code) tightly locked up. To overcome this seeming conflict of interest, the small software company proactively offers a software escrow agreement along with its licence contracts to all potential customers. This agreement foresees a handover of a copy of the source code to the licensees in the event that the licensor defaults on maintenance or any other of its contractual obligations. This way, potential concerns about the size or age of the developer are overcome and the licensor opens up new business opportunities for itself that otherwise would have been unavailable. Further, if the developer decided to offer its software and services under a cloud model, the case for escrow would be all the more true (see 'Escrow and cloud computing' below).

In the same example, when shifting the perspective to the licensees, companies in need of software applications open up additional options of potential suppliers for themselves by exactly the same means: an escrow agreement may permit additional, better-suited opportunities when identifying viable software solutions and suppliers for their various business needs that otherwise would be ruled out because of the concerns mentioned above. And in particular for cloud-based services, security concerns and accessibility of the services and one's own data that are stored somewhere out of control in the cloud often become the stumbling block even to considering this innovative type of business proposition (see 'Escrow and cloud computing' below for more).

When looking beyond the two parties involved directly in an escrow agreement – the licensor and the licensee – one soon comes across a number of external advisers who may also have a stake in the planned licence transaction, eg lawyers, consultants, auditors or investors. Any of these professionals could potentially facilitate the deal by suggesting an escrow agreement to either of the two main parties, thereby creating apparent value, which would benefit their own cause and reputation. In other words, having escrow in their professional toolbox helps advisers to create potential new business opportunities for their clients.

Escrow explained

So how exactly can you mitigate certain risks and open up additional business opportunities by using escrow? To gain a better understanding, we will first identify some basics concepts.

Software or technology escrow is a service offered by a trustee or a neutral third party (often a professional escrow specialist), who receives, for example, the source code of a software application from its developer and who keeps it in custody for and in the name of the licensee. A source code generally provides access to all the know-how and intelligence incorporated into a given software application. At the same time, the source code is needed to fix any bugs or to develop new functionalities within the software.

The same principle applies for any other form of intellectual property (IP), often of a technical nature, that a licensor strives to protect (ie keep secret) but that a licensee would need in the event that the licensor should default on supply or maintenance. Examples for technology escrow would be drawings and diagrams for (and/or samples of) electronic circuit boards, chemical formulae or production processes, or detailed specifications and supplier information for complex machines. For the sake of convenience, for the remainder of this chapter we will stick to the most relevant field of escrow, software applications, and one of its more recent developments, cloud escrow.

Definition of source code

When programmers design software, they break down a planned new functionality (eg 'adding a new customer record to the bank's central database') by writing a series of specific instructions for the computer. For this, they may use any of the manifold existing programming languages. The result is the so-called source code, and anyone capable of 'reading' it, ie understanding the instructions in that programming language, could extract the specialized know-how and expertise that the programmers put into it (hence the effort to keep it secret). Next, the programmers 'translate' the source code into machine-readable code called object code. This process is also called 'compilation' and as a result creates the executable programs (so-called *.exe files) that run on our computers. For any subsequent change to the software (either bug fixing or the add-on of new functionality), the original source code needs to be modified and the process of compilation repeated. Without the source code, the software running at the licensee's facilities could be used only on an as-is basis.

The licensor strives to protect the IP that went into the software. The typical instruments available for protecting IP, such as copyright protection or patents, have several severe shortcomings for software – among them the fact that the source code needs to be disclosed.[2] The particular know-how – often considered to be the most valuable asset of software companies – could possibly be extracted and reused in a number of creative and legal ways. The result would mean taking unjustifiable risks, with potentially dire implications for the vast majority of all existing developers. Consequently, most licensors will never allow their source code to be disclosed, either to the general public or to specific customers.[3]

So while licensors have every reason to keep their source code secret, what is the position of the customer, the licensee? From the licensee's perspective, risk management is just as crucial. The licensee is a mere user and fully depends on the licensor in order to exploit both the software's immediate benefit and its long-term potential. The issues at hand here are bug fixing, maintenance, and development of new features. In this traditional licence model, licensees often enough have to invest up to seven- or eight-digit euro sums in new software and its indispensable implementation process into an existing IT landscape. Typical costs include the regular licence and maintenance fees and further charges for individual adaptations, interface programming, and additional or new hardware plus surrounding IT infrastructure, time and effort to analyse and adapt obsolete or incompatible internal business processes, and training for employees. Therefore, licensees have a strong interest in mitigating the risks involved and in protecting their investments in IT against the eventuality of their licensors defaulting on maintenance or other critical deliverables.

ESCROW AND CLOUD COMPUTING

Cloud computing – and notably SaaS – serves as an ideal alternative to on-premise solutions (the traditional licence model) for more and more companies. The advantages are obvious: customers get to use high-performance IT systems and state-of-the-art software in the cloud on a pay-per-use model, without having to invest huge amounts in hardware, software development, IT human resources and maintenance.

Cloud computing is not only a capex[4] saving but also an innovative answer to the requirements of the modern working environment, as it allows flexible usage of capacity as it is needed or consumed and relies only on a fast internet connection and networks that provide access to applications and customer data hosted on the developer's or cloud provider's hardware.

But what happens if this access is interrupted or even denied? After all, the cloud is an IT system – and no IT system is infallible. Besides technical problems within the realm of the provider or with the internet or network access, the cloud provider may disregard service, maintenance and further development, inflate prices or even go bankrupt. Moreover, legal or commercial disagreements can result in an outage of software and data. In any case the impact could be dramatic: clients who cannot be supplied, served or informed are typically not interested in the details behind the scene. Ultimately, the company using the cloud service is responsible and liable for safeguarding the data of its customers and for delivering its products or services offered on time, independently of any third-party service it is using.

So far, this is one of the main reasons why cloud computing is still considered to be generally risky and why it is currently successful only in non-critical applications. Therefore, when intending to work with cloud providers, possibly even for one's core applications, hard-core security concerns require additional coverage on top of standard measures. This is where cloud escrow could come into play.

As with conventionally licensed software, the source code of cloud applications can be verified and held in trust in its latest version. In addition, as with any standard software, the development environment and build and implementation instructions plus other relevant details can be deposited with a trusted third party. In this context, the original technical architecture of the cloud provider might have to be scaled down to the reduced capacity needs of that one licensee who was beneficiary of the escrow. But the true new aspect of cloud escrow is securing the proprietary customer data and ensuring that they match with and fully integrate into the application.

Depending on various factors like data volume, update intervals and a cost–benefit analysis, the cloud data should be deposited at a minimum once a month, presumably more often. This regular 'dumping' of the cloud data could be done with the customer or with any other third party. However, in order to ensure the actuality and integrity of the backed-up cloud database, it should be tested regularly in combination with the actual application from which it originates so that, in the event of stipulated need (a predefined release condition), cloud customers will be able to install the SaaS application and use it together with their own proprietary data to continue operations. This procedure does not guarantee uninterrupted service, of course, but it offers the option to avoid a complete loss and the need for a fresh start from scratch.

Source: Deposix Software Escrow GmbH

Practical guideline: when to use software escrow from the licensee's perspective

Software escrow should be considered when any of the following questions is answered with a 'yes':

- Does the software administer or operate with critical processes and/or data?
- Would a short-term replacement of the software lead to significant costs?
- Can maintenance of the software not be guaranteed 100 per cent?
- Can security and long-term availability of the cloud data not be guaranteed 100 per cent?
- Is compliance with one's own contractual obligations vis-à-vis customers or partners dependent on the software at hand?
- Does the investment in the overall project exceed €50,000?

If one considers the different perspectives of licensor and licensee, the inherent conflict of interest between developer and licensee becomes apparent. Whilst the licensor prefers to keep the source code secret and not to disclose it to anyone, the licensee seeks to get hold of the source code as back-up for a potential situation in which the licensor defaults on obligations. Both sides have legitimate interests to limit the risks involved for them.

However, if both sides insist, they would never sign a licence agreement. The detriment would be loss of potential revenue and reputation for the licensor and abandonment of potential benefits offered by acquiring the functionality of the software for the licensee.

Depending on when, within the buying process, the parties start addressing this conflict of interest, a very costly situation could arise for both parties. The quarrel over the source code has been recorded as an insurmountable stumbling block in more than one case in the past.

Software escrow as the solution to this conflict creates a three-party constellation in which the escrow agent serves as trustee and holds the IP in custody (see Figure 2.5.1). In contrast to a notary or other legal services firm, which typically serves as trustee in similar situations, the escrow agent has the competency to understand and evaluate the software from a technical point of view. Further, the escrow organization holds the internal processes ready, for example, to accommodate regular updates or the particular safety requirements.

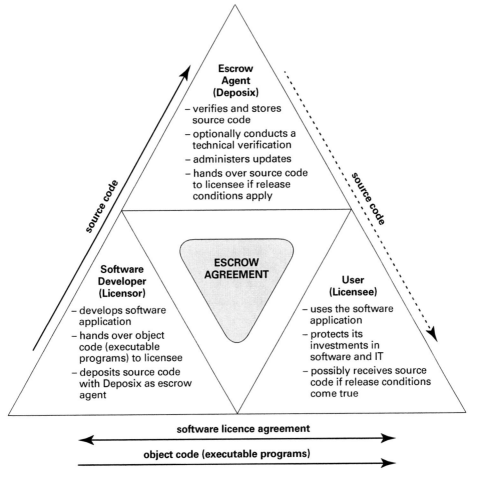

FIGURE 2.5.1 The software escrow triangle

As a vehicle to software escrow, a three-party escrow agreement is put in place, complementing the bilateral licence (or development, or maintenance) contract between licensor and licensee. Based on their expertise and experience, escrow agents typically adapt their standard agreement to the needs of licensor and licensee. Once the specific release conditions that could trigger the disclosure of the source code to the licensee as beneficiary are agreed and the escrow agreement is finalized, the software developer hands over the source code to the independent escrow agent. The agent verifies the content from a technical point of view and then transfers it safely into its specialized storage. If cloud or SaaS escrow is used, customer data are backed up and updated on a regular basis, too. From that point onwards, the agent ensures the quality and safety of the source code (and, if applicable, the cloud data) through regular maintenance and adherence to a strict contract management process and provides the licensee with access to the source code (and cloud data) in the event that one of the predefined release conditions occurs.

Six typical release conditions are:

1 bankruptcy of the licensor or termination of business activity;

2 licensor opening a case for insolvency protection;

3 default on maintenance;

4 decision to end the life cycle of the software;

5 loss of critical know-how (key programmers leaving the developer, 'brain drain');

6 change-of-control clause (eg competitors of licensees taking over the licensor).

Risk and opportunity management with software escrow

The licensee's perspective

A structured analysis of potential risks from a licensee's perspective would have to include a look at its industry and the specific type of technology or software in use. However, on a more abstract level, using a software application critical to its core business exposes the licensee to general IT and operational risks. The most relevant with respect to escrow, as mentioned before, is dependency on the source code (and, in the cloud, on the data) and thus on the developer or cloud specialist. When the licensor defaults on its contractual obligations in support and maintenance, one or several IT systems and the related operational processes are affected. Since we are assuming mission-critical software (and in case of cloud computing also data), this default implies some specific business or market risk. Related to the first example cited above, the bank's credit-scoring system, the business risk would be the lack of ability to score new credit applications and thus to acquire new business.

Using software escrow would mitigate or eliminate the above-mentioned risks; moreover, it could result in additional business opportunities. With respect to the credit-scoring application in our example, the bank potentially would have had additional options in choosing a supplier. Typical contractor and software selection processes evaluate among other things the standing of suppliers and often look at criteria like size (revenue, number of employees), age, balance sheet total, reference customers or similar factors. These criteria are only so-called secondary criteria, as the goal is always to try to derive a statement about the reliability of the products or services offered by the licensor. Through the use of escrow, the risk of default is mitigated independently of these criteria, and the potential result is an increased solution base from which to choose. In other words, the bank may place more emphasis on factors like functional fit, technological feasibility, level of service offered or price of an application, rather than decide primarily on the basis of the size or assumed standing of the supplier.

The very same applies to the selection of a cloud provider. Owing to known security concerns, some companies prefer on-premise solutions, whereas a simultaneously offered low-risk escrow agreement may result in the decision in favour of a cloud alternative.

The licensor's perspective

The licensor's perspective could be presented in a similar way, but as the converse of the licensee's perspective. As discussed before, the owner of an IP such as software has very good reasons for thoroughly protecting the underlying source code, but at the same time cannot ignore the needs and wishes of the (potential) customers for securing their investment in that particular technology and for mitigating the various risk types involved. If licensors did not address these needs, they themselves would face potential reputation and business risks, since customers would possibly look for more suitable alternatives in the market. By using a professionally administered escrow agreement, licensors address their own risks (IP, market, reputation etc) and open up new business opportunities by appealing to those customers who would otherwise look elsewhere.

The venture capitalist's perspective

VCs or other firms managing their stakes in technology companies are facing certain risks with respect to the IP incorporated in their investment portfolios. Often enough, the technology developed with the support of, or entirely based on, their funding is very volatile and at the same time represents the only tangible asset that exists. If portfolio firms fail for whatever reason, the VCs need to write down investments and bear the associated business risk. If, in cases with existing know-how and intellectual property (IP), these are lost completely and written off to zero, it might severely affect the VCs' reputation in light of their financial backers, the original investors. These investors entrust their money to the VCs, who are responsible for professional asset management. Unnecessary loss of an asset would risk damaging the trust and ability to raise future funds. On the other hand, VCs might open up new business opportunities by securing tangible assets of individual firms with an escrow agreement, since the IP could possibly be reused, either by transferring them to other portfolio firms or by selling them off to an external party.

The adviser's perspective

And, last but not least, the manifold advisers like lawyers, auditors or other consultants who work for and in the name of the main parties (ie licensors, licensees or investors) could use escrow as one instrument in their expert tool box. Since many clients by now know about escrow, they might expect the adviser to know about it as well. In any case, professional aides can demonstrate their specialized aptitude to their clients by 'pulling out' and recommending escrow from their tool kit whenever needed, thereby creating additional value. For the lawyer, a typical situation could arise when working on a licence contract or other key agreement – possibly involving IP – for his or her clients. For an auditor, it could arise under any circumstance related to financing or balance sheet optimization or due diligence. For a consultant – depending on the specialization – it could arise under circumstances ranging from giving advice on general risk management to helping with a procurement process (ie a software or supplier selection) to working on hands-on IT implementation. Whenever escrow is mentioned by the adviser, he or she will further his or her own professional reputation, thereby building the grounds for additional assignments in the future.

One final aspect of technology escrow that should be mentioned here is based on its general characteristic of reducing risks for its licensees. These beneficiaries – be they normal market participants or investors – often use external financing and specific insurance coverage for their normal conduct of business. The cost of this financing and insurance coverage, among other things, is typically based on a rating or screening of the applying company, and institutions lending money or insuring risks use or compile these in the process. In addition, banks or insurance companies have regulatory requirements like Basel II/III or Solvency II, which among other things analyse operational risks. All these frameworks try to quantify various different factors with the goal of putting a value (or from an applicant's perspective a price tag) to a potential deal. Naturally, anything that reduces risks will lead to lower costs. As shown above, technology escrow contracts help to reduce various risk types, and therefore users may benefit from reduced costs for financing or insurance coverage where needed. Tables 2.5.1 and 2.5.2 briefly summarize the potential risk types addressed by (software, technology and cloud) escrow, as well as the potential business opportunities opened up by using escrow, both distinguishing the different target groups.

TABLE 2.5.1 Risk types addressed by software and technology escrow, by potential target group

Risk type addressed	Target group			
	Licensees	Licensors	Investors, VCs	Advisers (lawyers, consultants, auditors etc)
IT risk	X			
Operational risk	X			
IP risk		X	X	
Business or market risk	X	X	X	X
Reputation risk	X	X	X	X

TABLE 2.5.2 Potential business opportunities arising from escrow usage, by target group

Additional opportunities gained	Target group			
	Licensees	Licensors	Investors, VCs	Advisers (lawyers, consultants, auditors etc)
Additional deals or business		X		X
Improved reputation		X	X	X
More business options or suppliers	X			
Improved financial rating	X	X	X	

Conclusion

The recent worldwide economic downturn caused by the crisis in the banking and financial industry has demonstrated once more in an impressive way that the stability of the overall marketplace, and in particular of individual firms or suppliers, is relative. As always, the proper management of risks and proactively seeking new opportunities are inevitable for protecting assets and securing the long-term survival of any market participant. In this context, this chapter has made the case that software, technology and cloud escrow are valuable tools for both objectives, effective risk management and opening up new business opportunities. In the case of cloud computing, escrow agreements may benefit an increasing number of companies, including smaller users, which benefit from the obvious advantages, and cloud providers, which may win new customers.

The key benefits of software or technology escrow for the two main parties to a licence transaction are protecting IP for the licensor and securing investments in IT or other technology for the licensee, thereby mitigating key risks and facilitating deal closure. Further potential beneficiaries are various types of advisers to the two parties (lawyers, consultants, auditors and so on), who improve their own service and professional aptitude and create additional value for their clients, and any kind of investors, who may improve the rating and/or exploitation of their portfolio's assets.

Finally, software escrow – which originated in the United States some 30 years ago – is slowly but steadily making its way across Europe and the rest of the globe and is becoming a commonly accepted best practice for business continuity. Cloud escrow, with its components cloud software and cloud data, is a comparatively young field, which will definitely gain significance in tomorrow's quest for managing risks and opening up new business opportunities.

Notes

1 SaaS (software as a service, sometimes also known as software on demand), PaaS (platform as a service) and IaaS (infrastructure as a service) together form the three service models for cloud computing, as outlined in the National Institute for Standards and Technology (NIST), US Department of Commerce definition (source: wikipedia.org).

2 In relation to shortcomings of copyright and patent protection for IP in software, the most intuitive step would be to rely on copyright protection and, in addition, to file a patent for the software, yet it is not that easy. While copyright protection and patents for software are generally available across most industrialized jurisdictions, typically only certain parts of today's comprehensive applications stand a chance of reaching the intended shelter. Copyright protection protects specific lines of code from being copied. This means that one can take no action against another code written independently that achieves the same effects. Patents for computer-implemented inventions offer a broader protection for a product or process regardless of the software language they are written in. Patents can be obtained generally for novel software-based inventions that, for example, guide a satellite in orbit, or manage more telephone calls through narrower bandwidth, or make a computer run faster through more efficient memory usage. But any competitor who finds a different way to achieve the same objective, perhaps even a better way, will not have to explain him- or herself to the patent holder. Furthermore – and this is true for other forms of tangible IP such as text, music or videos as well – software is an electronic and thus a very volatile good. Nowadays, there are very few physical restrictions on its dissemination. And as is often the case, unfortunately, being right and getting one's rights are two very different animals. This is why escrow has become a viable form of IP protection for many owners of software and other forms of IP.

3 A seeming counter-model to the licensing or 'closed-source' model described above is the well-known 'open-source' model. It is based on openly sharing all lines of code, which others can then reuse and base further developments on, for the benefit of the general public. However, what seem to be two incompatible (if not ideologically competing) models in reality have found a peaceful and even mutually stimulating way of coexistence and furthering one another. Often enough, open-source software is combined successfully with proprietary software, and both sides' components are put in escrow – well labelled for their originator and accompanying licence, of course. For the remainder of this chapter, however, we will focus on the traditional licensing or closed-source model.

4 Capex (capital expenditure) typically appears under 'Investments' in the balance sheet.

Reference

Raphael JR (2011) The 10 worst cloud outages (and what we can learn from them), *InfoWorld*, 27 June, www.infoworld.com

Frugal enterprise risk management and ISO 31000

2.6

STEVEN SHACKLEFORD, PETER MAGGS AND
IRVINE LAUDER, WMSNT LIMITED

Introduction

The primary purpose of this chapter is to focus on practical aspects of implementing risk management within an organization that is very resource constrained. It focuses on the third or charity sector; however, the findings are useful to practitioners in any sector.

The chapter first looks at the background of the organization. It then runs through ISO 31000, explaining how each stage of ISO 31000 was planned and implemented by the organization during a couple of months.

The context for frugal risk management in the present decade

The authors represent a risk consultant, internal auditor and chief executive of a large charitable company based in Birmingham, UK, which provides transport facilities for people who do not have access to public transport or private vehicles, usually because of age, disability or learning difficulties. For the most part the charity is funded from a range of local metropolitan councils (local government) within the region that the charity serves.

With the recent deterioration of the global economy, local government funding cuts have threatened the charity's funding. Alongside this problem is the fact that local governments themselves have had to cut back similar services for lack of funds and so more and more people are finding themselves in need of the charity's help. At the same time fuel prices for the charity's transport fleet have reached record highs.

Thus the charity finds itself in a funding squeeze on three or four different fronts, like so many other governmental and third-sector organizations. Sponsors naturally

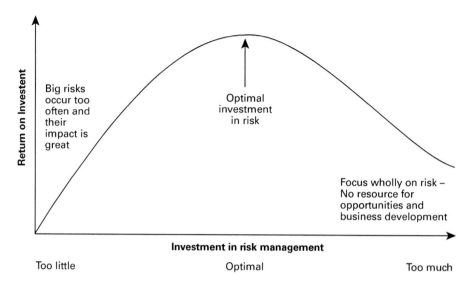

FIGURE 2.6.1 The limited benefits of investing in risk management

want assurance that their money is spent efficiently on front-line services, and never has the charity's external environment been so perilous.

Never too have the risks been greater, and never has the funding available to manage the risks been lower – the classic situation facing so many organizations during the 2010s.

The chief executive acknowledged that risk management needed strengthening, but he was aware that a balance had to be struck between investing money in developing risk management on the one hand and investing it in front-line business on the other hand. He was looking for a low-cost approach, which tended to conflict with most professional guidance, which indicated that organizations should be striving for the most mature level of risk management because only then could assurance be solid that risks were under control.

The solution was 'frugal risk management'; but where does 'frugal' lie in terms of investment? In fact frugal risk management is no different from good risk management; it's all about deciding upon the tipping point beyond which further risk management investment fails to yield a return, as Figure 2.6.1 illustrates.

The application of ISO 31000 to the charity

ISO 31000 is the newest approach to risk management, introduced in December 2009. The charity used the model to develop its first risk management framework in early 2012. Within two months all aspects of the 'framework' and the 'process' had been implemented, with the exception of the 'continual improvement' aspect. The approach is shown in Figure 2.6.2, and the rest of the chapter considers ISO 31000's approach and its application to the charity.

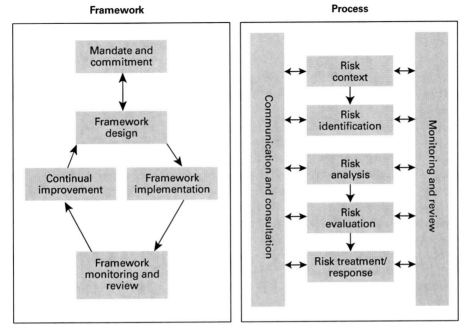

FIGURE 2.6.2 ISO 31000 risk management standard
SOURCE: Adapted from Airmic, Alarm and IRM (2010).

Framework: mandate and commitment

The first stage was that the chief executive employed both an internal auditor and a risk management consultant during the winter of 2011/12, both on a two-days-a-week, part-time basis. The idea was to create the framework by the middle of 2012. Just prior to this time, he spoke to the charity's managers about the need to develop risk management and that therefore they should expect the risk consultant and/or internal auditor to meet with them in the weeks to come.

Thus the scene was set and, when it came to undertaking the necessary meetings, the way had already been prepared and half the obstacles had been avoided.

Lesson one

For frugal risk management, if at the outset the person ultimately responsible for risk management (usually the chief executive) is able to provide both the mandate and the commitment (including a decision on resources), then the job of planning and implementing the risk framework is already half-done.

Process

Establishing the risk context

Establishing the risk context involved two clear aspects: 1) understanding where the organization presently was in terms of its risk management capability and knowledge; and 2) gathering the key strategic and operational objectives and then linking them together.

The chief executive quickly provided the new risk consultant with information that showed where the charity was. There was a recently produced set of high-level, purportedly 'strategic' risks and a SWOT analysis. There was evidence of earlier versions of this set too, because the annual report and accounts indicated that strategic risks were regularly reviewed. In fact, however, it was clear that some of these 'strategic' risks were more operational in nature, albeit potentially severe.

There was also some evidence that the risks were analysed using a Microsoft Excel five-by-five impact-likelihood grid, and there was evidence of inherent-risk analysis, response and residual-risk analysis. But what seemed clear was: 1) how difficult (or rather how almost impossible) it was to control strategic risks in the external environment; and 2) how those strategic risks seemed to be getting more adverse.

There was a strategic plan with a range of strategic objectives, but what appeared completely lacking was anything in the way of clear operational plans and objectives (and for that matter operational risk identification – which we talk about in the next section).

In short, the internal auditor, when applying the Chartered Institute of Internal Auditors' risk maturity model (see Table 2.6.1), considered that there was no formal approach adopted for risk management and that therefore the charity was presently at the lowest level of risk maturity.

So it was clear that the most logical next task was to consider developing a set of risk registers for operational risks too. The easiest way to do this was to create one

TABLE 2.6.1 Levels of risk maturity

Risk maturity	Key characteristics
Risk naïve	No formal approach developed for risk management.
Risk aware	Scattered silo-based approach to risk management.
Risk defined	Risk strategy and policy in place and communicated. Risk appetite defined.
Risk managed	Enterprise-wide approach to risk management developed and communicated.
Risk enabled	Risk management and internal control fully embedded into the operations, including management assurance.

SOURCE: Chartered Institute of Internal Auditors (2006).

risk register for each key department including the core services. It also seemed sensible to use the same Excel spreadsheet structure, as this was understood and accepted within the organization; it was also accessible because everyone had Excel; it was consistent in format and therefore quickly understandable and comparable for different parts of the charity.

Lesson two

If something is already in place, work with it if you want to be frugal. Do not reinvent the wheel, even if you believe your wheel will be rounder and smoother than the one in place; why create unnecessary battles?

Determining the objectives for each operational department could take months. The question was: what would be the quickest and cheapest way to identify the objectives of the departments that really mattered to the departmental managers concerned? The answer was a no-brainer: it was the managers' job descriptions (JDs)! The JDs succinctly captured all of the organization's expectations of the manager and, not only that, JDs existed for the managers' subordinates too! From these job descriptions the risk consultant very quickly obtained a pretty full set of objectives, from which one could begin to identify risks intelligently. And it was largely achieved in one day's work!

Lesson three

(This is repeated without apologies.) If something is already in place, work with it if you want to be frugal. Do not reinvent the wheel, even if you believe your wheel will be rounder and smoother than the one in place; why create unnecessary work and unnecessary battles?

Risk identification

Having reviewed the job descriptions, within one week of starting work the risk consultant was beginning to meet with departmental heads to clarify their objectives and talk through their worries about their objectives and the risks they faced.

The risk consultant said that he found the work to be both easy and pleasant. The chief executive had smoothed the road by talking to staff beforehand, and so everybody was always available and helpful and gave the risk consultant the impression they were engaged.

TABLE 2.6.2 Example meeting template used to identify, analyse and respond to risks

Staffing risk area			
Observation	**Risk implication**	**Recommendation**	**Manager's response**
a) Recruitment etc: There is a standard procedure for recruiting drivers that is followed. However, low turnover rates mean recruitment doesn't occur often. The DM recently had recruitment and selection training.	a) The sound recruitment of high-quality drivers is very important to the charity's users.	a) An independent review of driver recruitment procedure compliance. Inherent risk is quite high, even if the risk appears known and well managed (medium).	a) Agreed.
b) Etc.			

At the same time, however, each manager was different, and required a different interactive approach from the risk consultant. Some were more familiar with risk management than others, some seemed quite blind to some risks, and others added many risks to the set the consultant had prepared. Some preferred several short meetings over two weeks, while others could do it all inside a couple of hours.

After the risk consultant had taken copious notes, the meeting outcomes were written up into a table, which attempted to categorize risks within each department. See the example in Table 2.6.2.

The tables were then sent back to the departmental manager for approval and amendment as required. They were then used to draw up the operational risk registers for each key department of the charity.

Lesson four

For frugal enterprise risk management (ERM), consistency in the technical approach is essential to bring everything together, but variability in personal approach to deal with the different needs, objectives and personalities of different members of the organization's staff is equally essential.

Inherent-risk analysis

The same interview process was used to try to determine the relative severity of the risks identified by managers, based on their job descriptions. The manager talked around the issues and, from this, the risk consultant was able to some extent to form a view of the risk's likelihood and range of impacts.

With just the risk consultant taking charge of risk analysis, this facilitated a consistent approach across the enterprise. He was able to consider four areas, the last three of which might have been harder (and certainly longer-winded) had the manager undertaken a self-assessment process:

1 the potential severity of the risk directly to the relevant manager and his or her department;

2 the wider, indirect implications of the risk in terms of possible impacts on other departments;

3 the wider, indirect implications in terms of possible impacts on higher-level strategic objectives; and

4 the need to remove the possible problem of managers confusing inherent-risk analysis with residual-risk analysis.

The inherent-risk score was arrived at therefore on an organizational level, taking into account these four aspects.

Lesson five

Having one person, independent of management, undertaking risk analysis brings the quick wins of consistency in approach, while at the same time it enables a constant focus on the bigger and longer-term picture. Both of these things are an essential requirement of ERM, but at the same time can generate a lot of useful knowledge to the senior managers of the organization, and do so in an unbiased way. This lesson should however be exercised with caution – one person alone undertaking the process brings with it speed of completion, but also the risk of the personal risk stance of that person biasing the outcomes.

Risk evaluation 1

At this point the charity had not undertaken any risk evaluation in the form of a risk appetite statement in order for the consultant to assess the appropriate degree of response to the risks identified and analysed. This was to be considered later, in an informal way (see 'Risk evaluation 2' below).

Risk responses and residual-risk analysis

During the same interviewing process the risk consultant focused his questioning on three issues:

1 What were the existing responses (if any) to the risks that had earlier been identified?

2 How effective did the manager feel these responses were?

3 What further responses could the manager recommend as a result of conversations with the consultant?

The discussions here had the potential to be very political, because they required the managers to reveal both the strong and the weak in terms of their objectives management. This is why the intervention and support of the chief executive at the beginning of the process was so vital; it enabled managers to speak freely and honestly on their risk responses, and particularly where there were weaknesses.

From this work, the risk consultant was able to get some kind of view of each risk's net likelihood and impacts and thus was able to estimate net, or residual, risk.

Lesson six

This lesson repeats lesson one. Mandate and commitment for risk management by the chief executive are so easy to do and yet so vital in order to allow staff to reveal the truth, thus making the whole framework worthwhile. Their power is to cut through all of the possible political (or self-defensive) barriers that would otherwise completely block the flow of knowledge that is necessary to build risk intelligence. In that sense, it is the 'culture' that is the most crucial ingredient in frugal risk management.

Risk evaluation 2 (using the 2011 IRM approach to risk appetite)

From the discussions with the chief executive, and more particularly with the individual senior and operational managers, it became clear to the risk consultant that there were several risk appetites for the main risk categories facing the organization and that this was evident by the level of responses to risk already in place. Thus health and safety risks to the charity's users could never be accepted at any time; meanwhile financial risk had become much less acceptable as a result of the increasing prospects of squeezes on the charity's funding. What was encouraging was that all the senior managers generally had the same view on the level of acceptable risk for these risk categories.

From this intelligence, the Risk Consultant estimated the degree of acceptance of a risk on a scale of 0 to 5 for half a dozen of the key risks (a score of 0 being no acceptance in any circumstances and 5 being an almost cavalier acceptance of risk), and then equally weighted the scores for these half-dozen risks to form an overall, average level of risk appetite for the organization. Not surprisingly the level of risk appetite for risks that were important to the charity was fairly low.

Lesson seven

Risk appetite, typically considered as one of the most difficult areas of risk management, can actually be developed very rapidly, and if articulated in a semi-quantified form it can provide an easily understandable benchmark for reassessment in the future.

Monitoring and review: communication and consultation

As a result of the framework's rapid and recent development, there has been little time for a major process of review. However, this aspect was where the work of the internal auditor was very useful. From the work done by the risk consultant and chief executive in developing the framework, the internal auditor was able to review the work undertaken on the framework so far. More importantly, having been assured of that work, he was able to use the risk registers that came from the framework as the basis for building up his draft audit plan.

Using the Chartered Institute of Internal Auditors' risk maturity model (see Table 2.6.1), the internal auditor encouraged the charity to strive to achieve the 'risk defined' maturity level. He felt everything was now in place except for a risk strategy and policy, ie the risk communication tool. Taking the auditor's advice and using Hopkin's (2012, pp 79–80) approach, the consultant quickly wrote up a one-page draft policy for approval by the chief executive.

Lesson eight

As well as focusing on keeping the money investment as low as possible, frugal risk management requires us to consider the time investment, so try to keep risk-related documents short and to the point. The attention span of busy operational managers is limited, and rightly so. Time spent poring over risk information and data means less time and attention for their core focus – the organization's customers.

The benefits of frugal risk management

The work brought some really strong benefits to the organization, many of which would have been no better achieved had a massive investment of time, cost and IT applications been incurred:

- the building up of good working relationships between the chief executive, risk consultant and internal auditor, and a clarity to all operational managers that risk management is important for everyone;

- the speed of the process, which gave the opportunity for identifying and dealing quickly with any dangerous and unexpected risks that came up;
- the assurance afforded to users, sponsors and future business partners by greater transparency and disclosure of the charity's risk management in its annual report;
- the competitive advantage to the organization of an independent evaluation (in this case by internal audit) of rapid improvements in risk maturity, but at the same time knowing when to stop investing;
- the good publicity that was afforded by the fact that minimal investment was required to do this (in both time and money) and that consequently the organization could still state truthfully that there had been no decline in the proportion of resources focused on front-line services;
- the strength of a consistent approach, with consistent terminology and consistent presentation across the organization of risk management, which made it easier to keep the framework updated long after the consultant departed; and finally
- the fact that a whole range of risks faced by the organization were better understood, particularly in terms of their interconnectedness by risk type, by department and throughout the organization, leading to a true improvement in risk management!

There has never been a more important time to invest in risk management, yet during these cost-constrained times there has never been more pressure to seek value for money from any investment. To reap most of the benefits of risk management, it does not have to be expensive, but the onus is truly on the chief executive to ensure it is not.

References

Airmic, Alarm and Institute of Risk Management (IRM) (2010) *A Structured Approach to Enterprise Risk Management (ERM) and the Requirements of ISO 31000*, Airmic, Alarm and IRM, London

Chartered Institute of Internal Auditors (2006) *Gaining Assurance on Risks through Risk Based Internal Auditing*, Chartered Institute of Internal Auditors, London

Hopkin, P (2012) *Fundamentals of Risk Management*, 2nd edn, Kogan Page/Institute of Risk Management, London

Institute of Risk Management (IRM) (2011) *Risk Appetite and Tolerance*, IRM, London

PART THREE
Risk management applications

Understanding cyber security risk

3.1

**MARTIN SUTHERLAND, MANAGING DIRECTOR,
BAE SYSTEMS DETICA**

IT threats have been a feature of the internet for almost as long as it has been in existence. And yet 2012 was the first year that the World Economic Forum identified cyber attacks as a 'Top Five risk in terms of likelihood over the next decade'. What has changed, and why is cyber security now a risk that increasingly appears among the top 5 or 10 in corporate risk registers?

Some of it is inevitably down to organizations' ever-increasing dependency on information technology – with the impact of any disruption or damage growing in direct proportion.

There is an omnipresent risk from an organization's own employees, contractors and suppliers. These are individuals who have to be trusted with access to information and systems – inevitably opening up the opportunity for abuse of that trust. As the boundaries of the organization blur, both geographically and organizationally, the number of individuals in a position to abuse their privileges continues to grow.

Alongside this, indiscriminate external attacks – viruses, worms and their like – have long arisen either from the actions of hobbyists or as fallout from undirected, opportunistic criminal activity. Businesses have more recently learned to confront more targeted criminal activities, typically directed at the theft of large volumes of credit card information.

These are constant battles. But beyond those well-established risks, businesses must now also assess and respond to three new categories of external threats. Two of these have undoubtedly moved from the realms of the hypothetical to become widespread and mainstream concerns; the third remains today largely unrealized but is front-of-mind for governments worldwide because of the potential severity of the impact.

The new threats

'Hacktivism'

The first is the reputational risk associated with political 'hacktivists' – groups such as Anonymous and LulzSec that have gathered media attention worldwide with high-profile attacks on a wide range of organizations. These groups select specific targets, often announcing them in advance, and draw on all the tools at their disposal to embarrass them. Sometimes they succeed in nothing worse than a bit of low-level vandalism, such as taking a website offline for a short period. But on other occasions they have had devastating effect.

In today's world of global connectivity, social networking and 24/7 news, stories and political feelings can develop with astonishing speed. Even those businesses that face no apparent hacktivist threat today should be aware that a credible threat can develop rapidly, leaving very little time to put in place additional protective measures. What is more, threats can arise as a by-product of others' fights: in our interconnected world, one business can be targeted purely as a means of gaining access to another.

The efficacy of hacktivism as a means of embarrassing and damaging its targets has been proven, and despite continued actions by law enforcement groups it seems inevitable that the mainstream emergence of this activity will remain a significant feature of the cyber landscape. Any business with concerns about reputation can ill afford to ignore this aspect of the risk.

Advanced Persistent Threat (APT)

Second comes the very real, but poorly reported, threat of APT or industrial cyber espionage: the targeted theft of trade secrets or confidential commercial information by third parties gaining access to an organization's IT systems by connecting over the internet.

Many organizations are still finding it difficult to believe that they would be targets for espionage activities. Indeed, the word 'espionage' conjures up images of James Bond and the Cold War – very far from the concerns of contemporary business leaders. Yet in practice there seems almost no limit to the range of organizations that are being actively targeted for infiltration and the theft of confidential information.

By its nature, this sort of activity is covert and can take place entirely without the knowledge of the targeted organization. Even in those cases where the activity is detected, it is frequently found only after several months or even years of successful covert activity. And since it is often not in the interests of the affected organization to make a public disclosure of the findings, the level of public reporting of such activity is quite out of line with the true extent.

Businesses are therefore confronted with a need to understand and assess a new category of risk about which there is very little public information. What is clear however is that APT as a business model lends itself to industrialization.

While espionage has always taken place, the need for individuals who are in positions where they can access valuable data limits its scale; and there are real personal risks to those involved. By comparison, APT is cheap and scalable and can be conducted at minimal risk. The cost to gain access to even apparently well-protected systems is relatively low and, by connecting across the global internet, the perpetrators stand almost no risk of being identified – and are almost certainly out of reach of legal retribution even if they are.

The implications of this industrialization are stark, and are borne out by experience: businesses should not assume they are too low-profile to fall victim to cyber espionage. Far from the realms of spy novels, APT must be a mainstream concern for 21st-century businesses.

Cyber warfare and cyber terrorism

Finally, alongside the very real threats from hacktivism and cyber espionage (or APT) comes the threat of cyber warfare and cyber terrorism. Rather than the theft of information, these types of attack seek to use control over IT systems to have real-world effects, typically directed against elements of national infrastructure such as electricity distribution, telecommunications or financial payments.

By their nature, the effects of this type of attack tend to be apparent rather than covert, and we would expect to see evidence of at least some proportion of any incidents. However, to date, public reporting of such incidents has been limited to the case of Stuxnet – believed to have been an attack against the Iranian uranium enrichment infrastructure at Natanz.

What is clear therefore is that such attacks are not wholly theoretical: it is possible to have real-world effects using a cyber attack, and it would be remarkable if nation states worldwide were not investigating whether and how to develop this capability as part of their military arsenals. What is not clear is how difficult or how practical it is to use these techniques in order to generate an effective result, nor whether there is any reality to fears that terrorist groups might also investigate such approaches.

Businesses that operate in relevant sectors will certainly find it hard to ignore concerns around this type of attack. Indeed, there is increasing pressure on national governments to assess how vulnerable their national infrastructures are to this threat, and businesses in these areas should expect an increasing level of engagement with government bodies around this. At this stage, few nations have shown much appetite for explicit regulation, but this could change as knowledge increases, if further real-world examples are seen and as economic circumstances improve.

Businesses are at risk

What is perhaps shocking is how vulnerable most businesses are to these targeted threats. Time after time, there is evidence that even businesses that undertake recognized best-practice information security are breached by attackers with relative ease. Assessing vulnerability is an inexact science, but professional security-testing groups typically estimate that they can gain access to a well-protected commercial organization for a cost of a few tens of thousands of pounds.

Why is this? This is not the place for a lengthy technical discussion, but the root causes might be considered to be twofold. Firstly, complex software and systems are inherently vulnerable. 'Secure by design' approaches (still far from the norm despite the IT industry's 60 or so years of existence) can help to limit this level of vulnerability – but even here there is a point at which timescales and costs become economically prohibitive. Some residual level of vulnerability is an inevitable feature of the flexibility and innovation of information technology. Secondly, conventional approaches to information security presume a level of operational perfection in their execution that is near impossible to sustain in practice. An attacker needs to find only one weak point to exploit; the target needs to shore up all of them. In today's complex, connected corporate IT environment, there will inevitably be an omission or an accident, or an opportunity to cause one through careful social engineering.

Thus there are credible threats; and most businesses are much more vulnerable than they might imagine. What is harder to determine is how significant the business impact would be in the event of an incident.

Looking across the three categories of new threat:

- For organizations that manage large volumes of personal data, the reputational impact of a hacktivist incident can be enormous. Of course, the levels of effort that a hacktivist group may be willing or able to deploy in any given attack are very variable, and so businesses may be adequately protected against many forms of attack, but in general the risk should be considered significant by any organization of this nature that has a current or potentially credible threat.

- The impact of cyber espionage is much harder to estimate, but can in principle include very large business losses due to lost contracts, and reduced market share in the face of stolen trade secrets. Because cyber espionage is outside most executives' daily experience, many are fast to dismiss the likely impact, but in some cases businesses that have analysed the problem have discovered a potentially existent risk.

- Finally, in the case of cyber warfare or cyber terrorism, the potential impact is still very poorly understood in almost all cases. It is clear that an appropriately motivated attacker could cause system down times in what are sometimes highly critical systems, but what is less clear is whether that down time would be quickly recoverable at limited business loss, or whether it might be feasible for an attacker to create a more persistent, longer-term outage. Further research is a priority for those who need to engage seriously with this risk.

Managing the risk

There is great interest within the insurance industry in developing new forms of cyber risk insurance, but today's market contains a very limited range of products, and for the most part organizations are left with a decision as to whether to accept or reduce the risk.

Reducing the risk from targeted attacks will typically involve some mixture of two approaches: increasing protective measures in order to reduce the level of vulnerability, and deploying enhanced monitoring capabilities in order to detect successful attacks at the earliest possible stage.

Robust protective measures

Although the majority of commercial organizations are relatively vulnerable to targeted attacks, more robust protective measures are available and are tried and tested in high-security environments. For the most part, such environments tend to exist in a military and national security context, but examples are found also in the financial payments and transactions sectors, and in isolated pockets within other industries.

At the heart of these more robust protection approaches is greater separation of high-value data from high-threat environments such as the internet, going as far in some cases as complete physical and electrical isolation of separate, high-security networks (although intermediate levels are also possible).

This sort of protection approach is proven to be effective, but represents significant IT change and incurs costs in direct technology deployment, in business change and in the potential restrictions on operational processes that may result. Nonetheless, for the most valuable information this sort of approach is invaluable, and the Payment Card Industry Data Security Standard (PCI DSS) has driven extensive deployment for the protection of payment card details.

Detection

Inevitably, however, no defences are ever perfect and certainly, where conventional, highly connected IT architectures are used, organizations should plan for breaches of their defences. This need not however be a counsel of despair. Particularly in the case of cyber espionage, there is typically a significant period (weeks or months) following the initial breach of a network during which the attacker is looking for valuable information to steal. If this activity can be detected during the first few days, there is a good chance of evicting the intruder before any significant business damage is caused.

For this approach to succeed, however, it is necessary to detect intruders whose entire aim is to avoid detection. This is a sophisticated game of cat and mouse that requires investment in specialist emerging technologies and in capable investigative resources. Certainly, companies should not assume that existing technologies will suffice, although these systems can prove invaluable in detecting and responding to traditional, indiscriminate attacks.

Rapid response

Nevertheless, detection of itself will not solve the problem: it will be necessary to respond effectively when an incident is detected. The same is true whatever the means by which the incident has come to light: rapid and effective response will make a significant contribution to minimizing the business impact.

For this to be the case, businesses must prepare in advance to ensure they are best placed to respond. Of course, it is impossible to predict precisely what sort of incident is likely to take place, and so there is a limit to the level of detailed planning that can be done, but at a minimum organizations should:

- put in place technical measures to ensure that, when a real or suspected incident is under way, investigators have access to all the data that they might need, in particular ensuring the availability and retention of log data;

- ensure that they know where to find experts who can help with the investigation, and that relationships are in place to allow these experts to start work immediately;

- have clear chains of command and communication in the event of a crisis, so that decisions can be taken rapidly and clear definitive communications can be made to stakeholders.

Developing a strategy

Businesses face real challenges in developing their understanding of these risks. Assessing the threat presents particular problems in the face of APT threats, which are covert and poorly reported, and cyber warfare threats, which remain largely hypothetical. Engagement with governments can help to clarify some aspects, but nobody should assume that clear guidance will be forthcoming. Businesses will need to gather what intelligence they can, and interpret this through a geopolitical lens that is realistic about the lengths to which some global actors will go to support their economic development. Such discussions will inevitably fall outside the traditional comfort zone of most executives.

In evaluating vulnerability, the challenge is above all one of communication: detailed technical assessments need to be condensed and conveyed in a way that allows business evaluation and decision making. It will be incumbent on the business to temper bottom-up analysis with a top-down view that is honest about the levels of vulnerability to determined attack.

Finally, to understand the potential business impact of these risks, most organizations need to focus in two areas. They must improve their knowledge about the information they hold and the systems they use, and how these 'information assets' underpin their business success. They must then push the business to estimate both the direct and the consequential implications of compromises to those assets, while avoiding the inevitable tendency to assume that 'it won't happen to me'. A scenario planning approach can be an effective tool in this regard.

Against this backdrop, it becomes possible to assess proposed investments in security, informed of course by real understanding of what does and does not work against the different categories of cyber threat. Assessments and strategies will vary between organizations. What will be constant will be the growing recognition that the risks are too significant to be treated as a purely technical consideration.

Managing business risk in the life sciences industry

MUKADDER ERDÖNMEZ, XL GROUP

Introduction and overview of the life sciences sector

The life sciences sector is one of the fastest-growing industries in the world today. Life science is an extremely broad discipline and includes companies focusing on the areas of biotechnology, pharmaceuticals, biomedical technologies, food processing and medical devices. Across the globe, science is using sophisticated technologies to better understand and cure diseases, develop crops that are resistant to drought and pestilence, and improve imaging and diagnostic techniques.

According to research published in January 2012 by MarketLine, a global publisher of company and industry data, the global pharmaceuticals, biotechnology and life sciences industry group generated total revenues of $1,001 billion in 2010, representing a compound annual growth rate (CAGR) of 6.8 per cent for the period spanning 2005–10.

Pharmaceuticals proved the most lucrative for the global pharmaceuticals, biotechnology and life sciences industry group in 2010, generating total revenues of $733.1 billion, equivalent to 73.2 per cent of the industry group's overall value.

The performance of the industry group is forecast to accelerate, with an anticipated CAGR of 7 per cent for the five-year period 2010–15, which is expected to drive the market to a value of $1,405 billion by the end of 2015.

What is fuelling this explosive growth? Today, the global life sciences sector is in the midst of significant and rapid change, which presents both opportunities and challenges. Driving this change are supply- and demand-side pressures, lifestyle choices, longevity and a rise in chronic conditions such as diabetes, obesity and dementia. In confronting these realities, traditional ways of working will become quickly outdated and there will be constant pressure on companies to keep driving products and methodologies forward.

In addition, people in developed countries, where affluence rates are growing, are demanding a higher standard of healthcare and overall quality of life. This has resulted in more pressure being placed on governments to keep new and existing drugs at affordable price levels. Despite the harsh economic climate of the last few years, people have shown a willingness to spend money on a wide range of products – medicines, nutritionals and devices – that can help improve their quality of life and longevity.

Ernst & Young's 25th annual industry report, *Beyond Borders: Global biotechnology report 2011*, notes that diabetes and cardiovascular conditions are expected to escalate dramatically owing to ageing populations in developed countries and growing prosperity across emerging-market countries. In addition to the treatment of specific diseases, other growth areas include computer-assisted surgery, cellular and tissue engineering, rehabilitation, and orthopaedic engineering.

Risks and challenges associated with innovation

There are multiple developments that are playing a part in reshaping the life sciences sector. Consider the pharmaceutical sector, where finding new treatments for chronic diseases continues to place pressure on already stretched healthcare budgets. The emerging economies are demanding medicines in a much larger capacity than ever before, and healthcare manufacturers are struggling to keep pace with demand. At the same time, the pharmaceuticals market is becoming increasingly saturated, and healthcare organizations are regularly measuring the performance of products against each other.

In decades to come, it is expected that there will be more diverse product types and new therapies – many based on genetic targeting. Medicine will shift towards understanding the genetics behind diseases. Using stem cells and genetic engineering techniques, scientists are already learning to regroup damaged organs, tissues, muscles and bones to regenerate damaged bodies. In the future, we may no longer need the dentist to drill fillings or provide false teeth, because genetic engineers will have understood out how to stimulate the relevant genes so we can regrow and replace a missing tooth.

But all of this innovation comes at a high price, with financial and reputational risks coming into play. The life sciences sector faces a unique set of challenges, and those working in it need to understand how to manage these challenges effectively if they are to survive in the years to come.

An enormous amount of capital investment is required to bring a new product to market, whether it's a new drug or an innovative medical device. The life cycle process in life sciences is considerably longer than in many other industries. Lengthy research and development phases, typically in the region of 8–10 years, and a considerable testing phase, followed by trying to meet the intensive regulatory hurdles of different geographies all carry risks that can result in success or failure for the companies involved. All this is at a time when cash flows are diminishing while, at the same time, supply chains are tightening up and payment terms are being squeezed or made less flexible.

The Economist Intelligence Unit identified in a 2009 report that, too often, risk management is viewed by senior management as less important than other considerations, despite the continually evolving range of risks companies face every day, from regulatory

When things look like they might stop. We're the ones that'll help move your business forward.

MAKE YOUR WORLD GO

xlgroup.com

issues to fraud to counterfeit products and other threats to intellectual property. According to the report, many senior managers are so busy reacting to current risks that they fail to spot new and emerging risks.

While all companies in today's uncertain economic climate face risks to their business from shrinking credit, product pricing pressures and increased costs overall, the life sciences sector faces an additional and complex set of risks that few other industries need to address. These are discussed in the following sections.

Product liability

One of the most significant risks faced by companies in this sector is from product liability. The indemnification associated with drugs is high. We have seen a number of examples, in recent years, of drugs that have caused adverse side effects in a small segment of the population. This in turn can lead to class action claims, especially in the United States, being brought against the company. Associated with product liability is the issue of product recall, which is of considerable concern to pharmaceutical companies, which must manage these issues while trying to minimize their reputational risk.

In 2005, the recall of more than 420 products thought to be contaminated with Sudan 1, a red dye used for colouring solvents, oils and waxes, which had been banned for use in foodstuffs in the UK and across the EU, cost the parties involved more than £100 million, clearly illustrating the large risks associated with product liability and recall.

It also serves as a reminder that brands can be irreparably damaged if organizations fail to plan and manage recalls effectively.

New product safety regulation also increases liability. In the EU, legislation in the last few years has placed new obligations on manufacturers to share information and report any product safety issues in order for recall decisions to be made.

Clinical trials

For pharmaceutical and biotechnology companies, there are huge financial, scientific and technical challenges associated with bringing new drugs to market.

Clinical trials are essential for confirming the safety and efficacy of new medicines, and for testing new uses for existing medicines. They are an integral part of developing new treatments for unmet medical needs, but clinical trials can involve ethical issues and risks, and their impact for the patients involved must be carefully assessed. Once the clinical trial phase moves to human trials, the liability increases significantly. The targets of litigation are often the clinical investigators and research institutions that conducted the trials, yet the companies that sponsor trials are also at risk when something goes wrong. Pharmaceutical companies must take aggressive steps to make sure the clinical trials they sponsor are beyond reproach and to guard against even the appearance of conflicts of interest.

Those responsible for planning and conducting a trial must assess whether the beneficial results of a new treatment or trial will outweigh any risks the research may carry. The expenses and risks of testing a drug in clinical trials are considerable. It can cost hundreds of millions of dollars to conduct the clinical trials required to market a drug, and the vast majority of drugs entering clinical trials fail, making clinical trials an important contributor to the high cost of pharmaceutical R&D.

More than 3 million people worldwide annually participate in some 80,000 clinical trials to assess the safety and efficacy of new drugs, treatments and medical devices. While every effort is made to control risks to clinical trial participants, the experimental nature of these studies makes it impossible to eliminate all risks. Although 'new' may imply 'better' it is not known whether the potential medical treatment offers benefits to patients until clinical research on that treatment is complete. While new and powerful drugs targeting more serious illnesses undoubtedly pose risks, the potential benefits to patients suffering life-threatening and debilitating diseases are enormous. Clinical trials offer no guarantees, but they do offer hope when standard treatments fail or don't exist.

Business interruption

Given the highly sensitive environment in which life sciences companies operate, even small accidents can have a detrimental impact on the company's bottom line. Such incidents could take the form of room contamination or an accident with biological compounds. There is also the risk within companies that employees may become ill as a result of the work they are carrying out. For example, exposure over time to certain compounds or becoming injured during the manufacturing process is another issue that companies must face and be prepared for. While these incidents may not be hugely costly financially, they could have a negative impact on corporate revenues.

Patent expiration

Perhaps one of the biggest threats facing many companies is patent expiration. Many major pharmaceutical companies have been anticipating significant drops in both revenues and sales as a result of patent expirations in the coming years. Once a company's patents expire, generic alternatives enter the market, which leads to a sharp decrease in sales, as these generic companies often have lower overheads and compete primarily through lower prices. Drug companies now face: a drought of big drug breakthroughs and research discoveries; pressure from insurers and the government to hold down prices; regulatory vigilance and government investigations; and thousands of lay-offs in R&D.

Patents for a number of blockbuster drugs such as Seroquel, which is used in the treatment of bipolar disorder and other mental illnesses, and Tricor, used to treat high cholesterol, have expired or will be expiring in the United States in the near future. The Office for Life Sciences (OLS) estimates that this will be the equivalent of $140 billion in sales.

Environmental liability

There are also increasing risks from environmental liability, which has seen tougher sanctions worldwide in recent years. Environmental regulations, especially in Europe and the United States, force polluters to prevent and remedy environmental damage that they have caused. Fines and other costs can be steep, so companies need to take precautions to ensure they prevent and contain any environmental damage.

Shortage of skilled staff

Another significant and growing risk, especially in Europe, is the inability to attract and retain qualified staff. A study by Mergent in 2009 estimated that 40 per cent of the US scientific workforce comes from Europe, raising concerns that the European life science sector is simply not competitive enough to attract and retain the best people. R&D spend is still trailing that seen in the United States, despite increases in R&D being a top priority of the European Union.

Disease mutation

Finally there is the changing nature of diseases themselves. Diseases mutate over time, and drugs such as antibiotics that once reigned supreme are now losing their efficacy, thereby requiring pharmaceutical companies to rethink and re-engineer their treatment methods. Diseases such as Tuberculosis have made a reappearance in major cities like New York and London, while hospital 'superbugs', which have shown resistance to standard treatments, are presenting new challenges for scientists.

The life sciences industry must do more than merely be reactive. The stakes are high and, if the sector's full potential is to be realized, companies across the industry, be they pharmaceutical, biotechnology or medical devices, must remain alert to new risks that could jeopardize their bottom line and, more importantly, their reputation across the sector.

Independent assessment and certification: good for food safety – good for business

COR GROENVELD, LLOYD'S REGISTER QUALITY ASSURANCE (LRQA)

Food safety has been in the media spotlight continuously over the years, with deaths, illness and product recalls seeming to be an almost daily occurrence. That seems in stark contrast to the claims of global food retailers, manufacturers and government food agencies that 'food has never been safer'. Regardless of what the facts may be, in our world perception is reality. That is why it is of paramount importance for every link in the global food supply chain to demonstrate transparency, consistency and a commitment to food safety. Meeting that objective requires a very high level of interaction and integration between the individual elements, as the global food supply chain is exponentially more complex than it was just 20 years ago. Food is grown on one continent, processed on another, packaged on yet another and then distributed and sold all over the world. Retailers, manufacturers, suppliers and governments have all recognized that it is the responsibility of everyone in the chain to provide confidence in food safety, up and down the supply chain. Food supply chain stakeholders have invested heavily in a two-prong approach to food safety: 1) the development of thorough, harmonized global standards and certification schemes; and 2) competent, experienced, sector-specific auditors to deliver an independent, robust assessment of an organization's performance against those global standards and schemes.

How it all began – the emergence of food safety

Food safety is not a new subject, and neither are some of the standards and schemes that help to regulate it. It started with HACCP (hazard analysis and critical control

Assessors that see where you can both reduce risk and improve performance.

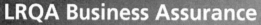

points), which was developed in the 1960s when the US National Aeronautics and Space Administration (NASA) asked Pillsbury to design and manufacture the first foods for space flights. Since then, HACCP has been recognized internationally as a logical tool used in the food industry to identify potential food safety hazards so that preventive actions can be taken to mitigate the potential risks. The system continues to be used at all stages of the food supply chain. As food safety systems and processes matured, global food manufacturers, suppliers and retailers realized that HACCP could be enhanced through the development of bespoke schemes specific to their individual organizations, supply chains and sectors. They also identified the value that having independent third-party certification bodies auditing their own facilities and suppliers against international standards offered in terms of building stakeholder trust and reducing risks.

An unintended consequence of organization-specific schemes was an abundance of similar auditing requirements. With separate audits being required for suppliers, a 'global silo mentality' emerged; continual improvement and best-practice outputs remained local instead of being used to drive change across the global food sector. Another impact was the rising cost from multiple audits. Suppliers were bearing the brunt of global retailer and food manufacturers' demands. They were being squeezed from both a cost and a time perspective with complex and costly auditing requirements.

The drive to harmonization

To eliminate duplication of effort and rising costs, there was a move to harmonize the auditing and certification process. In 2000, global retailers and manufacturers joined forces to form the Global Food Safety Initiative (GFSI). The GFSI delivered a recognition process for food safety certification schemes against a set of requirements set out in the GFSI Guidance Document. The principle of GFSI was 'certified once, accepted everywhere'. Put simply, when a food manufacturer was certified against one of the GFSI recognized schemes, all associated retailers would accept the certification. Today, an increasing number of organizations accept GFSI-recognized standards and schemes. A second important harmonization initiative came with the launch of the international food safety management system standard, ISO 22000, in 2005. The International Organization for Standardization (ISO) once again ensured that Deming's 'Plan, Do, Check, Act' cycle underpinned this new standard, making for ease of integration. Integrated, risk-based management systems and combined assessments were now a compelling proposition for organizations worldwide. ISO's historical success with the harmonization of standards meant that it was well placed to develop ISO 22000. ISO's collaborative approach saw it inviting feedback from key industry stakeholders. This ensured that the best elements from the many organization-specific schemes were incorporated into ISO 22000.

Since release in 2005, ISO 22000 has been implemented in thousands of companies worldwide. Applicable to any organization in the food chain – including suppliers of non-food materials and services – ISO 22000 can be applied 'from farm to fork'.

The shift towards ISO 22000 highlighted the importance of ensuring that food safety systems are established, operated and updated within the framework of a structured management system and incorporated into the overall management activities of the organization. This provides maximum benefit for the organization and interested parties.

The 2011 adoption of ISO 22000 by Carrefour – the world's second-largest retailer – to some of its key sites in Europe is a testament to the importance that retailers are placing on a transparent, globally accepted certification process.

ISO 22000's universal acceptance was hindered by the lack of prerequisite programmes, or PRPs as they are known. In 2010 this perceived weakness was addressed by Publicly Available Specification (PAS) 220. When combined with ISO 22000, PAS 220 offered a complete and holistic food safety management system for manufacturers of food ingredients and food products. Additional PRPs have been addressed through the development of PAS 222 (animal feed) and PAS 223 (packaging), which will extend the use of ISO 22000 and sector-specific requirements for PRPs throughout the supply chain.

Where we are today

In 2011 the launch took place of FSSC 22000, the ISO 22000 and PAS 220 based food safety certification scheme, which was benchmarked and approved by the GFSI. To be certified, a company must implement the requirements of both ISO 22000 and PAS 220 and have a certification audit by a FSSC 22000 approved certification body.

FSSC 22000 was developed by the Foundation for Food Safety Certification. Along with the copyright management of the scheme, this not-for-profit foundation also:

- focuses on the international compliance and adaptability of food safety standards;
- focuses on the development and maintenance of certification for food safety;
- promotes the international use of these food safety systems;
- provides services to support the certification of food safety systems;
- provides information on food safety issues.

The food supply chain scope of FSSC 22000 is growing. PAS 223 has already been implemented, so the scope of FSSC 22000 includes food packaging materials, and it is expected the same will happen with animal feed. These undertakings by the Foundation directly link back and address the key issues of putting independent third-party certification and assessment at the heart of food safety. The Foundation's commitments are directly driving a process-based approach, the harmonization of standards and, in turn, auditor competency. Through the harmonization of standards, the market at large can now easily benchmark against international standards and GFSI-recognized schemes such as ISO 22000 and FSSC 22000. As Mark Overland, Director of Global Certification at Cargill, explained, 'We are rolling out FSSC 22000 to over 1,000 plants in 67 countries. Having the same level of food safety execution at every plant is an expectation from our customers. We feel that having LRQA delivering a high level of consistency is the best approach to ensure that we are delivering on our promise to our customers.'

The value of harmonization is also supported by Wrigley, a subsidiary of Mars, Incorporated, which stated that, 'With the adoption of FSSC 22000, Wrigley's North American factories saw on average a 25–50% reduction of audits requested by retailers.'

Along with the Foundation for Food Safety Certification, both the GFSI and ISO have to be applauded as very important initiatives in driving effective benchmarking and the harmonization of standards. With now 12 approved standards from a starting point of 100, this is clearly a significant achievement, and we may expect the number will decrease in the future. The reason for this is that organizations in the food supply chain will make their choice from the internationally recognized standards, leading to further harmonization of standards and certification in the supply chain. The GFSI today is driven not only by retailers but also by other stakeholders like the food manufacturers, packaging manufacturers and storage and distribution companies.

There is also a shift in the approach to food safety – driven in part by the globalization of food supply chains – meaning that an organization's own supply chain is only as strong as its weakest link. Having a GFSI-recognized certification can be important to a company, especially when selling to one of the major retailers that requires a GFSI-recognized certificate. Because this list includes such giants as Wal-Mart, Carrefour, Tesco, Metro, Migros, Ahold and Delhaize, the GFSI recognition is very important to many food companies. In addition, global food manufacturers and food service companies have started to accept GFSI-recognized certification from their suppliers. So the GFSI principles are increasingly being used across the whole food supply chain.

A good example of this is second-party audits. Leading certification bodies are both recommending and ensuring that such audits, which are historically based around bespoke requirements, are underpinned with GFSI-endorsed standards to drive a holistic, process-based approach, which in turn delivers credibility and consumer confidence.

A further development is that the ISO recognized the need of the food chain to have international technical specifications for PRPs, and it published ISO 22002-1. This document has the same content as PAS 220 and is expected to be its international replacement. ISO has also decided to make these specifications for all sectors such as primary production, packaging material, transport and storage, animal feed and catering. Along with this, FSSC 22000 is able to extend their scope further in the supply chain.

The role of independent third-party certification

Never before have manufacturers and retailers listened to what their consumers and customers are saying as much as they do now. They are collaborating with their global supply network, which has grown from the local and regional suppliers of yesteryear into a complex global supply chain, or 'demand networks' as they should more accurately be called. To give an illustration of the complexity of the supply chain, a simple pizza can have over 100 different ingredients, and for some of them a manufacturer will have more than one supplier!

The certification industry is clearly one of the key stakeholders in the drive towards the harmonization of standards and schemes. The fact that many certification bodies are aligned with regulatory institutions, including my own role as Chairman of the

Foundation for Food Safety Certification, the organization that has ownership of FSSC 22000, is a testament to the importance that the industry as a whole is placing on certification.

Key components of a robust assessment process

Auditor competency

The delegates at the 2011 GFSI annual conference highlighted 'auditor competency' as the single most important issue concerning food safety. Auditor competency refers not only to the ability of auditors to perform a robust assessment, but also to the technical expertise of auditors and their experience in the specific industries and sectors that they are working in. For LRQA, it goes even further; our LRQA Business Assurance approach is built around ensuring that organizational objectives are directly linked to the objectives of organizations' food safety management systems and to the assessment process.

Put simply, if you are in the food sector, then food safety should be a top priority of every system and process that is a part of your organization. It should be identified and prioritized in both your corporate strategy and your management system. It should also be reflected in both the assessment process and the resulting report, thereby ensuring that continuous improvement and risk management become a part of corporate culture, not limited to the role of the food safety manager.

Those may seem like lofty goals for an auditor, but we believe that technically competent, sector-specific auditors with an in-depth understanding of their clients can have a fundamental impact on performance and the ability to manage risks. Organizations in the food supply chain that are prioritizing potential auditor CVs and certification body methodologies and credentials rather than focusing on price have clearly understood what is at stake. The food sector increasingly relies on independent, robust certification, not just to protect brands and businesses from prosecutions and health scares, but also to drive improvements and secure competitive advantage.

To these food organizations, large and small, certification is about a lot more than simply a piece of paper on the wall. They rely on the certification process to ensure food safety procedures are in place, but also to assess their business objectives, processes and management system(s). They need to trust their assessing bodies, and they need to have total confidence in the auditors.

Assessment methodology

At LRQA, we are committed to investing in our people and processes to ensure that we continue to deliver independent, robust assessment underpinned with best-in-class auditor competency to help organizations meet the needs and expectations of their stakeholders. It is this approach – simply called LRQA Business Assurance – that will help to drive trust and integrity on two key levels: from organizations towards the certification industry and from consumers towards the food industry through increased brand reputation.

The focus on continual improvement as an integral part of the assessment process will continue to add value to organizations across the global supply chain. Not only will this identify areas for focus and improvement, but organizations, through channels such as the GFSI and FSSC, will be able to share best practice to the benefit of the wider global food safety community.

Process-based approach

Both ISO 22000 and FSSC 22000 acted as catalysts for change, not only through the harmonization of standards but through synchronizing the whole supply chain management system approach to focus on minimizing risks and improving performance.

No longer just a single 'snapshot in time', the assessment process is now a holistic view on the whole network of interacting processes that are assessed and monitored. Let's take an example to illustrate this point: on 13 January 2009, the Peanut Corporation of America issued a recall for products it had made over the preceding six months, after five people had died and more than 400 had fallen ill with salmonella poisoning as a result of contamination. Two weeks later, the recall was extended to more than 400 consumer products made since 1 January 2007, while the toll from the contamination had reached eight dead and more than 500 ill in 43 states, half of them children. The company's factory in Blakely, Georgia, which was the source of the contamination, supplied some of the largest food makers in the nation.

The outbreak illustrated the complexities of the industrial food chain, and left consumers scrambling to figure out if some food in their cabinets posed a danger. It is scares like this that have ensured that retailers and manufacturers alike recognize that they are responsible for every risk in their supply chain. When food disaster strikes – and irrespective of who is to blame – inevitably it is the global brand that will become the focus of the media spotlight. Whilst the supplier at fault may disappear, it is the brand of the global retailer or manufacturer that will sustain the damage.

These risks are being mitigated through the global acceptance and use of ISO 22000 and FSSC 22000. What is also apparent is that, increasingly, global and national organizations alike are recognizing the benefits that independent third-party assessment against these standards and schemes can deliver in helping to minimize their risks.

Summary

Once viewed primarily as a tick-in-the-box exercise, third-party assessment and certification are increasingly seen as evidence of stakeholder engagement, risk mitigation and management best practice.

Collaboration, transparency and a strong focus on risk mitigation are at the heart of the food supply chain. Food safety is non-competitive; it is in the interest of all food stakeholders to reduce food safety issues to an absolute minimum. Two particular areas have worked together to bring about an increased confidence in the global food supply chain. The first of these is the harmonization of standards.

Harmonized, thorough food safety management system standards and schemes have brought increased transparency and best-practice sharing across sectors and geographies. Gone are the days of every large manufacturer and retailer having its own customized scheme, with little or no sharing of key positive or negative learnings. The GFSI-, FSSC- and ISO-driven initiatives led towards a smaller number of more powerful, more dynamic standards and schemes, which have benefited retailers, manufacturers and small suppliers alike, saving money while reducing risks across the supply chain.

The second area is that of an evolving assessment approach, one driven by the strategic needs of clients and the technical expertise of auditors, which has led to a transition in the role of assessments and auditors. The days of 'a single snapshot in time' checklist-style audit is fading into the history books and is being replaced with dynamic process-based management systems audits. Delivered through competent, experienced auditors with sector-specific expertise, these audits focus on the systems and processes that strategically underpin organizations and their supply chains, and it is this holistic approach that is gaining a foothold amongst retailers, manufacturers and suppliers.

Looking to the future, I think the next logical step is further harmonization of standards and certification schemes and the full mutual acceptance of the GFSI-recognized standards and schemes across the whole of the supply chain. This step would be appreciated by food manufacturers and suppliers, as it would avoid duplication of effort during the assessment process, thus improving the quality of audits and saving on time and money.

ISO 22000 and FSSC 22000, both gaining in acceptance by retailers and manufacturers alike, utilize a process-based management systems approach, one that offers stakeholders a more complete view of the organizations' food safety systems and processes. The expectation amongst food organizations is that this trend will continue, driving it to all parts of the food supply chain. To underpin these projected changes, what is of high importance is the need for the certification bodies to ensure that they can continue to deliver qualified sector-specific assessors to meet the growing demands of process-based management systems auditing. The responsibility for driving positive change across the food supply chain is not solely the responsibility of regulators, retailers and manufacturers. Certification bodies have a vital role to play in bringing confidence to the stakeholders of assessment and certification. With organizational objectives focused on delivering safe food, at LRQA we take our responsibility seriously. We are actively driving change by putting in place the mechanisms to train our existing assessors effectively to ensure that their sector and technical expertise is maintained and enhanced. In parallel, we are continuing to invest in recruiting new assessors to ensure that we can meet the stakeholder demands of tomorrow. Harmonization, a process-based approach and robust assessment have clearly acted as a force for change – a change for the better. Indeed, dare we dream of a future of a few schemes delivered by technically competent assessors that strategically link food safety objectives with corporate and social objectives alike?

Whatever the future holds, organizations across the food supply chain, including some of the world's leading manufacturers and retailers, are increasingly recognizing the benefits of independent assessment and certification, not only in terms of the costs, but also in terms of the benefits and value they bring. This approach is helping to drive consumer and other key stakeholder confidence, as well as ultimately helping to safeguard the lives of people around the world. On the road to food safety, this can only be seen as a positive step.

Opportunities and pitfalls of distance learning

ERIC LYNN, MYLIFEQS

A decade into the 21st century, we are fortunate to have the world wide web enabling a low-cost, high-scalability platform for combining a plethora of learning resources, thus providing an apparently unlimited range of learning opportunities. And these opportunities really are unlimited if they are harnessed appropriately. If not, this potential can just as easily become a graveyard for wasted resources.

Distance learning, however, is nothing new – it has been with us for a very long time. Correspondence courses were a standard medium of study for decades for those who could not afford university or college; the UK's Open University will soon be celebrating its 50th birthday; structured foreign language courses have been available in this form for longer.

Our focus in this chapter will be on ensuring effective use of distance learning opportunities while avoiding the pitfalls. The principles are not complex, and opportunities far outweigh the risks. As with most important things in life, and learning is important, the question cannot be reduced to an either/or syndrome. How the resource (technology) is used is critical.

Questions include:

- Where is distance learning appropriate and where not?
- What are the opportunities and risks to the multiple stakeholders in any distance learning interaction? Stakeholders include the provider, the programme developer, an organization that may be a paying customer, and the individual end user.
- What are the critical challenges for an effective programme and how can they be overcome?

To begin with, we need some clarity on definitions:

- *Distance learning:* programmes designed to be used predominantly offline (ie studies in the learner's own time in which face-to-face contact is a complementary component).
- *'Learning' in an organization context:* knowledge, skills and/or insights that can be beneficially applied in real life. Application may be broad based or detailed,

Aligned Leadership Development
Leadership Coaching
Cultural Integration
Asia
Positive Organisation Change
Management Teams
International Projects
International M&A

MYLIFEQS
Self-Coaching Positive Life Change

Refocus and Integrate
Business Integration is People-Driven

How we work ...
Deep Powerful Questions. Engagement. Responsibility. Results

Why we work this way ...
We believe in what we do.

In addition ...
mylifeQs Online Self-Coaching Programme:
Personal & Professional Development for Employees.

Let`s open a conversation ...

Eric Lynn
Berlin, Germany
Tel: +49 176 67889006
eric@mylifeQs.com
www.mylifeQs.com

fast or long-term, immediately apparent or emerging with time. The benefits are not always directly measurable and do not need to be. For those readers who do business according to the principle 'If you can't measure it, it's not worth doing', I would counter with a reflection from Albert Einstein, who most people agree understood a thing or two about the way the world works: 'Not everything that can be counted counts, and not everything that counts can be counted.'

When an organization stops learning and developing, it dies. Kodak is one of the better-known recent examples. Every organization needs to encourage learning, and the results of each initiative are not always directly measurable.

Attractions of distance learning

All forward-looking organizations are interested in continuously developing their workforce, and even the more conservative ones are generally aware of the necessity of doing so. All seek approaches that are both effective and economical. Individuals who sign up set similar parameters.

The potential benefits to the user are well documented and fairly clear, including:

- flexibility to study in one's own time;
- no travel time or expenses;
- relatively low per-person cost compared to face-to-face learning, with providers able to take advantage of product scalability;
- technology readily available and economical today.

For an employer, the benefits are vastly reduced non-working time and the ability to implement standardized programmes. For larger organizations, especially those with a global reach, there is the added attraction of standardizing organization-specific courses as well as outsourcing a non-core business component.

For providers, potential returns for good programmes are extremely attractive.

Programme developers with entrepreneurial spirit can take advantage of the internet's scalability; others engaged by providers may be attracted by potentially high commission earnings.

All opportunities are of course accompanied by risks, and by far the biggest risk to all stakeholders is in the inappropriate use of a distance learning approach.

Ideal vs less suitable contexts for distance learning

While distance learning can form the core of a programme for some topics, for others it is appropriate only as a supplement.

For information-based subjects where the focus is on specific technical skills, distance learning is an excellent tool. Examples include project management techniques, technical skills, computer-based skills, accounting, law and administration.

These are all knowledge-based fields where theory can be studied and then practised individually in the form of exercises, problems and case studies, which are relatively easy to set up. It is also fairly easy to assess progress, so both the employer and the learner can see how and where the learning can be implemented.

However, the approach is not a magic wand to wave over all organizational learning fields. Developing human interaction skills is essential for all organizations, and here the core element is human interaction. In relation to improving skills in communication, leadership, negotiation, presentations, conflict avoidance, languages or any other field in which experience is key, distance learning is at best a supplement and can never be a core learning platform.

Why? Management literature inevitably refers to 'communication theory' and 'leadership theory', which one needs to learn in order to be 'successful'. Similarly, you can find dozens of books propagating an 'effective', 'best' or 'successful' approach to negotiating, presenting, and avoiding and resolving conflicts. It is therefore tempting to consider the web as an ideal platform for learning these essential management skills, especially for organizations that wish to develop programmes underpinned by their corporate philosophy.

This is the trap. Neither 'communication theory' nor 'leadership theory' as such exists. There are numerous models, each based on the leanings of the authors. Approaches to negotiation, presentations and conflict avoidance are just as varied and subject to the same bias. Most importantly, the goal here is attitude and behaviour change, which can only occur via experiential learning, which may or may not be structured. While the learner can (and should) gain valuable insights from reading, listening to talks and discussions and watching videos, or be provoked by encountering and encouraged to reflect on alternative models, a personal exchange incorporating all our senses, preferably under the guidance of a professional facilitator, is required to bring out the deeper learning potential of any such programme.

For learning a foreign language, the situation is similar. Contrary to the approach taught in most schools around the world, the key to speaking a language fluently is not learning vocabulary lists and grammar rules, but actually speaking it. Simple. Granted, exceptional improvements in self-learning language courses have been made, and some individuals have the ability to learn a language quickly through self-study; they are a small minority.

The current trend in large organizations of handing responsibility for outsourcing decisions to the purchasing department, which is unlikely to have the know-how to judge the relative merits of programmes, increases the risk of inappropriate decisions being made on the basis of visible costs alone. Every organization development consultant encounters this syndrome in discussions with clients who are simply unaware of the enormous risk entailed in standardizing procedures that are incompatible with one another.

A good investment is defined by its return. Cost-based decision making risks waste.

Organization-specific learning programmes

Modern-day technology is creating enormous, seemingly unlimited potential for corporations, especially those that are internationally or globally oriented, to spread the reach of their learning programmes effectively and economically. Any initiative is now potentially available to anyone in the company anywhere in the world. A unified corporate philosophy can underlie all learning. Employees can theoretically contact any expert in the organization regardless of location. This technological resource is amazing, and development opportunities abound. Everything appears positive and is – if, but only if, it is used in the right way.

The technology is both the opportunity and the risk. The latter is the temptation to believe that technology can drive learning – it can't. Technology is a tool. It can do nothing more than make learning readily available. While the learner is responsible for his or her own learning, the provider, here the employer, is responsible for creating the platform to make it available in an appropriate form.

Issues that will be encountered internationally include not just language and web connection quality, but also cultural appropriateness. Is the content speaking to a Western learner brought up in an environment of individual responsibility? Or to a Western learner whose society and organization are geared more towards collective responsibility? Or to Asian, African or Middle Eastern employees where hierarchies govern decision making as well as perspectives on what constitutes 'knowledge' or 'correctness'? Or is the programme geared towards individual study while the users (eg in many Asian or African societies) tend to be driven by the opportunity to work collectively?

The potential list of pitfalls is endless. The message remains the same: the only way to benefit from the potential is to adapt the programme to local conditions.

Risks of distance learning programmes

Undoubtedly one of the biggest risks to the effectiveness of self-learning programmes is the innate ability of the learner to stick with the task. Even the most driven of individuals is prone to procrastination – after all, we can always find something else interesting to do. Motivation is intrinsic; the drive needs to come from within. To gain from a programme, learners need to have a natural interest, find the content stimulating, have the feeling that they are benefiting, have no issues with the technology and be the kind of people who learn easily by themselves. Even when all these parameters are met, risks remain, predominantly self-driven. The solution for programmes without interpersonal interaction is unclear.

Just as all humans have their own character, we all have preferences for learning. Some are more easily able to learn by themselves; others require human stimulation. For the latter group, distance learning is unlikely to be very effective. The ultimate risk here is that the learner will simply give up. Result: wasted resources. Possible solution: support learners to gain awareness of their natural personal learning styles, which may help them through heavier phases of a programme.

Age is an additional issue. The ability to work with rapidly changing technology comes far more naturally to a generation that has grown up with it than to those who have had to learn it as a new tool. Design programmes with the user group in focus. Possible solution: offer human support.

With the internet as the medium for the vast majority of (but not all) modern-day distance learning, effective technology is an essential element for programme success.

However, the technology is nothing more than a tool, meaning the platform needs to be designed to user needs. Countless course participants relate their frustration with technology that doesn't work. They give up. Result: wasted resources.

The risk carried by the provider is frequently ignored. Designing a very good, effective programme (all others are a waste) requires time and resources. Authors will need to feel reasonably sure that an adequate reward will ensue from their efforts. The need is for convincing market research and reach by the provider organization. Numerous colleagues have paid dearly for their trust and naivety in this area.

Overcoming the challenges

Content

Possessing subject know-how is of course essential. However, unless the designer has the ability to make it available in the form of a well-structured, clear, didactically sound programme, the learner will not benefit. No programme will be ideal following initial development. It will need to be tested, improved and retested before going live. To support learning, the learner will also require clear, easy-to-use working guidelines. Check before signing on.

Technology

The technology must be easy to use, available in a form and language appropriate to the user, designed for use by those with no interest in technology, and provided with clear, simple, non-technical user instructions. And, of course, it must work! If the above are not in place, the programme has no value.

Users everywhere will tell you of their experience of frustration with technology that ultimately led to their giving up on a programme. Muddling though with 'almost OK' solutions is not an option here. The provider is responsible for accessibility. Check!

Content and technology issues are relatively easy to solve. By far the biggest challenge is overcoming the lack of personal contact in distance learning programmes. As social animals, the vast majority of human beings require interaction to thrive. Countless users will explain that they struggle to find the drive to study alone, regardless of the programme quality and their level of interest in it. Content alone is dry. We need to apply it, play with it, exchange ideas and ask the questions holding us back. Solutions do exist, some obvious, others more innovative.

Below are some suggestions for incorporation into programmes, which, to be effective, need to be driven by the provider:

- Form learning groups who develop their own guidelines for staying in touch, supporting each other, dealing with open issues etc.
- Make people available to the learners. There will always be open questions, as well as learners in any group who require personal contact in order to progress.

- Have online tutorial sessions, which are relatively easy to organize using platforms that are readily available for all learning groups.
- Incorporate workshops into the programme to bring participants together.

Finally, when selecting a programme, ask yourself:

- How good is the provider I'm considering? Only good is economical. Cheap is expensive.
- Is the programme really using all the appropriate available possibilities (web based and face-to-face) to make it as easy as possible for the learner (therefore your organization) to learn? If not, which changes would improve quality and return on investment?

Learning programmes are for people.

Current risk issues in employment

KEVIN MCCAVISH, SHOOSMITHS

Two of the current employment law issues of concern where employers need to take care to avoid adverse awards are changes in the Employment Appeal Tribunal (EAT)'s stance on the effective dismissal date in the case of employee resignations and on TUPE service provision. In this chapter we bring readers up to date on the risk aspects of each issue.

When an employee resigns without notice, what is the effective date of dismissal?

The EAT has provided useful guidance on the effective date of termination for an employee who resigns without notice.

Background

Identifying an employee's effective date of termination (EDT) can be crucial to determining what their statutory rights may be. For example, whether an employee has the necessary length of service before dismissal will generally determine whether or not the employee can bring a claim of unfair dismissal. To calculate the employee's length of service it will be necessary to know the correct EDT.

Identifying the correct EDT is also crucial to determining the deadline for an employee to pursue a claim of unfair dismissal. An employee has three months less one day from the EDT to pursue an unfair dismissal claim, and tribunals apply this deadline strictly. If employees miss the deadline, they are unlikely to be able to proceed with their claim.

In the case of *Horwood* v *Lincolnshire County Council* UKEAT/0462/11 the EAT had to decide when an employee's EDT was in order to determine whether the employee had submitted her claim for unfair dismissal within the required deadline.

The law

The law states that an employee's EDT is: the date on which the employee's contract expires, where notice is given; or, where the contract is terminated without notice, the date on which termination takes effect.

Facts

Mrs Horwood worked for Lincolnshire County Council. She had appealed against a final written warning and a demotion but had been unsuccessful. As a result, she decided to resign and claim constructive unfair dismissal. On 28 January 2010 Mrs Horwood sent a letter by special delivery to her employer's chief executive and copied it to the practice manager and another director. The letter stated: 'I am resigning with immediate effect.' The letter arrived on the next day and was opened by administrative staff and date-stamped 29 January. On 1 February, the practice manager saw the letter and arranged for confirmation to be sent to the claimant. The practice manager's letter stated that Mrs Horwood's resignation would commence from the date of the letter, 2 February.

Mrs Horwood subsequently submitted a constructive unfair dismissal claim on 28 April. Her claim was submitted by first-class post, and it arrived at the tribunal on 29 April. Her employer argued that her claim was out of time because the EDT was 29 January, the date that the resignation letter was opened by administrative staff, and therefore the latest date an unfair dismissal claim could be submitted was 28 April.

The tribunal agreed, and the claim was struck out at a pre-hearing review. The claimant subsequently appealed, arguing that even if her original EDT was 29 January this had subsequently been varied to 2 February by the employer.

EAT decision

The EAT dismissed Mrs Horwood's appeal and agreed with the tribunal. It was sufficient that the letter had been opened and date-stamped by administrative staff on 29 January for this to be the date on which the resignation was communicated to the employer. The employer's subsequent letter had not varied that EDT.

The EAT decided that employers needed to know where they stood when an employee left and that this could be done through 'communication by words or by conduct such as to inform the other parties of the contract that it is at an end'. It was clear from Mrs Horwood's letter that her resignation was immediate, and therefore it was sufficient that her resignation had been communicated to the Council when it was opened and date-stamped by the Council's administrative staff.

The EAT also confirmed that an EDT could not be altered by the parties retrospectively. The EAT highlighted that this was different to a previous case in which an earlier termination date was agreed during the notice period. In this case, Mrs Horwood had effectively communicated the decision to resign with immediate effect, which fixed her EDT. It could not be retrospectively altered. Since the claimant's contract had ended on 29 January it was not open to the employer to change the termination date of a contract that had ceased.

Comment

This case confirms that when an employee resigns the EDT will be the date on which the resignation is *communicated* to the employer and that it is not open to the parties to agree an EDT after that event.

It is also worth noting that there is no need for the letter actually to be read by the individual to whom it is addressed. As long as someone at the employer's organization has seen the letter, the communication is effective. In this case, the administrative staff were not even Council employees but employees of the company contracted to provide business and administration services to it. The EAT was satisfied that they were acting as agents of the employer and as such were authorized to open and date-stamp all letters arriving for the attention of the Council's employees.

Employers should contrast this case with that of *Gisda yf* v *Barratt* [2010] ICR 1475, which confirmed an employee's EDT when she had been dismissed without notice by the employer by letter.

In Gisda, the employer had held a disciplinary meeting with the employee on 28 November 2006, after which it confirmed that she should expect a letter from the employer by 30 November confirming the outcome of the meeting. The employer sent a letter to the employee by recorded delivery confirming that she had been dismissed without notice. The letter arrived on 30 November; however, the letter was signed for by the son of the employee's partner, as the employee was away from home looking after a relative at the time. The letter was not opened by the employee until the following Monday, after she returned home.

The tribunal decided that the EDT was when the decision was communicated to the employee, which in this case was when she read the letter. The decision was appealed all the way up to the Supreme Court, which agreed with the tribunal, stating that the employee's EDT was the date on which she actually read the letter or had a reasonable opportunity of discovering its contents.

Employers should, therefore, ensure that, if they want greater certainty of the EDT when dismissing an employee without notice, they communicate that decision at a face-to-face meeting. However, employers should ensure that their decision to dismiss is communicated only once the evidence provided at the hearing has been properly considered and that the decision and the reasons for it are then confirmed to the employee in writing.

TUPE service provision changes: how to spot an 'activity'

The EAT has considered whether or not TUPE applied when taxi booking services were insourced.

Background

The Transfer of Undertakings (Protection of Employment) Regulations 2006 (TUPE) apply where there is a sale of a business and also where there is a 'service provision change' (SPC).

An SPC may occur where there is an outsourcing, an insourcing or a change in contractor providing services. However, for TUPE to apply, tribunals must first identify the activity being carried out by the original contractor. They must then determine whether the activities carried out by the subsequent contractor after any alleged transfer are the same as those carried out beforehand. If they are, TUPE may apply (although other factors such as whether there is an organized grouping of employees carrying out those activities must also be considered).

In the case of *Metropolitan Resources Ltd* v *Churchill Dulwich Ltd* [2009] IRLR 700, the EAT confirmed that the activities after the alleged transfer did not need to be identical to the activities carried out beforehand; they just had to be *fundamentally or essentially* the same.

In the case of *Johnson Controls Ltd* v *Campbell and another* UKEAT/0041/12, the EAT had to identify whether the tribunal had properly identified the activity.

Facts

The claimant worked for Johnson Controls Ltd as a taxi administrator. His job involved him taking bookings for taxis from clients, as well as performing other administrative tasks such as advising on journey timings, allocating jobs to subcontractors and checking invoices. One of the clients was the UK Atomic Energy Authority (UKAEA). UKAEA decided to insource this service by using its own secretaries to book taxis directly with taxi firms rather than using Johnson Controls. The claimant argued that 80 per cent of his time was taken up with UKAEA work and subsequently brought a claim for unfair dismissal and a redundancy payment against Johnson. As a preliminary matter, the tribunal was asked to decide whether the claimant's employment had transferred under TUPE from Johnson to UKAEA on the basis of a service provision change.

Decision

The tribunal found that UKAEA was not performing essentially the same service as Johnson Controls, which had carried out the taxi booking service in a centralized and coordinated way. The tribunal found that the central coordinated service no longer existed after UKAEA secretaries took on the function of booking taxis directly with taxi firms. The tribunal therefore decided that there was no service provision change under TUPE.

The EAT upheld this decision on appeal.

The tribunal had stressed that the service being provided by Johnson Controls was more than the sum total of the list of activities or tasks undertaken. The EAT considered that the tribunal had been entitled to reach the decision it had on this basis and that it was not just a question of whether the majority of tasks performed were the same before and after the alleged transfer. The EAT stated that identifying what an activity is involves a holistic assessment by the tribunal, and the employment tribunal in this case was entitled to place an emphasis on the centralized and coordinated nature of the service.

Comment

In the current economic climate, bringing services back in-house is becoming more common for employers in an effort to reduce costs. This case is a good reminder that TUPE will not always apply in such situations. However, each case will turn on its own particular facts. By taking a holistic, impressionistic approach, as endorsed by the EAT in this case, tribunals are less likely to be swayed by the simple percentage of similar tasks being performed before and after any putative transfer.

This is one of the latest in a long line of recent cases that has tested the application of SPCs. Whilst each case will depend on its own particular circumstances, the decisions are all providing greater clarity about how a tribunal will determine whether TUPE applies: as regards SPCs the trend is currently towards a restrictive approach, with the EAT seemingly more likely to decide that TUPE does not apply than has previously been the case. It should therefore not be assumed that TUPE will *always* apply just because there is an outsourcing, insourcing or change of contractor.

Tribunals have more latitude when it comes to interpreting the SPCs, because this is essentially a 'home-grown' provision; the UK was not required to implement the SPC by Europe as it was in respect of business transfers. The 'purposive approach' to legislative interpretation, which so often leads to decisions that are perceived to be employee friendly, therefore does not apply to the question of whether or not there has been an SPC.

Future developments of TUPE

As part of the government's wider review of employment law it is reviewing TUPE following concerns from business that it is currently too bureaucratic. The UK Department for Business, Innovation and Skills (BIS) issued a call for evidence in 2011, focusing on whether TUPE could be improved or whether improved guidance and best-practice examples could better address the issue.

As part of its consultation the government sought views on whether the increased certainty about the application of TUPE to SPCs has resulted in a reduced need for businesses to seek legal advice on the application of TUPE prior to contract tenders and consequently less litigation. The results of the government's consultation have not yet been released, but some commentators are predicting that the government will decide to remove SPCs from the ambit of TUPE altogether following the consultation.

It should be remembered that SPCs were initially brought expressly within the scope of TUPE to provide greater certainty to businesses when services were being contracted out or brought back in-house. Prior to their inclusion, SPCs could fall within the existing law on business transfers. However, there was a considerable amount of uncertainty over the law's application. This uncertainty led to costly and unnecessary disputes.

The rationale for including SPCs was to reduce that uncertainty so that businesses and employees knew where they stood when there was an SPC. The objective was also to ensure a level playing field for contractors bidding for service contracts so that tendering decisions were taken on commercial merit rather than differing views on the rights of employees and the risk of litigation.

Whilst the government is dedicated to reducing the regulatory burden on businesses to encourage growth in the current economic climate, removing SPCs from the scope of TUPE will, in our view, have the opposite effect. Removing SPCs is likely to lead to a greater degree of uncertainty for businesses and employees, which in turn will lead to an increased need for legal advice, protracted contract tenders and costly legal disputes.

PART FOUR
Risk assessments of high-growth emerging markets

Managing business risks in Brazil

GEERT AALBERS AND THOMAZ FAVARO,
CONTROL RISKS

Introduction

Whether the BRIC countries have more points in common than differences among them is subject to regular debate. One indisputable fact, however, is that each makes credible claims to a raft of superlatives, with Brazil entitled to its fair share. Just to name a few:

- Brazil is the world's emerging agricultural powerhouse. It is already the largest global producer of beef, sugar, coffee and orange juice, and is rapidly climbing up the ranks in the production of soya, poultry, pork and corn. With its innovative and cutting-edge agricultural technology, abundance of water, favourable climate and only 15 per cent of its arable land in use, Brazil will play a critical role in guaranteeing food security for an increasingly urbanized world.

- Brazil is home to the world's largest exporter of iron ore, as well as to a diverse group of multinational companies that are rapidly globalizing and climbing the ranks of the Fortune 500.

- Over 50 per cent of Brazil's energy is derived from renewable sources, which makes Brazil the industrialized country with the cleanest energy matrix. It is the leading producer and user of ethanol. Flexible-fuel cars constitute 90 per cent of newly sold vehicles, and 20 per cent of its total fleet.

- Between 2011 and 2014, Brazil plans to invest over US$500 billion in infrastructure to prepare itself for the World Cup in 2014 and the Olympic Games 2016. The country will also support one of the world's most ambitious oil and gas exploration programmes, which will make Brazil the sixth-largest oil-producing nation by 2020. By that time, according to IMF projections, Brazil will also be the fifth-largest economy in the world.

Given the above, it is no wonder that investing and expanding operations in Brazil has become a strategic imperative for most global companies. With all its allure and charm, however, Brazil remains a unique and complex country, and succeeding in Brazil requires companies to understand and manage a broad array of business risks, a selection of which will be addressed in this chapter. Before doing so, however, it is worthwhile to briefly place the changing nature of risk management in BRIC countries into context.

The changing face of risk management in the BRICs

The framework for managing risks in the BRIC countries has undergone a significant shift over the past few years. Three factors in particular underlie this change:

1 The growing geo-political and economic importance of the BRICs;
2 The changing nature of risks associated with investing in these countries;
3 The growing recognition that effective risk management is a key source of competitive advantage.

Global investors have demonstrated substantial interest in the BRIC countries since the term was coined just over ten years ago. At the time, these countries were projected to become the world's four largest economies by 2050. The jury is out on how fast and sustainably these countries can grow given that they each face a unique combination of internal economic, social and political challenges. However, it is undeniable that over the past 10 years a dramatic shift in economic and political power has taken place, and that this trend is set to continue.

Over the past decade, the BRIC economies contributed to over one third of global GDP growth in PPP terms; this is expected to increase to almost 50 per cent over the next ten years. In the global governance arena, further reconfigurations of the G20, IMF and UN Security Council are expected to reflect a more influential weighting of the BRICs and other emerging markets. It is exactly this increased capacity of the BRIC countries to exercise their power and influence on the world stage that is generating a host of new risks, as well as new opportunities. There has also been a marked change in the nature of the risks associated with investing in the BRIC countries: with their history of political and financial instability, traditionally the focus was on managing risks associated with sovereign default and to liquidity issues in the banking sector. Political risks such as expropriation and nationalization also featured prominently on investors' risk matrices. The former risks were typically addressed via multilateral financial arrangements, complex financial engineering and capital market solutions, whilst the latter risks were usually covered by some form of political risk insurance. Brazil, for example, only managed to break free from its historic cycle of oscillating between military dictatorship and democratic government when it restored civilian rule in 1985, and it was only in 1994 – after the consolidation of the Plano Real – that the country entered its current phase of institutional improvement and managed to overcome the cycle of hyperinflation that had plagued the country since the early 1980s. Moreover, as recently as 1999, Brazil saw one of its prominent states declare a moratorium on payments to the federal government. That same year, Brazil was forced to float its local currency and accept over US$40 billion in financial support pledged by the IMF.

The fact that the BRIC economies maintained relatively solid and robust growth throughout the recent credit crisis was a definite turning point in how these economies are perceived by investors. Substantial and long-term growth projections in the BRICs, compounded by continued economic fragility in the developed economies, have put the BRICs squarely in the centre of global corporations, sovereign funds and pension funds as they seek higher financial returns. For these investors, managing risks in the BRIC countries is less about hedging exposure to high-yielding investments in what were previously considered exotic and peripheral plays in their investment portfolios, and more about aligning their strategy to operate successfully in these markets, which are the core of their future growth prospects. In summary, fewer and fewer investors are focusing on sovereign and financial risk. Their focus has now shifted to managing a host of complex and less quantifiable strategic and operational risks.

Finally, there is a growing recognition that effective risk management is a key source of competitive advantage, providing enhanced resilience particularly to those organizations heavily vested in the complexity of the BRIC countries. Currently, Enterprise Risk Management (ERM) is the gold standard for risk management and is increasingly adopted by companies worldwide. The underlying assumption of ERM is that enterprises exist to create value for their shareholders, facing uncertainty in the process of doing so. Senior management is ultimately responsible for aligning risk appetite with strategy, and defining the type and level of risk the company is prepared to take. The aforementioned strategy needs to be combined with an ongoing risk management process that enables the company to identify those risks most likely to impact the achievement of its strategic objectives, helping the company effectively assess, respond to and monitor these risks. Organizations across the globe are increasingly acknowledging the strategic imperative of ERM: being better than your competitors at managing risks and capitalizing on opportunities associated with those risks are a key source of competitive advantage.

Business risks in Brazil

Business risks span the horizon of strategic, financial, hazard and operational issues. Companies have traditionally been adept at managing the first three. Operational risks, on the other hand, are often those with the greatest potential impact on companies' reputation, typically because they are not anticipated and therefore not appropriately prepared for. The remainder of this chapter will focus predominantly on operational risks in Brazil.

The World Bank annual 'Doing Business' report ranks countries on the ease of doing business. In 2012, Brazil was ranked 126th out of 183 countries, behind China (91) and Russian Federation (120), and just ahead of India (132). The report highlights some of the key challenges of operating in Brazil, which include the process of setting up and closing a business, obtaining construction permits and navigating through the complex and burdensome tax and labour requirements. Other risks related to the political and regulatory environment, integrity issues such as corruption and fraud, social movements, security and infrastructure are beyond the scope of the World Bank report and will be addressed below.

Despite the complexity of doing business in Brazil, and the recent slower pace of economic growth, the investment climate is likely to remain largely positive in the coming years. The main political parties have increasingly converged towards the political centre ground, and largely agree on the importance of macroeconomic stability. President Dilma Rousseff's personal approval ratings remain high, as her perceived determination to root out corruption has met with widespread public approval, allowing her to carve out an image and governing style distinct from that of her predecessor. On the other hand, her ruling coalition is beset by tensions between its fourteen parties. Support for government policies from allies has been made conditional on factors such as political appointments to key ministries and the approval of other pieces of legislation. This will make the passage of important legislation both time-consuming and inefficient, and effectively means that much-needed reforms will continue to progress at a painfully slow pace. As a result, investors will continue to face the so-called 'Brazil cost' of seemingly endless bureaucratic delays and excessive red tape.

Although the state's role in the economy may increase under Rousseff, there is no imminent threat of radical state intervention such as expropriation or nationalization. There are, however, a few developments pointing to greater state involvement in investment activity and increased restrictions on corporate organizations.

Trade policy and the application of commercial law

The first development is in relation to trade policy. Rousseff's administration has been marked by a series of protectionist measures such as local content requirements, new rules for government procurement, import tariffs and other barriers to trade. The new policies meet the pressures from local industrialists, who lost economic strength as the real (currency) appreciated and global demand declined in the global economic crisis, and more recently from unionists who fear losing their jobs. Labour-intensive sectors such as textiles and footwear have struggled to compete internationally, particularly against companies from East Asia, though more high-technology products such as vehicles and vehicle parts have also been affected.

The second development is related to the extractives industry, where the government is promoting an overhaul of the oil and mining regulations with the aim of exercising a more active role, increasing national-content requirements for exploration and maximizing revenues from royalties.

Thirdly, the Rousseff administration is a strong promoter of 'national champions' and of a strong local presence in 'strategic sectors'. The Conselho Administrativo de Defesa Econômica (CADE), the antitrust authority, has historically been anything but a fierce watchdog – allowing the formation of huge Brazilian conglomerates, and increasingly being accused of favouring Brazilian companies over foreign competitors. In order to succeed, companies need to recognize the sectors where the government is most prone to intervene and tighten rules, develop and implement a strategy to hedge against possible partial state intervention and conduct extensive due diligence on potential joint venture partners. There are also legitimate means available to circumvent some of the government-imposed restrictions. For example, foreign firms that have formed joint ventures with local partners have usually benefited from increased contractual security for their investments. The judicial system in Brazil is broadly fair. Contract enforceability has improved, with companies enjoying a healthy degree of predictability, even when contracting with government. However, judicial processes can be extremely slow and complex. Courts are overloaded, and simple commercial disputes can take years to resolve. According to the World Bank's 2012 'Doing Business' report, which includes an assessment of the general environment with respect to enforcement, enforcing a contract requires 45 procedures, takes 731 days and costs 16.5 per cent of the value of the claim. The report ranks Brazil 118th out of 183 countries in terms of the ease of enforcing contracts. Moreover, ambiguities and inconsistencies between constitution, laws, decrees and regulations can lead to arbitrary interpretations. Particularly in the more remote and less developed areas of Brazil, political contacts and personal influence can count for more than legal documents. Court-based settlements should be avoided and, where appropriate, international arbitration preferred.

Integrity issues

Brazil also continues to suffer from widespread integrity issues such as corruption and fraud. The issue of high-level political corruption has come back into focus under President Rousseff, whose government has seen a wave of senior government departures as a result of corruption allegations. Local anti-corruption legislative initiatives are moving in the right direction but are inconsistently enforced. This remains a significant concern for foreign investors, particularly in light of increased enforcement of international anti-corruption regulations such as the Foreign Corrupt Practices Act and the UK Bribery Act. Excessive bureaucracy and interaction with a large number of regulatory agencies make operational procedures painfully slow and create incentives for bribes and facilitation payments.

Significant opportunities for investments in the public sector are also a fertile ground for corruption. Corruption watchdog Transparency International's 2011 Corruption Perceptions Index (CPI) ranked Brazil 73rd out of 183 countries, where the first-placed country is that perceived as least corrupt. The CPI gave Brazil a score of 3.8 out of ten (where 10 is considered 'corruption-free'), well below Latin America's top performers Chile (7.2) and Uruguay (7.0). As the potential cost of non-compliance increases, companies that adopt risk-based anti-corruption programmes designed to proactively prevent, detect and remediate corruption risk are increasingly gaining a competitive advantage. Similarly, frauds such as asset misappropriation or fraudulent statements are commonplace and often go unpunished, partially as a consequence of highly protective labour laws. Again, companies with robust risk-based fraud management programmes – starting from pre-employment screening practices and broadly communicated ethics codes through to clearly defined investigations procedures and protocols – are best equipped to minimize the impact of this pervasive risk on their operations.

Social issues

Social movements by landless groups, unions, NGOs and local communities all have the potential to affect investments in a variety of sectors in Brazil, particularly in the mining, agriculture and infrastructure sectors. The Belo Monte hydroelectric dam, the most contested infrastructure project in the country, is a case in point. Plans for the Belo Monte dam have existed since the 1970s, but have been consistently blocked by environmental activists and indigenous protesters. Activists fear that the project will lead to the displacement of thousands of indigenous people and damage the local ecology. Indigenous groups claim that they have not been consulted on the implications of the project. However, the authorities insist the dam is needed to meet the country's growing energy demands, and the government has already made it clear that it will push hard for the dam's completion.

Companies are well advised to conduct assessments to map and evaluate the different levels of influence and interrelationship of these groups with other private and public interests. Moreover, in order to prepare risk mitigation and contingency plans, companies should obtain a thorough understanding of the means and capacity these groups have at their disposal to act against the company's interests. These could vary from targeted smear campaigns organized by NGOs, targeted strikes organized by unions, and disruptive and often violent land invasions staged by landless movements.

Labour activism is set to increase in upcoming years in the infrastructure sector, as the government invests heavily to expand energy supply and improve road and rail networks, port capacity and communications. Several projects are particularly time-sensitive, as they are scheduled to be ready before the 2014 World Cup and 2016 Olympics, adding pressure on workers. However, widespread labour unrest remains very unlikely in Brazil. Although trade unions retain considerable political significance, most of the main ones enjoy good relations with the PT government, and the working class is benefiting from a decade of strong economic growth and low levels of unemployment. Strikes are likely to be localized and evolve around very specific demands.

Security issues and crime

Despite Brazil's economic growth and stable foreign relations, security of people, assets and information continues to represent one of the most serious issues facing the current government. Successive government efforts to tackle security issues in the past 10–15 years have had limited success, although there has been a partial displacement of the most violent crimes from São Paulo and Rio de Janeiro to north-eastern states such as Pernambuco and Alagoas, and to the North. Security threats vary broadly by sector and location, and nature of assets deployed. Crimes such as street-level mugging and motorcycle-borne armed robbery in gridlocked traffic continue to be the main security threats in the primary metropolitan centres. Cargo theft has increased in recent years, facilitated by the poor condition of the road network. Organized crime gangs involved in drugs and arms trafficking and other criminal activities are also active throughout the country. These gangs are particularly well entrenched in the shantytowns of Rio de Janeiro and São Paulo, where they control lucrative local drugs markets as well as transit routes from Latin America to Europe and North Africa. Well financed and armed, these gangs frequently outgun the police.

Finally, the combination of being home to some of the world's most crafty hackers and a complete vacuum in information privacy laws makes Brazil particularly vulnerable to information security breaches. Companies can effectively manage the aforementioned risks by conducting threat and vulnerability assessments, and subsequently designing and implementing security management and business resilience programmes tailored to mitigate these risks.

Infrastructure risk and opportunity

Finally, it would be remiss not to mention the tremendous risk and opportunity associated with infrastructure in Brazil. Despite its precarious state, Brazil has invested a paltry 2 per cent of GDP in infrastructure over the past decade, compared to over 7 per cent in Asia. Poor transport infrastructure adds to the costs of doing business, particularly given the large distances that goods and supplies usually have to travel. Road is by far the most predominant means of transport in Brazil, but is vulnerable due to poorly maintained highways, sudden road closures by labour unions and other activists, and crime such as highway robbery. The rail system is extremely limited, while the canal network is poorly developed. Airport and port infrastructure is also substantially below the capacity required, particularly to support Brazil's booming commodities export business. As a result, both supply chain risks and logistics costs, as a percentage of GDP, are significantly higher in Brazil compared to more developed markets.

Of course, the flipside of the infrastructure risks is that the government has embarked on the second phase of its Growth Acceleration Program and earmarked US$500 billion for infrastructure investments through to 2014. If executed comprehensively and to schedule this would be a strong driver of growth and a tremendous opportunity for the private sector, in particular, to invest in the expansion of road and rail networks and port and airport capacity. Indeed, the infrastructure sector has experienced a different trend when compared to extractive industries such as oil or mining. Whereas in the latter case the government has sought to increase the state's control, both the Lula and Rousseff administrations have generally welcomed foreign investment in the infrastructure sector. This benevolence is largely due to pragmatism: a failure to deliver adequate reforms and to ensure smooth sporting events in 2014 and 2016 would be a political catastrophe for the government, with the potential to precipitate the opposition's return to power. The recent successful privatization of three of the country's main airports and the decision to increase the cap for foreign capital in local airlines are reflective of this trend. After the successful auction for airports, which raised US$14 billion, the government is considering opening tenders for 77 port terminals in the near future.

Despite this investor-friendliness, delays in establishing the mechanisms to support public–private partnerships have been an obstacle, while the government's relaxation of procurement procedures and laws in order to accelerate works is a recipe for substantial cost overruns and greater corruption risk. Companies planning to invest in this sector need to adopt appropriate and prudent measures as outlined above. A further latent risk for foreign investors lies in the fact that Brazilian construction conglomerates are amongst the most powerful businesses in the country, with strong links to national and state governments. In the past, these companies have been less than thrilled by the prospect of exposing their market share to competition from abroad, and have adopted defensive tactics to avoid the entry of new players. Foreign companies aiming to take advantage of the huge potential in the sector need to be prepared for 'smear campaigns' and heavy lobbying against their plans.

Intellectual property (IP)

As Brazil tries to diversify its domestic industry and improve the knowledge-based part of its economy, the country's record on intellectual property rights has become a focus in recent years. Brazil was the first country to take on multinational pharmaceutical companies in a campaign to break patents for HIV/AIDS drugs – a controversy resolved in 2001 by the World Trade Organization. As a signatory to the Trade-Related Aspects of Intellectual Property Rights (TRIPS) agreement, Brazil has a legal framework that is broadly in line with the minimum requirements expected from member states. However, a shortage of material resources and qualified personnel, a cumbersome bureaucracy, and a slow, overburdened judicial system stand out as the main reasons for a notoriously deficient enforcement in this area. Piracy, including the unauthorized distribution of illegal software, hard goods piracy, illegal photocopying and contraband imports, is a major concern for several copyright-based industries.

The outlook for IP setting is one of cautious optimism. The Brazilian government has shown increased commitment to IP issues, and several initiatives have been undertaken, both in terms of updating legislation and making law enforcement more efficient. However, government officials have also shown that they do not view IP infringements as a critical issue; in sectors such as the recording media and regarding internet piracy, public officials, police authorities and the general public consider infringements of IP rights a natural part of the country's informal economy. Improvements in law enforcement are likely to continue, but at a slower pace than most industry players would prefer.

Closing remarks

As the BRIC country that is generally seen as the most in tune with the political and institutional ideals of the developed West, Brazil is often praised for its continuing political stability and consolidating democracy. This admiration has led – rightly so – to substantial interest in the country by both financial and corporate investors over the past decade. However, wild praise from abroad often leads to complacency on the part of investors. With public finances relatively in order and a low risk of radical state intervention, many take the country's newfound stability as an all-encompassing guarantee of a successful venture. In doing so, investors forget the more obscure on-the-ground risks which can surface in an investment cycle, many of which are described above. Investing in a mine located in a small municipality in the northern state of Pará presents entirely different risks from investing in an infrastructure project in the interior of the south-eastern state of São Paulo. This fairly obvious fact is often forgotten within the context of the international spotlight under which Brazil is currently basking. Investors that adopt a holistic and rigorous approach to managing risks will not only find themselves at an advantage to their competitors but also in a unique position to maximize the rewarding opportunities Brazil offers.

China: balancing opportunity and threat

JONATHAN REUVID, HETHE MANAGEMENT SERVICES

Predictably, the spectacular downfall in March of Bo Xilai, Party boss of Chongqing, prompted crisis comment and speculation in the Western press. Even the most sober publications, such as the *Financial Times* and the *Sunday Times*, indulged themselves in dramatic headlines ranging from 'The threat to the post-Mao consensus... as Chinese corruption plays catch-up' to 'Ousting of China's iron fist signals power struggle within ruling elite'.

Certainly, the incident sparked a Chinese political crisis bigger than anything since the 1989 Tiananmen Square massacre and the timing was unfortunate, coming in the 10th and final year of President Hu Jintao's presidency and Wen Jiabao's premiership. The story of Bo's corrupt, autocratic administration of the municipality's 30 million people, his business activities and the spectacular charges against his wife, Gu Kailai, of murdering British businessman Neil Heywood ensured global attention and encouraged predictions that the legitimacy of the Communist Party of China (CPC) rule was fatally undermined and that the ruling leadership elite was riven by an internal power struggle.

However, as always in evaluating China, observers should not be swayed by *schadenfreude*. The fears (or hopes) of the doomsters that the public clash and subsequent purge of the ambitious Bo, a candidate for high office, would lead to infighting among the elite and paralysis within the political system were quickly confounded. Hu and his moderate Communist Youth league faction seem to have had little difficulty in maintaining ascendancy over Bo's hardliners, who included Zhou Yongkang, head of domestic security, the former president Jiang Zemin and allies in the upper echelons of the People's Liberation Army (PLA). Xi Jinping, the anointed president in waiting, who had previously shown signs of encouraging Bo's promotion to the nine-member standing committee of the Politburo, was careful to align himself rapidly with Hu, Wen and the future premier Li Kewiang and the decision to instigate Bo's purge. Unless something totally unforeseen occurs in the second half of 2012, Xi and Li will be appointed president and premier at the end of the year.

None of this is to deny that there are formidable risks in doing business with and in China. However, it is important to differentiate between the risks that are political and those that relate to the Chinese economy or the operational business environment.

It is the intention of this chapter to provide an overview in perspective of the overall business risk in dealing with China and Chinese enterprises.

Political risk

In practice, the principal threat to the CPC and one-party rule is the upward aspiration of China's rising middle class. For 2013, this is more of a time-bomb than a threat of immediate explosion. The steady rise of consumerism, foreign travel and cosmopolitan education is a potential detonator in the medium to long term, although it is impossible to predict when any tipping point will be reached.

However, the theory that continuing growth of the economy would inevitably cause democracy to replace single-party dictatorship soon holds less credence. As noted in previous publications, centralized autocratic government has proved an economic advantage and has certainly been a core driver in powering sustained growth over decades. Compare the 30,000-plus miles of motorway-standard roads constructed in China since 1990 against India's achievement of just 300 miles.

Nevertheless, in the next decade China will need to face up to the Damoclean social problem that has been hanging over the government's head for some years – the demographic outcome of the communist regime's one-child policy, which with some exceptions remains in force to this day. After 2012 the Chinese working population is expected to decline rapidly from five workers aged 20 to 59 supporting every citizen over 60 to two by 2032. The government has yet to declare how it will address the issue.

Legitimacy of the CPC

To Western governments any one-party political system, either a dictatorship or a superficially more benevolent form of collective autocratic government, is anathema, and the suppression of freedom and human rights in China is a constant source of friction. However, the argument is rather subtler, as Daniel Bell (2012) points out. While non-democratic regimes are perceived to lack legitimacy in the West, the present level of dissatisfaction with the regime in China is relatively low, and it can be argued that its legitimacy is therefore high. Legitimacy rests on three pillars: embedded in both socialist and Confucian values; the first pillar is described by Bell as 'performance legitimacy'. Certainly, the CPC can claim legitimacy with its ability to provide for the welfare of the Chinese people, as it has presided over historic poverty reduction during the reform period since 1979.

The second pillar is the perceived meritocracy of political leadership based on the belief that leaders should be endowed with superior ability to make morally informed judgements. Conversation with educated Chinese on leadership quality makes it clear that procedural arrangements to choose their leaders counts for much less than confidence in government by high-quality politicians. (In the West, it sometimes seems that the reverse is true.) On this test, the CPC has also done relatively well. Its organization has become more meritocratic over the same three decades, with enhanced emphasis on education and an open examination system as criteria for leadership selection. The Bo Xilai episode, had it played out differently, could have struck a serious blow to this pillar.

The third pillar is ideological legitimacy. The CPC was founded on Marxist principles, which were distorted by Maoism, in particular the Cultural Revolution, but few Chinese today believe in communism as a substitute for the traditional Confucian code of ethics. Lord Sacks (2011), Britain's Chief Rabbi, suggested there are now more practising churchgoers in China than members of the CPC, a reflection of the 'young, hard-working, mobile entrepreneurs for whom Christianity offers an ethical framework, a structured view of life and its disciplines in a society experiencing rapid transition'. In effect, the CPC has turned from communist ideology to nationalism, which chimes perfectly with China's resurgence as a global economic leader.

Longer-term regime change risk

On grounds of legitimacy, there is no reason to anticipate a short-term collapse of the current regime. However, there are two potential risks to political stability.

The first is the fear that the rate of economic growth will slacken so that it becomes unsustainable to support wage inflation (already a significant factor in China's industrial and commercial centres and conurbations) and to pay the wages of migrant workers who have moved from the countryside to more prosperous areas. By 2010 agriculture's share of GDP had dwindled to 9.6 per cent, and employment in agriculture to 29.5 per cent of the labour force of 780 million. Therefore the urban drift is certain to continue, given that industrialization is spreading steadily from the coastal provinces westwards. Economists have estimated that the critical level of growth below which Chinese society becomes vulnerable to disruption is 6.5 per cent, but although that seems less of a threat today than at the beginning of 2012 (see Table 4.2.1) the two interest rate cuts in June and July are the harbinger of a forecast slackening of growth to 7.6 per cent in the second quarter.

The second risk element, already referred to above, arises from the near elimination of poverty during the coming years when the pressures for participation in politics are certain to grow. For now, the leadership is still seen as providing the most effective management of the economy, and popular anger against corruption is focused on lower-level officialdom; but, as prosperity advances, the CPC will need to pay attention to the intellectual and ethical development of the people. In the meantime, there will be a continuing trickle of high-profile intellectual dissidents like Chen Guangcheng, whose plight became the subject of a diplomatic stand-off between the United States and China in May 2012. Hopefully, the Chinese government is learning that it must handle similar future incidents more sensitively.

Encouragingly, the leadership is showing signs that it is aware of the risks and intends to embark on change management. In an unexpectedly bold speech on live television in March 2012, Wen Jiabao indicated obliquely that China's leadership needs to take a new direction. Referring to the Bo Xilai incident, he stated: 'Without successful political structural reform... New problems that have arisen in Chinese society will not be fundamentally resolved and such historic tragedies as the Cultural revolution may happen again' (Lewis, 2012). Later in the same speech, he signalled the outlook for step-by-step reform: 'If the people can run a village well, they can run a township; if they can run a township, they can manage a county.'

External political risks

As discussed at length in a previous book (Reuvid, 2011), on its road to economic hegemony China poses no real risk to international security, except in its aspirations to extend its influence in its immediate geographical region of the South China Sea – of concern to the Pentagon but not perceived as a serious threat by the United States' NATO allies. China's foreign policy in Africa, East Asia and the Middle East is driven by economic considerations, specifically the consolidation of its mineral resource holdings. So far, it can be argued that China is not pulling its weight in international affairs and, wherever possible, holds back from commitment in the political issues of the Middle East where the United Nations is engaged. Nevertheless, in his recent speech quoted above Wen also stated: 'The Arab demands for democracy must be respected. It is a force that cannot be held back.' Such a comment from a Chinese leader would have been unthinkable even a year or two ago.

Economic risk

The interaction of China's economy with those of Europe and the United States in 2011 and 2012 is a reversal of the situation in 2008 when developed economies tumbled into global financial crisis. On that occasion, China had remained relatively stable and, with its massive stimulus of RMB4 trillion (about $570 billion) after the Lehman Brothers crash, helped to pull its Western trading partners through recession. This time around, while China remains a beacon of hope for Western economies tumbling into recession with a sustained period of low growth ahead, there is a risk that the fallout from the Eurozone crisis will drag the Chinese economy into severely reduced growth – China's equivalent of technical recession.

2012 – the first six months

In the final quarter of 2011, China's foreign exchange reserves fell for the first time since the Asian financial crisis of 1998 as its trade surplus decreased. However, although the reserves shrank by $20.5 billion, Beijing still controlled $3.2 trillion of official currency reserves, nearly three times more than those of Japan, which ranks second internationally behind China.

In January 2012, the government set about addressing a number of weaknesses in the financial sector of the economy. The first focus of attention was stock market regulation. Since its peak during the bubble of 2007 the Shanghai Composite Index had fallen 65 per cent. The China Securities Regulatory Commission (CSRC) now announced plans to improve the mechanism for initial public offerings (IPOs), a long-standing source of corruption inhibiting the listing of private companies. It also instituted an 'investor protection bureau' to boost confidence in the market, which had been subject to insider trading and manipulation. At the same time, there were indications that Beijing would allow money and credit growth to accelerate in order to improve liquidity. The Shanghai Composite rose 5 per cent in the week following in anticipation of a rally of 20 to 30 per cent to come. Also under the CSRC plans, foreign fund managers prepared themselves for increased investment quotas to be allotted to them by Beijing. A month later the Central Bank published a report setting out the path to a freely tradable currency and more open capital markets and signalled that the loosening of capital controls would be accelerated.

In March, the slowdown in the economy became apparent when the GDP growth target for 2012 was cut to 7.5 per cent. Against an earlier warning that Beijing had already set its five-year plan growth rate at a more modest 7 per cent, this was no surprise, and the lower growth target confirms a policy move towards a more mature economic profile in place of previous headlong growth. However, Beijing has a record of setting conservative targets, and the IMF April forecast of 8.2 per cent growth appeared more realistic then. The inflation target for 2012 was maintained at 4 per cent.

In April, China started to allow more volatility in the daily trade of its renminbi currency, which is now permitted to rise or fall by 1 per cent each day from the daily official trade against the US dollar, twice the previous trading range. The renminbi has now risen 31 per cent against the dollar since 2005 in nominal terms. Of course, the 'real' exchange rate has risen much faster over the same period as a result of inflation. Wages, particularly, have increased at an annual rate of more than 20 per cent – much in excess of productivity gains – so that Chinese goods have become more expensive and less competitive in international markets. Inevitably, global manufacturers of labour-intensive commodity-type products (eg clothing) have moved their production from China to lower-cost Asian or East European countries. Thus the contentious issue of the renminbi–dollar exchange rate has become less of a cause célèbre in Sino-US trade relations.

At the end of May, the official news agency Xinhua revealed the government's intentions: 'It will not unveil another massive stimulus plan to stimulate economic growth. Current policies to stabilize growth will not repeat the old way of stimulating growth three years ago.' This declaration removed any lingering hope among Western economies that China would ride to the rescue with a repeat of the 2008 remedy. Therefore the announcement by the People's Bank of China (PBoC) a week later of a cut in the one-year lending rate for the first time since 2008 by 25 basis points to 6.31 per cent and on deposit rates to 3.25 per cent came as a surprise. Inflation had slipped back towards 3 per cent, cutting the central bank more slack in easing rates, but the reduction was seen as a response to the first quarter slowdown in growth to 8.1 per cent from 9.2 per cent in 2011.

Most of the current indicators remain negative, although there was a surge of 15.3 per cent in exports in May compared to 2011 against growth of only 4.9 per cent in April, while May imports also advanced by 12.7 per cent compared to only 0.3 per cent, reflecting increased demand for iron ore, copper and crude oil. However, the economy remains at risk if China's exports collapse so that millions of workers lose their jobs.

Where China is now

On 5 July, the PBoC announced a surprising second round of interest rate cuts within a month, with the lending rate down 31 basis points to 6 per cent and the benchmark deposit rate down 25 basis points to 3 per cent, confirming China's concern at the fallout from the Eurozone crisis. If further measures are required to boost consumer demand and ensure that its full-year growth rate forecast is achieved, the government will run the risk of reviving higher inflation and speculative excess in the property market.

The first half experience of 2012 reconfirms the long-recognized imperative for China to progress from an investment and export manufacturing economy to a growth model driven by domestic consumption rather than investment. Nevertheless, significant additional infrastructure investment and possibly an additional stimulus to bank lending in the form of quantitative easing may prove necessary to relieve the economy from present peril.

Business environment risk

The downside

China's protectionism is the source of nagging complaints on both sides of the Atlantic. The United States in election year is the most vocal; although accusations of currency manipulation are more muted as the dollar–renminbi exchange rate in real terms has adjusted, complaints persist around export restrictions on rare metals, theft of intellectual property and the buy-China policy. (In the latter respect, the United States is open to similar complaints from its trading partners.) The following is a non-comprehensive list of protectionist measures that are of particular concern in these tough times, not just to the United States but to other major trading partners:

- import tariffs from 2.5 per cent to 21.5 per cent on US-made cars (said to be retaliation for US duties on China-made tyres);
- intellectual property theft, a thorny subject – particularly in ICT, where US companies are also engaged in fights to the death with other competitors, eg Microsoft versus Samsung;
- the crackdown on Chinese bureaucrats to stop buying foreign cars (mostly German) and substitute made-in-China vehicles, an annual spend of about $13 billion on 6.5 million vehicles;
- $30 billion subsidies per annum to Chinese manufacturers of solar panels and cells, again affecting German companies in particular;
- restrictions on the export of minerals, including rare-earth metals essential to the manufacture of high-tech products such as missiles, hybrid cars, mobile phones, camera lenses and computer disk drives – in some of these, such as graphite, and rare-earth elements such as scandium and cerium, China has from 80 per cent to 97 per cent of the world's deposits;
- opaque regulations and unfair restrictions affecting European companies. In a 2012 survey of 557 of the biggest European groups engaged in China, 40 per cent

complained that Beijing had discriminated against them; nevertheless 71 per cent of those surveyed ranked China in the first three of their preferred investment destinations.

The upside

In recessionary times, of course, it is to be expected that all countries will 'tighten their belts' in order to contain imports while at the same time redoubling their efforts to stimulate exports and build business with higher-growth trading partners, of which China is the biggest and most tempting target for most companies.

While Chinese manufacturing evolves up the value chain and quality is driven to international standards so that Chinese durables succeed in export markets (Lenovo computers and London taxis imported from China have become commonplace), there is an unquenchable thirst for luxury goods and expensive premium brands in China. The demand is driven by both the breed of mega-rich entrepreneurs (China is now the top export market for Rolls-Royce motor cars) and the growing population of upwardly mobile, middle-class consumers. For example, Burberry is a popular brand as a status symbol, largely because handbags and clothing can be shown off in public (an age-old Western phenomenon). British brands are also creating major new investment opportunities; most recently Jaguar Land Rover (now under Indian ownership) announced the formation of a joint venture with Chery Automobile, China's sixth-largest car manufacturer, in Anhui Province. Already, Land Rover four-by-fours are selling well in China.

So far, so good, but the UK has been slow to exploit the opportunities in China. When Wen Jiabao visited Europe in 2012 he placed £1 billion of orders in Britain but £14 billion in Germany. The disparity between the two emphasizes the opportunity for British business.

The UK has also been successful in attracting Chinese investment. In January, China's $410 billion sovereign wealth fund, China Investment Corporation (CIC), acquired a 10 per cent stake in Thames Water. However, Chancellor George Osborne's visit to Beijing at the time is unlikely to generate a rush of Chinese investors in UK infrastructure projects, although that was the focus of his talks with Lou Jiwei, CIC's chairman, and other Chinese financial institutions. Although the UK is rated highly for its open economy, sound legal system and relatively benign tax regime, the planning and construction cycles are so long compared to infrastructure development in China that the periods from commitment to investment payback in such projects in the UK are unattractive. The major opportunities for inward investment, as with export, are in the hands of proactive private companies.

Summary

The political and economic risks of engaging in business with China to take advantage of its growing consumer markets should not be a deterrent to British entrepreneurs. The macroeconomic argument in favour of China is highlighted by Table 4.2.1.

TABLE 4.2.1 Comparative GDP growth forecasts

	Analysis of output growth (%)			
	2010	2011	2012	2013
United States	3.2	1.6	1.4	2.0
Japan	4.4	−0.7	2.0	1.7
EU	1.9	1.4	−0.3	0.9
UK	2.1	0.7	0.8	2.0
Germany	3.6	3.1	0.6	1.5
Brazil	7.5	2.7	3.0	4.1
Russia	4.3	4.3	4.0	3.9
India	10.6	7.2	6.9	7.3
China	10.4	9.2	8.2	8.8

SOURCE: International Monetary Fund, April 2012.

Statistically, India offers similar attractions, but readers of Chietigj Bajpaee's devastating analysis of the contemporary Indian business environment in Chapter 4.4 may judge that risks there far outweigh the opportunities.

There are many factors to consider before engaging in China with a winning strategy. Those who are planning entry seriously may find some useful guidelines in *Business Insights: China: Practical advice on operational strategy and risk management* (Reuvid, 2011).

References

Bell, Daniel (2012) The real meaning of the rot at the top of China, *Financial Times*, 24 April

Lewis, Leo (2012) Great wall of silence cracks, *The Times*, 15 March

Reuvid, Jonathan (2011) *Business Insights: China: Practical advice on operational strategy and risk management*, Kogan Page, London

Sacks, Jonathan (2011) China is reversing the decline and fall of Christianity, *The Times*, 21 May

Russia: business risk in 2013

4.3

CARLO GALLO

Russia remains a compelling investment destination thanks to its resource wealth, geographic location and growing, educated middle class. While macroeconomic and political risks are likely to grow in the next few years (see 'Political risk' below), Russia enjoys greater political stability and more balanced economic management than many other resource-rich emerging markets. However, doing business in Russia continues to require thorough preparation. Even the most experienced emerging-markets investors face an uneven investment playing field characterized by opacity, excessive bureaucracy and often capricious regulation. These obstacles help explain why Russia continues to attract less foreign direct investment (FDI) per capita than other countries in the broader region, such as Albania, Kazakhstan, Turkmenistan and Montenegro, as illustrated in Figure 4.3.1.

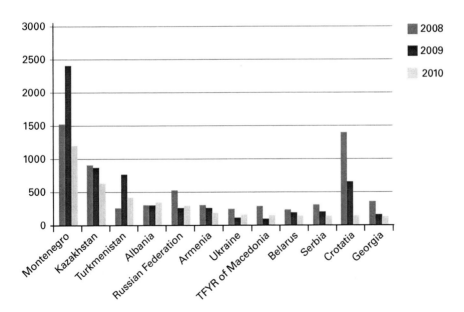

FIGURE 4.3.1 Selected transitional economics: annual FDI inflows
SOURCE: UNCTAD.
NOTE: USD at current prices and exchange rates, per capita.

Business risks in Russia are entrenched, as they derive to a large extent from structural features of the country's political, economic and social environment. Politically, power is highly concentrated in the hands of a narrow group surrounding President Vladimir Putin, and personalities dominate over weak and underdeveloped institutions. Rulers and bureaucrats' lack of social accountability allows for systemic corruption. Despite recent urban protests (on which more below), the majority of the population is disengaged from politics and, in part as a legacy of the Soviet era, expects paternalism from the state. Economic growth is dependent on constantly rising prices for hydrocarbons, raising serious questions around longer-term sustainability. These structural features underpin and reinforce a legal environment characterized by weak protection of property rights and unreliable courts. Moreover, these embedded problems are interlinked, making them very difficult to resolve.

This structural background produces a number of major risks for foreign business, for example high levels of official corruption, barriers to entry for foreign investment, uncertain regulation and dependency of business on politics. Companies can also encounter 'grey' business practices – essentially company-level financial mechanisms that can conceal tax evasion schemes, money laundering or attempts to defraud.

That said, not all companies are affected in the same ways. Business risks tend to differ according to sector, modes of investor entry and suitability of business partners, among other issues. Many companies make a success of their investments in Russia, particularly those with a high level of risk awareness, a solid understanding of their own vulnerabilities and risk exposure, and active risk management strategies that allow for a changing operational environment.

In a broad sense, risks for foreign direct investors in Russia fall into three categories: political, operational and security. Although the balance between the three will differ from case to case, potential investors should consider the full spectrum to enable them to choose the optimum entry strategy and highlight priority areas for risk management. As in other complex business environments, a risk management strategy for Russia should be integrated into the full life cycle of a business, rather than treated as a one-off exercise.

Political risk

Russian politics is changing. The political and economic system built by Vladimir Putin during his first two presidencies (2000–08), based on the centralization of political and economic power in the hands of a narrow circle of allies, has degenerated into stagnation and systemic corruption, and is increasingly unable to meet the requirements of a modern economy and just society. However, alternatives are very hard to come by. Major protests in Moscow followed rigged parliamentary elections in December 2011 and continued in the run-up to (as well as after) the March 2012 presidential vote. They demonstrate a new activism by progressive social groups – the relatively younger, better-educated, higher-income Russians who live in the larger cities. But they remain a small minority. Their call for civil and political rights is not shared by a majority of their fellow citizens who live in smaller cities and towns and tend to be more dependent on the state for their livelihoods and on state TV for their information. At least 50 per cent of Russians continue to support Putin as of mid-2012.

Putin was comfortably re-elected to the presidency in March and has countered the urban protests by relying on the support of the much larger, lower-skilled and state-dependent masses in the provinces (and on authoritarian voters' mobilization in the ethnic republics). To keep the support of industrial Russia, however, Putin needs to keep increasing social spending, including pensions, state salaries and various forms of subsidies to inefficient plants. But such populist economic strategy is not sustainable. The country derives half of the national budget from energy exports, and oil prices are unlikely to rise indefinitely.

Should oil prices fall below $70–80 per barrel (Urals blend) for a couple of years, the country would, by the end of that period, have exhausted its oil reserve fund, face rapidly growing budget deficits, and need to increase taxation massively and stop the rise in social spending. The first cuts would probably affect new infrastructure projects, but social spending would probably follow if the downturn were prolonged. Under such a scenario, widespread socio-economic protests in the provinces, involving ordinary Russians, would be more threatening for Putin than the recent urban protests. A nationalist, Soviet-style foreign policy rhetoric, based on the notion of a Western conspiracy against Russia, would probably offer only short-term legitimation for the regime.

The closer it gets to the above scenario, the stronger the incentives for Putin to refrain from modernizing the economy, which requires socially painful steps, such as reforming the pension system, further liberalizing domestic gas and electricity prices, improving market competition in sectors dominated by monopolies etc. At present, Putin and his entourage appear to lack a convincing strategy for sustaining growth, achieving economic and political modernization, and improving the investment climate. This casts a doubt on Putin's ability to complete his new presidential term (2012–18), as big business may seek to replace him with a collective ruling mechanism, better able to integrate diverging social interests while avoiding dangerous populism.

This strategic uncertainty is likely to translate into higher political risks in the coming few years. To the extent that Putin continues to boost social spending, this would probably continue to boost disposable incomes supporting the retail sector. On the other hand, the government has already announced higher taxes for the gas sector, as well as on very expensive cars and homes and on tobacco and alcohol. Higher taxation will probably add incentives to counterfeiting and push even more business into the grey economy. Uncertainty on the overall economic strategy will probably continue to fuel capital outflows, which reached $46 billion in January–May 2012, an increase of 44 per cent over the same period of the previous year.

Political reforms, even tightly managed and controlled ones, would also involve greater uncertainty. For example, Putin's 2012 decision to reintroduce popular elections for the heads of regional governments, while absolutely necessary in order to improve the quality of local governance and albeit tempered by a presidential right to vet candidates, is already shifting the centre-regional balance of power in favour of regional governors, by enhancing their independence vis-à-vis Moscow.

Regional politics is very important for business given Russia's federal system of government. For many investors, particularly those in prominent sectors such as extractives, political attitudes, stability and policy making at the federal level will be most relevant. For others, eg clothing, or food and beverage retailers with extensive distribution systems across the country, the politics of Russia's regions may be more relevant for the smooth running of day-to-day operations. Indeed, an investor's interaction with the local authorities on tax, security and regulatory issues can be crucial. Awareness of the local environment is essential to mitigating this risk, especially when relations between central and regional power are likely to become more unstable in the coming years following the reinstating of direct gubernatorial elections (see above).

At the federal level, government control over an expansive list of 'strategic sectors' is ensured via the Law on Strategic Sectors of 2008. The restrictions on foreign investment set in this law were somewhat relaxed in late 2011, but FDI levels have remain subdued. The law lists 42 strategic sectors in which the acquisition of controlling stakes (over 50 per cent) by foreign investors is subject to the prior consent of a government commission. These sectors include defence-related operations, nuclear installations, aerospace, natural monopolies and fixed telecom. If foreign investors are looking to invest in entities involved in the exploration and exploitation of large subsoil areas ('of federal significance'), then they also require government approval if the target stake is above 25 per cent.

World Trade Organization entry, achieved at the end of 2011, will promote Russia's further integration into the world economy, with long-term regulatory benefits. For the next five to eight years, however, the government has managed to negotiate the continuation of protectionist measures, such as import duties and government subsidies, to protect several sectors from imports, for example in automotive and agriculture. In addition to formal barriers, investors will continue to see strong government involvement in the private sector and, for many, a strong need to interact with state-owned entities to achieve business goals. Indeed, despite bold announcements, the government is likely to proceed very slowly with promised privatizations.

Under conditions of growing political uncertainty, as explained above, investors need to spend even more time and resources mapping the preferences of key political groupings, to forecast the likely direction of regulatory policy for any given sector of the economy. In particular, investors need to understand the attitudes of senior members of the political and business elites towards foreign investment in that area.

One effective political risk management strategy is researching the formal and informal links that exist between major political players and local businesses with which investors may be interacting, such as partners, suppliers or competitors. The end result provides investors with a 'power map' highlighting key political and business players, their roles and their relationships to each other.

Operational risk

The prevalence of official corruption is the dominant risk to a company once it has entered the Russian market. The country featured 143rd out of 183 countries ranked in global corruption watchdog Transparency International's Corruption Perceptions Index in 2011 (where the country ranked in first place is viewed as the least corrupt). Companies that are subject to the Foreign Corrupt Practices Act (FCPA) in the United States and the UK Bribery Act (UKBA) that came into force in July 2011 can be prosecuted for any corrupt dealings in Russia. The UKBA goes further than the

FCPA, introducing corporate responsibility for failure to prevent bribery within an organization. Both laws extend corporate responsibility to the behaviour of associates and agents. Similar anti-corruption laws exist in other OECD countries.

Corruption will not be stamped out overnight in Russia, whatever the level of political commitment over the coming years. However, companies can protect their businesses, reputation and legal standing by demonstrating genuine commitment to establishing corporate awareness of corruption, screening relationships, and introducing appropriate company processes and training.

Rather than opting for 'off-the-shelf' country corruption assessments, which can distort the picture, companies can conduct sector- or activity-specific corruption threat assessments that identify how corruption manifests itself in particular business situations. This type of assessment will then allow a company to focus its attention and spending on due diligence and background checks on agents, partners, employees and associates in high-risk parts of the business. Investigations and screening of counterparties can detect 'red flag' situations not uncommon in Russia, such as partner companies having deceased or fake shareholders, shareholders of distribution companies in fact being in charge of procurement at state-controlled entities (a clear FCPA risk), the use of a mass registration address as a legally registered address for a company, or numerous tax evasion schemes. Although this is a daunting list, companies can avoid engaging in bad practice without losing business if they use risk management tools effectively.

Companies can introduce appropriate policies and training to build a genuine anti-corruption culture and prepare management to respond appropriately should a corruption event occur. Training can include implementing measures to help detect malfeasance, for example devising an internal ethics code, planning regular and thorough audits, and implementing whistle blowing. Other mechanisms can help to prevent bad practice, such as drafting detailed procedures for working with contractors and government officials, hiring people known to be ethical and training them in the company's ethics policy, building cooperative relationships with regional authorities and coordinating anti-corruption strategies with industry associations.

Companies clearly should not attempt to 'outsource' corruption risk by hiring intermediaries or agents that are likely to engage in corruption when dealing with the authorities on behalf of the company. Such a strategy would not protect the company from the reputational, financial and even security risks posed by engaging in corrupt activity in Russia, not least because US companies or those with any activity in the UK would still be liable under the FCPA, UKBA and similar laws in other OECD countries.

Other operational concerns in Russia include the country's sprawling bureaucracy, infrastructure constraints, inadequacies in the legal system, and an occasional mismatch between the availability of skilled labour and private sector needs. The World Bank's 'Doing business' 2012 study ranked Russia 120th of 183 countries in terms of the ease of doing business. Putin's 2012 pledge to bring Russia to 50th ranking in the World Bank's study by 2015 appears ambitious but not impossible. It should be noted, however, that regulatory reforms narrowly aimed at improving a country's record on the few indicators on which these rankings are based may not bring as much improvement to the wider business environment. Therefore investors will probably continue to face the bureaucratic problem. Those more attuned to the Russian business environment can review the bureaucratic procedures that are essential to their business and employ appropriately skilled local staff to focus on those areas to minimize business delays and disagreements with local officials. Generally, red tape absorbs much more administrative and managerial time than in the average Western economy.

For a majority of direct investors, the lack of sufficient and upgraded infrastructure also continues to be a problem, particularly outside Russia's major cities or where levels of private sector investment are low. Poorly maintained and developed roads, slow and insufficient railway transport, inadequate fixed-line telecommunications, or outdated oil and gas pipelines can all present problems for investors dependent for a variety of reasons on well-functioning infrastructure. Investors need to factor infrastructure-related problems into route-to-market, supply chain and distribution strategies.

Another major operational issue for investors is the reliability of Russia's legal system, which has dealt with foreign (and Russian) investors inconsistently in the past. The experiences of Shell in the Sakhalin II project in 2006, as well as the dismemberment and de facto expropriation of Russian oil producer Yukos in 2003–07, underline continuing concerns around contract sanctity and the reliability of property rights. Many investors and lawyers argue that the quality of legislation is improving overall, and some foreign investors in Moscow point to specific instances where they have successfully defended their rights in local courts. However, the court system lacks independence from executive political power, which makes it unreliable when the interests of the state or of well-connected business players are at stake. Foreign investors need to try to minimize risks of unfair treatment by employing experienced local legal experts who have a solid understanding of the local political environment.

Depending on the extent to which a company's activities will require a local workforce, skills availability can be a problem. Although the population as a whole is well educated and well trained, the remote location of some of Russia's natural resources, the vast territory and uneven population distribution, as well as low rates of internal labour mobility, mean that companies can lack the appropriate skills in relevant parts of the country. Companies may find that the impact of the global economic downturn and subsequent rise in unemployment has led to greater labour availability in some cases. However, they are advised to review the local labour environment, particularly in remote parts of the country, to enable them to prepare for any labour shortages.

Security risk

Foreign investors in Russia do not, generally speaking, face as challenging an environment as they do in many more hostile emerging markets. That said, as with other risk categories, there are numerous physical and non-physical security threats that foreign investors need to consider, which vary according to their particular set of circumstances.

The physical security threat posed by terrorism emanating from the North Caucasus continues, despite the authorities' declaration in 2009 of an end to their counter-terrorism operation against rebels in Chechnya. Attacks take place regularly in the North Caucasus, and occasionally in public places in Moscow. Although foreign companies and individuals have not been targeted directly, the public nature of the attacks means that all personnel are at risk of being affected as bystanders. The likelihood of indiscriminate attacks in the North Caucasus – together with the threat of violent crime – makes that region particularly high-risk for foreign investors.

Two recent developments suggest that foreign investors should take the security threat posed by terrorism more seriously than in previous years. First, the January 2011 bomb attack on Domodedovo airport in Moscow – in which some 37 people were killed – suggests a change in tactics by terrorist groups. The attack inside Moscow's newest, business-oriented airport, probably timed to coincide with the arrival of international flights, was clearly designed to tarnish the city's image as a host for foreign business, as well as tourism.

Second, there has been an increase in suicide attacks by terrorist groups in the North Caucasus since 2009, particularly in Dagestan and Ingushetia and, more recently, in Kabardino-Balkaria. Although foreign companies may not be the intended targets, the introduction of suicide bombing as a tactic increases the potential for mass casualties and fatalities. Investors are advised to monitor terrorist activity around the country to enable them to understand and mitigate the specific threats in their location.

The Winter Olympics in Sochi in 2014 will be a major test of Russia's ability to contain the security threat in the North Caucasus and successfully hold an international, large-scale sporting event close to insecurity hot spots in that region. The related security infrastructure and procedures put in place for the event could, if successful, make the region more attractive for foreign investment over the coming years. Government efforts and incentives are already attracting more investment into the North Caucasus than in previous years, particularly in the local energy, transport and tourist infrastructure.

The risks presented by non-physical security threats, such as brand and intellectual property theft and fraud, are arguably more difficult to assess and mitigate. However, for some investors, these can present greater problems than physical threats. Pharmaceutical producers cite brand protection as a priority in Russia, given widespread reporting of counterfeiting of pharmaceutical goods and an apparent lack of political will to combat the problem effectively. The government's Pharma 2020 strategy focuses on the need to increase levels of manufacturing within Russia, rather than relying on imports, and to keep prices low to meet the needs of a population in the midst of both an economic downturn and a public health crisis.

Investors can take steps to limit exposure to counterfeit activity in the pharmaceutical and other sectors. Companies can conduct an assessment to highlight problem areas in their sector. For example, an assessment of brand protection risks in manufacturing may highlight the threat of 'third shifts' – illegal shifts producing counterfeit goods conducted after a factory's closing hours by complicit members of staff who then profit from their sale on the black market. Investors can choose a risk-averse mode of entry into the Russian market if counterfeit threats are high, for example limiting in-country manufacturing. The investor can also screen all relevant employees, associates, suppliers and partner companies, thus increasing transparency and boosting company awareness of the potential for internally generated threats.

Conclusion

The structural nature of the majority of risks for foreign investors in Russia will slow any major improvements in the business environment in the near term. Real investment incentives, improved rule of law, modernization of the bureaucracy and transparency will take time to achieve. However, some developments in the domestic private sector point to positive trends for the business environment overall. Many Russian companies are realizing that adopting greater transparency can benefit their competitive standing internationally.

Despite the many very real challenges for foreign companies, the investor who goes about doing business in Russia with sufficient care and discrimination can manage risks and achieve commercial success. Companies need to put risk management at the centre of their Russia strategies. A tailored approach to risk management, coupled with high-level corporate commitment at every stage of the business cycle, can set entrants into the Russian market apart from their peers.

Acknowledgement

This chapter is an update and extension of Chapter 4.4, 'Business risks in Russia', from the previous edition of *Managing Business Risk*, written in association with Tanya Costello of Control Risks.

India: the risk environment

CHIETIGJ BAJPAEE, VIVEKANANDA INTERNATIONAL FOUNDATION

Despite India's strong fundamentals – its favourable demographics, growing middle class, high savings rate and dynamic private sector – the country remains a complex and sometimes difficult operating environment. The World Bank's 2011 Ease of Doing Business Index places the country in 132nd place out of 183 countries, with its lowest ranking on enforcing contracts (182).[1] This can be attributed to well-entrenched bureaucratic, regulatory and political constraints that have translated into policy lethargy and complacency.

This has manifested itself in the case of several recent high-profile corruption scandals and prolonged inflationary pressures, which rather than indicating a few 'bad apples' in the system in the case of corruption woes or pressures from short-term exogenous factors in the case of inflation are instead indicative of the inability or unwillingness of the government to accelerate the much-needed second generation of reforms in India's economic liberalization (Dehejia, 2010).

Reform agenda on the back burner

The momentum of the economic liberalization process – which began in 1991 with the dismantling of the infamous 'Licence Raj' by lowering trade barriers and liberalizing the foreign investment regime in the face of a foreign exchange crisis – appears to have slowed amid a false sense of security that appears to have crept into the Indian National Congress (Congress) party since its re-election to a second consecutive term on a strengthened mandate in 2009.

Among the fundamental reforms that are necessary for realizing India's economic potential are:

- accelerating the process of disinvestment (privatization) of public sector utilities (state-owned companies);
- raising foreign direct investment (FDI) limits (in such sectors as retail, defence and insurance);
- improving transport, power and agricultural infrastructure;
- relaxing fuel and agricultural subsidies;

- dismantling the industrial licensing regime;
- addressing issues of corporate governance;
- other reforms aimed at improving the basic operating environment in India, including the development of a more flexible labour market;
- improving judicial efficiency;
- strengthening enforcement of intellectual property rights; and
- improving the provision of basic education services.

Among the most urgent of India's stalled reforms is the fact that the country still remains a largely agrarian economy held hostage to annual rainfall in the absence of much-needed investment in irrigation infrastructure. While the country is the world's second-largest fruit and vegetable producer it suffers an estimated 1 trillion rupees in annual losses of perishable goods, drawing attention to the urgency of making improvements to India's food supply chain infrastructure, including cold storage, warehousing, food-processing facilities and transport infrastructure (Hoque, 2011).

The fact that some 55 per cent of the workforce continues to be employed in the agricultural sector is itself not sustainable if India seeks to become a major industrialized power.[2] Related to this, restrictive labour laws (notably the Industrial Disputes Act, 1947, which requires a company that employs more than 100 people to seek the government's permission to lay off workers) also remain a barrier to unleashing India's full productive capacity. This has been illustrated by the relative decline of India's much-hailed business process outsourcing (BPO) sector amid rising labour costs, high attrition rates, and skills shortages. The number of call centres in India has halved over the last three years amid the rise of competitors in Asia and Eastern Europe.[3]

While the government continues to pledge rhetorical support for economic liberalization, actual progress remains slow, patchy and sometimes even counterproductive. For instance, the disinvestment process appears to be driven more by short-term concerns over filling the government's coffers than a genuine recognition of the need to reduce the role of the state in economic affairs.[4] Furthermore, several crucial bills aimed at improving the investment environment remain stalled in parliament. These range across the Insurance Laws (Amendment) Bill 2008, which proposes to raise FDI limits in the sector from 26 to 49 per cent, the Land Acquisition, Resettlement and Rehabilitation Bill, which amends the outdated 1894 Land Acquisition Act, and the Mining and Minerals (Development and Regulation) Bill.[5]

Political considerations have driven the slow pace of reform. For instance, recent policy flip-flopping over a decision to lift a ban on foreign investment in multi-brand retail is related to the fact that organized retail accounts for only 6 per cent of the country's 15 million retail outlets, with the rest dominated by *kirana* (corner shops) that employ 8 per cent of the workforce, making it the country's second-largest employer.[6] Meanwhile, the main problem plaguing India's mining and infrastructure sectors is the issue of land acquisition given the political sensitivity associated with the conversion of agricultural land for industrial use.[7] In the absence of clarity and consistency, the country's mining policy remains opaque, as demonstrated by the fact that a $12 billion steel plant in Orissa state, which is the single largest foreign investment project in the country, has been held up since 2005 by a number of political, socio-economic and bureaucratic hurdles, the most recent being a memorandum of understanding between the Orissa state government and South Korean company POSCO lapsing in 2010 (Bhattacharya, 2011).

Similarly, while the Planning Commission has set an ambitious target to attract $1 trillion in infrastructure investment over the period of the 12th Five Year Plan (2012–17), of which a third is expected to come from public–private partnerships (PPP), implementation remains difficult (Sikarwar, 2011). This is because of bureaucratic delays and the need to appease multiple constituencies, including environmental activists, local communities, state, local and federal governments, and competing ministries, though to be sure the creation of special industrial zones that are free of the shackles of the country's onerous labour laws is a step in the right direction

Beyond being slow in pushing forward reforms, the government's capricious policy making is also leading to the occasional reversal of the country's reform process. This was demonstrated by the government unveiling dozens of tax proposals in its 2012 budget, including taxing foreign takeovers retroactively to 1962 (General Anti-Avoidance Rule – GAAR).[8] This overturned a January 2012 Supreme Court ruling that rejected a tax bill imposed on British telecom provider Vodafone over its 2007 purchase of a local operator. This follows in the footsteps of the Supreme Court cancelling 122 telecom licences in February 2012 amid claims that they were improperly auctioned in 2008. While the government has suspended GAAR for a year, such policy flip-flops will have a detrimental impact on investor confidence and foreign capital inflows and will ultimately undermine the country's growth prospects.

Corruption reborn

Policy complacency and gridlock have in turn become deterrents of progress in improving governance and tackling corruption. Corruption is not a new dilemma facing India and remains standard practice in many aspects of conducting business in the country, which accounted for the country's dismal 95th ranking (dropping eight positions from the previous year) in the 2011 survey of Transparency International's Corruption Perceptions Index.[9] Adding to these poor rankings is a report by US group Global Financial Integrity, which noted that India lost $462 billion between 1948 and 2008 – more than twice the country's external debt ($230 billion) – to illicit financial flows (Kar, 2010). More than two-thirds of this capital flight has occurred since the start of the liberalization process in 1991, indicating that deregulation has actually been a catalyst for the illicit transfer of funds. Beyond the reputational risks of conducting business in India, corruption has also made it harder and more expensive for companies to conduct business in India given the need by foreign companies to undertake a more rigorous due diligence process during mergers or joint ventures with local companies in order to evaluate compliance with anti-corruption laws in their home jurisdictions and mitigate the risk of any successor liability.

The petty corruption of *babus* (junior government officials) during the 'Licence Raj' period that dominated the first four decades of the country's independence has been curtailed, as the role of intermediaries in such activities as tax filing and payments, acquiring permits and obtaining telephone connections has been reduced amid the streamlining and computerization of services (Rao, 2011). However, while petty corruption has been tackled somewhat, larger-scale corruption has grown during the country's economic liberalization process. This has been fuelled by well-entrenched collusion between the private sector and government. The fact that some 17 of the 30 companies on the benchmark Sensex index of the Bombay Stock Exchange are family controlled has also fuelled the prevalence of favouritism, nepotism and a lack of transparency in the conduct of business in the country.[10] The real estate, construction and telecom sectors are particularly prone to corruption given the high level of government intervention in these sectors, with multi-level approvals and the involvement of large capital investments (KPMG, 2011). Mining has also become a hub for illicit activities, with a draft report from government auditors in March 2012 alleging lost revenues of $210 billion between 2004 and 2010 over the sale of coalfields without competitive bidding.

Nonetheless, despite the well-ingrained culture of corruption in India, the string of recent high-profile corruption scandals at the upper echelons of government has come as a shock to many. The widespread support for social activist Anna Hazare, who called for the inclusion of civil society members in a government-established anti-corruption panel (as part of the Jan Lokpal (Citizen Ombudsman) Bill), and Baba Ramdev over demands for the repatriation of illicit funds stashed abroad has highlighted the growing public frustration over the government's apparent complacency in clamping down on corruption (Bhaskaran, 2011; Ramachandran, 2011a). Among the high-profile scandals that have plagued the government are:

- claims by army chief General VK Singh in March 2012 that he had been offered bribes of $2.7 million by a defence industry lobbyist for the purchase of sub-standard trucks;

- the resignation of Karnataka state chief minister BS Yeddyurappa in July 2011 after he was indicted in a mining scandal that allegedly cost the exchequer more than $3 billion as a result of illegal mining in the Bellary region;

- the arrest of former telecoms minister Andimuthu Raja in February 2011 over the alleged undervalued auction of 2G telecom spectrum licences that cost the exchequer some $39 billion in lost revenue;

- the misappropriation of funds for the Commonwealth Games in Delhi in October 2010, which was estimated at between $1.1 billion and $1.8 billion;

- revelations in November 2010 that flats in Mumbai designated for families of war veterans were being allocated to senior military officials and politicians; and

- whistle-blowing website Wikileaks revealing in March 2011 that the US embassy in Delhi was allegedly aware of vote-buying efforts by the Congress-led United Progressive Alliance (UPA) coalition government to secure the requisite number of seats to win a vote of confidence in 2008 (Akya, 2011; Ramachandran, 2011b).

The fact that PJ Thomas, the head of India's anti-corruption watchdog was himself forced to resign in March 2011 by the Supreme Court while facing corruption allegations demonstrates the weight of the problem.[11]

Anti-corruption initiatives

The growing backlash against the recent scandals has prompted the government to take some steps toward reform, though results have been mixed. The Prevention of Corruption Act, 1988, for instance, maintains a very low conviction rate with no form of public participation. Meanwhile, the Central Vigilance Commission (CVC) lacks enforcement powers and often operates at the whim of the administrative authorities. Similarly, the state *Lokayukta* (anti-corruption ombudsman) only has the power to recommend punishments. On the other hand, the Right to Information Act, 2005 has been hailed as a pivotal tool in the fight against corruption, along with the Bill on Public Interest Disclosure and Protection of Informers (Whistle Blower Resolution).

The government has pledged to follow in the footsteps of the United States and United Kingdom, which have implemented anti-corruption legislation such as the US Foreign Corrupt Practices Act and the UK Bribery Act 2011, to formulate its own anti-corruption law. This aims to clamp down on illicit activities in the private sector according to the United Nations Convention against Corruption (UNCAC). It follows the government's decision to sign up to the anti-corruption action plan unveiled at the G20 Summit in 2010, which is also targeted at corruption in the private sector. Other reforms under consideration include the proposed National Anti-Corruption Strategy and the revamping of the Central Economic Intelligence Bureau (CEIB), the nodal agency responsible for combating economic offences, including tax evasion, money laundering and smuggling.

Nonetheless, despite rhetorical support in the campaign against corruption, many of the initiatives that have been unveiled remain mere token gestures in the fight against corruption amid the prevalence of political interference and red tape. For instance, while the government is in the process of implementing the anti-graft Lokpal and Lokayukta Bill, the bill itself has flaws, including its failure to provide any right to appeal and its limited investigative powers (Salekar, 2011).

There are also concerns that the Companies Bill, which came under renewed attention following the corporate fraud case of Satyam Computer Services in late 2008, may be watered down, reflecting limited progress in strengthening corporate governance.[12] Among the proposed reforms of the draft bill, which aims to replace the Companies Act, 1956, is the introduction of class-action lawsuits to empower investors to challenge companies engaged in fraudulent activities and labelling insider trading as a criminal offence.

Amid the failure of the executive to clamp down on corruption, it has been left to an activist judiciary, the media and civil society to step up. However, this has not been without controversy, as noted by the publication of transcripts of conversations between corporate lobbyist Nira Radia and prominent journalists, industrialists and government officials in November 2010, which confirmed the well-entrenched collusion between the media, government and private sector.[13] Human resources and infrastructure deficiencies in the judiciary, which have contributed to a backlog of more than 30 million cases, have also led to judicial and bureaucratic delays, the poor enforcement of verdicts and the absence of harsh penalties (Murti, 2009). Concerns have also been voiced on the oversight of the judiciary and media, which have often used their growing influence for populist causes rather than fighting for a genuine improvement in transparency, accountability and governance. Furthermore, the use of extra-constitutional means to fight corruption threatens to corrode the very institutions that these means seek to strengthen.

Political pressures take precedence

The silver lining may come from the growing astuteness of the Indian voter, who can no longer be won over by merely exploiting caste, ethnic and religious rivalries, making token handouts to the poor and pledging rhetorical support for the *aam admi* (common man). The crushing defeat of the DMK party in state elections in Tamil Nadu in April 2011 amid allegations of corruption against several of the party's politicians relating to the undervalued auction of 2G spectrum telecom licences reaffirmed the view that an investor-friendly government need not be an unpopular government. This has also been noted by the re-election of reform-oriented governments in Bihar under the helm of chief minister Nitish Kumar and in Gujarat under Narendra Modi.

However, the other side of the coin is that recent state polls have reaffirmed the importance of regional parties, which retain the ability to hijack the policy agenda at the national level. This has served to tone down the irrational exuberance that followed the Congress Party's re-election to a second term in 2009, which led to claims that its strengthened mandate would lead to a cleaner and more efficient government amid the reduced reliance on regional parties. This was refuted by the government's slow and feeble response to Raja's improper auction of spectrum licences. Despite it being reported as early as 2008, prime minister Manmohan Singh reappointed Raja to the telecom portfolio following the UPA's re-election. This has tarnished Singh's 'Mr Clean' image amid claims that he was ignorant of this scandal or, more likely, unable to do anything about it given the need to appease the coalition partner, the DMK.

Similarly, despite the resignation of the communist Left Front group of parties from the federal government coalition in 2008 and its poor performance in state elections in West Bengal and Kerala in 2011, the bloc's traditionally pro-poor, anti-liberalization agenda remains alive and kicking. The Trinamool Congress – a coalition partner in the ruling UPA government and ruling party in West Bengal state – has emerged as more left-wing than the Left Front, as noted by its support for violent agitation against land acquisition for the famed Tata Nano automobile factory in Singur in 2009, the construction of a petrochemical facility in Nandigram in 2008, and more recently opposition to lifting restrictions on foreign investment in multi-brand retail (Dutta, 2011). The Congress Party itself retains its socialist ideological roots from the days of the country's first prime minister, Jawaharlal Nehru, and the party remains reluctant to abandon these roots, as it seeks to 'play it safe' in order to secure a third consecutive term on an even stronger mandate by 2014.

Ultimately when looking at India as an investment destination one is not looking at the country itself but rather the individual states, where policy consistency and continuity are often more important than the political ideology of the ruling party in ensuring the presence of effective institutions, infrastructure and law and order. This accounts for Gujarat state emerging as an investment hub under the leadership of chief minister Narendra Modi, who is the longest-serving leader of the state. This comes despite Modi's rise to power on a divisive and inflammatory Hindu-nationalist agenda.

Behind the slow pace of reform in India is the consensual nature of the country's politics. The need of any national government to appease its core constituency of rural voters and coalition partners from regional parties, and to fight off opposition claims that the government is selling its soul to foreign interests, makes reforms a slow-moving process by any ruling party in India. The current national political climate is particularly hostile to reform, as demonstrated by the results of polls for five state assemblies that were announced in March 2012, which failed to yield a conclusive victory for any single national or regional party. This alludes to the possibility of a return to the era of weak (and sometimes short-lived) coalition governments that plagued the country in the 1990s. In this context, while India may have finally escaped the lethargy of the 'Hindu rate of growth' that plagued the first four decades of its development, it is likely to continue to be held back by a slow-moving 'Indian rate of policy making' until the next economic crisis forces it to accelerate the next generation of reforms. Until then, India will remain a complex and difficult business operating environment.

Notes

1 Ease of Doing Business Index 2011, World Bank, http://www.doingbusiness.org/rankings (accessed 30 May 2012).

2 The government has set a target to increase the share of the manufacturing sector from 16–17 per cent of GDP at present to 25–26 per cent by 2020: 'Govt to soon announce manufacturing policy', *Economic Times*, 8 April 2011; 'Indicus Analytics: India's skill disorder', *Business Standard*, 26 May 2011.

3 Certainly, this is also a reflection of the Indian BPO sector moving up the value chain into knowledge process outsourcing industries, such as software development, medical record services and accountancy (Adriano, 2011).

4 Of the government's 213 state-owned companies (public sector utilities – PSUs) the government has pledged to divest interests in some 45 loss-making PSUs in 2011–12 (Tiwari, 2011).

5 'FM seeks allies' support for consensus on Insurance Bill', *Economic Times*, 28 March 2011.

6 Foreign investment in single-brand retail is currently limited to 51 per cent; it is 100 per cent in wholesale trade and barred in multi-brand retail: 'No decision yet on multi-brand retail: Pranab Mukherjee', *Economic Times*, 26 March 2011.

7 The main disagreements over the country's mining policy relate to sharing mining royalties between state and federal authorities, the competing interests of government ministries, notably the environment and coal, and appeasing populist pressures given that rural voters constitute the core constituency of voters for any government.

8 'Backdated takeover tax latest blow to investors', *Agence France-Presse*, 16 April 2012.

9 Transparency International, Corruption Perceptions Index 2011, http://cpi.transparency.org/cpi2011/results/ (accessed 30 May 2012).

10 'India's family groups groom future leaders', *Financial Times*, 5 September 2010.
11 'PJ Thomas resigns as CVC', *Indian Express*, 3 March 2011.
12 'Investor-friendly Companies Bill dropped', *Indian Express*, 28 March 2011.
13 'Outrage as Nira Radia tapes dent image of 4th estate', *India Today*, 20 November 2010.

References

Adriano, Joel D (2011) Philippines ousts India for top outsourcing spot, *Asia Times*, 9 March
Akya, Chan (2011) Crooked Indians, *Asia Times*, 13 April
Bhaskaran, Gautaman (2011) New 'Gandhi' takes on India's corruption, *Asia Times*, 12 April
Bhattacharya, Prasenjit (2011) Posco to resume buying land despite protests, *Wall Street Journal*, 13 June
Dehejia, Vivek H (2010) Where are the second-generation reforms?, *Pragati*, December, pp 5–7
Dutta, Ananya (2011) Nandigram–Singur: a tantalising tale of two West Bengal constituencies, *The Hindu*, 3 May
Hoque, Akram (2011) Off limit for over 600 million, *Business and Economy*, 17 March
Kar, Dev (2010) *The Drivers and Dynamics of Illicit Financial Flows from India: 1948–2008*, November, Global Financial Integrity, Washington, DC, http://www.gfip.org/storage/gfip/documents/reports/india/gfi_india.pdf (accessed 19 June 2011)
KPMG (2011) *Survey on Bribery and Corruption: Impact on Economy and Business Environment*, http://www.kpmg.com/IN/en/IssuesAndInsights/ThoughtLeadership/KPMG_Bribery_Survey_Report_new.pdf, p 10 (accessed 19 June 2011)
Murti, Mohan (2009) Dispensing justice, speedily, *Business Line*, 7 September
Ramachandran, Sudha (2011a) Yoga guru transcends Delhi's crackdown, *Asia Times*, 10 June
Ramachandran, Sudha (2011b) Vote scandal adds to Manmohan's woes, *Asia Times*, 24 March
Rao, N Bhaskara (2011) Kicked upstairs: corruption at the level of basic public services might be declining, *Pragati*, January, pp 21–22
Salekar, Amba (2011) Jan Lok Pal is both unconstitutional and unnecessary, *Pragati*, May, pp 18–23
Sikarwar, Deepshikha (2011) PPP policy gaps to be filled in core push, *Economic Times*, 29 March
Tiwari, Dheeraj (2011) Govt will review revival plans of sick PSUs, *Economic Times*, 2 April

Thailand: manageable business risk

ERIC LYNN, MYLIFEQS

Thailand is perhaps better known in the Western world as a tourist rather than a business destination, and this paradoxically is one of its attractions – it's a great place to be.

Paradoxes are ubiquitous in Thailand and can be encountered in all walks of life. The lived culture is simultaneously classical, conservative and traditional while being renowned for its liberal and open-minded attitudes. It is friendly – the friendliness may be apparent or real. Regulations are highly bureaucratic, yet if you encounter the right person Thais can display wonderful flexibility in getting things done quickly. You will generally receive a positive answer when making requests, which may or may not mean 'yes' as understood by Westerners – Thais prefer not to disappoint. Security guards are considered a necessity for all property containing valuable items, yet you will also encounter incredible honesty. (The author had his ATM card returned to his bank after absent-mindedly forgetting it in the cash dispenser!) It is a seemingly easy place to live and work, yet society and business regulations are exceedingly complex, with the latter liable to change at any time.

Welcome to 'Amazing Thailand' – a slogan of the Tourism Authority of Thailand. As a business destination it encompasses both opportunities and risks, which will be our focus here.

Background

With a population of about 67 million, low unemployment, a high literacy rate (although the quality of its public education system leaves plenty of room for improvement), good infrastructure (which makes travel relatively easy), a reliable and easy-to-negotiate banking system and a strong currency, Thailand has the potential to provide a good base for business.

With a large proportion of the population either self-employed or engaged in small businesses, a widespread commercial mindset and people who are generally open to new initiatives, opportunities abound. One well-connected person with decades of business experience in South-East Asia describes the Thais as 'very commercial'.

Together with the opportunities come issues that are likely to be totally foreign to the experience of most Western businesspeople. They are a part of life in Thailand and you will need to work with them.

Geography

The climate is sub-tropical, meaning property and physical assets require protection against monsoon rains. The topography varies from mountains in the north to beaches in the south, with the centre of the country effectively a garden, which partially explains why food is at the core of Thai culture and agricultural product processing is a huge industry. It's easy to be deceived by the size of the country when looking at a map: the distance between the northernmost and southernmost points is over 2,000 kilometres. Overland travel takes time. The well-publicized floods of 2011 illustrated the real risk that climate can pose for business in the region. While you cannot change the prevailing conditions, in business terms you are able to prepare for them. The government and local authorities came in for a great deal of valid criticism for their handling of the situation. Placing your trust in oral or even written 'assurances' when planning investments is risky, as numerous Thai and foreign businesses found to their cost. Research the environment thoroughly, design buildings accordingly and spread your options.

Infrastructure

The fundamentals are good, with reliable transportation, telecommunications and power available throughout the country.

An extensive, good-quality road system makes overland travel relatively smooth but time-consuming, simply because of the distances. The rail system works, is prone to disruption from landslides during the monsoons, and is in dire need of modernization. Plans now exist for high-speed links from Bangkok to the North, North-East and South. As to timing, don't hold your breath. Domestic flights are fast, convenient and relatively cheap, with numerous airlines competing on many major routes.

Phones work, and connections are easy and quick to obtain. Mobile network coverage is excellent, though the introduction of 3G has been delayed by a series of long, ongoing legal battles among the various competitors – the end is not in sight.

Economy

With the exception of agricultural processing, much of which is done in the provinces, most industry is located in or near Bangkok, with the Eastern Seaboard region (approximately two hours' drive from the capital) home to a significant automobile sector. Other important industrial cities are Nakhon Ratchasima and Udon Thani in the North-East. Lamphun near Chaing Mai in the North is developing into a high-tech centre.

The major sectors in the Thai economy are automotive, including parts, financial services, electrical and electronic appliances and components, tourism, agriculture and agricultural processing. Industry and services each account for over 40 per cent of GDP, while agriculture (the traditional foundation of both the economy and culture) is still significant at 11 per cent. GDP is approximately US$5,500 per capita. Thailand is now classified as an 'emerging economy'.

According to the World Bank's 2012 'Doing business' series, Thailand is ranked 17th of 183 countries in the 'ease of doing business' table. Notwithstanding this, bureaucracy is complex, although there have been significant improvements in recent years. If you find the right partner, display a willingness to cooperate and remain patient, you will discover an amazing ingenuity for skirting formal barriers.

Interactions

Learn some Thai, but you will initially need to use English as your business language. Complexity makes Thai a challenging language for Westerners, but you will be appreciated and respected for attempting to learn even a little. Be prepared for compliments on how well you speak after uttering a few words!

You will need partners and staff who are not only professionally qualified but also able to speak and understand English fluently. They are plentiful in Bangkok, less so in the provinces. While English is taught in most Thai schools, the standard in the public system is generally appalling. Self-driven young people (and you will find many in Bangkok) seem able to teach themselves to a reasonable level. Many members of the establishment as well as senior managers were educated abroad and speak well.

Business regulations for investors

Thailand encourages inward investment and is particularly interested in initiatives that provide meaningful employment, know-how transfer and skills development. The Board of Investment (BOI), which operates under the auspices of the Ministry of Industry, offers assistance with all regulatory procedures for investments that it formally approves. Full details of requirements are available on the BOI website, yet because regulations can change frequently and are not always completely clear it is advisable to establish a contact in the Board and address enquiries directly. Afterwards, double-check the responses you get. As well as regional offices throughout Thailand, the BOI has representations in Europe and the United States and throughout Asia.

The Foreign Business Act regulates which work can be carried out by foreigners and which professions are reserved for Thais. There are three lists: A (closed to aliens), B (closed to aliens unless promoted by the Board of Investment) and C. Only those on list C are 'open to aliens'.

Under Thai law, no foreigner may own more than 49 per cent of a business. The same applies to ownership of land. You may own the assets on the land but not the land itself. A registered Thai business may own land. You may also obtain land on a long-term lease. The ownership of large areas of land in Thailand is not documented; therefore, before entering agreements, ensure that your lawyer ascertains the correct status of the land in question. As with most things in Thailand, there are exceptions to these regulations. If you receive BOI approval for your investment, the Board may be willing to facilitate foreign ownership of the land on which you wish to build your facility.

Business ownership regulations have also been tightened in recent years, with the Foreign Business Act of 2006 placing additional restrictions on proxy ownership of businesses, with heavy fines and even imprisonment for those breaking the law. Changes are frequent, and the regulations often leave room for interpretation. The risk to investors is that you may find that you are operating illegally despite having obeyed the law at the time you set up your business. It's imperative to keep up to date, with this being such a critical risk factor. Bangkok has numerous consultancies with expertise in local conditions – you'll need to work with one anyway.

Buildings

Your place of work does not simply perform the function of a business location; it is also a site for social interaction among all who work there. Thais are very superstitious. Almost every building you see anywhere in the country has at least one spirit house in the front. The spirits are welcomed here and fed (rice, fruit, drinks etc), safeguarding the main centres of human interaction. New buildings need to be inaugurated by monks on an auspicious day, and you will definitely need to participate in the ceremony. Don't even think about dismissing or ignoring this custom. If Thais feel apprehensive about entering a building in which they sense the presence of evil spirits, they won't.

Political risk

Thailand has a history of political turbulence that dates back to the establishment of a constitutional monarchy in 1932. There have been no fewer than 17 constitutions and 18 coups in the intervening period. The past six years have seen a marked increase in political-related violence, which has, on occasions, briefly brought local economies to a standstill. The current conflict is simply a power struggle between the establishment and a section of the newly wealthy business community. It is neither, as inaccurately reported in most of the Western press, a conflict between rich and poor nor a conflict between so-called democratic forces and the military. Democracy as known in the West does not exist in Thailand. Vote buying is commonplace; most villagers have little access to objective information, with village heads frequently exercising their influence to encourage residents to vote for the candidate of their choice. Money buys influence. The military remain influential, though they claim not to seek power. An inherent distrust of their motives exists.

What are the consequences for business, and which risks does this entail? Generally, life goes on, and politics will not interfere greatly with your business. Populist Thai politicians like to activate the xenophobia switch, and conflicts provide fertile ground for populism. This may result in sudden changes in visa and business regulations, which more often than not are opposed by the business community, who appreciate foreign investment. Be aware, ensure your information is up to date, yet take care to avoid political debate. You may never discover the leanings of your partners, and a few poorly placed words could irretrievably harm your business. Relationships and good connections are a lifeline in Thailand.

Corruption is an issue in the vast majority of countries in the world and is acknowledged as serious by Thai business and political leaders. The extent of the problem is confirmed in the 2011 Transparency International Corruption Perceptions Index, in which Thailand is 80th of 183 countries, with a score of 3.4 (highly corrupt). Apart from the beneficiaries, nobody likes it. The challenge is to find a way to work around it; you cannot and will not change the system, regardless of the extent to which it annoys you. Of course, it is related to the political instability. Widespread corruption could not exist without the tacit understanding of ruling politicians.

Notwithstanding Thailand's lip service to democracy, accompanied by the sense of independence and individualism that you will observe, freedom of speech is selective. It is illegal to criticize the monarchy; Westerners too have been imprisoned for doing so. The internet is censored. Stories circulate of physical threats to those who challenge established and influential business interests; business and politics are interconnected.

People and everyday life

In a culture where a higher value is placed on relationships and status (people) than on function (the task at hand), the success of your venture will depend upon your ability to develop an understanding of the mindset and build meaningful relationships. As a foreign investor, you will be given an opportunity to attend functions and interact with the business community, observe how business works and extend your circle of influence. You will also be expected to contribute to business development locally.

Thai social hierarchy is automatically established through status and associated wealth. You will also experience deference for age. While as an outsider you will never be part of the structure, you will be expected to learn, recognize and accept the way things work. As an investor, you begin with a credibility bonus earning you initial respect – even more if you are fortunate enough to have grey hair. However, nothing is automatic. Your integrity will be tested; your willingness to support will be tried, as will your ability to withstand attempts at exploitation; your dealings with both business partners and staff will need to be human, cooperative, consistent and very clear. If not, you may well find obstacles appearing in your path – and never discover their origin or even how you can remove them.

Loyalty in Thai society can be broadly visualized in terms of three concentric circles. (Almost) automatic loyalty is given to family and very close friends with whom people have grown up – the inner circle, the safe protected world in which all are good to each other. A sense of professional loyalty exists towards those who may be important for the individual's progress in life – business- and work-related relationships fall into this category. As the boss, you will be expected to do good for the people within your sphere of influence and would do well to remember that their motivation is personal gain. The contract is merely a business document and does not imply automatic loyalty. The outer circle is for occasional random interactions where little personal regard is shown by either party.

Your challenges with staff will be manifold, yet all can be overcome. When you find good staff (well qualified, displaying initiative, with a positive attitude), value them, support their development and keep them. In everyday interactions, you are likely to encounter significant differences to Western business life in your staff's willingness to take responsibility, decision making and communication.

You are the boss and therefore paid to take responsibility and make decisions. The staff are paid to perform tasks that you initiate. Society is hierarchical. From early childhood, Thais learn to respect the hierarchy and not question decisions. Of course, they bring this into working life. They like to please and will readily agree to your suggestions. If you are looking for constructive critical input and independence, you can train them. Take time, nurture them, show appreciation and value them. Expecting fast change and using pressure are a formula for failure.

Your people will expect official holidays, which are mostly religious or associated with the royal family, to be respected. They will also need and expect time off for family affairs such as weddings, funerals, and significant birthdays of parents or uncles. As their boss, you may even be invited to weddings and funerals – if so, you are expected to go and take gifts.

When I first relocated to Thailand in 2004, I asked numerous acquaintances about the three most important things for the people: *sanuk*, *khao* and *mai pen rai* were the inevitable answers.

Sanuk implies easy-going fun, which Thais expect to experience in all walks of life. They may even distrust those who don't smile.

Khao means rice and is synonymous with food. Thailand is the world's largest rice exporter, rice is the staple food and eating is core to the culture: Thai cuisine is fresh, exceedingly diverse and necessarily delicious – poor food is simply not tolerated. A shared meal is a social interaction that helps to build the sense of community Thais seek. However busy you are, make time for meals with your people; they'll appreciate invitations and having simple lunches brought regularly into the office. A few centuries ago, a Thai king is reported to have said: 'If there are fish in the rivers and rice in the fields, the people are happy.'

Mai pen rai – never mind – is an expression you will often hear. Whatever happens, life goes on. Take it on board – you'll need it.

A hard-nosed businessperson may be tempted to dismiss the above as futile. Do so at your peril. You need your people on your side.

Summing up

If you perceive elements of the information here to be contradictory and even completely illogical, you're correct. The logical training that the majority of Western managers receive has limited relevance for navigating the Thai mindset.

You will need to find good, reliable Thai partners in order to establish a business in the country. The challenge is to find partners whom you can trust, but this is no different from doing business anywhere in the world. Research thoroughly, taking time to get to know people.

Of course, you will formulate and sign contracts. However, the Asian perspective of a contract is somewhat different from that in the West. A contract is valid on the day it is signed. Because circumstances may change, the contract may need to be renegotiated. It's simply a different perspective on the validity of agreements. Legal conflicts should be a last resort. Thai culture is cooperation oriented. While Thais will not shy away from conflict if they feel threatened, the danger of losing face should not be underestimated. In addition, for an outsider, the chances of success are limited if your opponent is well connected.

For specific advice on Thai business, property, accounting, trade, employment, work permits, immigration and other related regulations, find appropriate service providers with offices in Bangkok who can demonstrate a thorough knowledge of local conditions.

You will frequently find yourself quoting the tourist authority's 'Amazing Thailand'. It's a ride. The key question to ask yourself throughout is: 'How can I work with this system to ensure my business runs smoothly?'

South-East Asia: managing risk regionally through delegation

STEPHEN GILL, STEPHEN GILL ASSOCIATES

South-East Asia is a sub-region of Asia, consisting of the countries that are geographically south of China, east of India and north of Australia. It is one of the world's most promising and dynamic economic regions, which rebounded from the global economic crisis with medium-term growth prospects returning to pre-crisis levels.

Although not immune from global economic uncertainties and with localized natural disasters shedding a negative light from time to time on the growth prospects of the region, overall South-East Asia is predicted to have a solid growth performance through to at least 2016. Thus it has become particularly attractive when compared to many of the sluggish economies around the world, and high on the priority list of geographical areas for businesses wanting to expand their activities.

The countries that make up South-East Asia are also usually grouped together in international business terms, with many multinational companies treating the geographical region as a business region, with perhaps a head office in one of the major cities such as Singapore, Jakarta, Kuala Lumpur or Bangkok, with sub-offices (or country offices) located in a number of the other countries. However, the complexity and diversity of the region present anyone doing business there with as diverse a set of challenges as they will find anywhere in the world, and this chapter looks at delegation of authority as one business control measure that may be used to reduce risk when doing business in the region.

Geography and population

South-East Asia can be divided into two distinct areas. 'Mainland' South-East Asia includes Cambodia, Laos, Burma (Myanmar), Thailand, Vietnam and Peninsular Malaysia. The island (or maritime) nations include East Malaysia, Brunei, Indonesia, the Philippines (which is made up of more than 7,000 islands), Singapore and East Timor.

South-East Asia has a land area of approximately 4.5 million square kilometres (1.8 million square miles), which to put it into perspective is about half the size of China and 18 times the size of Great Britain.

The region's combined population exceeds 600 million, which in round terms is double that of the United States and just over half that of India. The Indonesian island of Java is the most densely populated large island in the world, with Indonesia itself being the most densely populated country. The metropolitan areas of Jakarta, Manila and Bangkok each have populations in excess of 10 million people, and are continuing to grow.

South-East Asia's economics

The region's economy greatly depends upon agriculture, with manufacturing, tourism and services also being important. Indonesia, as an emerging market, is now the largest economy in the region. Singapore and Brunei are established affluent developed economies, with the newly industrialized countries including Malaysia, Thailand and the Philippines. With the exception of Vietnam, which is notably making steady progress in developing its industrial sectors, the rest of South-East Asia is still heavily dependent on agriculture and tourism to some degree.

Growth for the six South-East Asian economies, Indonesia, Malaysia, the Philippines, Singapore, Thailand and Vietnam, was 5.0 per cent in 2011, and is projected to be 5.6 per cent during 2012–16. The so-called 'tiger economies' of South-East Asia have become active participants in the global market.

Political landscape

Although there is no single political voice for the region, the Association of Southeast Asian Nations (ASEAN) is an economic and geopolitical organization of 10 countries (Indonesia, Malaysia, the Philippines, Singapore, Thailand, Brunei, Burma (Myanmar), Cambodia, Laos and Vietnam), with aims that include the acceleration of economic growth, social progress, cultural development among its members, the protection of the peace and stability of the region, and the provision of opportunities for member countries to discuss differences peacefully.

Although the region is mainly focused on economics, there have been pockets of political tension, such as the 2010 anti-government demonstrations in Bangkok.

In Burma (Myanmar), the closed, state-controlled economy had been crippled not so much by unrest or regional crisis as by more than 30 years of disastrous military rule. US sanctions and the lobbying of human rights groups had reduced tourism and foreign investment to a trickle. However, since the 2010 elections, the government has embarked on a series of reforms toward liberal democracy, a mixed economy, and reconciliation. These reforms include the release of pro-democracy leader Aung San Suu Kyi from house arrest, establishment of the National Human Rights Commission, general amnesties for hundreds of political prisoners, the institution of new labour laws that allow labour unions and strikes, relaxation of press censorship and regulations for currency practices.

The consequences of the reforms in Myanmar are far-reaching. The ASEAN members have approved Burma's bid for ASEAN chair in 2014. US Secretary of State Hillary Clinton visited Burma in December 2011 to encourage further progress, the first visit by a Secretary of State in more than 50 years. Clinton met with Burmese president Thein Sein as well as opposition leader Aung San Suu Kyi. Domestically, Aung San Suu Kyi's party, the National League for Democracy (NLD), was permitted to participate in the by-election after the government abolished laws that led to NLD's boycott.

At the time of writing (June 2012), Aung San Suu Kyi is on the last leg of a UK tour during which she gave a historic speech within the 11th-century walls of Westminster Hall, imploring Britain and 'the world beyond' to reach out to help Burma at 'the moment of our greatest need'. The Burmese pro-democracy leader and Nobel laureate, the first woman apart from the Queen to address both houses of parliament, appealed for practical help to support reforms to bring 'better lives, greater opportunities, to the people of Burma, who have been for so long deprived of their rights to their place in the world'.

Social, cultural and spiritual diversity

The social, cultural and spiritual diversity of South-East Asia is as rich as other aspects of the region. All major religions are represented and also many lesser-known ones. Indonesia is the world's largest Muslim nation, and the Philippines is Asia's largest Christian country, while the northern areas are predominately Buddhist.

The region is home to hundreds of languages and peoples who suffer vast inequalities of wealth. The countries' governments range from democracy through to a military dictatorship and various forms of monarchy. The legal systems vary and include Islamic law.

Business approach and risk

The sheer size, disparity and diversity of South-East Asia makes a common business approach to the region problematical, but to have uncontrolled flexible procedures with varying standards for each country is an administrative nightmare, potentially impossible to manage, which exposes businesses to risks stemming from inconsistency.

As one may appreciate from this brief introduction to the region, the range and scope of the risks faced by organizations operating throughout South-East Asia are immense, well beyond the capacity of this chapter to describe individually or in detail. However, that doesn't prevent many businesses from operating successfully with proper control measures in place.

A primary focus of a successful business must be to form procedures that ensure the efficiency and effectiveness of organization functions and reduce risk by establishing and fully including additional authority, as needed, for managers whilst at the same time being workable and practical to implement. These procedures must ensure that managers fully understand them and always operate within their authority level while being held accountable for their financial, human and physical resource decisions. Approval authority must be clearly defined and allocated so that all individuals in the business understand whether they are authorized to approve certain business activities.

Authority, responsibility and accountability

Authority can be defined as the power and right of a manager to use and allocate the resources efficiently, to take decisions and to give orders so as to achieve the organizational objectives. Authority must be well defined. All managers who have authority should know what the scope of their authority is. The top-level management has the highest authority level. Authority always flows from top to bottom. Authority should be accompanied by an appropriate level of responsibility.

Responsibility is the duty of managers to complete the task assigned to them. Managers who are given responsibility should ensure that they accomplish the tasks assigned to them. Responsibility without adequate authority leads to discontent and dissatisfaction. Responsibility flows from bottom to top. The middle-level and lower-level management hold more responsibility.

Accountability means giving explanations for any variance in actual performance from the expectations set. Accountability cannot be delegated. For example, if A is given a task with sufficient authority, and A delegates this task to B and asks B to ensure that the task is done well, responsibility rests with B, but accountability still rests with A. The top-level management is most accountable. Accountability, in short, means being answerable for the end result.

Delegation of authority

The concept of 'delegation of authority' refers to senior executives giving the authority and responsibility for the approval of activities to direct reports and/or others in the organization. Typical examples of activities that may rely upon delegated authority can range from the signing of contracts for significant expenditure to approving leave or petty cash payments. The range of activities will depend upon the nature of the business and the functional position.

Both the delegation and the appropriate use of the authority reduce a company's risk. They reduce the risk of poor or hasty decisions that are not based on sound business judgement. They reduce the risk that employees will make commitments to activities that do not create a benefit to the company, and they also reduce the risk that fraud will be committed by unscrupulous employees.

The organization will have to develop and implement rules for those who have the authority to approve certain types of activities. The rules provide for when that authority must be used, delegated or shared with other business functions, and with which employees or departments it is to be shared. These rules will help to protect the organization and its employees from poor and hasty decision making.

A well-designed delegation of authority system will:

- be clear as to what delegations actually exist so that delegates and everyone who deals with them know the extent of their authority;
- allow only as much discretion as is needed to perform the delegated responsibilities;
- attach accountability controls to delegated authority;
- include a review mechanism to check the use of delegated authority over a given time period.

Effective delegation of authority implementation

If delegation of authority is to be effective, all employees must be notified in writing of the delegation levels of all members of staff, functions, departments and teams. A register of the delegations, which is available to the whole company, demonstrates who is acting on delegated authority and for what purpose.

The delegation system should provide for automatic reporting of decisions made under delegated authority. The system should include processes to verify that a delegation is still current, and to check that any temporary delegations are properly authorized, notified, recorded and archived. In turn, the system should remove temporary delegations, or permanent ones that are no longer needed, and store superseded delegations for future reference.

A regular and scheduled review of delegations (every 12 months, for example) should occur to ensure that they are still appropriate to the capabilities, qualifications and needs of the positions to which they apply. Equally, a process should also be scheduled to audit and review the performance of the delegated functions system and to ensure compliance with the organization's operating procedures.

Corruption risk and managing corruption risk

Of all the risks that a delegation of authority process is intended to reduce, one of the greatest ones that remains is that the process itself will be used by a manager to make a decision for corrupt purposes. There is also the risk that managers may stretch their authority to act outside their delegation for corrupt purposes. For example, they may use delegated authority to grant an approval that will benefit themselves, a relative or someone else with whom they are connected, which may include another member of the same organization. Examples of this type of action include awarding a contract to a contractor in exchange for a bribe, or discontinuing enforcement of a policy in exchange for some sort of compensation.

To minimize the risk of such abuse of the delegation process, the policy and procedures should be carefully designed in the first instance using a robust policy that contains elements that have all been tried and tested and proven to be effective. The policy should also include sanctions and corrective steps or actions for any breach of the policy and procedures.

It is recommended that the policy be reviewed at least every two years or less if appropriate. There should be an ongoing audit and monitoring procedure that can detect breaches or help to identify potential breaches.

The organization should train its entire staff on the delegation of authority process and policy and include the use of delegations in all relevant corporate documents such as employee codes of conduct.

The policy itself and all training should be in a language that the staff understands. Bear in mind the diversity across South-East Asia and that many staff may not be working in their native country or language.

The organization should ensure that the policy includes a requirement for records to be kept of all decisions taken under delegated authority and include the use of delegations in the organization's internal and external audit and any corruption management processes that it has. If and when using external third-party auditors, the delegation process must be used for their selection and hiring. It is not unknown for local managers to hire another local with whom they have a connection to carry out the external audit.

Examples of when things go wrong

Here are a couple of examples of risk that have occurred as a result of failure to apply the delegation of authority policy.

The first example is that of a sales team in the head office in Jakarta that negotiated a contract for a multimillion-dollar construction project with a commercial customer in Malaysia. The contract included a clause that stated that the seller would repay the construction loan if the owner or developer could not. The contract also contained a clause that it was subject to Malaysian law.

The sales team informed the operations team, including the general manager, of the negotiations, but did not include the finance or legal or any other department in the process. This was against their delegation of authority policy.

The sales team were successful in being awarded the project and signed the contract. Unfortunately, the economy took a downturn and, as a result, the owner defaulted on the construction loan and it became the responsibility of the seller to repay the lender for the remaining amount due. The seller filed several lawsuits in Jakarta in an attempt to recover from their client the millions of dollars it had to pay the lender, but they were unsuccessful as a result of it being under Malaysian law.

As a consequence of the lack of proper approval and multi-department review the project had a significant negative impact on the seller's financial results.

While there are several issues raised in this example, one important issue is the failure of the sales team and their leadership to comply with their delegation of authority policy, which required that all supporting documentation, or the contract language, must be questioned by the finance and legal departments. If the policy had been adhered to, the finance and legal departments would have seen the clauses and raised the appropriate warnings prior to the signing of the contract.

The second example is that of a country manager in Bangkok, who was able to influence all tendering decisions for third-party subcontract work within Thailand. The selected vendors then entered into sub-contract agreements that were also controlled by the same country manager. The manager also used his delegated authority as contract supervisor to give approval for extra services to be carried out under the contract that were not genuine or required for the actual contract. These works resulted in additional payments to the vendor and additional benefits for himself. He also approved the invoices submitted by the subcontracting company knowing he would receive a portion of all payments received.

The manager abused the delegation in place but was detected when an external audit followed the approval trail and discovered that vendors should have been approved by the head office, which was in Indonesia.

The manager demonstrated fraudulent behaviour that remained undetected for some time because he kept the size of the payments to within his delegated authority level of $50,000. In addition, because he was the country manager, the staff beneath him assumed that they must automatically authorize all payments requested by him because his authority level exceeded theirs, so they never checked that the procedures regarding selection of vendors was being correctly followed.

A final word of caution

When carrying out business in South-East Asia, one will quickly learn that bargaining is a way of life to many of the people and businesses there. They bargain on a daily basis for the purchase of groceries and other household goods, and it has become an automatic response to bargain and negotiate for favourable terms in both their domestic and their business world.

To compete successfully in business in the region, one has to join the bargaining and learn how to be good at it; don't make concessions quickly, but be ready to use a concession to extract a better bargain for yourself. Also, never lose your temper, shout or become overly demanding at delays in decision making or bureaucratic procedures that you do not understand. Be aware that saving face is the first rule, so let your local representative or colleague monitor progress and guide you. If you must criticize, do it calmly, gently and indirectly. The organization should be aware that their staff or representatives will sometimes naturally behave in this way.

While all this negotiating may be necessary to succeed in business (and at times fun), the organization and individuals involved must not bend the rules and limits rigidly laid down within the delegation of authority by exceeding the authority level in the heat of the negotiation process to secure business. It is all too easy to be drawn into negotiating on a risk that was not even present at the outset of the bartering process.

South-East Asia is a great place to live, work and carry out business successfully. A proper delegation of authority correctly applied and adhered to can greatly reduce operating risk while achieving effective operational business results.

APPENDIX

Contributors' contact list

Accenture Risk Management
1 Plantation Place
30 Fenchurch Street
London EC3M 3BD
Tel: +44 (0)20 7844 4000
Contact: Laura Bishop
Tel: +44 (0)20 7844 4650
e-mail: laura.n.bishop@accenture.com

BAE Systems Detica
110 Southwark Street
London SE1 0TA
Tel: +44 (0)20 7812 4000
Contact: Nick Wilding
e-mail: nick.wilding@baesystemsdetica.com

Chietigj Bajpaee
Fairmont House
Needleman Street
London SE16 7AW
Tel: +44 (0)74 3843 9140
e-mail: cbajpaee@hotmail.com

Control Risks
Corporate Investigations Latin America
Cottons Centre
Cottons Lane
London SE1 2GQ
Tel: +55 (0)11 5504 7900
Contact: Geert Aalbers
Tel: +55 (0)11 8536 7414
e-mail: geert.aalbers@controlrisks.com

Deposix Software Escrow GmbH
Innere Wiener Str 11a
D-81667 Munich
Tel: +49 (89) 189 1255 0
Contact: Stephan Peters
e-mail: stephan.peters@deposix.com

Det Norske Veritas AS
Ventasveien 1
1363 Høvik
Oslo
Norway
Tel: +47 675 9000
Contacts:
Sverre Danielsen
e-mail: Sverre.Danielsen@dnvkema.com
Gunnar Hauland
e-mail: Gunnar.Hauland@dnvkema.com
Anne Cathrine Johnsen
e-mail: Anne.Cathrine.Johnsen@dnvkema.com
Morten Bremer Maerli
Tel: +47 950 00 079
e-mail: Morten.Bremer.Maerli@dnvkema.com

DNV KEMA
Palace House
3 Cathedral Street
London SE1 9DE
Tel: +44 (0)20 7716 6546
Contact: Allan Gifford
e-mail: Allan.Gifford@dnvkema.com
Simon King
Simon.King@dnvkema.com

Financial Reporting Council
5th Floor
Aldwych House
71–91 Aldwych
London WC2B 4HN
Tel: +44 (0)20 7492 2300
Contact: Chris Hodge
e-mail: c.hodge@frc.org.uk

Carlo Gallo
Tel: +44 (0)79 6325 0069
e-mail: carlo74@hotmail.com
website: www.direct-analytica.com

Stephen Gill Associates
Stanton Lodge
Aston on Trent
Derby DE72 2AH
Tel: +44 (0)1332 793399
Contact: Stephen Gill
e-mail: steve@stephengill.eu

Institute of Risk Management
6 Lloyd's Avenue
London EC3N 3AX
Tel: +44 (0)20 7709 9808
Contact: Steve Fowler
e-mail: steve.fowler@theirm.org

KPMG LLP
115 Canada Square
London E14 5GL
Tel: +44 (0)20 7311 4885
Contact: Amanda Morrison
e-mail: amanda.morrison@kpmg.co.uk

LEGO Systems A/S
Aastvej 1
DK-7190 Billund
Tel: +45 (0)7950 6070
Contact: Hans Læssøe
Tel: +45 (0)7950 5051
e-mail: Hans.laessoe@LEGO.com

Lloyd's Register Quality Assurance (LRQA)
LRQA Centre
Hiramford
Middlemarch Office Village
Siskin Drive
Coventry CV3 4JF
Tel: +44 (0)24 7688 2386
Contact: Philippa Weare
e-mail: philippa.weare@lrqa.com

mylifeQs
Wilhelmshoeher Strasse 17
D-12161 Berlin
Germany
Tel: +49 (0)176 6788 9006
Contact: Eric Lynn
e-mail: eric@mylifeQs.com
website: www.mylifeQs.com

Jonathan Reuvid
Little Manor
Wroxton
Banbury
Oxfordshire OX15 6QE
Tel: +44 (0)1295 738070
e-mail: jreuvidembooks@aol.com

Shoosmiths LLP
Apex Plaza
Forbury Road
Reading, Berks. RG1 1SH
Tel: +44 (0)37 0086 4000
Contacts:
Paul Eccles
e-mail: paul.eccles@shoosmiths.co.uk
Rachel Reeves
e-mail: rachel.reeves@shoosmiths.co.uk

WMSNT Limited
80 Park Road
Aston
Birmingham B6 5PL
Tel: +44 (0)121 327 8128
Contacts:
Peter Maggs
e-mail: peter.maggs@wmsnt.org
Steven Shackleford
e-mail: shacklefordsteven@hotmail.com

XL Insurance UK
XL House
70 Gracechurch Street
London EC3V 0XL
Contact: Paula Wilson
Direct line: +44 (0)20 7933 7282
e-mail: paula.wilson@xlgroup.com

INDEX

(*italics* indicates a figure or table in the text)

INDEX OF ADVERTISERS

CPSIA information can be obtained at www.ICGtesting.com
Printed in the USA
BVOW061213070613

322734BV00012B/166/P

9 780749 466848